D0592583

940.54 Vau

Vaughan, Hal, 1928-

FDR's twelve apostles : the spies wh

33543009889379   wst

MONTGOMERY COUNTY LIBRARY

CONROE, TEXAS   77301

WEST BRANCH

FDR'S 12 APOSTLES

FDR'S 12 APOSTLES

THE SPIES WHO PAVED THE WAY FOR THE INVASION OF NORTH AFRICA

HAL VAUGHAN

THE LYONS PRESS
Guilford, Connecticut
An imprint of The Globe Pequot Press

MONTGOMERY COUNTY LIBRARY
CONROE, TEXAS 77301

To buy books in quantity for corporate use
or incentives, call **(800) 962–0973, ext. 4551,**
or e-mail **premiums@GlobePequot.com.**

Copyright © 2006 by Hal Vaughan

ALL RIGHTS RESERVED. No part of this book may be reproduced or transmitted in any
form by any means, electronic or mechanical, including photocopying and recording, or by
any information storage and retrieval system, except as may be expressly permitted in writing
from the publisher. Requests for permission should be addressed to The Lyons Press, Attn:
Rights and Permissions Department, P.O. Box 480, Guilford, CT 06437.

The Lyons Press is an imprint of The Globe Pequot Press.

10   9   8   7   6   5   4   3   2   1

Printed in the United States of America

Library of Congress Cataloging-in-Publication Data

Vaughan, Hal, 1928–
    FDR's twelve apostles : the spies who paved the way for the invasion of North
Africa / Hal Vaughan.
        p. cm.
    Includes bibliographical references and index.
    ISBN-13: 978-1-59228-916-5
    ISBN-10: 1-59228-916-9
    1. World War, 1939-1945—Secret service—United States. 2. World War,
1939–1945—Campaigns—Africa, North. 3. Roosevelt, Franklin D. (Franklin Delano),
1882–1945. I. Title. II. Title: Frankline Delano Roosevelt's twelve apostles.
    D810.S7V28 2006
    940.54'8673—dc22

                                                                        2006022143

Once again for Phuong . . .

CONTENTS

PREFACE AND ACKNOWLEDGMENTS

THIS IS THE INTIMATE, SECRET, and first-time-told true story of how Robert Daniel Murphy and a handful of dedicated men—America's first World War II spies—prepared the invasion of North Africa.

The tale came to me on a sunny autumn's day in 1998 as I strolled along the left bank of the Seine River past a bookseller along the Quai Malaquais. I couldn't resist the piles of old French books in their wood bins; my fingers plucked out a book here and there—and then my eye fell on a red and cheaply bound volume. Thumbing through its pages, I came across a name: Ridgeway [sic] Knight. I knew that name . . .

I paused. My God, I thought: Ridgway Brewster Knight was my chief in Karachi! The pages that followed told a fictionalized tale of OSS operations in North Africa.[1]

Over the years Ridgway (now deceased) and I had stayed in touch. I followed his career as he graduated to senior posts as a U.S. diplomat and as U.S. ambassador to Belgium. I was between books and he was delighted to talk about his North African adventures. Eventually he gave me a two-volume memoir of his life in North Africa and during World War II, when he served on the staff of General Mark Clark. We would meet at the American Club of Paris and at his home in Pas-de-Calais, where, over endless bottles of very good French wine (Ridgway was an expert on French and Italian wines), and often in the company of his charming wife, Christine, Ridgway took me back to the days before Pearl Harbor, when Robert Murphy set his men to work in Algeria, Morocco, and Tunisia. He confided in me details of Bob Murphy's life in Algiers and how Murphy and his team helped plan Operation Torch—

the U.S. invasion of North Africa, and the only time the United States had a shooting war with France.

Ridgway was a scholar and a student of American diplomacy in World War II. He was critical of how President Roosevelt manipulated U.S. diplomacy from the White House. And he told me what he knew about the assassination of Admiral Jean-Louis-Xavier-François Darlan, who, as the U.S. pro-consul in North Africa, got French forces to join the Allies and fight against German and Italian armies in Tunisia—a prelude to the invasion of Italy and Normandy.

The behind-the-scenes drama of how America prepared Torch and barely avoided disaster captivated me. Over many months I assembled the personal memoirs, reminiscences, and photographs of the men who served with Robert Murphy and Ridgway Knight in Algeria, Morocco, and Tunisia. Murphy's family—and relatives of former vice-consuls and OSS agents in North Africa—generously offered their help. I dug in the files of the National Archives at College Park, Maryland; the personnel archives of the U.S. Department of State; the Hoover Institution at Stanford, California; the French National Archives in Paris; the Italian National Archives in Rome; the Public Records Office in London; and the Franklin D. Roosevelt Library at Hyde Park, New York. And I was privileged to interview and correspond with four eyewitnesses to the events surrounding the Torch operation. The story that emerges lends conviction to the aphorism: Truth is stranger than fiction.[2]

I am grateful for the assistance of one of the leading historians of the period, Mr. Arthur Layton Funk, author of *The Politics of Torch* (University of Kansas, 1974), who corresponded with me and kindly gave me his handwritten notes: "Intelligence in North Africa, Oct. 1941–Oct. 1942."

I want to thank all those who contributed to helping uncover this story.

To my dear friend, Charles L. Robertson, professor emeritus of Smith College, ever-present when I needed to talk: *mes homages*. Phyllis Michaux, a former OSS operative now living in Paris, helped me find documents about the Princess de Ligne, a close friend of Robert Murphy, as did M. Ludovic de Polignac and la Princess Jean-Charles de Ligne. And to Maurice Bood: *Chapeau* for your good work.

Many thanks to Pamela Zimmerman, my energetic and efficient "mining partner," research assistant, and copyeditor in New York and to her husband, Gerry Cohen, who brought to me Anthony Eden's musings about Darlan's assassination. The generous help of Mr. John Taylor of NARA has advanced Pam's research. I am grateful to Rosemary Murphy for her help, and a particular *merci* goes to her sister, Mildred M. Pond, Robert Murphy's youngest daughter, for corresponding with me and sharing family photographs and documents about the Murphy family prior to 1942. Christiane Guerlain, of the Lesieur family, and a dear friend and colleague at the American Hospital of Paris, helped with details of her life in Algiers between 1941–1942, and events surrounding Robert Murphy's life and work there.

Rob Kirkpatrick, PhD, senior editor at The Lyons Press of Guilford, Connecticut, had a good grasp of the Torch story and a sharp pencil. His suggestions and comments were invaluable; and many thanks to his editorial and marketing team.

I am duly grateful to the following who shared with me family documents, photographs, anecdotes, and insights into the life and work of four of the important actors in the North African saga: Peter M. F. Sichel and Jacques Tétrault about Franklin O. Canfield; A. Derek Knox about his mother, Daphne Joan Fry Tuyl Knox and stepfather, John C. Knox; Donna Reid, PhD, about W. Stafford Reid; Maurice Hendrik Bood for his work in tracking down documents about General Weygand; and Mrs. Edith Kunhardt, daughter of vice-consul Harry A. Woodruff, deserves a special thanks for her last-minute interventions and a telephone interview with the author.

Finally, and with great admiration and thanks, I salute my agent, Edward W. Knappman, of New England Publishing Associates, for his generous and valuable help over many years; and thanks too, to his wife and partner, Elisabeth Knappman, a gracious hostess and thoughtful literati.

To the many others who helped along the way, including Leslie Presson, who held down the Westport fort, and Dr. Nadia Volf and Karen Kyker and Dave, who kept my body and mechanical brain working—a thousand thanks. I am solely responsible for any errors of fact.

PROLOGUE:
HOW A HANDFUL OF MEN
MADE A DIFFERENCE

THREE DAYS AFTER AMERICAN and British forces landed on French North African shores, Winston Churchill celebrated Operation Torch, the first real victory for the Allies in World War II. He ventured: "Now this is not the end. It is not even the beginning of the end. But it is perhaps the end of the beginning."[3]

Torch was President Franklin Delano Roosevelt's "great secret baby"[4] and the first joint major British-U.S. operation. The landings and what followed opened the Mediterranean roads leading to Rome and Berlin. FDR's "Twelve Apostles"—vice-consuls assigned under Robert Murphy to prepare Torch in Algeria, Morocco, and Tunisia—set the stage for a long string of espionage, sabotage, and psychological warfare operations that the United States would carry out in World War II.

Indeed, some eighteen months before tens of thousands of American and British soldiers were thrown onto Mediterranean shores, FDR agents under Robert Murphy worked secretly among French colonials and Arab and Berber peoples to defeat Vichy and Axis agents in Algiers, Casablanca, Oran, Rabat, Safi, and Tunis. They arrived when North Africa was a mosaic of nations and tribes—French colonials living amid the Babel of French, German, Italian, Arabic, and Berber languages with smatterings of Hebrew, Greek, and other ancient tongues. German and Italian agents, often security police with the Franco-German Armistice Commission installed after the French surrender, had made no significant progress in undermining French colonial rule in North Africa. And the Arab peoples wouldn't swallow Nazi-fascist philosophy.

Murphy's original team—the twelve—were mostly well-mannered gentlemen with outsized personalities drawn from upper-class Ivy League gentry. They came from a generation of Americans that sought something greater and grander than they could find at home. All had studied abroad in their youth, five had volunteered to fight in World War I, and three had served in the American Field Service before America entered the Second World War. Two had served in the French Foreign Legion, and four were married. All had the veneer of European sophistication, and most could have passed for Frenchmen. Still, the twelve were red, white, and blue Americans first and *toujours*; but they loved France for its culture, food and wine, conviviality, and insouciance—an "art of living" that comes only when speaking the language fluently. Most were in France when the country fell to the German invasion and, like those at home, were disgusted and shocked at the capitulation of the French government under Marshal Philippe Pétain. When a chance came to serve in North Africa, they were itching to be involved in a war that America had yet to join—eager to seek glory, romance, escape—a chance to get into the game.

As gifted amateurs, untrained in the clandestine arts, innocents to the world of dirty tricks, they preceded William J. Donovan's COI-OSS operations. They were also the first organized U.S. spy team in World War II to operate under diplomatic cover—an avant-garde CIA.

Torch was boldly conceived and executed by General Dwight D. Eisenhower. In the fall of 1942 massive flotillas embarked from U.S. and British ports, marking the first transoceanic amphibious operation and the first U.S. airborne operation in World War II.[5] In the events that followed, American, British, and French forces suffered heavy casualties during the Torch fighting and in defeating German field marshal Erwin Rommel's desert armies.

Torch opened French North and West Africa to the Atlantic Mediterranean routes and the Suez Canal, and led next to the liberation of Sicily, Sardinia, and Corsica—toppling Mussolini from power and causing Italy to surrender. Rommel's loss dealt a heavy blow to Hitler's armies and prepared American troops for the invasion of France at Normandy two years later—and the eventual defeat of Nazi Germany.[6]

The courageous acts of FDR's agents and their compatriots would change the course of the war. But their mistakes would cost dearly as they went about the business of learning the spy trade. Indeed, the Torch enterprise was an enormous risk and might have ended in disaster. Yet despite the blundering and the errors of omission and commission, the men Murphy finally chose to be in on the operation did make a difference and probably guaranteed its success.

Were these men heroes? We shall see. In the foreword to *Gentlemen Volunteers*, a book about WWI ambulance drivers, George Plimpton writes that "the word 'volunteer' is derived loosely from the Latin word *voluntarius*—one who undertakes an action without external constraint and who thus performs of one's own free will . . . a property that one often associates with heroism, especially if the cause is an honorable one."[7]

Here then, are a handful of Christian gentlemen, eager to taste the exotic life of Algeria, Morocco, and Tunisia in a Cecil B. de Mille–like adventure film with a cast of colonial Englishmen, refugee Poles, French colonialists (colons), Arabs, and Berbers, and with the production values found only on Mediterranean shores and desert outposts. We shall meet these men one by one.

FRONT MATTER ENDNOTES

1 Pierre-Charles Guillemot, *Les 12 Vice-Consuls. Afrique du nord 1942* (Paris: Editions Olivier Orban, 1977).

2 Anonymous.

3 Churchill's words, borrowed from a phrase spoken by Talleyrand in 1812 after the Battle of Borodino, were spoken at the Lord Mayor's Day Luncheon in London on November 10, 1942. Justin Kaplan, ed., *Bartlett's Familiar Quotations*, Seventeenth Edition (New York: Little, Brown and Company, 2002), 621.

4 Rick Atkinson, *An Army at Dawn: The War in Africa, 1942–1943, Volume One of the Liberation Trilogy* (New York: Henry Holt & Company, Inc., 2002), 31.

5 Atkinson, 159.

6 The Torch Allied assault forces as of November 8, 1941 numbered 107,453 Allied troops, 107 ships carrying 9,911 vehicles, and 96,089 long tons of supplies. By December 1, 1941, the strength of Allied forces landed in North Africa numbered 253,213 troops. A precise count of Allied and French casualties between 8–11 November 1942 in the Algerian-French Moroccan campaign does not exist even today; the best estimate is 526 U.S. killed in action and 939 wounded or missing in action. The British reported Allied losses at 2,225, including nearly 1,100 dead. The French may have suffered as many as 3,000 casualties, mostly at sea. George F. Howe, *Northwest Africa: Seizing the Initiative in the West* (Washington, D.C.: Center of Military History, United States Army, 1993), 173 and Appendix A; and from *VFW Magazine, Anniversary Issue*, November 1992, 15.

7 Arlen Hansen, *Gentlemen Volunteers* (New York: Arcade Publishing, 1996), jacket copy.

PART ONE:
BEFORE THE TORCH WAS LIT

What are we waiting for . . . The Barbarians are coming today.

—Constantine Peter Cavafy, *Waiting for the Barbarians'*

1

JUNE 14, 1940:
THE BUSINESS OF BARBARIANS

PARIS WAS DEADLY SILENT—its tree-lined boulevards, slate-gray River Seine, and fine monuments were enveloped in clouds of oily black smoke. Bits and pieces of charred paper floated in a light breeze.[2] Café life was suspended—snuffed out. It was as if some dreadful cataclysmic event hung over the city and its environs. Suburban roads were choked with refugees and reeked of petrol as the first mechanized evacuation in history ground on to the scraping of automobile gears and the wails and curses of those caught in the exodus. Fourteen million French men, women, and children fled from north to south.[3] The picture was of an unbroken stream of humanity underneath a hot sun: tens of thousands of Parisians and homeless refugees trudging south, fleeing the advancing German machine. "In that world of terror, panic and confusion, it was difficult to believe that these were the citizens of Paris, citizens whose forefathers had fought for their freedom like tigers and stormed the Bastille with their bare hands."[4]

Chaos ruled the streets. The French government and the city's mayor had fled—but U.S. ambassador William C. Bullitt, despite orders to follow the government, refused to be part of the exodus. He called on diplomats to join him to protect the city and organized a meeting of the diplomatic corps at the Cathedral of Notre Dame to pray for the city's salvation. Bullitt was seen kneeling in the first pew, weeping.

As all communications between Paris to the outside world were cut, Bullitt, in a dramatic gesture, assumed the role of the city's provisional mayor.

He managed to find an open line to U.S. consul Leland Harrison in Bern, Switzerland, and dictated an urgent message telling the Reich foreign office in Berlin that "Paris has been declared an open city . . . all possible measures are being taken to assure the security of life and property."

This was not the wish of Winston Churchill. He and General Charles de Gaulle in London urged "a suicidal resistance." Churchill wanted French forces to resist German attacks in and around the city and fight in the streets. His hope was that the Germans would bombard the city, cause widespread devastation, and ignite American anger. He expected that German barbarity would prompt Roosevelt to declare war on Germany.

It was not to be. In last-minute negotiations between the Swiss minister in Paris and the U.S. Legation in Switzerland, an agreement was reached to spare the City of Lights.[5]

It was just past midnight on June 14, 1940, when Bullitt's political counselor, Robert Daniel Murphy, and the U.S. naval attaché, Commander Roscoe Hillenkoetter, set out from the U.S. Embassy on the avenue Gabriel to walk the deserted streets of Paris.[6]

For Murphy and the staff of the American Embassy, it had been a long, hectic, and hot day. Murphy had fielded desperate calls from fleeing French ministers, while the staff had been besieged by a flood of Americans seeking last-minute documents and escape from Paris. Amid the chaos, the embassy files and codebooks had to be burned.

Alone now, Murphy and Hillenkoetter traded bits of information garnered from journalists, diplomats, and French officials. Many were shaken by the sudden drama of the day's events and feared that Paris would be "ground to a rubble" by the advancing German armies.

The situation seemed hopeless. British and French troops had already fled France at Dunkirk aboard ships sent from England; and now French forces were overrun.

Murphy and Hillenkoetter tried to digest the grim news. Over the past days, in the turmoil and confusion, the only information that Murphy, the senior political counselor at the embassy, had been able to send to Washington was based on official news bulletins, mostly wrong or purposefully deceiving. No one really knew what was happening outside Paris.[7]

That night, the last night Paris would breathe free of Nazi occupation for four years, the two friends walked on with heavy hearts. No light showed anywhere. They met no one. From a distance, toward the town of Melun, came occasional flashes of artillery fire. They must have wondered then how it could have come to pass, one catastrophe after another: Austria, Czechoslovakia, Danzig, Poland, and now Holland, Belgium, and France. It was a dark time for the soul.[8]

"This is a morning we will never forget."[9]

Murphy slept that night on his office couch. He woke early on June 14 to a tempest of sound: heavy motor vehicles, the rattle of bicycle troopers—and, amazingly, horse-drawn artillery advancing along the cobblestone plaza below. A section of Hitler's unstoppable army was in the city. From the French doors of his office, across the avenue Gabriel on the Place de la Concorde, Murphy watched German troopers swarm over the spot where Marie Antoinette had lost her head. Horse-drawn caissons lumbered past the Obélisque de Louqsor and the Tuileries. Earlier that very morning German troopers had raced to the top of the Eiffel Tower and torn away the *tricolore*; a Nazi swastika now flew over Paris.

The American diplomat was in a foul mood. Pale and exhausted from lack of sleep, he had been cut off from news of his wife, Mildred, hospitalized back home in Kansas, and his three daughters—his "queens," as he called them. He dreaded what Mildred, a diagnosed manic-depressive, might be going through.[10] And he was certainly not looking forward to making a courtesy call on the new commander in chief of occupied Paris, Lt. Gen. Bogislav von Studnitz, one of Hitler's star panzer leaders.

Murphy knew Germany and its people well. He had spoken German since childhood in Milwaukee, and had met Adolf Hitler in Munich in the mid-1920s as the U.S. vice-consul in that city. And he had no love for the Nazi machine. Indeed, because of a trivial incident involving his wife, Mildred, Murphy had been forced to leave Munich, banished to Spain.

Calling on von Studnitz was a disagreeable chore laid on him by Ambassador Bullitt, who was not about to personally honor the invading Germans. Murphy was given the unenviable job.

It was midmorning when the ambassador's three emissaries—Murphy, Commander Hillenkoetter, and Colonel Horace Fuller, the military attaché—

walked through the embassy gates, crossed the rue Boissy d'Anglas, and filed through a cordon of German infantry to enter a side door of the posh Hotel Crillon. (Twenty years earlier, U.S. president Woodrow Wilson had stayed at the Crillon during the League of Nations' talks after Germany's World War I defeat.)[11]

Inside the hotel lobby, Murphy was stopped by a French police commissioner whom he knew well. The man, clearly shaken and overexcited, spoke in a hoarse whisper, his face covered in sweat. He told how early that morning a German colonel had arrived at the shuttered hotel, summoned him, handed over a swastika flag, and ordered in perfect French: "Open the hotel, take down the French flag on the roof, and run up this German flag." The commissioner desperately tried to get into the locked hotel. He searched feverishly for a locksmith as precious time went by. When the colonel returned and found the hotel still closed, he erupted: "If that hotel isn't open in fifteen minutes and the French flag is not down, we will shoot it down—and you too." Fortunately, a locksmith was found.[12]

When Murphy and the attachés got to the Prince of Wales suite—the best apartment at the Crillon—they found a German colonel waiting for them.

"Murphy!" the man exclaimed in amazement. "What are you doing here? You don't remember me? I am Colonel Weber from Munich."

And like an old friend, Weber welcomed the Americans and introduced them to General von Studnitz. (Later, it came to Murphy that Weber was a Bavarian officer he had known fifteen years earlier.)

Murphy had expected to pass a few formal minutes with the general. Instead, von Studnitz ordered champagne from the Crillon's cellars: "The best in the house," he insisted. (It apparently was not, and the three American diplomats drank brandy).[13]

Von Studnitz, sporting a small mustache and a monocle, looked every bit the Prussian cavalry officer. The general said he had once been a military attaché in Warsaw, Poland, and was delighted to give the American attachés the information they needed to do their jobs. Then, sipping from his glass, he launched into an extraordinarily clear and concise summary of how the German army had overrun France—information that Murphy and the others had only gleaned from Western and Berlin broadcasts. When von Studnitz concluded, Murphy asked, "What happens next?"[14]

The general said that mopping-up operations in France might require ten more days; but, he emphasized, German armies would soon cross the

English Channel. Not a single English division was intact in France; their heavy armament was abandoned. He added categorically, "Further resistance [is] impossible."[15]

Murphy and the attachés listened in amazement as von Studnitz elaborated on the Nazi plans for the invasion of England. When Hillenkoetter asked how the Germans planned to cross the Channel, the general brushed the question aside. He assured them that since the British were exhausted, the war would be over in six weeks—by the end of July.

Finally, as the Americans rose to leave, von Studnitz asked Murphy to deliver an invitation to Ambassador Bullitt to join him that afternoon at a military review of the general's old unit: the "Green Heart," 185th Infantry Division. The men could only nod their assent.[16]

Walking back to the embassy, the three diplomats agreed that the general was convincing. Here was a man who had the confidence of Adolf Hitler, and who knew the secrets of the German general staff. They agreed that von Studnitz's news of an imminent invasion of England was startling information that Washington and London should have immediately; but how to reach Washington? The embassy had burned its codebooks the night before, and the Germans had cut all communications except through Berlin. The only way Ambassador Bullitt and his staff could communicate with Washington was through the German Foreign Ministry. It would be three weeks before Murphy was free to send the White House a report of the von Studnitz meeting.

That afternoon, von Studnitz paid a formal call on Ambassador Bullitt at the American Embassy. The general left the compound after a short visit amid the glare of flashbulbs as curious news reporters looked on. He walked directly to the center of the Place de la Concorde. Rigid, his monocle screwed into his eye, von Studnitz stood there for exactly an hour, reviewing his conquering "Green Heart" division. With U.S. political counselor Robert Murphy by his side, von Studnitz and other dignitaries watched as the troopers goose-stepped along to regimental marches, and listened to their shouts of "Heil Hitler!" as they passed.[17]

Walter Kerr of *The New York Herald Tribune* spied Murphy alongside von Studnitz. Kerr was shocked to see an American diplomat standing with a Nazi general while German army cameramen recorded every instant of the procession for the world's newsreels. Later, walking back to the embassy with Murphy, Kerr asked why he had allowed that to happen.

"The general wanted [to invite] the ambassador, and the ambassador told me to take his place," Murphy answered.

Kerr's inquiry must have come as a punch in the ribs to Murphy. He knew the reporter would write a piece about the event—and Murphy had been the fall guy.[18]

The next day, Bob Murphy and the U.S. attachés witnessed an ignoble event: the herding of French prisoners past the gates of the embassy in a cold, driving rain. Newsmen gathered behind the building's iron fence and reported, "a pitiful sight, the [prisoners'] faces were haggard, their uniforms dirty and worn . . ." The dejected crowd trudged right by, most of them carrying "long loaves of rain-soaked bread. As they dragged along the street bent in submission, several shouted bitter invectives: 'Look at the American flag! . . . Look at that American! . . . He looks well fed . . . Why the hell didn't you help us?'"[19]

In the days that followed, Ambassador Bullitt established a working relationship with Gen. von Studnitz, but only after the high-strung Bullitt had almost set off a very nasty incident: On the night of June 16–17, noise was heard on the embassy roof. A staff officer found German signal troopers crawling around, stringing telephone and telegraph lines. Incensed, Bullitt ordered his staff to arm themselves. He then sent an emissary across the street to the Hotel Crillon to warn von Studnitz that if the lines and the soldiers were not removed from the embassy roof immediately, he would consider it "a violation of American soil." Bullitt's emissary was ordered to say that the ambassador promised to "personally shoot at any German on the embassy premises."[20] Bullitt then posted himself, Murphy, and other aides at the embassy's French doors and windows. (This was pure bluff, because there were only two revolvers in the entire mission.)[21] The Germans removed the lines at once.

Meanwhile, Murphy took on the disagreeable job of working with German authorities to issue exit permits to American, French, and English residents who desperately wanted to get away from the German-occupied zone. He helped New York bankers keep their Paris operations going, and with great cunning saved the life of the head of the French police's intelligence services.

Deputy police commissioner Jacques Simon[22] had hidden confidential police records in a river barge outside Paris. The boat was deliberately sunk when the Germans advanced on the city. (The French later lifted the barge before the sodden documents dissolved.) When the German police arrived

8

to seize the documents, they found only the smoldering evidence of destroyed papers in the intelligence bureau's furnaces. This was a technical violation of the open city agreement, and Jacques Simon was arrested and told he would be shot. The man's chief begged Murphy for help. Murphy asked Ernst Achenbach, a German diplomat in Paris married to an American from California, to step in. Achenbach found Jacques Simon imprisoned in St. Cloud, and arranged for his freedom. Later, Simon claimed that Murphy had saved his life.

But mostly, Murphy, alone and bottled up in a city crawling with German troops, continued to fret over how Mildred and their daughters were getting on. He had not seen them for almost six months, since the Christmas holidays, when he had taken Mildred home to Kansas from a hospital in France, and he longed for news of her and the girls.

Instead, Murphy and Bullitt heard French Gen. Charles de Gaulle's BBC broadcast from London on June 18. The two must have been struck to hear de Gaulle pleading with Frenchmen to continue the fight against Hitler. Until that moment, de Gaulle had been a little-known junior French minister; and only months before that, he was a colonel who had successfully led a squadron of French tanks against the advancing Germans and had been cited for great initiative and courage in action. Murphy had never heard de Gaulle's name before that BBC broadcast, and he had to wonder how de Gaulle had become so important. (Later, thinking back, Murphy concluded that de Gaulle was "the most forceful French personality of his generation.")[23]

Murphy may have been irked, stuck, as he was, in German-occupied Paris when the ambassador and staff were accredited to the French government. Amid the staggering loss of life, the desperation of refugees fleeing the German armies, and the brutality of war unfolding around him, he must have questioned Bullitt's decision to remain in Paris, far from the political events that would shape Franco-German and Franco-American relations for four years to come.

Indeed, Ambassador Bullitt had no official status in German-occupied Paris. Still, he remained for over two weeks despite the stated wishes of President Roosevelt, U.S. secretary of state Cordell Hull, and French prime minister Paul Reynaud that Bullitt follow the French government when it fled the city.[24] Bullitt had FDR's private code for direct communications with the White House. But during the most crucial moments of the French Republic's final hours, Bullitt, Roosevelt's close friend and confidant in

France, and Murphy, the State Department's senior political adviser, were cut off from Washington.

Meanwhile, miles away, devastating events unfolded in the southern French cities of Tours and Bordeaux, where the French government took shelter from the advancing German armies. Paul Reynaud's staff first landed in the quiet town of Tours, only to be bombed out by German and Italian warplanes. Despite the chaos and the roads packed with refugees, the government relocated to Bordeaux, where British prime minister Winston Churchill caught up with them while Bullitt and Murphy remained in Paris.

In a dramatic effort to prevent a French capitulation, and with news that President Roosevelt could not have the United States intervene, Churchill dramatically offered to hastily arrange a meeting of the French cabinet, "an indissoluble union with common citizenship and a single united war cabinet with amalgamated armed forces," and perhaps a polyglot, single parliament for the British and French states.[25] Prime Minister Reynaud, Gen. Charles de Gaulle, and a handful of French cabinet members backed Churchill's proposal. They also urged the government to move to North Africa—Algeria or Morocco—and relocate all French army and navy forces there, too.

Marshal Henri Philippe Pétain would hear nothing of this. The eighty-four-year-old hero of the World War I Battle of Verdun, now a member of the Reynaud cabinet, and the powerful men who backed him—like French commander in chief Gen. Maxime Weygand—had already decided that Britain was finished and that France must seek an armistice with the Germans.[26] Pétain called the Churchill plan for amalgamation, "a marriage with a corpse . . . abandoning the country to the invaders." [27]Pétain hated the English and saw them as invaders—just as the English King Henry V had invaded Normandy in 1415, an event remembered in France as the ignominious defeat of French knighthood at Agincourt.[28]

Gen. de Gaulle and a handful of ministers close to Reynaud wanted to resist the Nazis and called for a "strategic retreat—a military-naval regrouping of French forces in North Africa."[29] The Pétain clique won: Reynaud resigned, and in a deal with Pétain was named Vichy's ambassador to the United States. (It almost cost him his life, as we shall see.) Churchill, his last hope of saving France from itself dashed, left France, not to return until after the Normandy invasion in 1944.[30]

Once in power Marshal Pétain installed his own men—led by Pierre Laval and Adm. Jean-François Darlan—as ministers of a French cabinet bent on capitulation. Charles de Gaulle fled to England. Nineteen French deputies and one senator sailed to Casablanca in anticipation of building a government in exile in French North Africa—in Algeria, Morocco, and Tunisia. Pétain had every one of them arrested in Morocco and deported to France.[31] He then had de Gaulle demoted—and eventually court-martialed and sentenced to death.

Cordell Hull believed that had Bullitt been at Reynaud's side, "We [U.S. diplomacy] should have had a reasonable chance to induce the French cabinet to continue the fight with the fleet and colonies."[32] Indeed, at the time, many in America and Europe thought that Bullitt and his staff were in the wrong place at the wrong time. De Gaulle never forgave Murphy's "grandstanding" when the Germans entered Paris. He believed, as other American, English, and French observers did, that had Bullitt and Murphy followed the legitimate Third Republic ministers, they might have convinced the Reynaud government to carry on the war from French North Africa.

Despite the heroic gesture to save the city, neither Bullitt nor Murphy brought credit to America's image by staying in Paris.[33] Before the eyes of the world, Murphy had been seen standing with von Studnitz as his troops paraded by on the Place de la Concorde, and it was broadcast that Bullitt had also met the conquering German general. The French were never able to understand why America deserted its World War I ally.

June 30, 1940, dawned a beautiful day as Ambassador Bullitt drove out of Paris and headed for Vichy and a meeting with Marshal Pétain, slated to be the Vichy head of state. The weather had turned splendid, and a caravan of limousines carried Robert Murphy (with Gofio, the Murphys' Maltese terrier), Commander Hillenkoetter, U.S. Third Secretary Carmel Offie, and two military attachés. Bullitt also included his friend, Dudley Gilroy, in the caravan. Gilroy, a retired English major who managed a racing stable near Bullitt's home at Chantilly outside Paris, and his American-born wife, feared internment by the Germans. Bullitt wanted to help them escape to England. He issued Gilroy an American passport and warned him not to open his mouth when they passed the German border control outside Paris. When the party got stuck in traffic, the ambassador, already on edge, began shouting. It unnerved Murphy, and he yelled back at Bullitt something like, "Who do you think you are, William Christ Bullitt?" The ambassador calmed down. Everyone took a deep breath after crossing the demarcation line separating occupied from unoccupied France. They passed the time joking about what they would find in Vichy: Murphy ventured that it was "wryly appropriate" that the government of a defeated France should have chosen a place celebrated only for its disagreeable medicinal waters used to treat unpleasant but not necessarily fatal liver disease.[34] Indeed, Vichy had been selected not for its waters but because it had so many rooms in its many hotels, gambling casinos, and villas. (Some of those villas would later become Gestapo offices, where French and American resistance fighters would be imprisoned and tortured.)

The party stopped for a roadside picnic lunch in a shaded grove along a deserted road in a setting that Murphy recalls, ". . . could not have been more peaceful. And none of us could know then that France was to become a battleground for almost five years, nor the profound changes that had been wrought by the German blitz."[35]

At La Bourboule, a town just outside Vichy, Bullitt stopped for the night. There he told Murphy and his traveling companions that he could no longer be useful in a Europe dominated by Hitler's Germany. Bullitt would not present his credentials; but before returning to the United States, he held a long meeting with Adm. Darlan, minister of Marine (the French navy), along with "informal" talks with Marshal Pétain.[36]

A few days later Bullitt, with vice-consul Offie and ex-Major Gilroy and his beautiful wife posing as butler and maid, drove across the French-Spanish frontier. At the border control, a hostile Spanish immigration officer ignored Mr. Gilroy (who apparently passed for a butler) but became suspicious of Mrs. Gilroy. A Philadelphia society matron and childhood friend of Bullitt's, she looked not at all like a servant. It was a very tense moment until Bullitt's trusted aide-de-camp, vice-consul Offie, solved the problem. He took the Spanish officer aside and whispered into the man's ear: "Don't you understand that the ambassador has a mistress?"[37]

One of the last acts of Ambassador Bullitt was to ensure that Robert Murphy took charge of the American Embassy at Vichy. It was the end of a climactic and depressing six weeks: Paris under Nazi rule, the U.S. presence in the capital reduced and impotent.[38] A new era had dawned for Murphy. After some twenty years in the Foreign Service, he was to command an embassy. From his arrival at Vichy to the end of World War II, the boy from a Milwaukee slum would live many a breathtaking moment and play a key role in the Allied defeat of Nazi Germany.

ROBERT DANIEL MURPHY: THE LUCK OF THE IRISH

Bob Murphy began his diplomatic career in 1917 as a twenty-three-year-old code clerk at the U.S. Legation at Bern, Switzerland. Murphy was no isolationist despite his Midwestern upbringing. He believed America should enter the European war—not a mainstream American sentiment at the time. He was, in his own words, "innocent," but possessed with "the valor of ignorance."[39]

Murphy crossed the Atlantic that first spring of America's entry into World War I aboard the SS *Chicago*—a tub of a freighter loaded with volunteer American ambulance drivers. At a stopover in Paris, he caught the first of many glimpses of what war was about. And it stayed with him, writing almost fifty years later: "I never have forgotten the faces of the people on the streets of Paris: elderly soldiers, subdued workers, anxious women, and solemn children. They had endured three years of having their men slaughtered in the trenches."[40]

Murphy had been incredibly lucky, and Lady Luck was to follow him for most of his life. One wonders how the stenographer-typist, working in the Washington, D.C., office of the third assistant postmaster general, managed to obtain a wartime assignment. His new job in Bern was a far cry from living at Miss Rose's $5.00-a-week boardinghouse in Washington. In plain fact, an unpretentious but ambitious Murphy had an appetite for work. Unfit for military service (a childhood accident left him with a permanent foot injury), he may have longed to somehow get into the war. He later said that he chose to become "a diplomat among warriors," albeit in neutral Switzerland.[41]

"ON THE INSIDE . . . RIGHT FROM THE START"[42]

Bern, Murphy's first station in the third year of World War I, was a hotbed of espionage and intrigue. The city's arcades and taverns were crowded with spies. The young embassy clerk was thrown in with men and women employed in the grand game of buying and stealing intelligence. The process was similar to the way the English novelist and spy, William Somerset Maugham, described the work of his British agent, Ashenden. Maugham wrote how Ashenden

> paid [spies] their wages. When he could get hold of a new one he engaged him, gave him his instructions and sent him off to Germany; he waited for the information that came through and dispatched it; he went into France once a week to confer with

his colleague over the frontier and to receive his orders from London; he visited the marketplace on market-day to get any message the old butter-woman had brought him from the other side of the lake.[43]

Ashenden called this work monotonous.

Not so Allen Dulles, who was stationed at Bern with Murphy in 1917, and would head the CIA years later. One of Murphy's jobs was to put Dulles's and other American spies' information into secret cipher (regularly broken by the German Black Chamber[44]). Murphy also translated German and Austrian publications into raw intelligence. Young Dulles and Murphy were apprentices in the spy trade, learning to play in the Great Game.[45]

And Bern was the place to play it, according to Dulles: "Bern is just full of agents. . . . It becomes quite an art to pick out the reliable and safe persons with whom one can deal."[46] Murphy knew of one of Dulles's sources: a German naval officer married to the daughter of the American consul general in Zurich. The German would visit his wife at her father's home every weekend, and their long conversations were not limited to "family chitchat." Dulles cited this German captain as one of his sources in countless dispatches in 1917–18 dealing with conditions in Germany and Austria-Hungary. But Dulles never divulged that his German source was married to the consul general's daughter. Rather, the source was purported to be "an Austrian of intelligence and education, whom I believe to be well informed" and someone who was "personally very friendly to the United States . . . and opposed to any close alliance between Austria-Hungary and Germany . . . a naval officer in close association with the ruling house of Germany." Allen Dulles had thus learned early the practice of many an intelligence officer to shade his sources—and Washington commended him for his "extraordinary" work. Such is the business of espionage.

Armed with Irish wit and good humor, Murphy was refreshingly different from the men with whom he worked in Bern and in the years that followed. The majority of career diplomats were educated at eastern seaboard Ivy League prep schools and universities. To the contrary, Murphy wrote, "There is certainly nothing in my family and educational background to suggest a diplomatic career." Indeed, Murphy's father had dropped out of school in the fourth grade, and "tried his hand at many occupations, including operating a saloon with a friend." This colorless information, taken from Murphy's autobiography (which he claims is "no account of my personal life") is the only reference to his upbringing. It is typical tongue-in-cheek Murphy.[47]

Armistice Day 1918 came at last. In Bern, American bureaucrats were packing for home—but not Robert Murphy. He had become romantically involved with a Kansas farm girl named Mildred Taylor, one of nine children and the only one who left home to serve with the Red Cross in Albania in 1917. Posted to Bern, the "very beautiful"[48] Miss Taylor seduced Murphy by beating him in a shorthand contest on a shaking Swiss rack-and-pinion mountain train.

Mildred believed that Murphy had "no intention of following a permanent career in the consular services."[49] But he had already tasted life abroad— "had a glimpse of wide horizons"—and had made up his mind to be a career diplomat; though he may have had difficulty selling Mildred on the idea of living a life overseas.

In early 1919 the U.S. State Department asked Murphy to stand by in Bern for an assignment to Germany as a vice-consul.[50] But in May, Murphy changed his mind and asked to return home for personal reasons. "Family matters of some urgence [sic] and importance necessitate my immediate return to the United States. I trust that the necessity of returning . . . will not interfere with an appointment [as vice-consul]."[51]

Murphy arrived home with Mildred, now his fiancée, in June 1919. One can deduce that their sudden return was due to Mildred's first of many nervous breakdowns. Bob Murphy may not have known how fragile her health was—and he couldn't have known that her illness would haunt his career for years to come.

During the next two years Murphy worked days in the Treasury Department in Washington and finished law school at night. He reapplied for appointment to the Foreign Service and sought a post as consul (one grade above a vice-consul)—marshaling supporters at the U.S. House of Representatives to second his application. In 1920 Murphy took the Foreign Service examination and passed with an 81.41 percent rating.

Bob and Mildred "tied the knot" on March 3, 1921. The following month, Murphy was commissioned by Congress a vice-consul *de carrière* (an early State Department title for a career diplomat), and the couple left for a post at Zurich. His starting salary was $2,500 a year.

In passing, Murphy admitted that he had been offered a well-paying job at a private firm and turned it down. The son of a Milwaukee saloon keeper "had found [his] niche in life"—and a career that would last another forty years.[52]

Mildred Taylor Murphy probably didn't share her husband's enthusiasm for overseas life, but she did have a curious nature—and she would work hard to be a good diplomat's wife. Mildred learned to speak French and German fluently and made considerable efforts to adapt to the rigors of life overseas.[53]

Murphy gobbled up work. He had the Celt's hot nature and the gift of gab along with "a very quick temper [that] may flare up easily."[54] He also had a facility with languages. For most of his early career he studied French and German for an hour every day and could "think" and work in both languages. There is no doubt that his aptitude and driving ambition set him apart.

Bob felt at home in exotic and foreign surroundings—always with half a smile on his lips and a bon mot, he felt equal to all men. Without even knowing it, Murphy had undergone a metamorphosis in Europe. Reading about the man, one can almost feel Murphy's determination to learn the trade, to acquire the skills, to rise above the "clerkship" and bureaucratic boredom—the dull, routine consular work, with its visas and stacks upon stacks of government forms—to move onward and upward from a desk job to that of a polished diplomat. He learned the right turn of phrase for dispatches and operations memoranda; how to use informal letters to "stay in touch." Words were capital weapons, as were culture, correct dress, small conversation, good manners, and proper bearing.

In November 1922, Murphy again had the "luck" with him. As Adolf Hitler rose to prominence, Murphy was transferred to Munich, the epicenter of Nazism. He spent the next four years observing and reporting on the maneuverings and intrigues of Nazis and Bolsheviks, and on some of the main actors in that chaotic city: Hitler, Erich Ludendorff, and Eugenio Pacelli (later to be Pope Pius XII). Murphy sent Washington an eyewitness report on Hitler's attempts to overthrow the government of Bavaria in 1923, and about how "the noisy ruffian Hitler" had fired shots at the ceiling of a Munich beer hall when he tried to trigger a Nazi putsch.

Typically, Murphy heard nothing back from the State Department. His 1924 report on Hitler's trial for treason and five-year sentence to the military prison at Landsberg Fortress (where Germany's future Nazi leader wrote his prophetic treatise, *Mein Kampf*) apparently went unnoticed. It is perhaps typical of the time that Murphy's Munich boss, though appreciative in 1924 of

Murphy's "political affairs" work, thought that his political reporting "was done at the expense of the commercial work."[55]

At this point, the world had little time to devote to an obscure Adolf Hitler. The French army had occupied a part of northwestern Germany's major industrial and coal mining region in the valley of the Ruhr River. Fascism had spread to Italy. The Soviets openly called for a world revolution. Calvin Coolidge won the U.S. presidential election. And the first Winter Olympics opened in Chamonix, France.

But Murphy's Washington masters were apparently impressed with his talents as a spy. At a time when Japan's naval armaments were limited under the terms of the Versailles Treaty, Murphy met a young German named Diesel (son of the inventor of the diesel engine) who wanted to immigrate to the United States. Murphy got the man to reveal that the Japanese were buying German diesel engines, shipping them to Japan as "agricultural machinery," and then secretly converting the engines to drive their submarine fleet.

Now Germany began to slide into a cycle of galloping inflation that would reduce the German middle class to beggary. In 1922, "a ticket on a train cost a crazy fortune; but there were no ticket collectors."[56] The prewar value of the *deutschmark* was 25 U.S. cents. And near disaster lurked: by August 1923, a dollar was buying millions, in September billions, in October trillions of marks. Murphy's thrifty Munich cook, Louisa, who had managed to invest the equivalent of $20,000 in German State marks-denominated savings deposits, lost it all. She ended up penniless.[57] Murphy saw clearly how economic and financial disaster promoted fascism.

In the late summer of 1925, Murphy's assignment to Germany came to a dramatic end when Mildred was involved in a nasty scene at a Munich shop where she had gone to collect a vacuum cleaner undergoing repairs. Apparently the shopkeeper overcharged her for the work, and she protested. When Mildred tried to leave with the appliance, the proprietress shoved and insulted her. Mildred then slapped the woman four times and then slapped a male customer—an off-duty police inspector who tried to intervene. The Munich "extreme right-wing" press offered a "one-sided" version of the incident, and Robert Murphy responded. In a *New York Times* story datelined Munich, Murphy stated:

> It is true . . . that my wife did slap two Germans—a man and a
> woman—in a store here, but she did so in self-defense and under

severe provocation. Both Germans had laid hands on her and used vile and insulting language to her . . . Mrs. Murphy, whose small bill at the store, needless to say, always was promptly paid, protested against the price demanded for some repair work, whereupon the saleswoman burst forth in a tirade of the most insulting language and started to push my wife out of the place. Thereupon my wife slapped her. Then a man, who described himself as a police inspector out of uniform and off duty, made grossly insulting remarks to Mrs. Murphy and also attempted to shove her outside, whereupon she also slapped him. We both are extremely sorry the incident occurred, but my wife's actions were absolutely justified by the circumstances.[58]

One wants to cheer Mildred Murphy on; but no matter the provocation, this was scandalous behavior for a Foreign Service officer's wife. The U.S. minister in Munich had Murphy transferred to Seville, Spain — though he did recommend that Murphy's career should not suffer. It was the beginning of a long personal trial for Bob and Mildred Murphy. From Seville, Murphy returned home so that Mildred could be treated at Johns Hopkins Hospital in Baltimore, Maryland. (Doctors later diagnosed Mildred as manic-depressive, with occasional recurrent loss of memory and hallucinations.)[59]

Murphy's restless energy and determination to make a career in the Foreign Service was not to be distracted. For the next four years in Washington, he worked diligently at "Old State." And he found time to earn a master of laws degree at George Washington University—despite the personal burden of a sick wife and three young daughters to raise and educate.

In 1930 Murphy's "excellent" performance earned him another overseas posting. He was offered the choice of Paris, Bremen, or Shanghai. Murphy asked Homer Byington, his chief of personnel: "What would you say, Homer?"

The next day, Murphy was transferred to Paris.

IN PARIS DURING THE GREAT DEPRESSION

Murphy would spend the next ten years at the American Embassy in Paris, working first in consular affairs and administration. By 1933, when Hitler became chancellor of Germany, Murphy was a rising star, and, when U.S. ambassador William C. Bullitt took over four years later, he appointed Murphy as the embassy executive officer, and then to the responsible and exalted job of counselor for political affairs.

And 1933 saw Hitler withdraw from the Versailles Treaty; French politics were in chaos as French families felt the squeeze of the global economic depression. The financial crash didn't spare the 30,000 American expatriates living in Paris.[60] Many were made poor in the months to come and were forced to return to the United States. The U.S. Embassy staff took a 15 percent cut in salaries and a reduction in living allowances. But they thought themselves lucky to have jobs—knowing they were better off than most expatriates living in France.

During the Depression years, riots, strikes, and street battles between warring political factions—communists and fascists—soured the sweet life of Paris. Murphy reported the election of a leftist popular front and the effects on France of the neighboring Spanish Civil War. "France," he wrote, "was politically paralyzed."[61]

Franklin Delano Roosevelt, running for a second term in office, told a Democratic convention in Philadelphia: "Here in America we are waging a great and successful war . . . It is not alone a war against want and destitution and economic demoralization . . . It is a war for the survival of democracy."[62] These were prophetic words. In Europe, as the Spanish Civil War raged, Roosevelt warned that "mortal danger came from Nazi Germany." He cautioned: "Let no one imagine that America will escape, that America may expect mercy, that this Western hemisphere will not be attacked . . ."[63]

FDR predicted to the visiting author H. G. Wells that a new world war would break out in 1941.[64] Indeed, in the face of global conflict, FDR stood out in the world as the "decisive, energetic, and benign" leader of a nation, whereas French and British statesmen seemed "dyspeptic, ineffective, and unimaginative," as they eventually proved to be.[65]

Tensions in Europe heightened when Nazi warplanes destroyed the Spanish town of Guernica. England was bent on appeasement, and Bullitt warned FDR from Paris that the new English prime minister, Neville Chamberlain, was "anti-American." Bullitt—brilliant, mercurial, conscientious, and highstrung—soon became FDR's spokesman in France and Europe: doggedly condemning Nazi aggression when "peace in our time" was the popular motto in England and on the continent.[66] Multilingual and vain—Bullitt was never without a fresh dark-red carnation in his buttonhole—the pink-skinned, blue-eyed, Philadelphia native tickled French audiences with his upper-class manners and aristocratic airs.

Robert Murphy freed Bullitt of the administrative tedium of a large embassy, allowing his boss to concentrate on advancing U.S. interests in political and economic matters. Despite being single, Bullitt entertained lavishly at his official residence behind the embassy on the chic Faubourg Saint-Honoré and at his beautiful home at Chantilly.

Between the terrible years when Hitler's Reich annexed Austria and invaded Czechoslovakia, Murphy formed friendships that would have a major impact on his future work. As the embassy's top political counselor, Murphy came to know the cream of the French establishment. Indeed, by the time he left Paris for Vichy in 1940, Murphy had dined at the table of every politician and bureaucrat who mattered—the men and their mistresses who made prewar France tick.[67] He was held in high esteem not only by his supervisor, but also by French prime minister Edouard Daladier himself.[68] And Murphy would work with these same Frenchmen—the fascist industrial elite and their wives and mistresses—later in Vichy.

Bullitt and Murphy knew war was coming and doubted the ability of the French to resist an invasion; they had concluded that France was probably lost.[69] In the summer of 1939, as Germany invaded Poland, Murphy sent Mildred and the three girls to La Baule, a resort town on the southwest Atlantic coast of Brittany, from where they could easily take a ship to America.

It was a breezy September's day when Mildred and her daughters sipped tea at a chic La Baule café. The other tourists enjoyed éclairs, cakes, and coffee—until a loudspeaker broadcast French prime minister Daladier's announcement that France had declared war on Germany.

The silence was stunning, frightening—and it may have been too much for Mildred. She suffered another nervous breakdown. Murphy made the urgent drive to La Baule—a five-hour trip from Paris—in the family's 1936 Buick. Exhausted from work at the embassy, he arrived to admit Mildred to an English army hospital (where already, wounded English soldiers were being treated). He then had to rush back to Paris, leaving seventeen-year-old daughter Catherine to take care of her sisters at the La Roseraie pension.[70]

Back in Paris, Murphy ordered Han, the family's Vietnamese butler/cook, to pack. The time had come to get the family out of France. Again back in La Baule, Murphy hectically drove the girls to Bordeaux without their mother, and saw them aboard the SS *Washington*, bound for New York. When ten-year-old Rosemary fretted about German submarines in the Atlantic, Murphy arranged for the ship's captain to personally guarantee that his "Rosemaruschka" (all the girls had nicknames) would arrive safely in America.

One wonders at how Murphy, in the space of a few months, burdened with overwhelming family problems and the stress of working in wartime France, managed to summon the stamina and resilience to cope. Again, Murphy drove to Baule. Mildred was now well enough to travel, and he took his frail wife to Lisbon, where they boarded the Pan Am Clipper for a transatlantic flight to New York.

After a brief Christmas visit with the girls at Mildred's family home in Kansas City, Murphy flew back to Lisbon to continue on to Paris. It would be a long time before the family was reunited.

Six months later, Murphy awoke on the couch of his embassy office to the sound of Wehrmacht troopers' hobnailed boots pounding along the Place de la Concorde. Four years of war lay ahead.

CHARGÉ D'AFFAIRES IN WARTIME VICHY

When Bullitt left Murphy in charge at Vichy, the Nazis had divided France into zones according to the terms of a Franco-German armistice agreement. Paris and the northern tier of France—from the Swiss border to the English Channel and south to the Bay of Biscay and the Spanish frontier—were occupied by Wehrmacht forces; and from Vichy, Marshal Pétain, head of state, ruled the unoccupied zone and France's overseas colonies, including North and West Africa. The Vichy regime may not have at first been fascist, but it was certainly authoritarian (except perhaps for the fascist Milice police, created in 1943, which would change the nature of the state). And it was immediately clear to Murphy that Pétain and most of his ministers were set on a course of collaboration with the Nazis. (Murphy's analysis was confirmed when, after Germany decreed the counting of Jews in the occupied zone, Marshal Pétain's Vichy government followed by banning Jews from "high public service.")[71]

In London, Gen. Charles de Gaulle established a Free French movement. The general was not totally acceptable to His Majesty's Government Foreign Office, but Churchill promoted him as the symbol of French resistance: the leader of a free France. Churchill would mostly support de Gaulle, hoping he would appeal to Frenchmen and to the French armed forces outside German control to reject surrender and to rally to the Allied cause. He let de Gaulle use BBC overseas broadcasts to make the general's early *Appels* of July 18 and 19, 1940.[72]

Amid the chaos, General Francisco Franco, Germany's ally since the Spanish Civil War, seized the Mediterranean port city of Tangier, at the west end of the Strait of Gibraltar in today's Morocco, while Italian forces held Ethiopia and Libya, threatening British Egypt and the Suez Canal. By June 1940, hundreds of Nazi Gestapo and fascist OVRA[73] agents—Italian security and intelligence operatives—flooded the principal cities in Algeria, Morocco, and Tunisia. As members of a German and Italian mixed armistice commission, they recruited spies among the Vichy bureaucracy and placed paid agents among Arab and Berber opinion leaders and tribesmen and in the news media. The Germans paid large sums for information about French political, economic, and military plans and for propaganda against the Allies. Gestapo agents put a twenty-four-hour watch on American businesses and diplomatic offices in North Africa.

Earlier, FDR had cabled Bullitt in Paris, expressing fears that the French fleet could "get caught bottled up in the Mediterranean." He asked Bullitt to warn Prime Minister Reynaud and French officials to get the fleet to safe havens in the West Indies and West Africa.[74] London and Washington dreaded the idea that the French fleet would fall under German control—that Germany and Italy would occupy French North Africa and hook up with Axis forces fighting the British in the Libyan and Egyptian desert.[75]

By midsummer 1940, all of North Africa and a mighty French fleet, mostly contained at Toulon and in Mediterranean ports, hung in the balance. The Allies feared the Mediterranean would become a German and Italian fortress.

Such was the state of affairs when Robert Murphy took charge of the U.S. Embassy in Vichy France on July 3, 1940.[76]

It turned out to be an infamous day for France: Winston Churchill, convinced that the Germans would seize or gain control of the French fleet in North Africa, ordered the seizure of French ships in British, Mediterranean, and Egyptian ports and at Dakar, West Africa. When the French resisted, British naval forces sank three French capital ships anchored at the Algerian naval port of Mers-el-Kebir, killing 1,297 French officers and seamen and wounding 351 others. At Dakar, the battleship *Richelieu* was torpedoed. There were no British casualties.[77] Then Britain's prime minister ordered the British fleet to blockade French ports.

Pétain broke diplomatic relations with Great Britain—France's ally in two wars—and tossed British consular officials out of French North Africa.

Had it not been for Murphy's intervention on FDR's orders, Pétain might well have declared war on Britain.

Murphy's appointment to Vichy was certainly one of the most complex and uncomfortable assignments an American diplomat had ever undertaken. Hitler's victories were so complete that millions of Europeans believed that Germany had already won the war—and many Americans agreed.[78] Nineteen-forty was an election year in America, and President Roosevelt feared that any move considered too warlike by voters might cost him his highly sought third term. Thus, Murphy received official directives that were classified "top secret"—to conceal Washington's plans from the Germans and from the American public.[79] He was to persuade the Vichy leaders—and particularly Marshal Philippe Pétain, Pierre Laval, Adm. Jean-François Darlan, and Gen. Maxime Weygand—that the war was not lost, that America backed Britain, and that Vichy had better not make concessions to Hitler concerning the French North African colonies and the French fleet. (Murphy's orders allowed him to offer American support to French leaders by every means permissible under the U.S. Neutrality Act, passed by Congress and designed to prevent American participation in Europe's war.)

French North Africa offered "the most promising opportunities to carry out anti-Nazi activities."[80] But Murphy's efforts to influence the eighty-four-year-old Pétain and his deputy, Pierre Laval (who was destined to be executed as a traitor after a summary trial by a postwar French commission), met with little success. Still, Murphy hammered away at Vichy ministers and Adm. Darlan that the French fleet had to be kept out of German hands.[81] The war was not over, Bob declared, and "Britain would prevail, the Allies would be victorious, and the French nation would eventually profit by refusing to make concessions to Germany beyond those already made in the armistice agreement."

It was a hard sell. Germany now controlled all of continental Europe. The hero of Verdun, Marshal Pétain, and most of Vichy's civil service, with Pierre Laval and Admiral Darlan (who controlled the French fleet) believed that Germany would defeat Britain.[82] The old marshal would tell Murphy in his cool, clear, and rather formal French that continuing the war would have been insane for France, resulting in the total destruction of the country; after all, the Germans were holding 1,850,000 Frenchmen in Nazi prison camps. Pétain argued that neither Britain nor France should have gone into a war for which they were totally unprepared. France could not afford to once again lose a million of its sons as it had in WWI. As for de Gaulle—in London, calling for resistance to the Nazis—Pétain called him "a viper I had clutched to my bosom."[83]

Despite the challenges and the horrid living conditions, Murphy, judging by his memoirs, seemed energized by the assignment to Vichy. Now in the prime of life, tall and handsome, he was at home with the upper crust of French bureaucracy and, indeed, French high society, bankers, and industrialists.[84] Behind the shirtsleeve workaholic was a shrewd, very perceptive, and sensitive man with a Gallic "temperament."[85] A dedicated civil servant, he backed FDR's policy to support Marshal Pétain and his Vichy regime.

Still, Murphy was not as cautious as he might have been given the time and place. In prewar Paris, he had come into contact with some shady moneymen who later turned up in Vichy. One, the Vichy secret police chief Pierre Pucheu,[86] had been an "infamous" pro-Nazi French businessman connected with the pro-fascist banks grouped around the Banque Worms et Cie in Paris.[87] Pucheu had close relations with a host of prewar fascists and monarchists: men like Henri, Comte de Paris, the pretender to the French throne; and business leaders like Jacques Lemaigre Dubreuil and his partner, Jean Rigault, editor of Lemaigre Dubreuil's *Le Jour-Echo de Paris*. These were men who wanted to establish in prewar France a totalitarian pre-Vichy elitism aimed at restoring "those ideas vital to the nation's health: authority, family, economy and country." They were dubbed, "fashionable in a totalitarian regime." And they echoed the slogans Pétain would adopt after the German occupation of France.[88]

Later, in Algeria, Murphy, the most powerful and influential American diplomat in North Africa, would be surrounded by Lemaigre Dubreuil and Rigault and a clique of fascist and royalist opportunists and their fashionable set of Parisian boulevardier ladies who sought a monarchist regime under Henri, Comte de Paris.

Washington was pleased with Murphy's work, and Ambassador William Bullitt urged the State Department to promote Murphy. Before the turn of the year, the former Bern code clerk was named to a Class 1, senior Foreign Service officer position at Vichy. It was apparent that Bob Murphy was marked by Washington for the most demanding jobs in the U.S. Foreign Service.

Finally his own boss, Bob Murphy was free in Vichy to conduct the business of his masters and to try to discover the business of others.[89] But for the time being Murphy was confined to the Vichy Spa, which swarmed with an inbred group of 130,000: French politicians, diplomats, and secret agents installed in hastily built cubicles in former gambling rooms or in unheated hotel rooms transformed into offices. Their archives were stuffed into bathrooms, and the old marshal's photo was hung or pasted everywhere—sternly looking down at his disciples as they shivered with the coming of winter. The place took on the air of a tacky and tawdry commercial fair. One observer declared that Vichy was "pulsing with energy, sexual and otherwise, where life went on at cabarets, nightclubs and brothels"[90] that served the needs of Vichy's high civil servants, experts, and professionals.

Murphy had known these men in prewar Paris; they were all products of the most rigorous education and curricula in any public administration in the world. In American terms, they were a brain trust; in British terms, a regime of "double firsts."

"This was the elite of the elite, selected through a daunting series of relentless examinations for which one prepared at expensive private schools."[91] But the Vichy mandarinate would soon discover that France was involved in a curious kind of civil war, from which even the bureaucracy could not remain aloof. Eventually even the elite would have to choose between the Allies and the Nazis.

Murphy lived a bachelor's existence at the Hotel Lutetia. More alone than ever, with Mildred again hospitalized in Kansas and without his three other "queens," he must have felt terribly isolated. It is impossible to know what he thought of the loose life in Vichy. Despite his acquired veneer and sophistication, there remained in the man a certain "reticence of Irish Catholic prudishness that inhibited him."[92]

Among the Vichy ministers, one man stood out: the minister of defense, Gen. Maxime Weygand. A devout Catholic like Murphy (and a confirmed anti-Nazi), he and Murphy would develop a solid working relationship and a friendship later in Algiers, when Weygand took over as delegate general of French Africa. President Roosevelt made the erroneous assumption that General Maxime Weygand might somehow head a conspiracy against the Axis sometime and somewhere in the future.[93]

The winter of 1940–41 was to be one of the coldest and harshest in ninety years. France, along with all of Europe, was destined to suffer: freezing temperatures, no fuel, dire shortages, and the 1940 harvest had been reduced to a third of its normal output. When Murphy ordered the American Red Cross in France to report on conditions throughout the country, they turned in a bleak picture. The Germans held hundreds of thousands of Frenchmen in prisoner-of-war camps. Every known commodity including wine was rationed, and German units organized for looting began to systematically strip the countryside and cities as they had done in 1914. Berlin put grievous economic pressure on France; the Reich choked off commerce between the two zones, imposing an unfair currency exchange rate and a penalty of twenty million *reichsmarks* per day for occupation costs. It was "a monstrous exploitation of the French economy."[94] Murphy told of all this in a dispatch to Washington, and predicted disaster for the twenty million people crammed into unoccupied France. (Six million were refugees: French fugitives from the occupied north of the country and refugees from the Benelux countries, anti-Franco Spaniards, anti-Nazis, and Jews from all over Western Europe.)

With Britain blockading French ports, France faced a grievous six months without heat, proper food, warm clothing, or jobs. Railroads, trucks, and buses were at a standstill from lack of fuel; and as the days grew shorter and colder, Vichy residents and their unwanted refugee visitors began scavenging the countryside for anything to eat or drink. Murphy repeatedly asked his masters in Washington to pressure the English to free up food by lifting the blockade; it made no difference to the present war situation. He insisted that France held enough French gold and assets in the United States to pay for urgently needed food and fuel that would avoid disaster in the unoccupied zone and in French North Africa. No sooner had his report arrived at the U.S. State Department than Murphy received a secret cable summoning him immediately to Washington.

Robert Murphy had no idea that it was President Franklin Delano Roosevelt who had ordered him to the nation's capital. FDR had read Murphy's reports on French North Africa and the Red Cross assessment of the dire conditions in France. But the president wasn't interested in French shortages; he wanted more information about the French fleet, French North Africa with its strategic ports along the Mediterranean basin, and French colonies in West Africa. As he headed for Lisbon to board a Pan Am Clipper for New York, Murphy could not have known of President Roosevelt's strategic interest in this exotic part of Africa, nor imagined that in a few months' time he would become a vicar to FDR's Twelve Apostles—Roosevelt's political instrument for the invasion of North Africa.

2

VICHY—WASHINGTON—ALGIERS: A NORTH AFRICAN STORY

FROM LISBON TO WASHINGTON . . . it must have seemed a divine transition. Murphy had gone from rubbing elbows with sycophants, profiteers, anti-Semites, spies, and pro-German hangers-on at Vichy to the sanity of the U.S. capital. And at the end of the voyage, there would be Mildred and daughters Catherine, Rosemary, and Mildred to greet him.

Robert Murphy was forty-six years old when he settled into the luxury of Pan Am Yankee Clipper flight 202 bound for New York. It was September 4, 1940. Strapped into a cushioned seat, he may have sipped Scotch or a glass of wine as he looked out at the heavy islands of autumn clouds that scudded by over the Bay of Lisbon. Then the Clipper turned west and headed to a refueling stop at Horta in the Azores. It was the beginning of what Murphy called, "the be all and end all of my existence." It was also the beginning of an undeclared war waged by America's first WWII spies against the Axis powers in the French Empire. "The odds against winning seemed overwhelming in 1940."[95]

"THE LIGHTS HAVE GONE OUT ALL OVER EUROPE"[96]

If Murphy looked back, he had little to feel good about: Indeed, the lights had gone out all over Europe. In thirty-eight appalling days, a bilious, psychotic Adolf Hitler had achieved what the German armies of 1914–1918 had failed to gain in four years of bloody war that cost two million casualties. The

27

"Little Corporal" (as opponents dubbed Hitler) had realized a German dream: Paris was at his feet. Hitler strutted up the steps of the Paris Esplanade at the Trocadéro as the world's cameras panned slowly over his conquest: the historic Eiffel Tower, now topped by the Nazi swastika, the gardens of the Champs de Mars, and the 800-year-old twin towers of the Cathedral of Notre Dame.[97]

Now five months later and over the Atlantic, a very American and clean-cut Pan Am Clipper cabin staff dressed in crisp whites offered Murphy a lunch of turtle soup, roast beef, potatoes, French pastries, and a *millésime* of French champagne served in the airplane's dining room. Coffee and cocktails were served in the lounge, after which Murphy might have retired to one of the plane's thirty-six sleeping compartments.

During the tedious hours of flight, Murphy, ever the inveterate storyteller, probably rehearsed some of the spicy Parisian anecdotes he was storing up for his friends and colleagues in Washington. One, a vaudevillian boudoir set piece, involved French prime minister Paul Reynaud's tragicomic dénouement and the death of his mistress, French countess Hélène de Portès.

Their liaison was the talk of prewar Paris. Their high jinks were cause for anxiety at Paris embassies—not the least when the countess and Madame Reynaud showed up simultaneously at American Embassy dinners. It was a protocol nightmare, and the rather "untidy" countess[98] had a sinister influence in the halls of power. Being openly pro-German, gossip had it that she was a paid Nazi agent; she was overtly Anglophobic, known to influence the prime minister's decisions, persistently urging her lover and his ministers to negotiate peace with Nazi Germany. The man that fate had put at the helm of France during the final months of the Third Republic couldn't seem to do without his countess. "She makes me feel big," he said.[99]

Destiny intervened. After the Armistice, Reynaud was appointed by Pétain to be Vichy's ambassador to the United States. He left his wife in Vichy and drove with the countess in an automobile crammed with baggage headed toward the Spanish frontier and the Pan Am Clipper station in Lisbon. On the way, the car Hélène was driving hit a tree. A suitcase in the back of the car careened forward and struck de Portès in the back of the neck, killing her instantly. The unfortunate Reynaud was taken to the hospital, unconscious. His head swathed in bandages, he eventually returned to Vichy—and to the tender care of his unforgiving wife.

"FROM THE DARK CONTINENT OF EUROPE TO A LAND OF LIGHT"[100]

Murphy's flying boat landed on the water at Horta for refueling. There, the pilots would check GMT time, and set their clocks three hours back before taking off for Darrell's Island, Bermuda, and a seventeen-hour nonstop flight: the Clipper's final leg of the journey to New York's LaGuardia rotunda of the Marine Air Terminal. Murphy and the other passengers landed at LaGuardia at 2:12 P.M., September 5, 1940. He was already news: A *New York Times* reporter asked him at dockside if he believed the newly named Vichy ambassador to Washington, Gaston Henry-Haye, was pro-Nazi. It was unlike Murphy, already the polished diplomat, to respond vehemently to such a question; but for this time at least, he went out on a limb, telling the newsman with a certain passion, "Henry-Haye . . . stood at his post as Mayor [of Versailles] in the face of the German invasion. I consider him a courageous man and a patriotic Frenchman and I am glad to call him a friend of mine. I consider him the best man for the position and any thought of his being Nazi or pro-German is . . . bunk."[101] This would not be the last time Murphy was wrong about his rich, French, high-society friends. A few months later, Ambassador Henry-Haye and Countess Josée de Chambrun, another acquaintance of Murphy's and the daughter of Pétain's prime minister (the pro-Nazi Pierre Laval), were denounced by British intelligence.[102]

GET REELECTED, AID BRITAIN, AND MARSHAL U.S. MIGHT[103]

When Murphy arrived in Washington, FDR was busy campaigning for a third term. A Gallup poll would show that 64 percent of the American people believed the U.S. should stay out of the war in Europe.[104] Murphy realized how angered and sickened the American public was at France's defeat, and "disgusted" by the news of Adolf Hitler's flaunting of his conquest of Holland, Belgium, and France.[105]

It was clear to Murphy that Washingtonians, like most Americans, "were uninterested in the plight of France."[106] It was the Roosevelt-Willkie election campaign, and baseball, rather than the Battle of Britain that held the public's attention that late summer and fall of 1940. There was no television to show America the terrors of the German blitzkrieg as the cities in England, Scotland, and Wales were devastated by Luftwaffe bombers. Roosevelt's secretary of the interior, Harold Ickes, wrote in his diary at that time: "Literally millions [in France] will die of starvation . . . But we ought not to send a pound of flour to any country that is controlled by Germany."[107]

Americans shunned the idea of intervention, much less war. Only the persuasive Roosevelt could manage to get Congress to pass a Selective Service Act mobilizing the U.S. military, as well as "lend-lease" aid to Britain. Despite his jaunty public image, FDR faced a tough election campaign and a Congress hostile to any involvement in Europe's troubles. He even feared impeachment by powerful domestic political enemies who labeled FDR, "a would-be dictator." He worried how far he could go to supply military aid to Great Britain as it faced a German invasion.[108]

Still, Roosevelt was determined to acquire for the United States a significant level of military might. He wanted to engineer "righteous hostilities" against the Axis, and then win an eventual war leading the world to a post-imperial Pax Americana. In this way, Woodrow Wilson's goals of safety for democracy and international legality would be established in some sort of American-led apparent international organization.[109]

It was Murphy's work as chargé at Vichy that had struck Roosevelt. The president had read his cables to Washington and was intrigued by a report prepared by Commander Roscoe H. Hillenkoetter, the U.S. naval attaché to Vichy France.[110] The naval attaché reported that French military and naval forces based in North Africa amounted to 125,000 combat-trained men on active service and 200,000 more in reserve. Hillenkoetter emphasized that army, navy, and air force officers and men had not lost their "traditional fighting spirit." And Murphy confirmed that, "if France was going to fight again anywhere in this war . . . North Africa will be the place." (This hypothesis held, despite the catastrophe of the British attack on the French fleet at Mers-el-Kebir.)[111]

A RENDEZVOUS WITH DESTINY

In the middle of FDR's election campaign, relations with Vichy France and French North Africa were secretly on the president's agenda when Murphy was summoned to the White House in mid-September 1940.[112] Undersecretary of State Sumner Welles, a close personal friend and confidant of President and Eleanor Roosevelt for forty years, would accompany Murphy to the meeting. It was a delicate moment for the president, Welles, and Murphy: for at that very moment a battle was being waged between William Bullitt, Murphy's old boss in Paris and his mentor, and Welles. As Murphy navigated the corridors of the Old State building off Pennsylvania Avenue, waiting for an audience with the president, he certainly met with Ambassador Bullitt, who wanted Welles's job (or to be secretary of the navy). Indeed, Bullitt had demanded that FDR fire Welles, claiming that the man was a degenerate and security risk ripe for blackmail. His claim arose from a nasty incident involving Welles, a married man. Bullitt had circulated in Washington "a description of Welles intoxicated on a rail trip in September 1940, [when] Welles had made indecent advances on a black railway porter." The man had complained to his employer.[113] (FDR refused to heed Bullitt's demand, hushed up the scandal, and eventually shunned Bullitt.)[114]

Murphy knew how to turn on the Irish charm. With his great toothy smile, he reminded FDR that they had already met briefly in 1920, when Bob was introduced at Hyde Park by another Irishman, James A. Farley, chairman of the Democratic National Committee. The president genially said, "You must have been in short pants," and then got down to business.

And the important foreign business for the United States that autumn of 1940 was how war had engulfed the European continent and the Middle East. Hitler had attacked Romania. Italy was going about devouring East Africa, Egypt, and Greece. In the Atlantic, German submarines were operating from the Gulf of Mexico to Labrador, threatening U.S. shipping, while at home isolationists and pro-Nazis exploited American fears of getting involved in a foreign war.

High on the president's list of decisions to be made was the question of a "Vichy policy." FDR saw Murphy as an instrument to somehow bring the French Empire and its fleet of warships and a rearmed French colonial army into war against Nazi Germany and fascist Italy. Using a large map displaying French North and West Africa spread out on his desk, FDR sketched out the geography: the Mediterranean and Atlantic coasts. He ordered Murphy to be his eyes and ears and asked him to go back to Vichy, France, obtain travel permits for Dakar, French Algeria, Morocco, and Tunisia, and work "unostentatiously" to prepare an urgent secret report for FDR's eyes only. The president told Murphy to bypass the State Department and the U.S. military, and report directly to the White House on economic conditions in the French North African colonies and the attitudes of the French bureaucracy, French businessmen, and North African Arab and Berber peoples and their leaders. It was a tall order.[115] (Roosevelt dictated that no record be made

of the Murphy meeting, at which only he, Murphy, and Welles were present—and no record exists. This extraordinary procedure would remain in
force for the next twenty-four months.)

Roosevelt made no bones about his choice of Murphy. He knew the career diplomat had worked in Germany and France, spoke both languages,
and was familiar with the politics and personalities of both nations. The president even ventured that as a Roman Catholic, Murphy might get on with
the Catholic Gen. Maxime Weygand, who had just been appointed by Marshal Pétain to be French Vichy delegate general (governor) of the colonies.[116]
With a wink, Roosevelt added, "You might even go to church with Weygand!" (Murphy later said the remark by FDR showed an exaggerated idea of
the bond existing between Catholics.)[117]

Murphy's assignment would have been dynamite, had details of their conversation leaked out in the press at the time. The president had campaigned
on his party's commitment to nonintervention and keeping America out of
the war. He told Murphy, with typical FDR humor, "American mothers don't
want their boys to be soldiers, so nothing really big can be done at present
about expanding the Army. But the Navy is another matter; American mothers don't seem to mind their boys being sailors." As a result, said the president,
"Naval rearmament was the only form of preparedness politically possible."[118]

Robert Murphy left the White House with no doubts about his mission
and his empowerment by the president. He was to be FDR's personal representative in North Africa; he was to bypass FDR's secretary of state Cordell
Hull—indeed, the whole State Department bureaucracy—and report directly
to Roosevelt. Murphy was now convinced that FDR meant to lead the United
States into war against the Axis powers. He learned in that short meeting that
the president considered Gen. Charles de Gaulle in London to be a comical
"mountebank," and that FDR thought even less of de Gaulle's "Free French,"
despite Winston Churchill's support for the young general's movement in
France and in the French colonies.[119] (It would be many years before Roosevelt
shared Churchill's belief that de Gaulle was morally and politically the only
French devotee of uninterrupted and unconditional war against the Nazis.)

Roosevelt's attitude toward de Gaulle would later turn Murphy away
from Gaullist Free French resistance fighters in North Africa. Indeed, Roosevelt's Vichy policy left Murphy little choice but to deal with marginal
groups—including one headed by Lemaigre Dubreuil. It was a serious future
impediment that later proved to be a major political error.

As privileged as Murphy may have felt to be the president's confidential agent, and as determined as he was to carry out FDR's instructions, he left Washington sick at heart. Despite the warm family reunion with Mildred and his daughters, who were now settled in a house in the Maryland suburbs, it was clear that Mildred was still ill and that Catherine, as the oldest daughter, was bearing a heavy burden.[120]

THE PROMISED LAND

Seven hundred fifty miles due south of Paris across the Mediterranean Sea in Algiers, and five time zones east of Washington, a stunningly beautiful Daphne Joan Fry Tuyl sat shaded from the typically brilliant North African sun, at lunch with the resident British consul general, Captain Galrow, and his wife.

It was Daphne's birthday, but "a day of anxiety, fear, and sadness," for she had just received news that Germany had overrun Holland. Gerard (Gerry) Tuyl, her husband and the father of their two children, was fighting there— a reserve officer in the Dutch army.[121] Daphne had fled a devastated Europe in 1940 to return to her home in Algiers and her widowed artist mother. She told her friends on her arrival from Holland that with Europe in Nazi hands, she did not know how she and her children, Tony, age four, and Derek, two, would survive. "My reserve of money was small and the Germans now cut off the small amount of funds that had been coming from Gerry. What could I do for a living?"

During lunch, Daphne wrote, "I heard little of the conversation going by me. I felt numbed. Was this the end of our adventure? Until then, our married life had been an adventure few people have experienced: we had dairy farmed an oasis in the Sahara for five years where Gerry and I had brought up our two small sons."[122]

Captain Galrow interrupted Daphne's somber thoughts with a startling, "How would you like to join the Military Mission?" Daphne stared at the big man and then looked at his wife.

"What do you mean?"

"I mean," Galrow said, "that we know enough about you to feel you might be useful to us. The war is only just beginning, you know. We have good reason to believe that North Africa is going to be a very important seat of operations. We need people like you who have been here several years and know both the language and the inhabitants. Well? What about it?"

"Yes, a thousand times, yes. If you really think I will be useful," Daphne gasped.[123]

And so began an adventure and a love story that would plunge Robert Murphy, key members of his team of Apostles, and agents like Daphne Tuyl into the frenetic political environment of French North Africa: where French families might be divided in their complex loyalties between the aging and pro-fascist Marshal Pétain and the vibrant young resistant, Charles de Gaulle; and where German and Italian authority was ever-present and universally detested. In French-dominated North Africa, racist attitudes put down the Jews, the Moslem Arabs, and Berber peoples; and French colons competed for scarce resources with the growing number of refugees from metropolitan France. Indeed, the tangles and twists of North African politics, ethnic strife, and power plays by Vichy opportunists would nearly sink Murphy's and Roosevelt's plans to free North Africa.[124]

Still, for French refugees like Daphne and war-weary British expatriates, North Africa in 1940 was a land of plenty, and Algiers, white beneath the haze of heat—a God-sent haven.[125] Europe offered an atmosphere of abysmal defeat: German occupation with the lack of fuel to heat, turnips for every meal, long lines at the butcher's, and near starvation.

Renée Gosset, a newswoman who knew Daphne and Murphy in 1940 and 1941, had arrived in Algiers from Lyon in April 1940. She described Algiers as a magical kingdom where one could buy a magnificent leg of mutton weighing five pounds for 60 francs 80 centimes (unheard of in France). Scarlet tomatoes, eggplants varnished deep purple, yellow-green garden peas, onions, leeks, and oranges were heaped on the stalls with hills of tangerines, vast quantities of lettuce, French beans, and mountains of potatoes that overflowed on the pavement. "Farmers and traders were prosperous, and generally North Africa was happy being out of the war."[126]

For many in 1940, Algiers was "the Promised Land."[127] But the wealth and abundant food would soon disappear. In 1941, Vichy obeyed its masters and stripped the North African land to feed German and Italian industry.

Daphne began work as a clerk at the British Military Mission at a time when resistance to the Axis was almost nonexistent, and de Gaulle's Fighting French movement was a growing phenomenon. She soon graduated to reporting the attitudes of her Arab and French acquaintances in Algiers—and with the aid of an anti-Nazi French air force officer, managed to copy French air force signals and codes and deliver them daily to the Mission. But this foray into espionage was not to last. Scarcely a few weeks into her undercover work, her job ended. Daphne was leaving home one morning when Captain Galrow, the British consul general, drove to her house. "Burn everything and lay low," he shouted and drove off. Daphne rushed back into the house and did as she was told. Then, suddenly she was gripped with the realization: "I had started to do something I knew very little about. Things could go wrong . . . and then what?"[128]

As it turned out, the excitement was about no less an event than the British ultimatum to the French fleet at Mers-el-Kebir; and it meant the breaking-off of diplomatic relations between England and France.[129] Daphne never saw British consul general Galrow again. When he stopped for the brief second to warn Daphne, he had been on his way to the British Consulate to burn the compromising documents in his safe. But Galrow apparently had the time to tell Murphy's colleague, Felix Cole, U.S. consul in Algiers, that Daphne was a trusted employee of the British and might work for the U.S. Consulate.[130]

Daphne then joined an informal resistance network run by Maurice Escoute, publisher of an underground newspaper. With Escoute's help, Daphne arranged to steal a small un-decked sailing boat, located a skipper to sail the craft, and managed to get a number of Allied pilots and seamen out of Algeria to British Gibraltar.

The Escoute embryonic resistance cell was made up of government officials and ex-army officers, physicians, and dentists who, like Daphne, hated "the enemy"—the Nazis, Vichy sycophants, German collaborators, and members of the local German and Italian Armistice Commission—in reality, Gestapo and OVRA agents. They began spying on the French Vichy administration and military and naval operations in Algiers, providing political, economic, and military intelligence to a Polish major who was a British MI6 agent in Algiers: Rygor Slowikowski.[131]

Slowikowski turned out to be an amazing character and real-life hero. Within a few weeks of Murphy's permanent assignment, and upon the arrival of the Twelve Apostles in North Africa, the Pole and his team would render enormous services to Murphy and to Washington. As a Polish officer serving France before the German occupation, Slowikowski was picked by London after France fell because he had managed to enter North Africa. On arrival in Algiers, Slowikowski devised a way to cover his spy network with a legitimate business that might have made him a millionaire. The cunning Pole bought large quantities of unprocessed oats from Morocco and installed a factory in Algiers, rolling a kind of "Quaker Oats" product. It was an immense success, and the French and native Algerians bought tons of his cereal. As Major Slowikowski's scheme began turning a profit (money he felt ashamed of earning), he bought a pig farm located close by an Algiers airfield named the Maison Blanche. The farm used oat husks to feed its pigs; and the farmer and one of the Polish network spies went about spotting Axis aircraft flying in and out of Maison Blanche, reporting valuable aircraft intelligence to the Allies.[132]

Later, when he set up shop at the U.S. Consulate in Algiers, Murphy used Slowikowski's network and recruited one of the Pole's agents, a singular French counterintelligence officer. He named the blue-eyed Basque "Scotty," as he looked more like a footballer than the crafty spy that he was in real life.[133] Scotty helped Daphne to penetrate the Vichy bureaucracy, but all the while—and unbeknownst to Slowikowski and Murphy—Scotty served several masters: the Poles, Murphy at the U.S. Consulate, and secretly, the British Secret Service, MI6 (as did Slowikowski). London supplied Scotty with an independent secret radio transmitter presumably to report on not only the Vichy French regime but Slowikowski's spy-net, and Murphy's work at the U.S. Consulate General in Algiers. (Murphy had some limited experience in WWI Switzerland on how "the Great Game" of espionage was played—but he was over his head in intrigue in North Africa.)[134]

COUNTRYMEN, O, HOLD UP YOUR HEADS. RESIST![135]

As Christmas 1940 approached, Daphne was not alone in devising intrigue. Felix Cole, the U.S. consul in Algiers, learned in early December of that year that Murphy was to visit North Africa on behalf of President Roosevelt. With great secrecy and diplomacy, Cole set about arranging a series of clandestine meetings for Murphy with Gen. Maxime Weygand—Marshal Pétain's newly appointed delegate general to French Africa and hero of World War I and the man Roosevelt had targeted to cooperate with the United States against Nazi Germany when he met with Murphy at the White House.

Cole arranged for Robert Murphy to make a whirlwind tour of North and West Africa. (Murphy would quietly visit Algiers and Mers-el-Kebir in Algeria; Dakar, West Africa; Gao, French Sudan; Tunis in Tunisia; Casablanca and Rabat in Morocco; and Tangier in Spanish Morocco. He would then fly to Lisbon, from where he could cable a secret report for President Roosevelt's eyes only.)

Murphy arrived from Vichy by seaplane at Algiers on December 18, but alas, despite Cole's efforts to keep his visit secret, the Nazi Gestapo members of the Axis Armistice Commission had their agents tracking Cole and knew of Murphy's arrival in Algiers. (Murphy was well known in Nazi circles for his early work in Munich and his diplomatic work in Paris and Vichy. The Nazi security services relentlessly trailed Murphy—as did Italian OVRA agents. In North Africa the Germans and Vichy agents intercepted his telecommunications and read his mail.)[136]

Murphy flew immediately to Dakar, French West Africa, in a rickety Air France trimotor Dewoitine transport plane to meet Gen. Weygand—who struck Murphy as willing to cooperate. He ordered his staff to assist Murphy on his tour of the French-African Empire. Murphy's first impression of Weygand was that the general's move to Algiers, with a change of climate and a healthy diet, had done wonders for the old soldier's morale—and his notoriously ill temper. Roosevelt had ordered Murphy to probe Weygand's real authority, his plans, and what the United States could do to encourage him.[137] But when questioned about a possible "defection" of North Africa and the territories' conversion to an anti-Axis redoubt, Weygand responded with the rhetoric: "Where are the [American] divisions coming from? Will the United States provide them?" Of course, Weygand knew full well that President Roosevelt could not yet enter the war.

Murphy had no answer. But he did tell the general that, "short of war," Roosevelt intended to support the British by all means. (Pearl Harbor was eleven months away.) To Murphy, Weygand would emphasize that he believed, as did other French officials, that Britain would never again be a world power and would be quickly surpassed by the United States. But the general did confirm what Murphy was eager to hear: ". . . that French forces under [Weygand's] command—100,000 trained soldiers, airmen, and sailors—and a reserve of 200,000 more—would resist a German effort to occupy North Africa, expected for the spring of 1941."[138] (Secretly, Weygand and Pétain were determined to resist all invasions of French territory—even if Allied forces were to invade to liberate North Africa.) He did urge Murphy to get the United States to supply equipment, petroleum, and arms. And he warned that time was running short—that his position was precarious. (Hitler knew that the old soldier was a determined anti-Nazi, and

Weygand believed that it was only a matter of time before the Nazis would see to it that he be eliminated.)

At this point, and for complicated political reasons involving the British and the U.S. Congress, all Murphy could offer were nonstrategic materials and goods. Still, Murphy and Weygand set about drafting a protocol to be known as the "Murphy-Weygand Agreement." The accord would unfreeze French assets in the United States so that Weygand could receive essential consumer goods to feed and clothe French expatriates, restive colons, and the Arab-Moroccan Berber populations in North Africa. (Because of British mistrust of Vichy, war materials were always excluded from shipment under the protocols.)

Then, as a matter of good faith, a member of Weygand's staff revealed to an amazed Murphy the location of hundreds of tons of French, Belgian, and Polish gold that Murphy, earlier in Paris, had helped the French to ship to Africa via a U.S. cruiser just before the Germans entered Paris. The gold had arrived safely aboard the ship and was now being kept at a fortress in Kayes in the French Sudan, some 400 miles east of Dakar. Murphy learned too that some of the Belgian and Polish gold was being flown back to Paris at Germany's insistence, as stipulated in the terms of the armistice.

When Murphy confronted Weygand about the bullion and the possibility of the French fleet falling into Axis hands, the general assured him that the Germans would never get control of either the gold or the French fleet. (And they never did.)

Finally, Murphy learned that the French military was concealing artillery, ammunition, and other military equipment—in excess of what France had been permitted by the German-French armistice agreement—in mountain hideouts. These arms could be used to fight a German or Italian occupation of Algeria.

Later, Murphy would say that the visit and Gen. Weygand made a tremendous impression. "I was fascinated with the immensity of the French possessions, their vast potentialities in war and peace, and their complicated problems . . . well handled by the French military and bureaucracies. I was delighted to meet Frenchmen who were strongly anti-Nazi, who were more pro-British than I had anticipated, and who acted as if they would really fight for their independence in their African Empire."[139]

Murphy, from the beginning, was led to believe, or wanted to believe, President Roosevelt's credo: If America entered the war, the French military establishment in Africa would fight the Germans. Nevertheless, Murphy came away with a Weygand-approved economic agreement. And he got Vichy French permission to allow U.S. officers to supervise the delivery of U.S. goods at ports in North Africa. This agreement laid the groundwork for the assignment of the Twelve Apostles to posts in Algeria, Morocco, and Tunisia as consular officers. Weygand had agreed that Murphy's vice-consuls could transmit coded messages, use diplomatic pouches, and employ diplomatic couriers. Murphy had thus taken a giant step forward to form a promising, embryonic U.S. spy network that would help make the Torch invasion successful and less of a bloody struggle against French forces.

In his biography, Murphy describes how Gen. Weygand and his associates were straightforward, "giving me not only the material facts of their situation but also confiding their sentiments and intentions." He then adds a cautionary note written twenty-four years after his first mission to North Africa: "It was not their fault that misunderstandings developed later."[140]

For whatever motive, Weygand took great pains to assure Murphy that the war was not over and that Germany remained France's enemy; and in Vichy, Roosevelt's envoy, Adm. William Leahy, would be told that, "Marshal Pétain himself [would] in his own right time give the signal to resume the good fight."[141] That Weygand was faithful to his oath to obey Marshal Pétain was not appreciated by Murphy and the State Department in Washington.

Washington chose to ignore the dynamic contradiction among the French officer corps, who were eager to erase the shame of defeat at Germany's hands—but could not and would not override their oath to obey their superiors. French officers had, after all, sworn to obey Marshal Pétain. The "misunderstandings" to which Murphy referred centered around questions of loyalty to Pétain, the oath of an officer, and French traditions of family and honor. Alas, this powerful persuasion would cause Frenchmen, traditional allies of the United States, to kill American "liberators" by following the orders of their legitimate leaders.

This was not the first in a series of costly errors of appreciation by Murphy and other Americans. Indeed, despite evidence to the contrary, Murphy, the White House, FDR's newly appointed ambassador to Vichy, Leahy, and the U.S. military wanted to believe that Pétain would turn the tables on the Germans and renew the fight in North Africa. It was not to be.

Gen. de Gaulle was not deceived. He claimed that Marshal "Pétain died in 1923."[142] But de Gaulle had no advocate in Washington.

★ ★ ★

EN ROUTE TO LISBON, where he would write his cable report to FDR, Murphy passed through Algiers. He stayed at Consul General Felix Cole's villa, where the two men must have discussed Marshal Pétain's recent shuffling of Vichy leadership. The old marshal had sacked the pro-Nazi Laval and brought Adm. Darlan to power. Then they learned that Darlan had met with Hitler in the German-occupied zone at La Ferrière-sur-Epre. What did it all mean, was the question bruited about in Algiers, London, and Washington.[143]

It had been a long, arduous, and sometimes dangerous three-week trip for Robert Murphy. He was exhausted and homesick for his family. And New Year's Eve 1940–41 turned out to be a fateful moment of decisive consequence for him.

The evening of December 31, 1940, Felix Cole took his newfound friend to a dinner party at the villa Dar Mahieddine in Algiers (which would later be the scene of many secret meetings with Murphy and Vichy-French agents). Their host for the soirée turned out to be Captain André Beaufre, an assistant to Weygand, who at the moment was secretly against Weygand's pro-Vichy attitude. On the side, Beaufre was hatching a complicated insurrection scheme involving the French industrialist Jacques Lemaigre Dubreuil—whom Murphy may have known in Paris.

Beaufre, a militant and impatient patriot, and Lemaigre Dubreuil, a passionate opportunist, had earlier met (probably without Murphy's knowledge) with Lemaigre Dubreuil's prewar business colleague, now Lt. Colonel Robert Solborg, a U.S. military intelligence agent visiting North Africa.

Solborg's mission was to encourage men like Captain Beaufre and Lemaigre Dubreuil to believe that the United States would support an insurrection in North Africa.[144] Solborg, like Murphy, was sure that Weygand would "come around" to the Allied cause.[145] And at that very moment Beaufre and Lemaigre Dubreuil were working to form a clandestine group among French officers to back a coup d'état and create a North African state independent of Vichy—all in violation of the protocols of the Franco-German armistice. Solborg may have led them to believe that the United States would supply arms to support the insurrection, to be headed, they mistakenly hoped, by Weygand.

The beautiful Daphne Joan Fry Tuyl, now working as an agent for the U.S. Consulate in Algiers, attended the Beaufre dinner party. She later said that Murphy was "very direct and charming . . . [And] he probed for my reactions and opinions. It was characteristic that he used these same tactics on everyone with whom he came in contact, leaving no stone unturned."[146]

Alas, Capt. Beaufre's New Year's celebration turned out to be a disaster. It would be typical of the North African imbroglio and intrigue that Murphy would have to deal with in the years to come.

Just before midnight, Vichy police burst into Beaufre's villa and arrested everyone. Gen. Weygand had betrayed his own officer, Beaufre.[147] While Murphy's diplomatic status prevented his arrest, Beaufre, Lemaigre Dubreuil, and others were not so lucky. The little nucleus of French military resistance was wiped out.

Beaufre (who would later be rehabilitated by Gen. de Gaulle to become General Beaufre under the Free French) and others were sent to Vichy, tried, and given relatively light sentences thanks to the help of British-Polish-Vichy-French counterespionage master and double agent André Achiary.

Lemaigre Dubreuil escaped arrest probably through Achiary's help. He then took over Beaufre's villa, Dar Mahieddine, where he installed his family and sister-in-law, members of the wealthy French Lesieur family—which owned the country's most important peanut-oil producer, Huiles Lesieur. From villa Dar Mahieddine, Lemaigre Dubreuil, his wife Simone, and sister-in-law, Christiane, both stunningly beautiful young women, would become active in a conspiracy that would weave a web of intrigue around Robert Murphy. The Lemaigre Dubreuil and Lesieur families and a coterie of monarchist and wealthy industrialists believed they could, with American assistance, come to power if America invaded North Africa.[148]

This was Murphy's first brush with the fascist Vichy police, but not the last—and his connections with Lemaigre Dubreuil were certainly reported to the Gestapo and to Vichy agents. Later, de Gaulle's agents would track Murphy's movements and tap his personal and official telephones at the Cole villa and at the consul general's, despite his diplomatic status.[149]

Murphy left all this behind and flew off to Lisbon on January 5, 1941, after visiting Mers-el-Kebir to inspect the damage done to the French fleet by the British. Twelve days later, he cabled FDR a preliminary report of his findings and a copy of the agreement with Gen. Weygand. The original report of Murphy's trip bears FDR's notation: "I have read this with great interest." Murphy's work was to be the basis of President Roosevelt's North African policy and the first step in the planning of Operation Torch.

★ ★ ★

VICHY FRANCE AND NORTH AFRICA never got on the agenda of official Washington that winter and spring of 1941. It was a moment when the United States needed an organized professional intelligence service and a paramilitary organization to aid patriotic groups prepared to advance America's war effort. But no agency existed to deal with secret war operations, black information and propaganda, espionage, sabotage, clandestine communications, arms running, and to generally engage in the business of dirty tricks.

In June 1941 President Roosevelt assigned chunky, fifty-eight-year-old William J. Donovan to build a White House-based spy agency named the Office of Coordinator of Information (COI), later to be called the Office of Strategic Services (OSS).[150] Donovan, like Sergeant Alvin York and General John J. Pershing, was a fearless hero of World War I fame. Known as "Wild Bill" Donovan, he led his Fighting Irish, 69th New York Regiment, on the Western Front.[151]

After Pearl Harbor, Donovan recruited U.S. Marine Corps colonel William A. Eddy, the U.S. naval attaché at Cairo, to be his chief agent for North Africa stationed at Tangier under the cover of military attaché to the U.S. Legation. Eddy spoke Arabic and French and was a close carbon copy of Wild Bill. Eddy had an enviable record of combat in WWI, and had lost a leg fighting with the marines at Belleau Wood on the Western Front of France.

Eddy's arrival would be a godsend to Murphy. This "superb soldier," who made a squeaking noise when he walked on an artificial leg of his own design, was in fact an intellectual and linguist who would spearhead all intelligence and special operations work in North Africa, coordinating with Murphy and the vice-consuls.[152]

Donovan ordered Eddy to build a spy network in North Africa and arrange for agents to be left behind if the Americans should be excluded from the area. Eddy and his agents were to prepare for "sabotage, guerrilla warfare, and organized armed resistance" against eventual Axis forces.

Donovan warned Eddy, "Our whole future may depend on the outcome in [North Africa of Torch] and the accuracy of our intelligence estimates."[153] As a consequence, Eddy would work desperately for the rest of 1941 with Murphy's men to supply Washington with reliable intelligence about every aspect of French North Africa.

★ ★ ★

AS THE NEW YEAR OF 1942 UNFOLDED, Washington cabled Murphy at the U.S. Embassy in Lisbon and ordered him to return to Algiers to reassure Gen. Weygand that the United States government was "prepared in principle to go ahead with extending economic aid to the North African territories."

But when Murphy met with Weygand, alarm bells began ringing in London and Washington. It was typical of the French North African stew: lies, half-truths—a bouillabaisse of disinformation. Radio broadcasts from London and New York reported that "hundreds of Germans were swarming into Morocco, many of them disguised as tourists." (The presumption was that German or Italian agents were about to take over the French administration.) A British report claimed that a German delegation, including specialists in preparing airfields and submarine bases, had taken over the French air force in Morocco. Felix Cole, U.S. consul general in Algiers, cabled Washington (without consulting Murphy), stating that: "All reports here indicate massive German infiltration of Morocco, maximum 6,000, with 800 officers and men at Casablanca." And: "Germans have been given submarine bases in Casablanca and Tangier, plus three major air bases." A British source reported, "60,000 German troops massed in Spain, poised for an imminent attack on Gibraltar and Morocco."[154]

None of this was true. It was all a package of British disinformation and Nazi propaganda to prevent the U.S. from aiding the French in North Africa. One lone German civilian had appeared in Morocco with a tourist visa issued in Paris. The visitor was promptly shipped back to France, and French authorities issued orders that similar visas were to be rejected. In fact, only fifty-three new German members of the official Armistice Commission—mostly clerks and noncommissioned officers—arrived that spring. French officials even gave Murphy a complete list of the Germans on the Commission, with detailed descriptions of the background, habits, and the characteristics of each individual. Still, wild rumors persisted.

Then, on June 22, 1941, it was all over: Nazi Germany invaded not Morocco but Soviet Russia. (Any German feints toward North Africa had been ruses intended to deceive the Soviets and Great Britain.)

Murphy had spent the first six months of 1941 traveling back and forth between Washington, Vichy, France, and Algiers via Lisbon. He now knew that Gen. Weygand's future in North Africa was doubtful: Adm. Jean-Francois

Darlan, Pétain's vice president, would use Weygand's relationship with Murphy as a reason to have Gen. Weygand recalled from Algiers.

Nevertheless, as Murphy left Algiers for Washington, he believed he had made progress. He had established relations with Jacques Lemaigre Dubreuil and a Group of Five: anti-communist, rightist dissidents eager to work with Murphy and the United States.

Murphy spent the weeks that followed working at Old State, persuading and cajoling the bureaucracies of the war and navy departments to recruit suitable candidates to fill the posts of his vice-consuls ("intelligence agents") in North Africa—the first organized U.S. overseas intelligence operation in World War II.

3

HOW TO BECOME A VICE-CONSUL

WASHINGTON IN THE SPRING of 1941 was an exhilarating place to be. The country was stirring. FDR's Selective Service program had been launched: sixteen million American men were registered for the draft, and the first batch would begin compulsory military service in June. The long, gray winter of depression was fading: jobless men were leaving mean streets and entering military service or finding employment in industries gearing up for war.

Across the Atlantic, the coming of spring brought new reasons to despair. The first roundup of Jews had begun in occupied Paris; Bulgaria, Greece, and Yugoslavia had fallen to the Wehrmacht; and Hitler proposed that Spain seize Gibraltar, and that France, along with its fleet and African Empire, join the Axis.[155]

When Robert Murphy returned to Washington that spring, he was optimistic that even if Gen. Weygand weren't ready to "fight the war," the general would resist any German moves in North Africa.[156]

But Murphy knew that the British would try to sink the quid pro quo agreement he had negotiated with Weygand. He feared they would oppose the release of French assets in the United States so that Weygand could buy nonstrategic materials. Thus, Murphy worked tirelessly to get American "control consuls" assigned to North African ports, where they would inspect shipments of French goods as an assurance to the British that the cargoes would not fall into German hands.

But Weygand was finished in North Africa. Unbeknownst to anyone in Washington, the Germans were reading Murphy's personal "for Welles's eyes only" cables to Roosevelt, including one relaying an appeal from Weygand to FDR asking for arms if the Germans were to attack the French Empire. The Germans had a spy in Algiers or Washington. (Weygand would be recalled, retired, and arrested by the Gestapo.)[157]

And where were the twelve vice-consuls?

It turned out that State Department officers were unsuited and unwilling to do the irregular and dangerous work in North Africa. Adolf Berle, the assistant secretary of state responsible for finding the men, turned to the army and navy for help. Murphy quickly realized that he had to deal with a "timid, parochial" army and navy intelligence service, "operating strictly in the tradition of the Spanish-American War."[158]

Finally, a frustrated Bob Murphy "pleaded" with Berle and the army and navy powers to get at least two vice-consuls recruited, processed, trained, and dispatched to Africa by air.[159] What he got was the full twelve.

A SECRET MISSION ON FOREIGN SOIL

David Wooster King, a forty-eight-year-old Connecticut Yankee with a "sloppy" look about him, was the best and the bravest of the twelve vice-consuls.[160] In 1914, he left Harvard College at the age of twenty-one, and was nearly buried alive in a trench on the Western Front, where he fought as a French Foreign Legion infantryman—a poilu (or hairy-one). King suffered an eye injury there in 1915, and was wounded again at Verdun, where trench warfare was fought with bayonets.[161] When America entered the war in 1917, he was commissioned a first lieutenant in the U.S army.[162]

Another WWI officer was W. Stafford Reid, known as "Staff," who, like King, had fought as an infantry officer in WWI. Unlike King, Reid was impeccably dressed and looked like he might have just finished a round of tennis with Katharine Hepburn. King and Reid would spend the next two years together. But for now they were the first of Murphy's men to meet Lt. Colonel Ralph Smith of the U.S. Army Military Intelligence (G-2) Service in Washington. They would be the first to navigate the bureaucratic labyrinths of the U.S. War Department.

King and Reid impressed Col. Smith with their World War I records and their language skills. He told the men that the army and the State Department were planning a limited, secret joint mission on foreign soil. Barely ten days later, on April 15, 1941, King and Reid were offered posts as army reserve officers in military intelligence.

A few days later, David King telephoned a friend from his World War I days, Leland Lasell Rounds. Like King, Rounds was eager to join up and get into the fight, and at Col. Smith's urging he met with an army officer in New York's Roosevelt Hotel. On the basis of his WWI record and French-language skills, Rounds was offered a job as an intelligence officer-cum-vice-consul in North Africa.

Another legionnaire followed King. Forty-one-year-old John Crawford Knox was an alumnus of Groton, Harvard, Oxford, and the French military academy, Saint-Cyr. He had fought and was wounded in the Riff Mountains of Morocco. Col. Smith rushed him through the system so that Knox could join Murphy in Algiers (where he would immediately fall in love with Murphy's agent there, Daphne Joan Fry Tuyl).

A fourth World War I veteran, John Harvey Boyd, the former manager of Coca-Cola in Marseilles, France, was recruited in late April. Boyd, King, Reid, and Rounds were given routine physical examinations and then ordered to the Rockefeller Institute in New York City for cholera and yellow fever vaccinations. (The New York location was chosen because it was considered "insecure to alert Army medical departments.")[163] The four were then cleared to handle secure material and commissioned as captains in the U.S. Army Reserve. They were briefed to go to North Africa by officers from air, ground, and naval intelligence services (collectively known as MIS for Military Intelligence Services). The new recruits were instructed on what reports to send to Washington. Incredibly, for it was the spring of 1941 and America was still at peace, they were told they would assist in planning a future invasion of North Africa. And they learned that army and navy intelligence, the only American spy services in 1941, didn't have up-to-date maps or telephone books of major North African cities—and knew practically nothing about the region.[164]

MIS urgently needed maps, photographs, and sketches made of all ports in West Africa, from Agadir, Morocco, to the Spanish frontier—detailed reports on the conditions of roads, bridges, railroad trestles, roundhouses, and rolling stock. The four future vice-consuls were instructed to obtain the strength, disposition, and equipment of French armed forces in Algiers, Morocco, and Tunisia and to monitor the movements, activities, and contacts made with the French and locals by German and Italian members of the Armistice Commission. "Keep your eye on this Axis Fifth Column and their agents," MIS stressed. The neophyte agents were urged to quickly select potential agents among the French whom they would come to know: men and women who would spy for the United States.[165]

Staff Reid, ever conscious of being properly outfitted, took leave in New York to purchase military uniforms and paraphernalia. When he returned to Washington, he and the others learned that the U.S. State Department refused to issue passports to army officers traveling into Axis-controlled territory. "Someone had pointed out that commissioned officers, if they performed civilian functions while on active duty, could be shot as spies," Murphy wrote.[166]

Bob Murphy finally prodded the State Department to agree that the officers assigned to him in North Africa would be known as "vice-consuls." So the military uniforms went into storage, and as the first days of May approached, Boyd, King, Reid, and Rounds were issued "special passports"[167] that offered them little or no protection in case of war or arrest. Nevertheless, they went over to State where they met Robert Murphy, the man who would lead them in the great "North African adventure."[168]

Mid-May found King and Reid (Boyd and Rounds were delayed) at the LaGuardia rotunda of the Marine Air Terminal in New York, preparing to board the Pan Am Clipper for Lisbon. The vanguard of an "American Fifth Column" was at last on its way to the Old World.[169] When the plane stopped to refuel in Bermuda, King and Reid were amazed to see Bob Murphy board the plane. He had been bumped from an earlier flight because of heavy mail priorities, which spoke volumes about his status as the personal representative of the President of the United States.

Murphy had all but refused to go back to North Africa in April. Mildred and the girls were now settled in a new home in Chevy Chase, Maryland, a lovely suburb of Washington, D.C. But Mildred was sick again. (Her health was described as "very precarious.") Bob finally agreed to return to Algiers when Secretary Welles promised him the assignment would be limited to two months, and that the State Department would keep in touch with his wife.[170]

FROM WINE TO WAR

Ridgway Brewster Knight took a more convoluted path to becoming an "Apostle." After France fell, he wrote: ". . . by leaps and bounds I became restless, eager, with a pressing sense of urgency to be involved."[171]

And it must be said that Ridgway Knight looked the perfect pre–World War II spy—with family connections on the European continent and a gift for languages. Born and educated in France, he was the son of Aston and the grandson of Daniel Ridgway Knight, two successful and well-known American landscape painters who lived in France from 1859 to 1940. Ridgway returned to America to graduate from Harvard Business School at age twenty. Now, ten years later, believing that the air force would be the first to see action, he decided to learn how to fly. Several times a week during the summer of 1940, Knight rose from his comfortable bed in New York City at 5:30 A.M. to drive across the George Washington Bridge (linking Manhattan Island to Fort Lee, New Jersey) to a small private New Jersey airport to take instruction.[172]

Meanwhile, marriage loomed: Ridgway's exquisite good manners, patrician bearing, Harvard education, and considerable fortune made him a very sought-after young man among Manhattan's Park Avenue elite. After Harvard, Pierre Cartier, the famous Fifth Avenue jeweler to the rich, selected Ridgway to be his "dauphin" and to run the company's magnificent, chic emporium on Fifth Avenue in New York City. But "Mr. Pierre" expected Ridgway to marry his beloved and only daughter, Marion Cartier. Instead, stubborn Knight, ever a man of his own tastes, married Betty Spalding. He then left Cartier's and went into a partnership in the liquor business—the first firm in the U.S. to import wine bottled on French estates. Ridgway and his colleague, Freddie Wildman, made a sensational purchase early on for their Madison Avenue store when they bought at auction 10,000 cases of Château Mouton Rothschild, 1929— "a marvelous year; and for a little less than $11 the case."[173]

But the wine business was not all a bed of grape leaves. Just before France was invaded, their company was struck by a local labor union run by ex-bootleggers—gangsters who had served time in the federal penitentiary in Atlanta. Fights broke out on a picket line in front of their Madison Avenue store. Ridgway was nearly killed at a riverside freight yard by a "very large and wild-eyed Negro armed with a bailing hook," when he tried to defend one of his delivery trucks against a squad of union "goons."

Nevertheless, Ridgway's business affairs prospered. Betty delivered three sons, two of them twins, and the Knights lived well, very well—to the point that "when I came home to decant the wine for dinner with Eliot's help [the oldest of the Knight boys] it was in a home where the cook was making the dinner, the maid setting the table and the nurse giving the twins their evening baths before putting them to bed in their cribs." Ridgway was not in the least shy about his surroundings, and judged that though ". . . [my life]

may sound like Rockefeller or Vanderbilt standards . . . this was not the case. While we were indeed well off, there were many, many other couples as well off as we were in New York City."[174]

Ridgway persevered with his flying lessons while applying for a pilot's commission in the Army Air Force.[175] When he was turned down due to poor vision, he applied to the U.S. Marine Corps. When they offered to commission Ridgway as "a recruiting officer," he applied to the U.S. Navy. Again, he was rejected.

The navy, however, passed his application on to someone interested in recruiting men for intelligence work. An official in Washington had noticed that Ridgway was fluent in French and had knowledge of German and Italian.

The next thing Ridgway heard was that FBI agents were knocking on the doors of family and friends and asking all sorts of personal questions. Friends were whispering: "Ridgway, what have you been up to?" In mid-March, the State Department cabled him to appear for an interview for a possible assignment overseas.

In Washington, Ridgway may have, for some reason, received a more detailed briefing than the other vice-consuls. He learned that the United States, under the agreement Murphy had negotiated with Gen. Weygand, had committed to supply and ship nonstrategic goods for distribution through the Vichy North African government to help feed the peoples of Algeria, Morocco, Tunisia, and West Africa. Ridgway's role, and that of the other vice-consuls, was to act as a merchandise control official and monitor the program. This must be done, he was told, to meticulously protect his cover. He was warned not to speak to family or friends about the real nature of his mission: "spying."[176]

Ridgway was told that MIS needed information about the area's "delicate targets"—military bases, coastal batteries, location and movement of military and naval units, equipment and morale of officers and troops, ammunition dumps, communications networks, and the movement of ships. And in dealing with Vichy officials, he was instructed to make clear the U.S. government's "profound opposition to Hitler, Mussolini and the Axis; and America's determination to help Britain by all means short of hostilities." Murphy's men were to avoid all contact with German and Italian officials.

(Later, Ridgway would criticize the sketchiness and haphazard nature of the briefing he received in his barely five days in Washington. He thought that given the clandestine nature of his work and danger of the mission among experienced and ruthless German and Italian agents, all of the men going to North Africa should have had better training.)[177]

No one bothered to tell Ridgway Knight or the other vice-consuls that at U.S. embassies and consulates in North Africa, career American diplomats, who did not know the nature of the president's brainchild, resented the assignment of noncareer officers. On President Roosevelt's orders, the U.S. State Department was kept in the dark about the real role of the vice-consuls as America's first spies and about FDR's secret option to invade North Africa. However, this didn't stop career officers from asking: how had these upstarts become vice-consuls? Who were these men who had been sent overseas without oral or written examinations, little vetting, and with no knowledge of consular affairs—the issuance of visas or consular invoices? How had they escaped the rigorous screening that candidates for career posts were subjected to? And those American officials who guessed that the twelve were spies under cover of consular officers resented their presence even more.

Indeed, in 1941, outside the Donovan organization, spying was against the policy of the State Department and the ethics of U.S. Foreign Service officers. Diplomats did not spy. They were wedded to the belief of former secretary of state, Henry L. Stimson, a gentleman to his fingertips and of "the old school," who declared in 1929 that "Gentlemen do not read each other's mail."

Ridgway was sworn in the first week of May 1941. His pay, like the others, was $3,600 a year, with a per diem allowance of $7 a day while traveling and while in North Africa. On this pittance, he was expected to entertain, and without any allowances or access to special funds, to pay agents and carry out clandestine activities. (Only later would Murphy obtain authority from the State Department to finance undercover operations.)

Ridgway must have read one of the State Department's typically outdated post reports that painted a grim picture of North Africa. Mail could not be relied upon. Morocco, for example, was singularly unhealthy, damp, and unwholesome. The inhabitants were said to be suffering from malaria and bubonic plague. Communications had broken down all over the country. Railroad traffic was disrupted and petrol was not to be found.[178]

At home in New York, Ridgway's rather bewildered wife helped him pack what turned out to be all the wrong clothes for an absence of indeterminate duration. (He would later manage to shed his American garb in exchange for European suiting and local mufti.)

Finally, it was time for the Knights to part. It was a tearful goodbye. Betty and the children were anxious and stressed. Ridgway's friends at the La-Guardia rotunda of the Marine Air Terminal, including the Wildman brothers, tried to be entertaining. Freddie had shown up with a chilled bottle of Perrier Jouët 1928 champagne, which he'd quickly poured into glasses.[179]

And so Ridgway joined the second wave of neophyte spies—aka vice-consuls.

Aboard the PA 201 bound for Lisbon, he found himself enjoying the comfort and luxury of Pan Am Clipper service along with newly minted vice-consuls, John Ellrington Utter, Leland Rounds, and John Boyd.[180]

Boyd had served in the American Field Services in France from 1939 to 1940, and later he and his wife were trapped in France for ten months under the German occupation (and Mrs. Boyd died there). John got out of the country with ninety-four other Americans in a harrowing six-day trip traveling from Marseilles to Madrid.[181]

Harvard alumnus John Utter had taken the Foreign Service exam in 1928, failed the oral portion, and went to work for National City Bank of New York in the U.S. and France. He was with the bank when the Germans occupied Paris, and, like Boyd, spent a torturous time trying to flee first France and then Spain. Utter's harrowing experiences were typical of what refugees suffered attempting to get out of German-occupied Europe: it meant sleeping in overcrowded train stations packed with refugees from many lands—terrified Jewish families fleeing Nazi persecution; the men, women, and children desperate to reach a port city like Marseilles and board a ship bound for the United States. (Any port would do; and some refugees ended up in unlikely port cities such as Shanghai, China.) With the German occupation and Vichy fascist rule, French ports were closed and refugees in southern France desperately tried to gain passage on trains bound for Spain.

John Utter finally reached New York from Spain in the spring of 1941, when he immediately applied for work with the State Department.

OVER THE SPANISH SIERRA

Meanwhile, Reid and King had flown to Casablanca after spending some time at the U.S. Embassy in Lisbon, where the two men were introduced to the esoteric science of coding and decoding. They managed to hop a flight to Tangier via Madrid—the only air route to Morocco—aboard what Reid described as an ancient and decrepit aircraft, run by an obscure Spanish outfit. When the plane ran headlong into a severe storm over Seville, they were soon in trouble. The aircraft shook and yawed, rapidly making great arclike movements. The lyrically minded Stafford Reid wrote about the trip: "I was sure the antique plane would be wrecked against the red-tinted Sierra Morena Mountains, and the careers of two untested fifth columnists wrecked trying to get into the Great Game. The wings of the relic Spanish Civil War aircraft began to quiver and wrinkle like palm leaves before the approaching storm."[182]

Most of their fellow passengers were Spanish officers returning to their garrison in Spanish Morocco. The man sitting behind Reid "slumped over with his head in his lap, completely passed out in a real rodeo . . . [as] hailstones the size of camphor balls pelted the wings to the tune of distant drumfire, and flashes of lightning and chains in rolling tunnels of black clouds."

Then, Reid says:

> Out of nowhere, the northern peaks of the Sierra sprang into view. Through the open door of the pilot compartment we saw [the] co-pilot and radio operator pumping frantically on a handle—spilling gas from the fuel tanks to lighten the ship. The enveloping spray of gas arched colorfully into a rainbow off wing surfaces and disappeared into the slipstream. We watched the exhaust sputtering like blowtorches below the wings and sat in mute silence wondering how long this pregnant combination could hold out.

Now the crew began to throw excess weight overboard. "The plane lifted and we sighed with relief to see the Sierra Morena peaks fall behind into the landscape . . . with the last rays of sun over the Mediterranean reaching out through the storm . . . outlining the approach to Tangier, picturesquely straddled across the gateway to North Africa."[183]

Harry A. Woodruff, thirty-eight and a former Paris banker, and Franklin Olmsted Canfield were the next vice-consuls to leave New York on board another Clipper flying to Lisbon en route to Casablanca. Their family lineage, education, and references qualified the two close friends as decidedly "black shoe," blue-blood, elitist. Harry and Frank were questioned at LaGuardia air terminal by a *New York Times* reporter—it seemed the paper covered every Atlantic Clipper departure. They told reporters they were vice-consuls going to North Africa and were "connected with the relief thing." This seemed to raise the curiosity of the *Times* man. A story, on page seven of the paper, announced that, "their departure recalled the Administration's reported preparations early in May to send food to French North African colonies provided the Vichy Government withstood pressure to 'collaborate' with Berlin, particularly as to the passage of German troops to Spain."[184]

Canfield, then thirty-one, was a New York and Paris lawyer, a Columbia Law School graduate via St. Paul's School, Harvard College, and the University of Vienna. He spoke French like a Frenchman and did well in German. His references included no less a person than John Foster Dulles, who would be secretary of state under President Eisenhower, and Supreme Court justice, Harlan F. Stone. The two friends had signed up as vice-consuls bound for North Africa with the permission of their wives.[185]

AMONG AXIS SPIES AT THE EL MINZAH

Aboard the Pan Am Clipper, a deluxe "flying railroad car" bound for Lisbon, Boyd, Knight, Rounds, and Utter must have enjoyed the in-flight luxury: wide and deep seats, sleeping berths, and a saloon cabin to move about in and take meals. But despite the pleasant surroundings and spacious quarters, it seemed that Ridgway Knight was having second thoughts about his new job. He couldn't put aside the notion that he had made a terrible mistake. He was flying across the Atlantic to an unknown fate, far from his family for an indeterminate length of time. As the great Clipper dipped its wings and headed for a landing on the Tagus River, Ridgway was not at all sure he had done the right thing.

At the Lisbon air terminal the four men were greeted by a surly secretary of the U.S. Embassy, who announced in icy and sarcastic terms, "They're taking pretty good care of you noncareer vice-consuls. When I joined my post I traveled on a dirty old Portuguese liner." It was the first of many run-ins between career and noncareer staff.[186]

The four stayed the night at a crowded, second-class Lisbon hotel, but managed to get a flight to Tangier the next day. Their plane, not unlike the aircraft Reid and King had boarded, was a broken-down WIBOT aircraft dating back to the early 1920s. Its windows had to be pulled up with a strap as in an old horse-drawn hansom cab. The flight was as dramatic as King's and Reid's traumatic journey over the Spanish Sierras.

In Tangier—a Moroccan city occupied by Spain since 1940—Boyd, Knight, Rounds, and Utter hooked up with the earlier arrivals, Reid and King. Now their accommodations were at the sumptuous El Minzah Palace

Hotel, which Ridgway described as "a monument to mid-Victorian conceptions of Moorish architecture and discomfort" overlooking the Bay of Tangier.[187] The hotel featured a large palm court that served as a patio for meals, entertainment, and a rendezvous for spies. Italian and German diplomatic and army staff and members of the Gestapo mixed daily with British diplomatic and intelligence officers (and later, Americans) who lunched daily and shared false rumors and scraps of gossip. (David King and OSS agents working for Murphy would later plan to murder these Axis agents but would be refused permission.) Ridgway was "thrilled to [hear] the sound of German and Italian spoken around the hotel pool." Neophyte that he was, Knight believed he had gone into "action; and the conversation was often, 'Monsieur is German?' And: 'Where is Monsieur from? Where is Monsieur going?'"

Ridgway believed that the chambermaids, porters, and barmen, cum amateur spies, earned an extra few francs from the Germans and Italians "by reporting daily that I was an American."

The six vice-consuls now spent weeks at the American Legation office in Tangier, waiting to get to Casablanca and Algiers.[188] They thought that even going to work at the Tangier Chancery was an "exquisite exotic experience." The office was housed in a 200-year-old Moorish building—a palace of mosaic and colored marble located down a noxious, narrow alley of the Medina. It could be approached only by foot or on the back of a donkey, mule, or horse; and a narrow and busy street separated the embassy—the residence—from the chancery. It was hardly convenient and even less secure from the prying eyes of Gestapo agents.[189]

Ridgway Knight describes how his group of vice-consuls tussled with the U.S. minister plenipotentiary to Tangier, J. Rives Childs, an "unimaginative stickler for protocol . . . pompous and the very epitome [of what was to change in the U.S. diplomatic service during World War II] of a striped-pants diplomat."[190] (The State Department had not informed Minister Childs of the intelligence and psychological warfare aspects of the vice-consuls' mission.) Childs was one of those Foreign Service officers who "thoroughly disapproved of spies; spies and spying were not gentlemanly, and therefore spies were not decent company."

Nevertheless Ridgway Knight was amused by Minister Childs.

> After considerable harrumphing and looking our group up and
> down, Childs declared in solemn tones: "For the life of me, I fail

to understand why the State Department thought I needed you and accepted you on its rolls. We have high standards to maintain. From what I know of your records, none of you gentlemen fit the bill."

Letting his eyes rest slowly on each one of us in turn, he went on: "A banker and a lawyer, perhaps; but a wine merchant and a soft drink salesman . . ." Looking at John Boyd and me, his voice trailed off. Then with a vengeful glint in his eye, our unwilling host went on in severe tones: "However, gentlemen, I must warn you. You are now in Tangier, in my area of responsibility, and I must disabuse any one of you who might think that he is going to enjoy a holiday at Government expense. I intend to put you to work."

Ridgway felt that Childs had "destroyed any illusions that any one of us might have entertained. We were then dismissed with a wave of the hand and a 'that will be all for now.' "[191]

The cable traffic at the Tangier mission was unusually heavy in May 1941; so the men, "parachutists" to the diplomatic staff, were sent to the code room to learn the rudiments of the one-time pad coding system[192] used in those days for confidential messages—a skill they would not regret mastering later on. After days sequestered in the legation code room and appeals to get them on the next flight to Algiers, Boyd, Knight, Rounds, and Utter finally abandoned the idea of flying to Algiers.[193]

Instead, the group headed for Algiers via Sidi Kacem-Casablanca-Oran in a train burning poor local coal. It was not a cushy trip for these well-heeled gentlemen, as they crammed into standing-room-only cars with unwashed Arabs, their wares, and animals.

Ridgway describes a breakfast at a stopover at Oujda before reaching Oran and Algiers, where Murphy waited impatiently to assemble his Twelve Apostles:

. . . we had miniature eggs—probably fed on fish—and cooked in foul native oil having a peculiar rotten odor of its own. After a sleepless night, my heart sank as I had visions of the months to come . . . why had I given up a perfectly comfortable life, a caring wife, lovely

children and a darn good cook, to volunteer for an assignment . . .
that would mean reeducating my palate completely? [194]

In the first week of June 1941, the intrepid four arrived at the Algiers train
station—forty-eight hours after leaving Tangier and a distance of 500 miles
as the crow flies. Still, they had watched "a glorious sunrise over an Arizona-
like landscape"[195] and had their first tastes and smells of North Africa.

Vice-Consul Orray Taft Jr., the pompous career diplomat who had taken
the British agent, Daphne Joan Fry Tuyl, to the New Year's Eve party six
months earlier, met the group at the station with Murphy.[196]

The men had leaped six time zones and landed at an outpost of the U.S.
Foreign Service—in an exotic French beau geste–Arab and Berber corner of
the world. The former was ruled by strict protocol; the latter, a land where
Arab and Berber customs prevailed and where the cultural texture and reli-
gious attitudes of life were unfamiliar to Americans.

Over time the vice-consuls would see how the French colons, with their
veneer of French bourgeois manners, and the career French military officers
were "Arabized" by years of service in the Maghreb—not unlike the English,
who spent a lifetime in the Indian Civil Service.[197] And they would learn that
life at a State Department outpost was ordered above all by protocol and etiquette, with a capital "P" and a capital "E."

By June 1941 all of the original vice-consuls had managed to cross the seas and
were first assembled in Casablanca and Algiers under Murphy's command. The
Casablanca contingent was originally composed of: King, Kenneth Pendar—
who was the last man to fly over—Reid, C. Denbeigh Wilkes (also a late arrival),
Canfield, and Sidney Lanier Bartlett, who with many mishaps traveled by tramp
steamer. Murphy placed Woodruff and Utter in Tunis, Tunisia, and assigned
Knox, Boyd, Knight, and Rounds to Algiers. In a short time Knight and Rounds
would be moved to Oran, near the Mers-el-Kebir anchorage where British warships had attacked the French Mediterranean fleet a year earlier. Finally, Murphy was able to get Annapolis graduate and WWI hero, Frederic Culbert, who
had been in Dakar, Senegal, transferred to Casablanca. As a young naval officer,
Culbert had dove into the sea to save two American aviators who were caught
in the wreck of a French dirigible that had broken up and was sinking.[198] His
naval experience would be invaluable to the "Casa" (short for Casablanca) team.

The game was afoot . . . and fit for treasons, stratagems and spoils.[199]

4

CASABLANCA:
OF PET MILK, GREEN TEA, AND SUGAR

CASABLANCA—*DAR EL BEIDA* in Arabic, or *Maison Blanche* in French—was the jewel of Morocco. And despite the war, "Casa" was still a modern commercial metropolis and a model of French enterprise and the latest European ideas for city planning, architecture, and conveniences. It was a magical place bathed in the Atlantic breeze—a place where Humphrey Bogart and Ingrid Bergman might fall in love.

"Casa" lay just beyond the Pillars of Hercules—the nearest port in North Africa to American shores and the gateway for receiving American supplies shipped from the United States under the Murphy-Weygand Agreement. This beautiful city would play a major role in the pre-invasion preparations of Torch.

But when Dave King and Staff Reid got there in May, fear permeated Casablanca and the staff of the U.S. Consulate—a dread that Hitler's armies would, in those pre–Pearl Harbor days of feigned U.S. "neutrality," move through Spain, cross the Mediterranean, bypass Gibraltar, and invade Morocco.

Reid, King, and the other vice-consuls who arrived in Morocco found that the "career guys" at the U.S. Consulate General were living in a perpetual state of "anxiety and confusion"—anticipating some catastrophic event.[200] In turn, the old-timers feared that Murphy's novice, uneducated (in the ways of diplomacy) interloper-intruders would upset the Vichy bureaucrats, the German- and Italian-staffed Armistice Commission, and make their jobs more difficult. The new arrivals were clearly unwelcome.

Chained to the coding desk, stretched by the strain of adapting to the heat, the exotic Oriental food, and the hostility, Murphy's newcomers—King, Reid, Wilkes, Canfield, and Pendar—soon came down with multiple cases of "GIs" (known locally as the "Casa crud"), and quickly tired of being warned by the "professionals" to "stay out of sight" of Vichy authorities and the Gestapo. The tedium of enciphering messages, the weeks of being penned up in the code room, put tempers on edge, and good manners soon gave way to office brawls.

Alerted, Murphy hastily flew to Casablanca from Algiers. Without taking sides, the master of oiling moving parts straightened his men out. He let the newcomers know that they had acted like spoiled children. To their relief he removed them from boring code work and assigned them in teams of two as consulate control officers. As a cover for their clandestine work, they were to appear to be low-level consular ship inspectors, checking invoices and verifying that the cargoes of American goods coming into the Casablanca port from American cities reached needy Moroccans. It was an early version of the postwar U.S. aid program. The consuls were to do audits to be sure that the cloth, cooking oil, and foodstuffs didn't end up in German or Italian hands.

Murphy knew that shipments would be sporadic. This would leave plenty of time for the men to carry out their real work: spying. He identified their targets: French officials—the military and naval establishment; the expatriate community and German officials; and Gestapo and Italian OVRA agents and Japanese consular officers.

Under diplomatic cover as U.S. vice-consuls, their real mission was to collect political, economic, and military intelligence and to scout out the Arab-Berber hinterland—forbidden territory to anyone outside the Vichy French administration. Murphy's men were to do in peacetime what was forbidden to "gentlemen": read another's mail and spy on a friendly government that the United States considered "sovereign."

Murphy says in his inimical Irish way that his team essentially "winged it . . . and that one or two of us, with luck, might be able to distinguish a battleship from a submarine on a particular day."[201]

The arrival of six new faces did not go unnoticed. They had barely shown up in the casbahs of Casa when the Gestapo reported to Berlin that "the vice-consuls whom Murphy directs represent a perfect picture of the mixture of races and characteristics in that wild conglomeration called the United States of America. We can only congratulate ourselves on the selection of this group of enemy agents who will give us no trouble. In view of the fact that they are totally lacking in method, organization and discipline, the danger presented by their arrival in North Africa may be considered nil. It would merely be a waste of paper to describe their personal idiosyncrasies and characteristics."[202]

★ ★ ★

PHYSICALLY SCARRED FROM FIGHTING Germans in the trenches of the Western Front in 1914, David King had killing Germans in his soul. He referred to them as *les Boches*—a pejorative World War I term, among others, that the French used to describe the Hun. Under Murphy, he would take over the dirty work of "special operations" in Morocco. King's fellow Western Front veteran, Staff Reid, became his partner. And if they didn't always see eye to eye, they worked well together in the first months in Casa. King was the "Elizabethan adventurer,"[203] plain talking and a bit rough; Staff Reid, ever the well-groomed Yale man, was suave, handsome, and polished. Their undercover work in Casablanca suited them to a "T."[204]

Early on King heard that a spectacular villa in the chic Casablanca suburb of Anfa was available to rent—but the Gestapo wanted the handsome house, too. King and Reid managed to outmaneuver them, and moved in overnight just as the Germans sought to rent the place. When their competition arrived to inspect the property, King and Reid's houseboy, Abdullah, told them in pigeon French: "Sorry, big Americans move in now; no room for more."[205]

It was a good life in the villa. Abdullah went out at dawn each morning on a rickety bicycle to shop at the local market, while his wife, "Fat Mah" (presumably Fatima—one of Reid's puns), cooked breakfast. And Reid went about the village of Anfa on a rented bicycle, too. He figured he would need two wheels to avoid the Gestapo, who invariably followed consular cars marked by diplomatic license plates. One can only imagine how German and Italian spies viewed the aggressive new arrivals.

Then King landed his first agent: a Frenchman who was able to deliver the plans of port buildings and the scheduled changes of the port's naval guards. The schedules would allow Reid and Frederic "Teddy" Culbert, the ex-U.S. naval officer, to sneak into the harbor's perimeter and spy on the French dreadnought *Jean Bart*, a capital ship reportedly preparing to go to sea. Culbert, fresh from Dakar, became the team's naval expert.

Indeed, major warships of the French Mediterranean fleet anchored in Casablanca harbor—the best French anchorage south of Toulon. The French sailors aboard the ships and the naval men and women working ashore were a spymaster's dream—while the German, Italian, and Japanese officials were a spook's reverie.

As the summer of 1941 unfolded, Murphy's team took to the chase. There was no absence of helping hands. In the months that followed their arrival, King, Reid, Pendar, and Canfield were assailed by a collection of characters: Polish refugees, pro-Gaullists, anti-Gaullists, ex-fascist *cagoulards*, and communists. They were all willing to help for a handful of dollars—priceless as the French franc devalued. Often what was offered, however, was a worthless rumor or disinformation planted by Gestapo agents.[206]

casse croute

French workers have always venerated the sacrosanct Gallic habit of *casse croute*—the breaking of bread at midday. The naval personnel at Casablanca harbor, solidly blue-collar, were no different. Everything stopped when the noon whistle blew. It was not the call to the Angelus that sounded along the waterside quays. It was but the call to bouffe, as the workers religiously observed the *midi* two-hour pause for a hearty lunch and a good swig of red pinot.

King and Reid used these precious hours to wander through the dockyards and warehouses, taking in the geography of the port and naval defense installations.[207] Under the heat of a noonday sun in June, the harbor unloading stopped. Not a mouse stirred while French customs and police officers took to their homes or nearby restaurants for lunch. Native stevedores opened their lunch pails in the shade of empty warehouses. Later, with their hunger slaked, they stretched out for a midday snooze.

The two dodged among the long shadows of the docks to take photographs and make freehand sketches of harbor defenses, concrete pillboxes, and military and naval warehouses, marine stores, and arsenals. All the time, they observed the large number of French destroyers, submarines, and cruisers that lay in the Casa harbor, and the arrivals and departures of the French fleet.

The 35,000-ton battleship *Jean Bart* drew particular attention all through that summer and fall of 1941. A year before, at the time of the Armistice, she had run to Casablanca from Toulon. Now, lying at anchor, her bottom covered with barnacles and her speed reduced to some 12 to 15 knots, the battleship was no less deadly; *Jean Bart* was a "ship-killer." Just as King and Reid had predicted in cables to Washington, at the time of the Torch invasion sixteen months later and in one of the most intensive naval battles of the Atlantic war, *Jean Bart* would throw red-hot salvos at the USS *Massachusetts* from her four powerful 15-inch front batteries.[208] In riposte, *Massachusetts* laid her 16-inch guns on the *Jean Bart*, punching fat holes in the French ship's forward turret, armored decks, and keel. She was finally sent to the bottom of Casablanca harbor by U.S. warplanes from the carrier *Ranger*—but not before *Jean Bart* nearly destroyed the U.S. command ship, the USS *Augusta*, with General Patton aboard.[209]

All that summer *Jean Bart* remained a target. If she left her anchorage to sail the Mediterranean or the Atlantic, U.S. naval intelligence needed to be alerted and Britain warned. Reid says that on one night's mission with Ted Culbert, they went about "with flashlights and .45 automatics . . . in our raincoats . . . we . . . drove to a deserted clearing along the seawall . . . the harbor was barely visible in a settling mist and blackout."

It was a waste of time. He and Culbert instead went to "a high point overlooking the harbor . . . the rooftop elevator cable shed of the Plaza Hotel." They climbed the hotel's twelve flights of stairs in bare feet. (German members of the Armistice Commission and the Japanese Consul lived there.) "We had to sneak past the watchman . . . in the pay of the Germans . . . to get to the rooftop . . . There with powerful Navy binoculars we watched the *Jean Bart*'s crew apparently preparing to go to sea."[210] (If this were the case, Reid had already drafted a cable to be transmitted from the consulate wireless station, to advise U.S. naval operations.)

At 3:15 in the morning they heard "the sound of the anchor chain echoing over the port as the crew winched the mastodon aboard—the hours dragged on. A stray dog in the Arab quarter began barking; a clock on the minaret tower now showed 5:00. Suddenly a woman's voice rang out sharply from behind us on the roof, saying in French, 'What are you doing up here in the middle of the night—who are you?' "

It was the wife of the Austrian proprietor of the Plaza Hotel—a lady intimate with its roster of Axis guests.

Reid brazenly yelled back, "We heard that the German fleet was entering the harbor at daybreak and would take over Casablanca."

The woman laughed. "No, no," she answered. "When the Germans come here no one will even have a whisper ahead of time . . . go back to bed. Why do you Americans pull chestnuts out of the fire for the British? They are finished—that blitz we have given them will finish them for good!"[211]

A few days later the *Jean Bart* did leave her moorings and anchored alongside the harbor breakwater, from where she engaged in long-range target practice.

★ ★ ★

IN THE LATE SUMMER FRENCH ships from U.S. ports began unloading canned milk, sacks of sugar, bulk tea, oil, and cotton cloth: the first shipments under the Murphy-Weygand Agreement to aid North Africa. King and Reid would take small craft out of Casa harbor to board the incoming freighters and inspect their cargo manifests. The ships' captains offered a traditional noon aperitif and information about Atlantic traffic sighted during the crossing. From the pleasant surroundings of the captains' decks, King and Reid would watch barefoot Arab stevedores, clothed in discolored filthy rags, swarm about the cavernous ships docked at quayside and haul the cargoes onto waiting trucks. When sacks broke, spilling their contents, the Arabs fought for a handful of sugar or rice with knives and hooks. In the blistering heat countless riots broke out, with Arab workers wrestling over stolen cargo until they were brutally beaten by French police. Reid tells that the Arabs "had been reduced to a semi state of nakedness" for lack of cloth. Yet they would use their last garment to wrap their dead, "a sacred ritual in the Koranic faith [sic]."[212]

As only Americans can, King and Reid mixed with the French sailors, painters, and machinists, befriending them with cigars, canned milk, cigarettes, and sugar. In turn, their "newfound friends" became agents and reported on the arrivals and departures of shipping and the condition and cargoes of French, German, and Italian naval and merchant ships—all grist for the vice-consuls' dispatches to Washington.[213]

COBALT

As news spread of German and Italian victories in the Mediterranean—as General Rommel's armies battled against British forces in the North African desert—Murphy's men wanted to act. The pretended neutrality of the U.S. seemed absurd to the vice-consuls as evidence grew that Vichy was actively helping the German war effort against Britain.

In Washington, President Roosevelt still hoped that Marshal Pétain or Gen. Weygand might turn against the Axis. It was a touchy moment, and any act that might offend Vichy or Weygand was proscribed by Washington.

Morocco was rich with metals dug out of the mountains of French North Africa, including zinc, copper, and aluminum. But the Germans were particularly desperate for cobalt—a mineral agent used in electronics and to make synthetic fuel and metals to harden the steel armor of German tanks. Staff Reid warned Murphy from Casablanca that Germany, Italy, and Japan were exchanging quantities of green tea and cotton goods for these minerals and secretly shipping them out of Casablanca. He could only hope that Washington would alert London.[214]

It angered Murphy and his men that the Italians and Germans were stripping the North African land of minerals and foodstuffs—wheat, fresh vegetables, fruit, wine, and livestock. The Germans were in great need of potatoes. Murphy learned that Vichy was offering a premium to North African farmers to grow potatoes, destined for Germany, instead of harvesting their customary vegetables. The local population quickly began to suffer from food shortages.

In Algiers and Casablanca, the vice-consuls discovered that a vast network of French and Axis agents were trafficking in strategic materials and food—truly adding to the penury of eatables for the hungry natives. The goods were being sneaked onto French ships labeled for transport to France, and then diverted to Italian and German ports. Murphy's agents reported that the freighter *Algerie*, ready to sail from Algiers, contained 2,640 tons of manganese hidden in her hold under a cargo of fish and vegetables. In Casablanca, the French freighter *Carimare* was loading 4,200 tons of manganese; and German officials had a hidden depot of monazite and antimony oxide near the Casa port. Finally, in Oran, John Boyd and Ridgway Knight discovered that the Germans had stored 300 tons of cobalt at Nemours and were preparing to ship the ore to France.

Murphy's team had uncovered even more alarming information: quantities of aluminum, lead, zinc, and copper stored at Casablanca had in fact "disappeared." In addition, a mine at Epinat, in Morocco's southern Atlas Mountains, was discovered to contain 10,000 tons of manganese ready to be moved by truck to Casablanca. Indeed, Reid found that German specialists were secretly working at mines in southern Morocco, supervising the production of cobalt. The Germans held special French military visas to enter and leave these forbidden militarized zones.

Murphy must have known that Adm. Jean-François Darlan, head of the Vichy Directorate (and by constitutional act, the marshal's successor), was eager to gain concessions from Nazi Germany that would free French soldiers from German prison camps and spare the lives of hostages held in Nazi jails. Trade-offs were made—with or without the approval of Gen. Weygand. For the Allies, concessions to the Germans undermined the war effort. Indeed, Darlan yielded to German demands to allow the shipment of strategic minerals from North African ports to war factories in Germany. He permitted the enemy to use the Rhone Valley waterways to bring military supplies to Mediterranean ports, where they could be transshipped to the port of Bizerte, Tunisia, and Rommel's desert army. The trade-offs might have tipped the scales that summer of 1941, and later, as Britain struggled in the Libyan Desert to keep Rommel from taking Suez. Indeed, the German Luftwaffe operating from Sicily and Italian submarines had closed the Mediterranean to British convoys to Alexandria, Egypt. The British Eighth Army fighting in Egypt was being supplied by convoys forced to travel the long route around the Cape of Good Hope into the Indian Ocean and the Red Sea. The Vichy French were violating the British embargo and helping the German and Italian war effort against Great Britain—which was not part of the armistice agreement.

Murphy and his men were forbidden to supply British agents data about French ships carrying contraband, though some information leaked out, aiding British patrol boats to locate and torpedo the offending ships.

Washington's policy of appeasing Vichy effectively prevented the vice-consuls from helping Britain; and Murphy's reports of contraband shipments and his agents' discoveries never got to London. It was an intelligence officer's dilemma and a spy's catch-22. But in the months that followed, their diligent work would pay off.

★ ★ ★

KENNETH PENDAR, ONE OF THE LAST of the vice-consuls to join Murphy's group, looked every inch the St. Paul's school "preppie" he was. His first meeting with clandestine intrigue came while on a courier trip to Tangier in the summer of 1941. He was approached in the lobby of the Hotel El Minzah by a British agent who couldn't enter Vichy-controlled Morocco. Very politely, the man wondered if the ever-obliging Pendar might render a small service to "Her Majesty's government" by delivering a package to a friend in Casa. Despite assurances that the package was "okay," Pendar opened it in his room and found it contained a bomb. The accompanying letter showed the device was to be used to sabotage a stock of Vichy government rubber lying in Casa harbor and ready to go aboard ship. Pendar dumped the package into the sea.[215]

Ken Pendar, a one-time antiques dealer, had been friendly since St. Paul's school with his partner in Morocco, Franklin Canfield, an inveterate card player and gambler. Murphy paired the two men to show the flag among Moslem tribesmen in the Moroccan hinterland. Kenneth Pendar, in his biography, thought it the most "fascinating assignment" of his life.[216]

The Arab and Berber communities in Morocco were targets of Murphy's design to influence native North Africans. He wanted to cultivate the leaders of the Moslem groups despite French warnings that such contacts were taboo. Looking at the ethnic mix of the peoples of North Africa in 1941, Murphy saw that French colonials were a minority—one million out of fifteen million living racially separated in enclaves of Jewish communities and Arab and Berber tribal villages—all controlled by a harsh Vichy French administration. Algeria, Morocco, and Tunisia formed an exotic galaxy—though separated tribally and ethnically—where one heard the babble of French, German, Italian, Arabic, and Berber with smatterings of Hebrew and Greek.

Indeed, the Arabs were betting that Britain would lose the war to Germany. They saw Hitler's legions as hosts of valiant fighters who had already defeated the French and British in battle—the Holy Koran, after all, preached that God rewarded the victors. Though the Arabs despised the Italians, they were receptive to German propaganda. It was all the more reason in Murphy's mind to have Pendar and Canfield visit the Arab hinterland despite French opposition.

The duo had a boundless taste for the exotic. Far from being "quiet Americans," Pendar and Canfield negotiated with French officials to occupy La Saadia—an ostentatious villa owned by an American heiress and one of the showplaces of Marrakech. There, the two men reigned for months, making frequent trips in a consular automobile to display a U.S. presence in the other French-pacified Moorish cities of Salé, Fez, and Rabat. It was "little-known country," and they worked at "getting to know the dark faces under the draped burnouses." They dined in the townhouses of Arab chiefs and the

Berber *caid* and visited their casbahs, set like medieval castles on the lofty heights of the Atlas Mountains.[217]

Almost as a sideline, the two supervised the distribution of cotton goods to Arab children and checked the delivery of canned milk, green tea, sugar, oil, and fuel, along with cloth used for burial shrouds.

Pendar's travels made him feel far removed from western civilization. Separated from "a stormy French world," he was "deeply affected by the fantastic intrigues and plots" he discovered under "hot blue skies; listening to secret whispers and gossiping" in the tight alleys of the casbahs. Curious and "romantic, often given to indiscretions" and enjoying every minute of his travels.

At this time Pendar became friendly with Henri, Comte de Paris, the Orléans-Bourbon pretender to the French throne. Pendar and Canfield would drive to Larache, eight kilometers outside Rabat, where the glossy, soft-chinned Henri lived a semi-regal life in a large villa surrounded by his numerous children, his blonde "royal" Brazilian wife, and the remnants of a small court.[218]

That summer of 1941 Comte Henri was drawn into a secret and "quite fantastic" plot hatched by the British SOE—the British Special Operations Executive. He agreed to issue a manifesto under his royal seal, calling on French peoples of North Africa to rally to a royalist coup d'état backed by the British monarchy. The plot, hatched at the British Embassy in Lisbon, was leaked to newspapers there and in Spain. It came to nothing—except outrage from the Vichy French authorities. And the Comte de Paris would try again a year later in Algiers and cause Murphy grave problems.

Canfield's affinity for gambling "huge stakes" of money with British SOE agents along with his and Pendar's relations with Comte Henri did not go unnoticed by German agents.[219] That the two Americans had invited native Arab leaders in the holy city of Fez to "cocktails" grated on French and Arab nerves; the pair had served alcohol at the event, offending pious Moslems, whose virtue and Puritanism were their stock-in-trade. It was a dramatic faux pas that rang alarm bells in Casablanca and Algiers. Despite Murphy's caution to be discreet and maintain a facade of neutrality for the sake of Vichy-American relations, Canfield's association with British agents and the vice-consuls' work among the Arabs and Berbers angered the French officials. A final blow was dealt when the lawyer for the owner of the villa La Saadia in Marrakech complained bitterly to the U.S. State Department that Pendar had occupied her Marrakech "winter" palace without permission. (Pendar claimed that he had moved in to protect the American woman's property from eventual requisition by French authorities.)[220]

As it turned out French, German, and Italian authorities protested to the U.S. Consulate General in Casablanca about the men's behavior. The U.S. minister to Tangier, J. Rives Childs (the nemesis of many of Murphy's vice-consuls), recommended that Pendar be recalled to Washington. The Pendar and Canfield incidents were embarrassing to Murphy; he feared they might signal to Morocco's five-star resident general Auguste Nogues that the vice-consuls were unreliable or untrustworthy. Murphy intervened and tried to end the affair by transferring Pendar to Algiers, out from under Moroccan authority. (Pendar would return later to set up a radio transmitter connecting Marrakech with Algiers.)

Canfield's trouble was more serious, and he would commit a final—and ultimate—indiscretion that would cause Murphy to transfer him out of North Africa altogether.

RUMOR, ROUGH STUFF, AND DIRTY WORK

Once more, persistent rumors swirled about Algiers, Casablanca, and Tunis that the Germans would invade Morocco. When Adm. Jean-François Darlan met with Adolf Hitler at Berchtesgaden, the event was widely reported in the French press. It appeared to the world that Vichy was betting Germany would win against the Allies and create a Nazi "Eurafrican" Empire. (The Zurich press reported—falsely—that the Führer had bestowed the Nazi military decoration, the *Kriegsverdienstkreuz*, on Pierre Laval and Adm. Darlan).[221]

By now, the Allies were harassed in the eastern Mediterranean; the Libyan Desert campaign was going badly, and the island of Malta was threatened. The war offices in London and Washington were gripped with fear that Spain's fascist *Caudillo*, Francisco Franco, would permit the Wehrmacht to enter Spain—allowing Hitler to take the rock of Gibraltar, cross the Mediterranean, and swallow North Africa. If Hitler moved south, Rommel's desert army would enter Egypt and seize the Suez Canal.[222] In the corridors of Whitehall and Old State, it was whispered that the Germans controlled all aviation fuel in Morocco; Vichy France was supplying Rommel's army through Bizerte; fifty-three French ships had been requisitioned by the Wehrmacht to transport troops to North Africa, and German troopers were garrisoning Marrakech.

Meanwhile, the fascist Spanish press, proclaiming how Franco hailed the Axis as his spokesmen, warned neighboring Portugal to "play ball" with Hitler. Indeed, Spain and Portugal held the strategic Cape Verdes, Canary, Madeira, and Azores islands, threatening neighboring Dakar, the capital of Vichy West Africa. If Dakar fell, passage along the Atlantic sea lanes to South America might be denied.[223]

The war appeared to be approaching a final stage. A *Time* magazine article from May 26, 1941, headlined VICHY CHOOSES, reported that "Unless the whole world was deceived, the Vichy government last week squarely and publicly placed its bet on Germany to win World War II." From Algiers, Robert Murphy reported to Washington that French officials avoided him. One vigorously advised Murphy "not to waste his time talking about a British victory."[224]

It was the moment for Otto Abetz, the Nazi *gauleiter* in Paris, to complain to Marshal Pétain about Murphy's close relations with Weygand and about how freewheeling U.S. vice-consuls were traveling all over North Africa. Abetz forced Vichy leaders to forbid French administrators and staff from having unofficially sanctioned contact with U.S. Consulate personnel.

It was good fortune then that U.S. vice-consul John Knox was able to introduce David King to a circle of Knox's former classmates and officers. Knox, an alumnus of Groton, Harvard, Oxford, and a 1923 graduate of the French West Point, Saint-Cyr, kept a wide circle of friends from his days fighting as a French Foreign Legion officer in the bloody Riff campaign in the mountains of Morocco. Knox put Dave King together with French army major Michel Despaix, codenamed "Pinkeye," who led a handful of other mid-grade French officers. They had all sworn allegiance to Marshal Pétain, but were ready to fight if Germany occupied Morocco. Pinkeye's group eventually encompassed reserve officers and professionals stationed throughout Morocco who were willing to risk spying for King.[225]

Pinkeye led King to an officer who was the technical chief of the French aviation workshops in Casablanca. Under the codename "Penguin,"[226] he would regularly feed King specific details of the disposition of French aviation: the number of planes and their locations, the plans of airfields and their defenses, states of readiness, and attitudes of pilots and staff. Overnight at the Casablanca consulate—out of sight of other U.S. officers—King copied the material and returned the documents to Penguin hours later.

King's and Reid's clandestine work had now turned perilous. The vice-consuls and their agents, Pinkeye and Penguin, had no diplomatic protection from arrest by Vichy counterintelligence officers. And King's French agents ran the risk if betrayed of being "eliminated" by the Gestapo; they faced disgrace, trial, and long prison terms at home if exposed. Had they been caught, the damage to Vichy-U.S. relations would have been incalculable; at the very least, there would have been grave embarrassment to the U.S. government. Neither U.S. consul general H. Earle Russell nor any of the career consulate staff knew of the vice-consuls' covert activities in the guise of ship inspectors and control officers. King and Reid secretly and personally coded the intelligence information under harrowing and rudimentary conditions in their consulate office, and then cabled or pouched documents to the U.S. naval attaché in Tangier for transmission to Naval Operations in Washington.

To protect his network, King employed a "cut-out" and liaison agent named Miss Dorothy Ellis. The intrepid Miss Ellis had taught English and French privately at home, and at the Lycée Jeanne d'Arc in Casablanca for years. She carried notes for King, coded to appear as a confirmation of the times and dates of English lessons—when in fact they were schedules of covert meetings. King also used Miss Ellis in his secret work with a British officer (Captain "K"), who slipped in and out of Casablanca from his post in Lisbon. Captain K's agent in Algiers was Daphne Joan Fry Tuyl, the beautiful ex-British spy who was now in contact with John Knox. K's principal work was to head a network that rescued British, French, and Belgian servicemen and Allied sympathizers in hiding from Vichy police. The men and women were smuggled from Algiers to Casablanca and thence to Gibraltar and Lisbon.

(After the British attack on French warships at Mers-el-Kebir, ex-servicemen and refugees, sympathetic to the Allies, were sought by Vichy police. If caught they were interned in French concentration camps set up in the desert.)

King had his agents hide the refugees on Portuguese schooners sailing between Casablanca and Lisbon. He used the brave Miss Ellis to deliver escapees, in various disguises, to King's agents, who would then convey the group aboard the schooners. King termed this work "underground rough stuff."[227]

★ ★ ★

IT IS HARD TO IMAGINE TODAY how primitive telephone and telegraph communications were in 1940—between cities in North Africa, and within and between Europe and the United States. Murphy depended on an archaic telephone system (when it worked) to talk to his vice-consuls—but the telephone was monitored by the Vichy French and Axis agents. (And Felix Cole's Algiers villa, where Murphy lived, was certainly wired to tap all conversations.) In an emergency, his team talked to Murphy using an unreliable and potentially confusing verbal code: for example, the diplomatic pouch was referred to as "new trousers."

There was cable traffic to the U.S. through Tangier but not between consulates, and all messages had to be coded and decoded. (We have already seen that Berlin somehow had access to Murphy's coded cables.) The diplomatic pouch was the most efficient means of exchanging letters and reports; though slow, it was reliable and secure. It was always carried by two vice-consuls, and Murphy used it to communicate with his group and to stay apprised of their work.

But in Washington, the Office of Naval Intelligence (ONI) was desperate for a reliable communications grid. Murphy assigned Staff Reid to run an ultrasecret project, undisclosed to the other U.S. officers and employees at the U.S. Consulate in Casablanca. Reid's assignment would eventually link the North African consulate offices by wireless radio to Gibraltar. It was a tactical priority if reliable and fast communications were to be available for dealing with urgent matters. Consul General H. Earle Russell learned of the first phase of the project—setting up a wireless transmitting station connecting Casablanca and Tangier—when Reid was forced to seek his permission to install a transmitter in an old "water closet" in the basement of the consulate building. It eventually became known to insiders as "Staff's outhouse." (After Pearl Harbor, Reid would further extend the communications network.)[228]

★ ★ ★

TANJA

Tangier—*Tanja* in Arabic—was known in Eddy and Murphy's days as "the African Gibraltar"—the first Oriental city when leaving Gibraltar bordering the Atlantic Ocean—and in its time, the most Moorish city between Egypt and the Atlantic coast. Tanja's powerful lighthouse at Cape Spartel sweeps twenty-five miles across the Strait of Gibraltar, a beacon for convoys entering the Mediterranean and a constant point for German submarines eager to sink the British ships desperately trying to provision the island of Malta and reach British forces in Egypt and Libya. Along the nearby Atlantic coast lay

Casablanca, and Rabat to the south; and to the east on the shores of the Mediterranean Sea, lay the city of Oran and the French naval port of Mers-el-Kebir. Inland, and directly south of the Mediterranean coast, the Atlas Mountains stretch east from the Atlantic across the borders of Morocco, Algeria, and Tunisia. Great battles had been fought here to control the fertile plains and access to the seas from black Africa through the Sahara—and great battles lay in the near future.[229]

In June 1940, Spain had seized Tangier but let the sultan of Morocco control the Moslem and Jewish inhabitants—some four-fifths of the population. The town might have inspired a chapter from a John Buchan spy novel, with its walled Arab quarter and narrow streets where veiled women, camels, smugglers, and spies plied their trades.

It was Bill Eddy's kind of place: a town where anything could happen—and did—without causing so much as a raised eyebrow. The city was a critical intelligence cockpit for North African events, where Spanish authorities "looked often upon the comic espionage interplay between the [British, Germans, Italians, and Americans] with a mixture of cynicism and bemused incomprehension."[230]

Col. Eddy tells about daily life in Tanja: "When war came to Tangier the last bars of discipline descended in the Open City, touts offered you their sisters . . . cheap . . . and millions were made by money-changers in the uncontrolled market."

Indeed, in Tangier, anyone could get ahold of foreign currency without identification. "When Germany was counterfeiting U.S. banknotes, and our government placed an embargo on import of U.S. currency across the Atlantic, I could go downtown in Tangier and get two ten-dollar bills for a personal check for ten dollars."

It seems that Tangier was populated by persons "who had been, or ought to be, in jail. As Lisbon was [to] Europe, so Tangier was [to] Africa—the escape hatch from prison, banking laws, justice, persecution, morality—there was no neighborhood without sin fit to cast the stone."

Because "the Spanish Army had taken over the policing of Tangier at the outbreak of the war . . . mayhem was rare. Otherwise, the lid was off . . . Allied and Axis personnel mingled freely without ever speaking. Consuls, military, and naval and press attachés downed drinks and hors d'oeuvres elbow to elbow, served impartially by smiling Spanish debutantes, and were greeted with equal suavity by Spanish authorities."

Col. Eddy was miffed that in Tangier, the Axis had the place of honor at public functions. Certainly due to the fact that fascists and friends of Franco ruled the roost, but the protocol was always correct and "we . . . took care not to show any resentment at the precedence given our enemies. The Axis, on the other hand, threw their social weight around; uniforms sparkling with braid and decorations (the Japanese military attaché looked like a Christmas tree), German dress-swords and Italian cockades were conspicuous."

But in one incident, Eddy notes:

> . . . the Germans presumed too much for the proud Spaniards. Invitations to the diplomatic corps to a High Mass in the Cathedral (as with the commemoration of Franco's victory in the Civil War) specified that all must be in their seats five minutes before the procession began. We went from the American Legation (five strong) and were shown to seats with the British in the third row—the first two rows being for the Germans and the Italians. At 10:58 we moved to the front row. The procession came down the aisle, went up into the sanctuary, and the Archbishop began to say Mass. Thereupon with clank and clatter, down the aisle came the Germans, booted and spurred, to be offered the third row. Indignantly they about-faced and stomped back up the aisle and out in high dudgeon. This snub was the delighted talk of the town for weeks. One does not trifle with Spanish pride.

Eddy wondered why Spain did not openly join Hitler while the Germans were winning, and let them station troops astraddle the Strait of Gibraltar. He says that "after the war the world learned what may well have been a decisive factor: Franco and Hitler met briefly on the Spanish-French frontier, talked and parted. Before entering his auto Franco looked back and saw Hitler aping and mimicking his (Franco's) gestures to his laughing staff of Germans." Franco's Spanish pride was devastated.

The Riff Hotel was reserved for Axis agents, while the Hotel El Minzah was for Allied spies and hangers-on. Regardless, "both hotels, along with bars, restaurants and lodgings, were staffed by double agents who took money with both hands impartially. Our hotel bureau drawers were ransacked regularly, as we proved many times by placing 'confidential papers' in marked positions. A Gestapo agent followed Dave King everywhere, and once lost him in a station crowd. Seeing his obvious distress, Dave went over to him and said, 'Here I am; you are supposed to stick with me.' "

And not infrequently, serious dirty work would occur: "An Axis submarine-signal station, on Cape Spartel, which regularly signaled [the position of Allied ships] to German submarines for targets, was blown up, killing the Hun in charge, his concubine, and his two assistants; a time bomb went off when one settled into the backseat of his car; an Allied diplomatic pouch just unloaded on the pier from the SS *Mayne* exploded and fragments killed two innocent Tangerines mending a roof on the port warehouse nearby."

Of course, Spanish authorities were very angry, "but never got to the bottom of the matter. The Axis claimed that defective explosives in the pouch went off when a suitcase fell to the ground. The British story was that an Axis agent added a suitcase containing a bomb to the baggage being unloaded."

As for the Italians, Eddy recalls:

> A nephew of Badoglio [Italian Marshal Pietro Badoglio], the Italian Military Attaché, forgot the rules one night and tried to push my Assistant Naval Attaché, Frank Holcomb, son of the Commandant of the Marine Corps, off a sidewalk. The Italian was forced the next day to apologize. . . .
>
> Tangier was crawling with German and Italian officers. But the local balance was maintained by a band of friendly gorillas, the "Gibraltar Boys"—200 strong civilians who had been evacuated to Tangier when it appeared that Gibraltar might have to withstand a siege and would need to ration food and drinking water. These Gibraltar Boys, of Spanish blood but British subjects, took no nonsense from the Germans, nor did they feel at all bound to avoid Axis haunts.
>
> A group of them were one evening sitting in the bar of the Riff Hotel near to a table where the German Military Attaché, Colonel Reiner, and others were squiring a German beauty-queen from Berlin (rumored to be a trusted friend of Hitler). This lovely raised a laugh by insulting the British in a loud voice, whereupon one of the Gibraltar Boys arose languidly, crossed to where she sat, and slapped her hard across the face. Reiner drew his sword and his comrades leapt to their feet. They looked around the room, saw they were outnumbered, thought again, and decided to leave.

Col. Eddy, ever the cynical spy, did regret that there was "no special moral superiority for the Allies in wartime Tangier—a former retired Allied diplomat was ostracized for his open preference for a German victory over the French; another had a wife, a notorious lesbian, living in Tangier while he retired cozily to a villa with a plump, nubile eighteen-year old Spanish heiress-mistress. 'Concubinage' was no novelty in Tangier; the oddity was to find a good family man. Such a man was the German vice-consul Sonnenhall, who lived at Larache with his lovely, blond wife—a charming, devoted couple, to whom I [was forbidden to] speak to, though I could speak to wife-beaters and perverts if their politics were passable. The secret service makes strange bedfellows: one must at times consort with scoundrels, and ostracize one's own ilk."[231]

COON AND BROWNE—ADDITIONS TO THE DONOVAN BROTHERHOOD—ARRIVE

Tangier as the "sin city" of North Africa, and Bill Eddy as its ringmaster, now received two past masters in deceit and men—intellectual pranksters and brave warriors. They arrived in the person of a Harvard professor of anthropology, Carleton S. Coon, and Captain Gordon H. Browne, after an extraordinary voyage through the Washington paper warren.

Coon arrived at Tangier after Browne because he spent some weeks training in small arms and demolition practices in Canada. The two were key additions to Eddy's staff, for together they had explored Morocco in 1939 as field archaeologists for Harvard University. They knew the country well, and spoke French as well as local Arab dialects. Their job was to do undercover work for Eddy as special assistants to the legation. To cover their tracks, they worked part-time doing research, propaganda, and translations from Arabic. (They produced a voluminous and "useless" compendium on propaganda in Morocco, which impressed the American diplomats.)[232]

Coon immediately ran into trouble with U.S. minister J. Rives Childs, whose first ploy was to refuse to allow Coon and Browne to use diplomatic plates on their only official automobile. (They eventually kept a set of plates hidden in case of emergencies.)

Eddy's new agents set to work building an underground organization among Arabs and Berber tribes. They recruited a leading Moroccan leader in the Riff who was given the codename "Tassels."

In traveling about Morocco, Coon developed an acerbic attitude about the French with whom he dealt, and made the following observation:

Frenchmen do twice as much work as is necessary to achieve a given result, provided that this work involves human interaction rather than muscular activity. Frenchmen find it necessary to talk incessantly and are as a rule incapable of maintaining security. Frenchmen worry enormously about [codes of behavior] and chains of authority, particularly in the Army and Navy . . . the personal loyalty of each man to his superior officer is . . . conditioned to react to superficial symbols; ribbons and decorations mean a great deal. . . .

Meanwhile, Tassels began feeding Coon and Browne valuable material about politics in the Moroccan Riff and about the French military administration of the region.

Meetings with Tassels were sometimes hair-raising. If the Spanish saw them together, their new agent would be shot; and the Americans would certainly be banished. To protect their man, Coon worked out the following bit of tradecraft:

One of our trusted agents, Gusus,[233] would run into Tassels by coincidence in the Tingis café, where Gusus and Tassels ate noontime lunch; Gusus would then slip him the details of the rendezvous—always held at night. . . . [We] would then drive someone's car to a prearranged place on a lonely street at a prearranged hour. Seeing Tassels walking along, if no one was about, [we] would stop and have him get into the backseat; if there were too many people around, [we] would come back and pick him up a few minutes later.

Once in the car, Tassels would be transformed into a *fatma*, or Arab woman, with a veil; or a uniformed porter of the U.S. Mission, sporting a tall fez on his head, garnished with the U.S. seal in gold metal. It was to seem as if they were taking one of their servants to a villa to work at an evening party. They were never able to eliminate the baggy trousers that Tassels always wore; but when he left the car, Coon and Browne would walk beside their agent so that his pants could not be seen. Sometimes they met at Col. Eddy's villa on the mountainside of Tangier, where a clandestine OSS radio station was hidden, and sometimes at a local small hotel run by an American.

At some meetings, Coon had to hide in the bushes beforehand in order to later lead Tassels to the hotel or villa. Eddy or Browne would hide on the roof to spot if Tassels were being followed, and warn him away. On one trip Coon, in his words,

> lay in the bushes next to a reed fence, and spiders and ants crawled over me and spun webs over me. Meanwhile, a pair of Spanish lovers lay down on the other side of the fence; I was treated to all their physiological noises as well as their periodic inane conversation . . . after what seemed to me a distinguished effort (compared to the graph on sexual intercourse published by Boaz and Goldschmidt in *The Heart Rate American Journal of Physiology*), they left, and I was able to move and brush off a few cobwebs. I retired to the roof and Gordon made a sortie, finally picking up Tassels, who was wandering about lost several blocks away.

With Tassels's help, Eddy and his acolytes laid out plans for a possible revolt of the Riff tribes. They plotted how Allied troops would land; the dropping of parachutists; and the delivery of guns and cutting off of roads and garrisons with prearranged signals, by which the Riffians would assemble, seize various key positions, and await the arrival of the Americans.

Coon says, "Tassels gave us much combat intelligence, battle order, troop movements, etc., in great detail, and most of this we passed on to U.S. G-2 in Washington. Most of it checked with other sources; it was seldom that Tassels was inaccurate."[234]

Later with the help of Arab agents, Coon and Browne would polish the Arabic version of a proclamation FDR was to broadcast on Torch D-Day.[235] It was all part of a great game that Coon and Browne relished.

THE SUMMER STORM: BARBAROSSA

On Sunday, June 22, 1941, Murphy's men woke to the news of a cataclysmic Nazi strike against Stalin's Russia: at 0300 hours, German Wehrmacht troopers on motorcycles and in armored cars dashed over the Krzna bridge into Brest-Litovsk in Russian-held Poland, today's Byelorussia. Luftwaffe planes struck deep into the Soviet Union, and German armored Panzer divisions swarmed toward Leningrad, Moscow, and Kiev. The Nazis called it Operation Barbarossa,[236] and it achieved complete tactical surprise—outwitting United

States, French, and Soviet intelligence services—and rolling up Soviet defenders from the Baltic to the Black Sea. (The British were craftier; their spies in Germany warned their English masters, who in turn warned Stalin, who in turn took the warning as an anti-Soviet British trick.) The greatest military assault in history came as a lightning bolt out of the summer skies. In London and Washington, senior intelligence officers believed that only an "act of God" could save the Soviet Union, as German troops occupied an area of Russia only slightly smaller than the United States east of the Mississippi.[237]

In Algiers, Murphy breathed a sigh of relief. The Germans would not now invade North Africa.

5

AN ODD COUPLE:
ALGIERS-ORAN, SUMMER-FALL 1941

YEARS LATER, Ridgway Brewster Knight would grimace when he told of how one of his agents, a Catholic priest, had murdered a German officer in a prison cell at Oran, Algeria, using the man's own necktie.[238]

The dark waters of Algerian intrigue closed around Ridgway in mid-June 1941 when he, John Boyd, John Knox, and Leland Rounds assembled in Murphy's office to hear Knight and Boyd tell of their scouting trip to Oran, Algeria's second city some 210 miles west of Algiers as the crow flies, and some 47 miles again to the Moroccan border at Oujda.

One can almost imagine the conversation:

Murphy, listening to Boyd, a former Marseilles Coca-Cola dealer with a Mississippi drawl: "I hear tell the water is putrid, salty, and undrinkable."

Knight: "It's true. And Oran is the dullest, ugliest, most uncouth town."

Rounds, a pal of David King's from his days as a WWI Lafayette Escadrille pilot; poetic, pointing to Murphy's window, toward the port below: "Oran isn't the white cascading crescent you see out there, Bob."

Knight: "There is, of course, the naval anchorage at Mers-el-Kebir, an army airfield . . . a navy seaplane base."

Knox, the ex-French legionnaire wounded in the Moroccan Riff twelve years before: "I hear the town's crawling with Germans and Italians; and the Brits may have something going there."

Murphy, grinning: "Well then, we should set up an outpost in Oran."

Everyone nods.[239]

And what was Oran like? Despite the vast nearby navy installations at Mers-el-Kebir (meaning "great port" in Arabic), the city was only notorious for its tomatoes, citrus fruit, vineyards, strong wine, and the fact that French philosopher Albert Camus lived there in 1941. The town of some 400,000 souls was infamous for its shoddy buildings erected on a flat plateau above the Mediterranean Sea—the European quarter unimaginably built with its back to the blue waters, facing the somber mountain range of the interior that rose to a thousand feet. The city was dull and functional. Its odorous souk huddled in a narrow ravine that went to the water's edge, to the east of the naval port where, in 1940, a British fleet had sunk French warships.

Instead of seeing Oran as a tourist site, Ridgway viewed it as "a slum—*la bled*" (literally, a "godforsaken place"). The French considered it a hard land of desert villages with occasional palm groves. Set on an arid plain stretching endlessly to the Atlas Mountains, Oran is an oasis beyond which the drifting sands of the Sahara stretch to Niger and Mali in black Africa.

The Oranese (a third Arab stock; the majority, Spanish immigrants) drank from over-pumped subterranean pockets that had been infiltrated with seawater. It was said that when away from home, the good people of Oran added salt to their coffee rather than sugar to recapture familiar tastes. And the peasants who had come from Spain were happy to sell their wine and citrus to German dealers, and for a handsome profit, too. They easily accommodated to Vichy France's policy of collaboration.

If ever there were an ill-matched couple, it was Ridgway Brewster Knight and Leland Lasell Rounds. Ridgway, the proud and handsome scion of a privileged family that had for generations lived as successful painters in France, was a Harvard man and New York's "silk stocking" Park Avenue resident who thought each main meal should be accompanied by a master French millennium wine. Leland was schooled at Montclair Academy in East Orange, New Jersey, and served in the Lafayette Flying Corps in France during WWI. Leland believed the best thing a man could drink at meals was the reddest, coarsest, cheapest Algerian wine.

And yet, a sea of difference frequently makes a couple—and this one clicked. It may be that Murphy decided to pair the two because he thought that thirty-year-old Ridgway needed the weight of Rounds's twenty additional years—and his experience. After all, Rounds had fought with the French in WWI and knew about war—and death.

In the end, Ridgway began seeing his new partner as the solid, tough man he was, eager to get the job done. He ended up calling Leland, quite extraordinarily, "his twin." He did, however, think Rounds was a little bit too quick to go for the .45 caliber Browning stashed under his pillow or in his waist belt—a weapon Rounds boasted General Douglas MacArthur had carried and used when "dugout Doug" made his first and only kill: a Huk insurgent in the Philippines in 1890.[240]

★ ★ ★

AT THE GRAND HOTEL: A NEST OF VIPERS

It was a very tired and very hot Ridgway Knight and Leland Rounds— soaked in sweat and "inconspicuously" dressed in American-made seersucker suits—that descended from the worn, dusty railroad car that brought them from Algiers. A beaten-down automobile-cab with broken springs took them to the cool interior of Oran's Grand Hotel and to their rooms overlooking the noisy Place de La Bastille in the center of town. Their bedrooms, and a reception room-cum-office, were sandwiched between a contingent of Italian (on the first floor) and German (on the third) members of the Joint Armistice Committee—some were certainly "dangerous element" agents of the "sinister" OVRA and Gestapo.[241]

After weeks of apartment hunting Knight and Rounds concluded they should settle at the Grand Hotel:

> It was convenient and comfortable. Indeed, the sheer brashness and seeming unconcern of our choosing to share the same quarters with the senior Germans and Italians in town should tend to encourage the thought in their minds that we were not very serious fellows . . .
>
> Whenever we did not feel like going downstairs, we had our meals sent up. Not only was it more restful, but it also was less embarrassing to enjoy the occasional extra course, to which we were entitled as foreign officials, and which caused an occasional raised eyebrow when served downstairs in the hotel dining room.

At the hotel, it took only minutes for Leland to develop a raging allergy to a handsome specimen of the German master race, a Major Beck: a very

Hollywood cinema image of a Gestapo officer: tall, thin, steel-blue eyes, immaculately dressed, his features frozen in a perpetual sneer. (Ridgway remarked, "I couldn't help thinking how unpleasant it would have been to fall into his hands.") Beck, the chief of the German mission in Oran, was everpresent in the hotel, and always accompanied by a blond "Adonis," a youthful boyish creature, an even more handsome replica of himself.

Leland couldn't stand the pair. In the privacy of their rooms, he exploded, his naturally florid complexion turning a purple hue as he pounded the table: "Maybe you can stand the sight of these *Heinie* bastards and the Dago smoothies[242]—it's a nest of vipers. I cannot. And it won't be long before I have a heart attack or a stroke."

But there was yet another ordeal to contend with at the Grand Hotel: the daily, unnerving, sleep-busting bedlam of noise from the square below and the Catholic Church across the way. There were the shouts of street hawkers, the creaking of donkey carts, the noxious fumes from traffic, the incessant ringing of the church bells, and from sunrise until late at night, an unending murmur, punctuated with shouts from the crowds of Europeans and Arab folk who used the square as a town hall. The Europeans were in western dress, always standing apart in a shaded corner of the square; the Arabs were clad not in the imagined flowing, clean, white robes and turbans but in threadbare cast-off European vests with dingy *seroual*—the baggy Moslem trousers. Their women wore nondescript European hand-me-down robes or dirty white *haiks*—large, cloth rectangle wraparounds, a corner of the cloth frequently held between their teeth as a makeshift veil.

It was all very far from the *Thousand and One Nights* fantasies of either man.

Knight, the Cole Porter celebrant from New York's Park Avenue, and the tough, no-nonsense, fifty-year-old New York union buster and professional anti-communist, Leland Rounds, began to get a taste of the adventures that awaited them.

Their routine at the Grand Hotel was unpredictable and sometimes perilous.

Arriving late one night, Ridgway found that his key was not downstairs. Upstairs, the door to their room was locked. Ridgway gently knocked at Leland's door. Immediately, Rounds yelled, "*Qui est là?*" (Who's there?)

Knight remembers:

> It was a boiling hot night . . . I found Leland stripped down to his athletic shorts on the bed and, near him his [armed] Colt .45 . . .

he explained that he had been warned by one of our friends in the French G-2, a Captain Shellenberg, that Vichy thugs planned to attack us, hoping we would leave Oran . . . Why hadn't Leland spent the night with friends until we could ascertain what was up? Leland Rounds replied: "What, pull out of here and leave all our coffee, cigarettes, whiskey and supplies to those S.O.B.'s?"

(Weeks later, Shellenberg, ever loyal to Rounds, would attack fleeing Germans when Torch was launched. He would be imprisoned and court-martialed when the U.S.-sponsored fascist French regime returned to power in Algeria.)

Rounds and Knight soon decided to play the game they dubbed, "living in a glass house"—brashly choosing to share quarters with the Germans and Italians, and feigning disinterest while going about their "routine business" of inspecting cargo. They realized they couldn't hide—they had no security or place to safely store documents. Indeed, the best course was to play happy-go-lucky fellows delighted to land a cushy job in wartime. Knight recalls that apart from the calculated risk of living surrounded by our enemies, ". . . life at the Grand Hotel was convenient for many minor practical reasons, such as the telephone service and the taking of messages. One of the very first things I had done was to drop by the operators' hideaway on the mezzanine with a much-appreciated gift of chocolates and cigarettes. Because of the importance of their goodwill, what with the frequent bottlenecks at their switchboard, I made it a practice of bringing them small gifts from time to time, and always at Christmas and Easter."

As a result, the vice-consuls enjoyed the best telephone service of any of the Grand Hotel guests. And in line with developing "our playboy image, we gave a champagne party two weeks after our second arrival, inviting people whom we had met so far, including as many pretty girls as possible."

Thanks to the champagne, the evening was a success. "And we included among our guests two French liaison officers with the Italians and Germans to reinforce our image of insouciance . . . While engaging in such social activities, we were, of course, also carrying out a significant part of our mission, i.e., making an enhanced U.S. presence felt, with all that this signified in the way of an American interest in the area, with its implied anti-Axis message."

It had taken a week for Knight and Rounds to get to know each other. But by then, Ridgway admits, "Leland was already revealing that extraordinary capacity for letting time pass happily and without physical exertion. He had bought a lightweight white *burnouse* of very finely spun wool. After lunch, during the hottest part of the day, he would take off his clothes, put on his *burnouse* over his triangular slip and, Buddha-like, recline on his bed with a book, more often than not a detective story or spy novel. Where and how he had acquired this quasi-Oriental capacity for the enjoyment of leisure was forever to remain a mystery!"[243]

Leland made an impression in the hotel dining room—shocking some, including Major Beck and his partner, but amusing the barman, Bruno—when Rounds did a fair mimic, with nasal tones, of the French physician who had shared their railroad compartment from Algiers: "I shun politics as Marshal Pétain advises . . . was it not the cheap politicians, Jews and Freemasons that brought us defeat . . . Pétain saved us once at Verdun . . . he will shield us from the Germans and the English—the treacherous bastards that hit us at Mers-el-Kebir when we were down. I find the Germans are more correct."[244]

Knight and Rounds soon befriended Bruno, the hotel's barman, who would go on to play an important role in helping the U.S. cargo inspectors and neophyte spies.

It took no time for Ridgway to stow away his seersucker suits and adopt an Algiers look in his dress. "In the hot, beautifully sunny weather, and umpteen pounds lighter than Leland, I would take a bicycle to explore the country and seaside with an extensive U.S. War Department checklist of information Washington needed. The list called for maps and information about beaches—their characteristics: the width of roads, their surface composition and foundation, their strength, and specifications of bridges and culverts."

Ridgway combined pleasure with work. "I would bicycle off with a bathing suit and bath towel, returning quite exhausted at the end of the day. I remember how delicious the grapes tasted, to which I unhesitatingly helped myself from the abundant vineyards along the roadside."

MADAME "S"

Life as a supposed bachelor offered not only intrigue for Knight, but, "At the age of thirty, living alone [in Oran] I was credited with several *bonnes fortunes*, as the French say, and as the Germans believed, according to the records which we seized in their offices after the landings. But I had only one affair during the entire time . . . in sharp superficial contrast with the photos I sent back home through the open mail, replete with beaches and attractive girls, which may have made my wife, Betty, share the Germans' opinion about my many feminine adventures." (Knight knew the Vichy French opened his mail, and thought they would be impressed with his "playboy" image.)

Ridgway tells in his memoirs about "S":

> She was a woman of the world, married, with three children and a husband with whom she had a sophisticated understanding. "P," the husband, was cultivated and somewhat precious. He was much interested in his books and obviously unhappy to be relegated in the backwaters of provincial Oran . . . "S" belonged to my group of social friends. (Until after the landings . . . she never knew what I was up to, beyond my control officer functions. Politically, she and her husband were "mainstream," i.e., pro-Marshal Pétain, while not pro-German.)
>
> Things developed quickly. "S" had her feet on the ground and told me early in our relationship that she had no intention of divorcing . . . I listened to this declaration of principle with unalloyed relief. I often ate [at her home] and with considerable embarrassment. For it was in that home that I was best able to feel how poor the food situation was and how difficult it was for an urban housewife, even with above-average means, to feed her family—and I was really shocked by the first entirely "family" menu which I ate in "S"'s home: a thin vegetable soup, followed by a platter of lentils and a piece of fruit. Once again, I was thankful that wine was not rationed! Needless to say, a fair share of the food, which I brought back from my trips to Algiers, found its way to "S"'s kitchen.[245]

Ridgway Knight's description of the beautiful Ingrid Smadja, who would later assist in his secret work, tells much about his taste for elegant, attractive women:

> When Ingrid showed up on consular business in what we somewhat pretentiously called our office, I was speechless. She was clad in a light-colored dress with its flowing skirt, which perfectly suited her tall, supple figure. I was painfully aware that my confusion must have shown. All I could think of saying was, thanks for calling . . .

After thanking me in perfect English, Ingrid burst out in a torrent of words: "You can't imagine what it means to me to have you and Mr. Rounds here. For me, it is a symbol of hope. I loathe the Germans. I feel sick at their very sight. That is why we left France. But, I feel in exile here. Pierre's [Ingrid's husband] family could not be nicer to me, but I can't stand all these Oranese who could not care less for the war. For me, it is a constant torment. And don't forget," concluded Ingrid, "that the more often Pierre and I see you and Mr. Rounds, the better it will be for our morale."

In short, Ridgway was "bowled over by the beauty and outspokenness of my visitor. Yet as I showed Ingrid out the door and watched her walking gracefully down the corridor towards the elevator, with her short light skirt swaying around her long legs, I could not but entertain some suspicions, notwithstanding the excellence of her credentials, her passionate anti-German profession of faith and the striking loveliness and distinction of my caller, that all struck me as being too good to be true."

Indeed, Mr. Knight was beginning to acquire the traits of any good professional: a dose of suspicion and a warning sense of disbelief.

As it turned out, Ingrid became an invaluable messenger and liaison agent between Knight's and Rounds's intelligence and resistance contacts. Ridgway thought: "What could be more natural than to have this Nordic beauty come up to the rooms of the *unattached* young vice-consul that I was? Meanwhile, Pierre patriotically sacrificed his husbandly honor on the Allied cause's altar. To be completely honest, I did occasionally have thoughts of attempting to give substance to this apparent liaison but to be equally honest, I never did, however much this may strain credulity."

Leland Rounds took on the job of regularly searching their rooms for hidden microphones. He found none. But he did discover that he and Ridgway were being followed by Vichy agents and others, too—men who hung out in the shadows and in the same Citroën sedan, certainly Gestapo thugs, seen once too often. At the time the Vichy French security services were nervously on guard following the surrender of Vichy forces to an Anglo-Gaullist army at Acre in Syria. The question was on everyone's lips: would the Free French Gaullists try to rise up in Algeria?

Rounds devised ways of breaking away from the constant surveillance. He and Ridgway tried various subterfuges: moving separately in different directions by taxi (and joining up later by foot); walking from the hotel and then ducking into a building with a separate entrance and exit and then jumping into a waiting car. The pair was perfecting their own methods of clandestine tradecraft and operational procedures.

By the late summer of 1941 Knight and Rounds began making contact with Frenchmen they believed could be trusted to join in covert operations and likely to supply information—two French priests, Father Théry (a Dominican "white Father") and Abbé Pierre-Marie Cordier (a Jesuit); and Henri d'Astier de la Vigerie (a distant cousin of vice-consul Harry Woodruff's)—all of whom were devout Catholics and royalists. (Knight and Rounds would later introduce these men, and a handful of French-Jewish patriots and French Freemasons, to Murphy in Algiers. Some would play a key role in the liberation of Oran and in Robert Murphy's political maneuverings.)

Rounds then recruited Colonel Pierre Tostain, a senior French army officer who supplied secret information about Vichy French forces. (Alas, Tostain would fail the vice-consuls at a critical moment.)

Through secret documents and information supplied by this group, Knight and Rounds assembled the battle orders of French forces in the region; the location of shore batteries, ammunition supplies, and depots; and the plans for Vichy counterintelligence units to spy on Gaullists and British agents. Knight and Rounds covered every road in the region, noting on a scale map the information requested by Washington: airfields, coastal fortifications, and armaments; fuel depots, prisoner concentration camps, water, fuel, electrical supply points; the course of high-tension wires, transformers, and areas mined by the French; and the position of armed forces and police headquarters. And they noted the location of German Armistice Commission personnel and their residences.

By September 1941 all the information had been sent incrementally to Murphy in Algiers via State Department couriers, who made regular pickups from the Oran airport. After copying the material in Algiers Murphy pouched a vast amount of secret intelligence to Washington. He could be pleased with his Oran outpost. (And Knight and Rounds co-authored a comprehensive seventeen-page political analysis of the political groups operating in the Oran region: Franco-German collaborators; those who "watched and waited;" and the outright partisans of "Anglo-Saxon victory."[246]) To spread confusion among the population Nazi propaganda organs claimed that the Gaullists and the communists planned to assassinate Admiral Darlan, Pétain's new vice premier.

AT YOUR ORDERS, SIR

One lazy autumn morning in the breakfast room of the Grand Hotel, Ridgway was informed that he had a caller. Immediately he was approached by a man in civilian clothes, with a ramrod-stiff military bearing. The visitor came to attention before Ridgway, clicked his heels, saluted, and loudly proclaimed, "*À vos ordes, mon Commandant!*" (At your orders, Major!)

Ridgway was stunned. Fearing that he was being set up and that German or Italian officials would appear at any moment, he exclaimed, "What the hell do you think you are doing?" He pulled his caller into a side room, where the man squeamishly whispered, "Sir, I am sorry. I am Captain Stanislaw Sczewalski, Polish Army, reporting for duty."

"There is some grave mistake, Captain," Ridgway said. "I am an American vice-consul supervising American economic aid to Algeria. Why have you come to see me?"

"Sir, we Poles were tricked by the French to come to Oran; we want to continue to fight the Nazis, but Vichy keeps us in camps in the desert."

Ridgway, more relaxed now, sympathetically replied, "I admire your sentiments, Captain, but I fail to see how I can be of help."

The Pole went on to explain the predicament of hundreds of Polish soldiers—prisoners of the Vichy French in desert camps. He was adamant. "Seeing you, I know you and Mr. Rounds want to wage the good fight." He presented his card, insisting, "No matter what you say, I consider you to be my commanding officer!" Captain Sczewalski left with a formal bow.

Later, Ridgway learned that his visitor was the senior liaison officer between the Polish prisoners and French authorities. He realized that the man was sincere—and later he would learn more about the terrible conditions in which the Poles were held by Vichy French police at a camp at Méchéria, on the edge of the Sahara Desert. Ridgway told Leland Rounds that he thought the Pole's rash impulsiveness and sense of honor were reminiscent of days gone by—of the Polish horse cavalry charging German tanks in September 1939.

Captain Sczewalski remained true to his word. When Ridgway and Leland failed to get ahold of navigational charts showing the depth of water alongside the port docks of Oran harbor, they enlisted his help. And Sczewalski and his assistant, Lieutenant Polanski, did the job.

Afterward, grinning ear to ear, Sczewalski met Ridgway in the Grand Hotel bar. It was always crowded and frequented by German and Italian officers and "professional ladies." Ridgway, perhaps naively, thought it a safe place to meet. Sczewalski came to the point in a hoarse whisper: "Mission accomplished," he said, and slipped an envelope to Ridgway under the table. Ridgway was aghast. But the Pole went on: "It was simple. Last night, Polanski and I go down to port with a pair of pliers. We walk along fence until we find spot out of sight of sentries, cut barbed wire . . . we walk along docks and see small steamer with light out, no one around gangplank. We board ship, go to bridge, break into captain's cabin, search through cabin and find chart."

Ridgway remarks in his memoirs, "It was as simple as that; those brave Poles belonged to another age."[247]

★ ★ ★

ALL SAINTS DAY was a national holiday in Algeria. On the frigid night before the holy day feast and some thirty-five miles from the Grand Hotel in Oran, groups of Polish soldiers began slipping into hiding places near the beaches of the village of La Macta, hoping to be picked up by a British-Polish manned ship and to escape to Gibraltar.

The arrangements for the escape had been made by Knight and Rounds when their Polish "friend," Captain Sczewalski, devised the following plan: The men were to steal out of their prison camp over a few days' time, hide by day, and make their way to La Macta. The vice-consuls used the U.S. diplomatic pouch to inform the British navy of the details of the plan, including timing, secret signals, and how to make the pickup from a boat anchored offshore. After an exchange of ship to shore signals, the Poles were to swim in small groups from the La Macta beach into the surf using safety lines laid by the boat's crew. They would then be taken aboard dinghies by trained seamen, and ferried to a large fishing trawler disguised as a Spanish commercial vessel. The operation had been done successfully before at other sites along the Moroccan coast. Captain Sczewalski was to coordinate the beach-to-boat operations using signals equipment. It was all very perilous.

The man who would direct the operation from the trawler at sea was already a legend in the rescue of Polish escapees and Allied resistant fighters. He was Polish naval lieutenant Marion Kadulski, who used "Krajewski" as his codename when operating for the British Military Intelligence Evaders-Escapee Service (SIS-MI9) based in Gibraltar. Krajewski had successfully operated various sailing craft and Feluccas that traveled from Gibraltar to Morocco and Algeria to pick up Polish, Czech, Belgian, and French servicemen escaping from Vichy or German prison camps.

Between Friday, October 30 and Sunday, November 2, some 200 Polish prisoners trickled out of the Vichy prison camp on the edge of the Sahara Desert and gathered near the La Macta beach forest and in the nearby sand dunes. Aboard the disguised trawler, all was ready: the dinghies were launched, lines rigged to the beach, signals confirmed. The holy Catholic holiday was to bring the Poles to freedom.

Alas, when dawn broke on that Sunday morning of November 2, 1941, misfortune struck. The French prefect of the region had arranged a Sunday charity hunt to benefit French POWs in German captivity, and the hunt took place in exactly the same La Macta area where the Poles were concealed.

It was a disaster. The French hunters and their dogs turned up not wild game but Polish soldiers hidden in the bush and sand dunes of the La Macta forest. The alarm was sounded by the hunters; the police were alerted, and in no time, a large force of French troops was sent to the area. It seemed the French high command feared a British landing.

By afternoon several companies of soldiers and police, walking abreast through the forest and shore, caught the Poles; those who were not caught gave themselves up during the next few nights.

Captain Sczewalski was saved by his quick wit. When he reported to Knight and Rounds after being detained for some weeks, the vice-consuls were horrified. Lt. Polanski had been arrested and imprisoned. Most of the escapees were back in the prison camp. Many were put in small cells, to subsist on bread and water.

Lt. Kadulski, by luck and thanks to very bad weather, barely escaped to Gibraltar with his boat and crew. He would sail again on rescue missions and participate in the invasion of North Africa aboard a Polish ship.

★ ★ ★

LELAND ROUNDS REMEMBERS Bruno, the barman at the Grand Hotel, as being a thin, sharp-faced Italian who served an inferior ersatz gin and whiskey—the only drinkable "booze" in town. The British blockade had successfully deprived Algeria of hard liquor.

For many months Leland and Ridgway had been unsure of where Bruno's sentiments lay. Notwithstanding his snide references to fascism, he was an Italian who maintained cordial relationships with several of his Italian compatriot customers.

One day after the dramatic "Polish escapee fiasco," Rounds had an appointment with one of the vice-consuls' run-of-the-mill local informants in the barroom. The man was a routine contact. But stupidly, without warning, the man persistently tried to pass an envelope under the table. His grimaces and winks went unnoticed by Rounds. Finally, Leland realized what was happening when Bruno, who had eyes for everything, signaled him. Rounds reached for the envelope.

After the caller had departed and Rounds was paying the check, Bruno whispered dryly, without cracking a smile: "Monsieur Rounds, I thought you would never catch on." It was then that Bruno told Leland that a colonel commanding the military section of the Italian Armistice Commission "harbored anti-fascist sentiments." And, announced Bruno, the colonel wanted to make contact with the American vice-consuls.

"The colonel would like to meet you; and I can arrange a discreet place where you could talk," concluded Bruno.

But Knight and Rounds were under orders to have no direct contact with Axis officials "under any and all circumstances." Much to Bruno's disappointment, they declined to see the man. (As it turned out Ridgway learned later, during the Italian campaign, that this colonel had been killed while fighting Germans in the Genoa area. Bruno's instincts had been right. Later, Bruno the barman would risk his life to aid the vice-consuls.)

TRIP TO CASA

In an early-morning phone call from Murphy in Algiers, Ridgway and Leland learned that the vice-consuls' official automobile, a gray, hard-top, two-seater Studebaker, had arrived at the port of Casablanca and was being offloaded from an American freighter.

A tin of Chesterfield cigarettes (available through diplomatic channels) slipped to the Air France manager at the Oran airport got the vice-consuls seats on a flight from Oran to Casablanca. (The Air France manager, Mr. Paul Quirot, had already told Leland Rounds that they both suffered from the same affliction: neither man could stand the *Boches*. Quirot began to feed Leland information about Germans traveling to and from Oran on Air France flights, as well as the movement of German and Italian military aircraft.)

Winter was approaching when Knight and Rounds flew to Morocco to pick up their official automobile that had arrived from America, and to observe how the other vice-consuls lived. The car was a U.S. government-issued gray Studebaker sedan, and it allowed Ridgway to drive Leland around the town. They found that their colleagues lived very well indeed—in well-furnished apartments and villas not unlike the one Reid shared with King. And they ate well and seemed to be free to play as they wished and with whomever they wished. According to Ridgway Knight, "They were able to circulate freely and act in a more unrestrained manner than we could in Oran, or that Knox and Boyd could in Algiers." For unlike Algeria, Morocco was not legally part of France. Morocco had an international status as a French Protectorate ruled by Sultan Mohammed V—and in Morocco, the Vichy French had to be more constrained in their use of power.

Morocco was a far richer country. In Casablanca, the vice-consuls ate "thick juicy steaks, golden French fried potatoes." Olive oil was plentiful and the beaches delightful, as were the very pretty girls in scanty bathing costumes. (The inventive bikini would have to wait for six more years.)

On the return to Oran in their new Studebaker, Ridgway and Leland traveled like first-class tourists:

> We spent the night in Fez at the ancient and finely furnished *Palais Jamai* which overlooks the old city—gray and mysterious in its [small valley] hollow—unchanged over the centuries. The hotel garden gave on the old town with a postern in the wall giving onto the *Al Madinah*. There Leland and I had an early dinner, in the twilight of late summer. I then went alone through an odoriferous maze of garishly lit and noisy lanes and byways. Most shops were open in the souks. The *Fassis*, as the inhabitants of the ancient capital of Fez are called, are sophisticated and used to seeing foreigners in their midst. I was fascinated and exhilarated [I had entered] the mysterious world of Islam . . . I returned to the hotel via the walled gardens to the faded glory of the *Palais Jamai* . . . feeling that at last I had been able to step into the world of the *Thousand and One Nights*.[248]

During their absence, Bob Murphy had temporarily assigned Harry Woodruff and John Utter from Tunis to Oran to carry on with Knight's and Rounds's routine work and to ensure an American consular presence in Oran. Ridgway had known Woodruff—and his wealthy widowed mother, who had remarried a French physician—since boyhood in France. He was fond of Harry but knew him to be "high-strung and sensitive, idealistic, and even somewhat tortured emotionally"—but Harry Woodruff was above all "an intensely scrupulous and intellectual man."[249]

In Ridgway Knight's memoirs, he tells how when he and Leland returned to their hotel at Oran, Woodruff and Utter were still there along with "the pettiest, most obnoxious member of the U.S. career personnel in North Africa, Vice-Consul Orray Taft, Jr." Taft, a career consular officer stationed in Algiers, had met Knight and Rounds when they first arrived in Algeria. Now he had popped in from Algiers for a visit. (Taft did not know that Murphy's team was on a secret mission to collect intelligence.) Ridgway tells how on their return and during a dinner at Oran's Brasserie Grillon, Taft "lost no opportunity to ridicule us and sneer at our job of checking merchant cargoes." Taft thought "our presence [in Oran] quite unnecessary." As dinner progressed, the mood at the table turned sour. "Caustic remarks were exchanged . . . influenced by the heat, the wine and the fatigue of a long day's drive." Ridgway began questioning Taft about whom he had seen during his visit to Oran. He pointedly asked Taft about the nature of his current business. With an unpleasant smirk, Taft replied that "as a career Foreign Service Officer, I wanted to ascertain whether you are conducting yourself in a manner befitting a representative of the United States abroad."

Ridgway tells how Woodruff became "white-faced with anger. Ever my loyal friend, Harry jumped up, seized an amazed Orray Taft by the arm and dragged him into the adjoining bathroom hissing, 'You bastard' through his clenched teeth. Then he hit Taft hard on the jaw. Taft lost his balance, fell, his mouth hit the edge of . . . a basin . . . breaking two teeth."

Taft never again appeared in Oran.[250]

Looking back on their trip and the extraordinary encounter with Taft, Ridgway declared to Rounds that he was not disappointed to be assigned at Oran. On the contrary, he said, "We have our own operation here." Indeed, though Ridgway envied the cosmopolitan life in Casablanca, not to mention the weather, he had come to realize that Oran had a great advantage: He and

Leland were their own bosses, far from the bureaucracy of consulates and legations—the hassles, protocols, and petty administrative tasks.

Ridgway began to realize that back at headquarters in Algiers, there were two Robert Murphys: the jovial, ever-agreeable Irishman and the shrewd diplomat. (And it may well be that at the time, Murphy saw in Ridgway an all-too-perfect Ivy League Franco-American snob.) It's also possible that Murphy, "the poor Irish Catholic boy from the Midwest"—schooled at night—had himself become "Grottier than the Grotties." (This was an allusion to the black-shoe prep school Groton, where Endicott Peabody instilled "The Groton Ethic," a notion of duty and honor practiced by men like W. Averell Harriman and Dean Acheson—men close to Murphy's heart.)[251]

NECKTIE

Robert Murphy never referred to the "Orray Taft" incident.

And Rounds and Knight forgot about it. As well they might, for after Woodruff and Utter had returned to Tunis, Rounds was warned by Abbé Cordier, who doubled as an agent of the French intelligence services and one of Ridgway's agents, that the Vichy security services were going to use Vichy agent provocateurs to attempt to lure the vice-consuls into a trap and arrest them if they could prove they were collecting military information.

Indeed, a French physician, Dr. Couniot, with a medical practice in Oran, showed up one day at the hotel. He asked for Leland Rounds and crudely offered him an envelope that he described as, "information to help our Allies." Rounds refused to touch the envelope and told the man he had no idea about this kind of thing. "Why don't you send it to Algiers to the U.S. consul general?" he suggested. It was to be one of many efforts by the Vichy French to compromise the vice-consuls.

A few weeks later Ridgway met secretly with Abbé Cordier and Henri d'Astier de la Vigerie. Over the previous months Ridgway and Leland had developed close relationships with the two men, and they met often but in secret. Ridgway covered these meetings by letting it be known that he was conferring with Abbé Cordier because he was thinking of converting to Catholicism. Over time d'Astier and Abbé Cordier and others in the d'Astier group had fed the vice-consuls valuable military intelligence about the Oran region, and supplied insight into how Vichy French G-2 undercover operations worked.

What the two men now told Ridgway "jolted" him out of his normally sheltered, well-ordered, and law-abiding life he was used to—a life "where violence was not fashionable." Indeed, at the time the spy novels of E. Phillips Oppenheim only rarely employed murder as a "tool of the trade."

D'Astier told Ridgway how a German spy named Schmidt (a pseudonym) had been caught in the act of spying with the help of Vichy French military officers in Casablanca. Schmidt had been caught *in flagrante delicto*—for he had learned that deep in the Middle Atlas Mountains, the French were hiding heavy weapons and ammunition—tanks and other military equipment for-bidden under the limitations of the Franco-German armistice agreement. While being secretly interrogated as a prisoner in Casablanca, the man's Ger-man superiors had been tipped off about his arrest and all hell broke loose. The Germans demanded his release and return to duty, threatening reprisals against French officers held in German prison camps.

Ridgway relates how d'Astier, ever the professional soldier, and the gaunt Abbé Cordier, then stopped talking and sat grinning like Cheshire cats.

Finally, d'Astier broke the silence. "My dear Ridgway, Schmidt is never going to make it back to his bosses in Germany."

Ridgway asked, "How can you be so sure of that?"

Abbé Cordier, not batting an eye, replied, "Sadly, I must inform you that he has committed suicide."

Taken aback, Ridgway studied him. "You received news from Casa?"

D'Astier turned to him. "Well, Herr Schmidt was not in Casa last night. He was right here in our own military prison."

Finally, d'Astier related the whole story. Instead of turning Schmidt over to the German mission in Morocco, "we succeeded in getting German officials to agree to have Schmidt transferred into German hands on French soil at the line of demarcation—at a border point between the two zones that now separated France. We told the *Boches* that surrendering our pris-oner in Morocco would be impossible . . . would cause us grave problems, as Morocco was not France. The German consul general finally saw reason, and agreed."

D'Astier went on. "Schmidt arrived here last night under guard. He was to sail today on the steamship *Ville d'Oran* for Marseilles. When I learned of his arrival, I arranged to call on him with Abbé Cordier to give the poor man moral solace . . . As the G-2 [military intelligence] here and with the Abbé, as a military chaplain, we have access to the prison day and night . . .

"We managed to be . . . alone with Schmidt, overpowered him, gagged him, and hanged him with his own necktie to a bar of the prison window."

Cordier laughed. "The man must have had a very guilty conscience to have committed suicide before returning home."

Ridgway relates in his memoirs how he sat for a minute, stunned and dismayed, facing the two men who had become his agents and friends. Seeing his discomfort, d'Astier ironically added, "If you are concerned about the sin of suicide, let your conscience be put to rest, Ridgway. Our friend, the Abbé Cordier, gave him absolution before he died."

A few months later, Henri d'Astier de la Vigerie was transferred to G-2 headquarters in Algiers; his permanent chaplain and the d'Astier family confessor who lodged at the d'Astier home went with him. Ridgway wrote a letter of introduction to Robert Murphy, recommending the two men as dependable agents of the United States. Later, Abbé Cordier was given the codename "Necktie." And sometime later, he would again give the sacrament of absolution, but in quite different circumstances. It would not be the last time d'Astier and Cordier would be involved in murder.

★ ★ ★

MEANWHILE, FROM HIS HOME in Rabat, Morocco, the exiled Bourbon pretender to the throne of France, the Comte de Paris, praised Marshal Pétain announcing, "This providential leader had accomplished a miracle and saved France from disappearing."[252]

Miracles indeed: As Monsieur le Comte was speaking in Rabat, his fellow Frenchmen at home were suffering terrible privations and German exactions for their resistance to the Nazi occupation. At Versailles that September 1941 German security forces shot sixteen Frenchmen and decapitated two other *Résistants*. Their crime had been operating an underground printing press.

Then the German occupation authorities announced that Adm. Jean-François Darlan would be the next Vichy official to be assassinated.[253]

6

THE MAN IN BLACK:
ALGIERS–TUNIS, SUMMER–WINTER 1941

IF SOME OF THE vice-consuls were mismatched—and if Leland Rounds and Ridgway Brewster Knight were rather an odd couple—John Knox and Daphne Joan Fry Tuyl seemed to have been made for each other. John Knox had had a turbulent early life as a student, wounded Legionnaire officer, and playboy in France before the war. Now the forty-two-year-old vice-consul had fallen "in love at first sight"—struck by the beauty and charm of Daphne. But Daphne, a sophisticated, widowed, English mother of two with a French education and a penchant for intelligence work, "took longer," she says.[254] Indeed, over many weeks the dry, somewhat stiff and jaded ex-Legionnaire officer had found every excuse to be in touch with the English beauty. And Knox soon realized that Daphne Joan Fry Tuyl was a sensitive, courageous, and no-nonsense lady. He wooed her in a hundred ways, and finally connived to ask Daphne and her mother if he could take his midday meal with them. In return, he would contribute American supplies to the household larder. The ever-practical Knox suggested that the family desperately needed fresh milk, and that he and John Boyd would pay to purchase a dairy cow to supply a daily milk ration—a rare commodity in Algiers that winter.

Daphne says the "cow could hardly be kept in either the consulate or in our small apartment, so we got Yusuf—for thirty years a doorman at the now-defunct British Consulate, currently employed by Robert Murphy (and decorated with the Medal of the British Empire)—to keep the cow."

Daphne had kept a dairy farm in the Sahara before the war. She and Yusuf ended up housing the "half-Swiss, half-native animal on Yusuf's small property."

"The beast supplied milk for all, for as long as it was well fed," she remembers, "until it went dry just before the landings." But in order to buy hay or fodder in Algiers, at the time of rationing, certificates were needed for each purchase.

"Yusuf never reported the lack of food in time, and he would appear in front of Robert Murphy, asking for a signature, with a piteous expression on his face and begging that the beast was starving." According to Daphne, "There would be a roar from the inner sanctum."

Murphy would complain, "Let the war be, and get Yusuf food for the cow. I cannot work with his woebegone face around the door."

John Knox was not alone in offering food to feed Daphne, her mother, and Daphne's boys, Tony and Derek.[255]

Daphne remembers:

> One evening we were settling down to an illicit listening-in to the BBC when the door opened and a friend of mine—a large, Norman sailor—walked in, startling John Knox. His name was Cramoisan, and he grinned amiably, depositing a sack of sugar on the floor.
>
> "You need not pay me for it. I stole it out of the ship's hold for you," he said. Then catching sight of the radio, he added: "You have a cheek, listening to London, so near the police station." (It was in fact just down the road.)
>
> "Don't worry," I replied. "I met the police sergeant the other day, and he told me to dim (the sound) down." [Apparently, a member of the Italian Commission complained about the volume when passing the house. The French sergeant had explained that the Fry-Tuyls were of British origin, and that what he heard was the family shouting at each other.]

Daphne recalls that Cramoisan was curious about Knox's presence at the house.

" 'Who is this?' " Cramoisan asked, pointing at John. I introduced them . . . The Norman's face brightened. He remarked, 'He can help me then.' "

Cramoisan wanted to know the date when a certain French ship would sail. He knew it would be loaded with minerals destined for Italy. So, he explained, if the British knew this, they would stop the ship and he could slip or transfer aboard—an easy way to get to England and join de Gaulle's Free French and fight the Germans.

Soon after, John Knox informed the Tangier Legation of the ship's name, cargo, and destination.

It was a few years later that Daphne and John Knox learned what had happened to their friend. The ship was torpedoed. Cramoisan could not swim but managed to get to a raft. He was picked up by a French ship, taken to Tunis where he was arrested by the Germans, and transported to Germany. He again escaped and made it to Spain—where he was again arrested. He remained in a Spanish jail for six months, broke out of prison again, and reached Morocco. There, Cramoisan joined the Free French Leclerc Division. He was eventually shipped to England, where the division was reorganized and rearmed.

Cramoisan landed on the Normandy beaches at D-Day.

Much later, he appeared at the Knox home (in London). Daphne says, "He showed the scars of wounds earned at the Normandy beachhead—and the Croix de Guerre with Palm."

Daphne concludes the retelling of her life at Algiers: "In spite of the lighter side supplied by people like Cramoisan, I felt the net was closing in on me . . . With luck, an agent can only hope to last a certain time. Marked [by the Vichy French] as I had been . . . I had already been lucky."[256]

EVERYWHERE, POLES[257]

From the early days of his arrival in North Africa, Robert Murphy had kept an eye out for "British agents who might help."[258] John Knox had unknowingly come upon such a group. By midsummer 1941 Knox was spending all his free time at the Tuyl home. And it was *chez les Tuyls* that Knox first came into contact with a Polish journalist who regularly visited Daphne to take English lessons.

The man was none other than Lieutenant Count Henry Lubienski (Agency Africa Intelligence Officer cryptonym, "Banuls") sent by Polish Major Rygor Slowikowski to scope out Murphy's vice-consuls. At the time, Murphy believed Slowikowski and his Poles to be agents of a "Polish underground or the Polish G-2."[259] He would later learn, however, that the men were part of an extraordinary British MI6 spy network: Agency Africa—run by the Polish-British agent Rygor Slowikowski.[260]

Banuls (Lt. Lubienski) was one of a handful of Polish officers who had worked with Slowikowski in Toulon and Marseilles in 1940 after the German occupation of France, when Rygor was running an intelligence and Polish evacuation network targeting Vichy authorities and the Gestapo.[261]

These brave men had managed to obtain French visas and German permission to travel to North Africa—in itself a disheartening task—and they became Slowikowski's trusted intelligence officers who then recruited agents all over North and West Africa. They were selected by Rygor for their ability to secure North African visas and their expertise in spying, evacuation, coding/radio transmission, and "wet work." This meant liquidating Polish-speaking German spies that the Gestapo sent to infiltrate Slowikowski's evacuation operation in France since 1940.[262]

In one dramatic case, a Polish artillery officer, one of Rygor's early agents, informed him in late 1940 that he had met another Polish officer in Marseilles who claimed to be from his same artillery regiment. The man also claimed to have escaped from a German prisoner of war (POW) camp and was demanding speedy evacuation to England. He was an imposter. The real regimental "friend" had been wounded in battle and died in German captivity.

Slowikowski set a trap: When the "escapee" reported to Rygor along with two of Rygor's officers—themselves posing as evacuation candidates—the man's identity papers were checked. They were authentic, but Rygor saw that the stamp on the photograph was forged. Unbeknownst to the escapee, the artillery officer confirmed, under oath, that the man was a spy. Rygor ordered all three evacuees to be sent by taxi to a French demobilization camp as a first step before evacuation to Spain via a route through the Pyrenees Mountains.

The road to the camp passed through a dense forest that ran along steep cliffs, where the dirty (or wet work) was carried out by Rygor's two men and the chauffeur. The German spy was shot and his body thrown over a cliff. (If the man's body had been recovered, the case would have been investigated by a French police official working with Rygor's group.)[263]

★ ★ ★

TUNISIAN OUTPOST

All of this was unknown to Murphy and the vice-consuls assigned to Algiers—John Knox and John Boyd. But Murphy, who had by now acquired the moniker, "The Man in Black" for his perennial black Homburg hat and somber black suits, had reason to be pleased. He could now see a North African network beginning to take shape.[264]

In Tunis, Murphy had installed at the U.S. Consulate General two bankers who had lived in Paris for many years: thirty-nine-year-old Harry Woodruff, a dark, poised, emotionally sensitive boyhood friend of Ridgway Knight's and French-speaking banking executive, along with thirty-six-year-old magna cum laude Harvard grad John Ellrington Utter. (Utter, like Woodruff, spoke impeccable French; he was also fluent in Italian, Spanish, and German.) Unfortunately, Utter had no sooner arrived in the city than he became ill with an interminable series of boils—sheer torture in that humid climate. Pendar thought him "the bravest man in Africa," as Utter carried on from day to day with hardly a word about his affliction.[265]

Tunis, the capital of Tunisia, was a strategic target with its principal port city of Bizerte, facing Italy's Straits of Sicily across the Mediterranean Sea. Through Bizerte's port the Germans supplied Rommel's desert fight against the Allies.

Tunis and its environs had great potential for the organization of guerrilla warfare against Italian occupation authorities and garrisons of hated Italian troops. Dave King, stationed in Casablanca, saw this immediately when he visited Utter and Woodruff to convey diplomatic pouches between the two cities.

King would urge Murphy to set up a clandestine French underground network among disaffected French officers—a fifth column inside the police, railroads, stevedores, and post, telegraph, and customs offices.

Later, on another visit to Tunis, King met a British merchant marine officer who was convalescing after being wounded in a submarine attack on his ship. The man told King to get to know U.S. vice-consul L. Pittman Springs, a visa officer who had joined the U.S. Consular Service in 1920 as a clerk, and like King, had served in World War I. He had been assigned to Tunis in 1935 after working in France and Great Britain.

"Springs," as he was known to his colleagues, had made solid connections over the years with the French and multinational communities in Tunisia. Murphy recruited Springs to serve with Utter and Woodruff.[266] While in Tunis, King put his experiences at Casablanca to good use. He, Woodruff, and Utter, with Springs's help, identified men and women sympathetic to the Allies and French officers who hated the Italian officials and garrison troops that strutted about Tunis.

The nucleus of secret resistance cells was formed in Tunis and the port of Bizerte. Agents were instructed to feed information through the three vice-consuls about German and Italian activities, shipping movements, airport activity, landing and service facilities, and other vital intelligence. Some of the French officers were prepared to carry out sabotage in case of a German invasion. And all this had to be done without the knowledge of U.S. consul general Hooker A. Doolittle—another career Foreign Service officer who, at the time, opposed spying from a diplomatic post.

The Italian security services (OVRA and SIM) filed volumes of reports about the U.S. consuls' work in Tunis. In one report, Italian agents called the political, military reporting, and propaganda work of the Americans: "childish, given to fantasy, and inefficient." The Italians noted that U.S. agents followed closely the movements of members of the Italian-German Armistice Commission but were "clumsy." But neither the Italians nor the Germans seemed to have discovered that King and Springs had put into place a secret radio transmitter, codenamed "Columbus." The station would be one of a chain of American-run clandestine radio transmitters and receivers that would eventually link Tunis with an OSS-run mother station, codenamed "Midway," in Tangier. Midway station would have a full-time operator to send and receive messages to and from London and Gibraltar. Columbus also linked Tunis with Malta, and this link was used to transmit coded operational intelligence. A second station, Pilgrim, would link Tunis with Gibraltar and Midway.

Within a few months other secret transmitters, with operators, would link the vice-consuls at Casablanca (station "Lincoln"), Algiers (station "Yankee"), and Oran (station "Franklin") with Midway in Tangier.[267]

ALGIERS: EL DJEZAIR

Miles away and far from the Atlantic breezes that swept Casablanca, life in Algiers that summer and fall of 1941 was decidedly unpleasant and akin to living in a Turkish bath. With the massive influx of French refugees, Algiers had become a city of 275,000 souls, of which 30 percent were poor Arabs jammed into too little space and air.

Algiers was an extraordinary mosaic of Continental and Arab life: a metropolis owned by well-heeled colons and transient Europeans. The colons rarely mixed with the people of the streets—the impoverished Arabs in tattered, filthy, European-style clothes, wearing the red fez, or Berbers in their hooded wool capes, called *burnouses,* trailed by their Moslem women in long, flowing gowns—their smoldering eyes peeping out of their veils. The city somehow managed to find a not unpleasant equilibrium despite the competition for its scarce resources. But that summer a new breed came through its quays: hordes of refugees straight off the steamships that plied between Toulon, Marseilles, and Algiers ports—French families and men and women fleeing the harsh continental winter, the still harsher privations of an occupied France branded with defeat, reduced to eating turnips, deprived of fuel, food, and wine. They were lean; their oversized clothing hung on nearly skeletal bodies. Their women were decked out with gold jewelry—a security against inflation, for paper money had lost its value. And every one of these men, women, and children dreamed of obtaining a visa to travel or immigrate to the United States. The U.S. consul general's offices were besieged daily with lines of people, most of whom would be turned away.

A climate of fear now pervaded Algeria. In June, the successful German invasion of the Greek island of Crete had hit the city hard. It seemed that the Allies couldn't do anything right. Crete was too far away to be a strategic threat to Algeria, or for that matter, to neighboring Tunisia in the east. But English, Australian, New Zealand, and Greek forces, and the British navy had suffered a stunning defeat at the hands of the Wehrmacht. Following on, one constantly heard rumors of other menaces: that Gen. Franco would let the Wehrmacht descend through Spain to invade Morocco; or Franco would, as Knight recalled, "openly join forces with his Axis friends and declare war on Great Britain." Spain as an Allied belligerent would seriously menace Atlantic and Mediterranean shipping and the British outpost at Gibraltar.[268]

In the space of a few months, the character of Algiers had changed. The city was now packed with refugees from France; and whereas the year before, when Daphne Joan Fry Tuyl and Renée Gosset had found a cornucopia of good things in the city's markets, now the price of staples, fruits, vegetables, meat, and fish had skyrocketed—the countryside was systematically being looted. By the end of 1941 Algeria and Morocco would be stripped bare by the Germans and Italians and the people left to starve.[269]

However, the civil servants coming from France and the German and Italian Armistice Commission agents—with their plump wives, their good salaries, and petrol to run automobiles—still found Algiers to be an exciting attraction: an exotic place, a city of many faces, many facades. It could sometimes be a bit "spooky" with the labyrinth of alleys, noisy as hell, where Arabs flogged bony horses and donkeys pulling carts and wagons up and down steep streets between shiny white buildings that rose tier after tier above the azure-blue sea.

The Germans delighted in dinner parties and dared penetrate the inner casbah, where the atmosphere was of a clinging, suffocating heat. It was very much like Julian Duvivier's 1937 film, *Pépé Le Moko*, shot in Algiers with Jean Gabin as Pépé—a romantic hero navigating the dangerously claustrophobic streets, where friendship and trust were everything, yet betrayal and duplicity lurked around every dark corner. This portrayal was not far from the real Algiers, where the actors and protagonists were Italian OVRA and Gestapo killers who never hesitated to eliminate Allied undercover agents.

Murphy, Boyd, and Knox were forbidden to enter the casbah and the twisting city slums of Bab-El-Oued.

So what was life like in Algiers that summer and fall of 1941 for Bob Murphy and his two acolytes, John Boyd and John Knox?

Murphy lived well: he shared U.S. consul general Felix Cole's home in the heights above Algiers, which had a splendid view overlooking the city and the sea. They employed two Polish servants, a holdover from Cole's diplomatic service at Warsaw. Marianna the cook and Lutzina the maid "were treasures," and looked after the two men while producing "extraordinary" formal dinners and organizing for their two charges informal evenings on the villa's terraced gardens. (Gofio, the Murphy family's Maltese terrier, brought from Vichy, shared the quarters with Cole's terrier, "Miss.") The villa, covered with purple and pink bougainvillea, was set back on the chic rue Michelet heights, not far from Murphy's favorite golf club, the Algiers' Bois de Boulogne and Weygand's summer palace. Indeed, Murphy had a comfortable life.[270]

John Boyd and John Knox lived at the deluxe Aletti: "Algiers' largest, newest and finest"—a watering hole located on the chic boulevard Carnot, with its municipal gambling palace, beautiful ladies that inhabited its salons, and German and Italian clientele. The "*Boches* were forever toasting their successes" in the hotel dining rooms and the Aletti bar; visibly celebrating victory, so much so that the Italians who played there as well avoided their noisy allies. Still, in the chic salons with the ever-present "ladies of the night," one constantly heard whispers of an imminent German invasion somewhere in North Africa.

Murphy, Boyd, and Knox kept offices in the former British Consulate building opposite the French Admiralty. The building stood on a finger of land that projected into the sea on the first of the tiny islands that encircled the port of Algiers.[271] From there Murphy ran his not-so-little fiefdom of twelve vice-consuls. He communicated by constant visits around the country and via hand-carried pouch mail—the only secure way of contacting his men and overseeing the quality and suitability of their intelligence-gathering production. Murphy supervised their reporting, giving guidance and following up when it looked like they had missed a target. But it was all very loose and much was left to the initiative of the individual officer. The major problem was communication between Algiers, Oran, Casablanca, Marrakech, and Tunis—the principal stations; and the U.S. official missions at Rabat and Tangier. Murphy and his men knew that Vichy agents and German and Italian operatives watched their movements. They suspected their telephone conversations were monitored by Vichy. (But Murphy could not have known that the Germans were reading his official mail to Washington.) He and his men did use the crude spoken and awkward code in telephone conversation, but it was given to misunderstandings; so Bob Murphy had to be on the move all the time and everywhere.

Knox and Boyd had no difficulty adapting to life in Algiers. They were veterans of foreign living and took quickly to the complex multicultural Mediterranean city, where one's ear was constantly besieged by sounds of French, Polish, Italian, German, English, Arabic, Berber, Greek, and Hebrew. In some ways for Knox, Algiers was like coming home; his French *savoir faire* and rough living as a French Foreign Legion officer in the Moroccan Riff made Knox the perfect aide to Murphy and a man adaptable anywhere.

Algiers was a welcome change for John Boyd, the forty-five-year-old widower from Mississippi and former Marseilles soft-drink salesman. He threw himself into undercover work, forming a close bond with John Knox. For almost two years, regardless of authorship, all of their political and military intelligence reports were signed: "Boyd and Knox."

A HOMESICK IRISHMAN

Despite the long absence from home, Bob Murphy managed to exude a seemingly endless cheerfulness. But it may have been too much grit and grind on his nerves. In the summer of 1941 Bob Murphy came down with a dose of old-fashioned homesickness and stress, probably because the constant work and travel gripped him that summer. Life in Algiers was finally catching up with Bob Murphy. Indeed, by late summer Murphy was homesick with a capital "H." He confided to Felix Cole that he needed to go home—his three queens were growing up: wearing high heels and lipstick, but without a loving father. And Murphy fretted over the burden his oldest daughter,

Catherine, was bearing back in Washington, D.C., caring for a sick mother and her two younger sisters.[272]

In August, Murphy cabled the State Department, reminding his masters in Washington of their promise when he left in April to keep him in Algiers for only "two months."[273] The State Department cabled back on August 21 that "in view of the developing situation," he must remain on post in North Africa.[274] Murphy would be condemned to remain in Algiers for the next twelve months until President Roosevelt summoned him home for an urgent White House meeting.

Ken Pendar, who was close to Bob Murphy that summer, never saw Murphy's distress. To the contrary, he observed that his boss never seemed to run out of energy; and despite flying about the country, between Algiers, Casablanca, and Tunis in very shaky aircraft, Bob was always eager to visit his outposts. "He was a superb crisis manager with an enormous flair for handling people . . . ever relaxed, efficient, friendly . . . with a gaiety that brought out gaiety in others, a tremendous gift for friendship, affectations that were almost too easy-going and warm." Pendar thought Murphy "wanted to . . . believe the best in everybody . . . [As] a devout Roman Catholic . . . something of his deep faith seemed to be reflected in the loyalty and liking he showed toward acquaintances, colleagues, and even the men with whom he negotiated."[275]

Ridgway Knight saw Murphy in a harsher light, though Ridgway's first impression of his new chief that summer of 1941 was positive; he saw a "tall, lanky [man] with longish and already thinning flaxen hair and pale blue eyes over a large nose, speaking ever in a cheery drawl." For many months, Knight recalls being captivated by Murphy's "superficial charm." This would soon change, however.

It seemed to Knight that Murphy "had a knack of always seeming to be in agreement with you while he said very little himself." Knight knew this was a tactic of negotiators, but it was "hardly the friendliest attitude to take with others who are day-to-day partners." As time progressed, Ridgway says he had trouble "ascertaining where Bob stood on an issue until at last, it became clear that his genial attitude masked a cold and self-centered personality. Bob Murphy played his cards close to his chest."[276]

And what did Robert Murphy think of his vice-consuls?

There is no record of his evaluation of Ridgway Knight in State Department files. But of Ken Pendar, Murphy wrote in 1942 that Pendar was, "energetic, dependable with a high sense of duty"—but "indiscreet." Equally cryptic, Murphy's colleague in Casablanca, Consul General H. Earle Russell, off the record, thought Pendar, "definitely a problem child."[277]

In contrast, Murphy had nothing but the highest praise for John Knox, whose contacts among French military officers provided "valuable intelligence" to the War and State Departments. And Murphy thought John Boyd "a hard worker" who spoke slowly with a pronounced southern drawl, but who had trouble writing and expressing himself clearly.

★ ★ ★

IF PUBLIC LIFE and private living were problematic for U.S. officials in Algiers in 1941, the political world was a savage jungle.

Murphy strove to manage the intricate politics of North Africa. With a velvet hand, he manipulated both his colleagues and the Vichy French officials. And he kept North Africa on the Washington menu, frequently intervening through Admiral William Leahy, the U.S. ambassador to Vichy, to urge Washington to advance the shipment of badly needed supplies for Weygand. It was a Herculean task to oversee the vice-consuls' work and to maintain contact with Vichy officials in Algiers, Morocco, and Tunisia: the Pétainists, the Darlanists, the Weygandists; the refugees, the collaborationists, the clandestine Gaullists; the hangers-on, and political, industrial opportunists ever in need of a favor from Roosevelt's man in North Africa. And not the least of his preoccupations was keeping in contact with Adm. Jean-François Darlan. Darlan's friend and agent, Adm. Raymond Fenard in Algiers, kept Murphy apprised while a battle was raging in Vichy between Marshal Pétain and his Nazi masters as to the fate of Gen. Weygand.

★ ★ ★

LOSERS AND WINNERS: WEYGAND AND DARLAN

Returning from Vichy in the summer of 1941, Maxime Weygand came home to his summer palace in the heights above Algiers, with get-tough orders to impose tight control over the colonial empire of North and West Africa. Weygand's powers were now diminished as Darlan consolidated his hold over the Pétain government. The admiral was now not only the marshal's successor, but also the French Vichy vice president, foreign and interior minister, and head of the armed services.

Weygand ordered new government controls for all North Africa—inflicting food and fuel rationing on the peoples. The German conqueror needed to be fed from the North African abundance, and Vichy was set on trying to reach a comfortable working arrangement within Hitler's Europe.

Immediately, the French extremes of colonial nationalism were compounded. The Vichy bureaucracy, ever dedicated to suppressing the legitimate hopes of the Arab and Berber peoples, and the French colons, dedicated to controlling the land, water, and commerce, turned the screw. Private enterprise was strictly controlled, and all forms of democratic protest or opposition were repressed. Civil servants, teachers, and military and naval personnel, who were already sworn to obey the eighty-four-year-old Pétain, were brought to heel. Contact with foreign persons and certainly with American officials was forbidden.[278] With Weygand's program of strict rationing and the effect of war, there was a growing food and clothing crisis and shortages of everything, a breakdown of communications, and a lack of morale. Ken Pendar thought Algiers had lost "the romantic quality it apparently had before World War I." He found the prevailing atmosphere, "one of degradation, lack of ambition and sheer dirt."[279]

★ ★ ★

MURPHY, FORTY-SEVEN at the time and certainly one of the most attractive and powerful men in Algiers, was a sought-after dinner companion. Despite his homesickness, Murphy relished good company. It's easy to imagine a lonely Bob Murphy, ever gregarious, born under the sign of Scorpio, enjoying intimate couscous suppers at Bouseres, one of his favorite restaurants, or Chez Cassar for oysters and fish. He dined often with Ken Pendar and the very pretty Boule Rodier and Christiane Lesieur, the sister-in-law of Jacques Lemaigre Dubreuil. Murphy enjoyed most of all spending time with good friends from his days in Paris and Vichy: le Comte de Rose, La Princess Marie de Ligne, and La Comtesse de Polignac—all titled members of Parisian prewar café society.[280] He was a frequent visitor to Jacques and Simone Lemaigre Dubreuil's villa, Dar Mahieddine, just outside the city, where he had nearly been arrested at Captain André Beaufre's New Year's party the night he had first met Daphne Joan Fry Tuyl.

It is easy to imagine, in those penultimate days before Pearl Harbor, how various groups—many of them sub-rosa, and some inherited by Murphy from Lt. Col. Robert Solborg—sought to influence Murphy. Solborg, who had been in Tangier briefly in 1940 as a U.S. military intelligence operative assessing potential underground agents (and later in Spain as a COI-OSS officer), introduced his contacts to Murphy. As he began to get acquainted with them, Murphy learned that some—despite Weygand's disapproval—were bent on insurrection against the Vichy state of affairs. Among those who sought Murphy's patronage was the so-called Group of Five, headed by Jacques Lemaigre Dubreuil. Murphy metaphorically described him as being the business of selling peanut oil... "sure of himself, speaking loudly...and displaying an innate taste for being observed, he moved about [between Algeria and Vichy France] freely disguising his conspiracy, like Ali Baba, in so many barrels of oil."[281] Lemaigre Dubreuil was the major figure and Murphy's interlocutor with the Group—a mélange of anti-Nazi patriots who were mostly elitists, royalists, and right-wing industrialists. Now installed in Algeria, the group contemplated a coup d'état, after which they would establish a provisional form of government (led by them). The men, some of whom were senior Vichy French officials, secretly lobbied Murphy for military and economic aid from the United States, contemplating a temporary separation of French North Africa from Metropolitan France.

As the wealthy manager of the Lesieur family oil business, Lemaigre Dubreuil played a "very controversial" part in North African politics. He was an intimate of Weygand, under whom he had served in the French military, and of the pro-German Pierre Laval. (In 1943, Lemaigre Dubreuil would try to broker a peace agreement between Laval and Roosevelt).[282]

But in the role of a determined patriot, Lemaigre Dubreuil would become extraordinarily useful to the politically conventional Bob Murphy— and Murphy shared Lemaigre Dubreuil's and his colleagues' traditionalist political leanings.[283]

The Group of Five soon assured Murphy that they were eager "to undertake action to resume hostilities against Germany and Italy." Indeed, an elite conspiracy was already launched: a race to find and offer the Americans the indispensable man—a figure (unlike Gen. Weygand, so wedded to the principles of his creation, the Franco-German armistice) that "would ride in on a white horse and rally French and African troops and lead them into battle against the German Hun."

Murphy kept his Washington masters informed of the group's activities; he assured the State Department that he considered the group an ideal instrument for implementing U.S. (Allied) policies in North Africa.

In the months to come, Lemaigre Dubreuil and Lt. Henri d'Astier de la Vigerie (who would move to Algiers) became the principal protagonists in the Murphy political entanglement. Both Frenchmen stood out as skilled manipulators and leaders.

If Lemaigre Dubreuil was a schemer, then Henri d'Astier "was a character from the Italian Renaissance." Henri was a brilliant, charming, reverent Catholic, nephew of a cardinal, with black feline eyes and the delicate bronzed features of a Spanish aristocrat who radiated charm and "militant royalist activist even before the war. [He] could and did use his hypnotic influence on the young men who surrounded him, not the least his own son Jean-Bernard, a young officer in the *Chantiers de la Jeunesse Française*—a Pétain youth movement, more paramilitary than Explorer or Sea Scouts and run by an ex-French Foreign Legionnaire named Colonel Van Hecke who was nicknamed 'Robin Hood.' "[284]

★ ★ ★

NOT ALL WOULD SERVE

Summer faded; the days grew shorter, and Murphy had his first of many nasty personnel problems to sort out. All was not well. In truth, Murphy's Twelve Apostles were in a state of flux; and Murphy soon determined that three of the men assigned to him in North Africa were unsuited for the work that lay ahead.

The first to go was a vice-consul with the unlikely name of C. Denbeigh Wilkes, whom Murphy sent home almost immediately (August 1941) because "he was inclined to listen to the remarks of his friends in high society" and repeat gossip.[285] Wilkes had sinned by challenging one of Murphy's reports to Washington (always carefully researched) as being "improbable"— certainly a mortal sin. Dave King thought Wilkes, "a snooty, impossible, useless individual." Finally, Murphy fired Wilkes and sent him home to Washington.[286]

Later, Franklin Canfield in Casablanca would be sent home, as we shall see, for "indiscretions and undue exuberance" that continued to have serious repercussions.[287]

Sidney Lanier Bartlett, who worked for Shell Oil in Paris and was a volunteer ambulance driver in France in 1940, turned out to be another "problem" vice-consul. In the spring, Bartlett had left New York via a French oil tanker with the unlikely but prophetical name of *Scheherazade*—for the fictional wife of an Oriental king in an *Arabian Nights* fable. The freighter, with Bartlett aboard, got caught up in a British blockade of North Africa, and he didn't arrive in Algiers until the end of June.

Bartlett fell desperately in love with a sultry French lady in Casablanca—later proven to be the Vichy-German spy named "Nikki." (Dave King accused him of "spilling" State Department cables to her.) In July 1942, Bartlett would be sent home by Murphy.[288]

Donald Coster, a Princeton graduate and native New Yorker and another late arrival to the group, would play an important role in Casablanca but would fail to get along with Murphy. In August of 1942, he resigned from his post in Casablanca to return to Washington and join Donovan's OSS.[289]

★ ★ ★

WORKING UNDERGROUND

Not far from Murphy's offices at the modest Hotel Arago, on the rue Arago, Slowikowski's Polish intelligence services (an arm of British MI6) had set up an ultrasecret radio transmitter, operated by a Polish officer under the name of Mr. Miller (Major Maximillian Ciezki). Miller's transmitter/receiver was hidden in his hotel room conveniently located on the same floor as Rygor Slowikowski's apartment. The transmitter linked Algiers with a Polish (also ultrasecret) radio intelligence outpost (cryptonym "Whirlwind") located at Uzes near Nimes in the unoccupied zone of southern France. As the Uzes station received Rygor's ciphered messages, they were retransmitted to Polish intelligence headquarters in London and then hand-carried to the British MI6 offices nearby.[290]

Through this channel Rygor communicated almost daily with London, sending short coded and urgent messages. After midnight, he would sneak along the hotel corridor and slip messages to be sent under Miller's door. When the two men met, it was never at the hotel but at a series of secret locations— and they were careful never to be seen together. From the Hotel Arago suite, Rygor's wife, Sophie, and son, George (then fourteen), helped prepare the pouches of documents that were forwarded by couriers via friendly Polish merchant seamen. The bulky reports, containing confirmation of radio signals, maps, and plans, were received by the head of Polish intelligence in Marseilles, who would then send the materials on to London by courier. (Pouches would eventually be secretly delivered to Murphy, Knox, and Boyd at the U.S. Consulate, as we shall see.)[291] All this took place, for the moment, without the knowledge of Murphy—and under the tightest security.

Slowikowski imposed a rigorous code on his intelligence officers and in turn, the officers on their agents; it was a matter of survival and could mean death if caught in the act of espionage by Vichy, German, or Italian agents. Security ruled that nothing was ever committed to paper and no real names were ever used. Couriers unknown to each other picked up mail from "mail boxes" set up around North Africa (frequently at doctors' or dentists' offices, where the courier could call on a physician without arousing suspicion), and using a different code word for each delivery or pickup. The networks were run by Rygor's eight Polish intelligence officers—men who may have worked together elsewhere but who didn't know their colleagues' assignments in North Africa, and certainly didn't fraternize with each other there. The eight officers ran nine principal outposts. Those who ran the outposts knew their intelligence officers, though they usually did not know the other outpost agents. Indeed, Rygor's chief salesman in Rygor's oatmeal manufacturing and distribution business, known as *Floc-av* (an acronym for flakes of oats in French), was also an agent of one of Rygor's intelligence officers—and until after the Torch landings, the man never knew that Rygor was running the show. Only the officers knew of the existence of Rygor, with the exception of André Achiary, who worked directly for him on certain projects in Algiers and later at Sétif, an important military base in the east of Algeria near the border with Tunisia. Achiary headed up a Vichy intelligence outpost there; but unbeknownst to Rygor, Achiary, Murphy's Scotty, had earlier set up a clandestine transmitter to work directly for British MI6.

Slowikowski's targets and intelligence collection priorities paralleled those of Murphy's men—strategic, tactical information from military and naval sources and financial, economic, and political intelligence from diplomats, bureaucrats, and politicians. The only difference was that Rygor's Agency Africa operated quasi-invisibly underground. As such, Rygor had access to targets, information, and subagents that Murphy and his vice-consuls—operating under diplomatic cover and being watched constantly by Vichy counterintelligence and the Gestapo agents—couldn't possibly have obtained.

In fact, as we shall see, Agency Africa became a kind of unwitting subagency for U.S. intelligence and at no cost to America, except for the minor fees for transferring clandestine pouches from consulates to consulates and then to Washington and London.[292]

★ ★ ★

DARLAN'S CHANGE OF HEART—WEYGAND IS OUT

Personalities and overdeveloped egos would haunt Murphy's work in the months to come. And no greater ego existed than that ascribed to freethinking, left-leaning, sixty-one-year-old Jean-Louis-Xavier-François Darlan, Marshal Pétain's right-hand man at Vichy.[293] On taking control of the Vichy government from the deposed Pierre Laval, Darlan had warned Adm. William Leahy, FDR's ambassador to Vichy, that he would be forced to make concessions to the Nazis if the Germans were to be kept out of Africa and the port of Bizerte were to be kept under French control.

But by October 1941, Darlan's attitude toward the outcome of the war had undergone a profound change, and the tough little admiral, who was more of a politician than a seaman, reached out to Murphy in Algiers, aiming to improve his image with the White House.

In the first of many secret meetings, Darlan's friend and emissary in Algiers, Adm. Raymond Fenard, met with Murphy and made it plain that Darlan wanted to gain "American favor." In the background was the deteriorating Franco-German relations following the German invasion of the Soviet Union. (And an ugly crisis had broken out in France—the assassination of German officers in Paris and elsewhere in the country by French Resistance fighters had led to German reprisals: the taking of hostages and the threat of mass executions.)[294]

Now in the fall of 1941, a U-turn in North African politics was being plotted in Berlin and Vichy. Adolf Hitler wanted Maxime Weygand out of Algiers—in fact, out of power in the Vichy bureaucracy. (Darlan was also on Hitler's short list of annoyances to be eliminated.)

The Germans had long wanted Weygand out of North Africa. His relations with Murphy irked them, and U.S. aid to North Africa was making a mark with the native Africans. Berlin had read Murphy's communications with Washington. They knew that Weygand had given Murphy a precise estimate of what the general believed was the size of the Allied force needed to successfully carry out an invasion of North Africa.[295]

On November 13, 1941, Jacques Lemaigre Dubreuil, just back from Vichy, and forever the *éminence grise,* told his former chief, Weygand, at a long lunch that he knew from German friends that Weygand was to be recalled and would not be allowed to return to North Africa. The Nazis wanted him out. Lemaigre Dubreuil tried to convince Weygand to remain in Algiers and to lead a North African resistance movement against the Nazis. But the old general wouldn't hear of it. He proclaimed his oath and honor as a French officer—which forbade him from opposing Marshal Pétain.

A few days later, Hitler's agent-ambassador in Paris, Otto Abetz, finally got his way: On November 17, Pétain ordered Weygand to Vichy. The next day, the old general resigned and was retired.

But the morning he flew from Algiers to Vichy, Weygand secretly gave Murphy a copy of a personal "testament" he expected to read to Marshal Pétain. It read: "The U.S economic accord for aid to North Africa made France . . . the only European power retaining its economic relations with the United States . . . a power which, in any event, will be one of the arbiters of the situation at the end of the war."[296]

Murphy had lost a man whom he had trusted and considered a friend. It was to be the beginning of a new era in North Africa. Weygand's supreme office was suppressed, and Darlan's friend, Adm. Raymond Fenard, was made secretary general of North Africa. Yves Chatel, a close friend and golf partner of Murphy's, was promoted to governor general of Algeria, and General Alphonse Juin inherited Weygand's military functions.

In Washington, there were calls to sever relations with Vichy. The State Department and others urged that Adm. Leahy at Vichy and Murphy at Algiers be recalled, and that all aid to Vichy France and North Africa end.

Murphy was deeply affected by Weygand's departure. He cabled Washington that he hoped the general's removal would "calm Nazi apprehensions regarding French Africa and give us a breathing spell." Then he asked the powers at home not to abandon the supply to North Africa and "wait to gather all essential facts."[297]

Two hours before his cablegram reached the State Department, Murphy heard the announcement that the American government had suspended its French North African program. He wrote about the incident twenty-five years later: "I did not get much sleep, turning over in my mind new arguments for resuming the Accord." He had received a secret handwritten message from Weygand via a trusted officer that read, "Continue, I beg of you, to favor the supply program. As the Marshal told Adm. Leahy, nothing is changed in French policy by my departure. My messenger will tell you how much I count on the maintenance between our two countries of the union necessary for the near future of the world."[298]

Murphy continued to explain to his Washington masters that by giving up the accord, the United States was losing its unparalleled "diplomatic courier service, use of cipher messages, and the presence of our own trained observers in this strategic area." As it turned out, Adm. Leahy, probably on the strength of Murphy's recommendation, changed his mind and cabled his sentiments to Washington.

In his memoirs, Bob Murphy reflects on his relationship with Maxime Weygand.

> I had become intimate not only with Weygand . . . but with his principal associates in Algiers. I had come to understand that, much as I admired the General personally, the African hierarchy was not just one man upon whom we should pin our hopes. I had grown to trust some of Weygand's associates as I did him and, with Leahy's support [in Vichy], I was eventually able to persuade Washington that we could deal with many Frenchmen remaining in Africa on the same basis as we had dealt with the General himself.[299]

Indeed, all those arguments were persuasive. But the real reason that Washington would decide to keep Murphy and Leahy in place was a Japanese armada secretly gathering to destroy American forces at Pearl Harbor.

The man who would momentarily profit from Weygand's demise was Adm. Jean-François Darlan—now in control of the Vichy government and the French navy, its officers, and seamen.[300] He had long sought Weygand's recall, for Gen. Weygand was the principal obstacle to Darlan's plans for North Africa. Darlan wanted and appointed only men he trusted, like his close friend, Adm. Fenard, who, with other allies, he named to key posts in North Africa. Fenard would keep in close contact with Murphy.

Back in March 1941, Murphy had talked at length with the admiral after his elevation to the post of foreign minister and vice president of the Council of Ministers. (Following the March meeting at Vichy, Darlan arranged sub-rosa to communicate with Murphy through Fenard and later, through Darlan's son, Alain, who visited Algiers not infrequently.)

Darlan's tack was to continue to attempt to soften the Nazi hold on France by allowing concessions to the Germans and Italians and by negotiating deals. It would be a losing battle. In contrast, Charles de Gaulle, the man Vichy considered a "traitor in London," believed that to resist was to preserve France's honor and would guarantee the country a say in the inevitable end game, while restoring France and its colonial empire to glory. Darlan's opinion about how the war would end, about Hitler and Germany, about France's awkward and tragic situation, and about the Allies was well known in Washington, thanks to reporting from Murphy and Ambassador Leahy and their staff in Vichy.

Darlan, according to Ambassador Leahy in Vichy, was viewed as early as January 1941 "as a well-informed, aggressive, and courageous naval officer, incurably anti-British." Leahy said Darlan "believes that the Nazi regime cannot long survive after the passing of Hitler, and that the French people will then attain a position of great influence or control in a new Europe that will emerge from this war." And Darlan thought that "the Nazi invasion of the British islands . . . even under the existing condition of British inefficiency" would fail. Still, Leahy reported that Darlan "is confident that the Germans will win the war and establish a new order in Europe."

Leahy, who enjoyed the complete confidence of President Roosevelt, went on: "All that was left for the Germans to do, [Darlan] concluded, was to attack Russia, and the moment Germany starts that, it means her downfall."[301]

Indeed, the German invasion of Russia and the stalemates on the Russian front by the time Weygand was recalled enforced Darlan's belief that Germany would eventually be defeated. It was time for Adm. Darlan, ever the clever naval and political tactician, to prepare for the future.[302]

It would soon be December 7, 1941, and the world would never be the same again.

PART TWO:
THE TORCH IS LIT

Heroism feels and never reasons and therefore is always right.

—Emerson, *Heroism*[303]

7

PEARL HARBOR:
THE OSS ENTERS THE "SNAKE PIT" [304]

ALGIERS, DECEMBER 7, 1941

It was early Sunday evening when Robert Murphy arrived at the villa of his good friend, Comte Tricornot de Rose, for cocktails, polite conversation, and dinner. The radio played in the background, but not everyone heard the news flash. Not everyone understood.

John Knox heard it when he entered the casino of the Hotel Aletti with Daphne Joan Fry Tuyl on his arm. Fellow colleague John Boyd was there, too, as were German and Italian officers separated only by the width of a roulette table. There was a startled pause and then everyone went back to playing "*27 en plein*" or the "last dozen."

Ridgway Knight and Leland Rounds heard it in Oran when Bruno rushed to their room and told the vice-consuls to turn on their radio wireless. David King and Stafford Reid got the news at the bar of the Hotel Transatlantique in Casablanca.

Later, Ken Pendar would be told, "Now you will understand what war is, and can't go on with your rich Yankee attitude of 'business as usual.'"

At the table with Comte de Rose, Robert Murphy, the only American present, told the dinner guests he "could hardly believe the Japanese could be so reckless; but it would solve the principal problem which weighed on President Roosevelt . . . the United States would enter the war! America no longer need pretend to be neutral."

Slowly, hour by hour, friend and foe learned what the Japanese had done at Pearl Harbor. Still, in those first days after December 7, 1941, unless you were in the Pacific under Japanese attack, few grasped what war would mean. And few imagined that the first battles to free Europe from Nazi domination would bloody North African soil.

In Washington six days after Pearl Harbor, William Donovan, FDR's intelligence czar, told the president that "the United States must seize North Africa to make a German invasion impossible; and they [the Germans] may occupy Spain and Portugal with the consent of those countries and [thus] the passage to Africa of large [Axis] forces . . . will make impossible the sending of anything more than a token army by the United States."[305]

Allied leaders immediately seized upon the significance of events. In London Gen. de Gaulle, soon to be scorned and despised by the White House, thought the Axis fate was sealed with the Japanese attack on Pearl Harbor. In an uncanny, almost supernatural prediction, he told a member of his staff: "Now the war is won; and in the future, the Americans will save the Germans and there will be a war between the Americans and the Russians."[306]

After exclaiming "so we have won after all . . ."[307] Winston Churchill boarded the newly launched British battleship *Duke of York* for a strategic conference with Roosevelt (codenamed "Arcadia"). It was 112 days since their first historic meeting at Placentia Bay, Newfoundland, aboard the battleship *Prince of Wales*. And it says something about Britain's disastrous position after a year at war with Germany—for now the gallant *Prince of Wales* lay at the bottom of the sea off the coast of Malaya, sunk by Japanese dive-bombers.

In preparation for the Arcadia meeting, Churchill noted:

> . . . now is the moment to use every inducement and form of pressure . . . upon the Government of Vichy and the French authorities in North Africa. The German set-back in Russia, the British successes in Libya, the moral and military collapse of Italy; above all, the Declarations of War exchanged between Germany and the United States, must strongly affect the mind of France and the French Empire. Now is the time to offer to Vichy either a blessing or a cursing. A blessing . . . a promise by the United States and Great Britain to reestablish France as a Great Power with her territories undiminished. It should carry with it an offer of active aid

by British and United States Expeditionary Forces, both from the Atlantic seaboard of Morocco and at convenient landing points in Algeria and Tunisia as well as from General Auchinleck's forces advancing from the East. [Sir Claude Auchinleck was command-ing British forces in the Middle East.] Ample supplies for the French and the loyal Moors [Moroccan tribesmen] should be made available. Vichy should be asked to send their fleet from Toulon to Oran and Bizerte and to bring France into the war again as a principal.[308]

Thus, Churchill and Roosevelt's Christmas White House conference laid out the priorities for the Allied war strategy. North Africa was high on the agenda.

When Churchill left Washington unwell but pleased, he had obtained most of what he wanted, not the least of which was "a fair wind" to advance plans for an Anglo-American invasion of North Africa, first codenamed "Gymnast," then "Super Gymnast," and finally, "Torch." It was to be an au-dacious, amphibious invasion that would be planned and executed by an un-known Gen. Dwight David (Ike) Eisenhower—General George Marshall's man for the job.

At home, Franklin Delano Roosevelt was near to "making the most pro-found American strategic decision of the European war in direct contraven-tion of his generals and admirals."[309]

PERILOUS TIMES: WOULD HITLER INVADE MOROCCO?
As Churchill made his way secretly to the United States, fears abounded in London, Washington, and in Algiers and Morocco that Germany would fi-nally convince Gen. Franco to allow German troops to enter Spain and at-tack Morocco. In Algiers, Murphy and his vice-consuls heard rumors that Adm. Darlan, on a mission to Berlin, had done a secret deal to help Hitler: At the right time he would order the French fleet out of Moroccan waters, aiding the German seizure of Casablanca airports prior to an invasion.

December 1941 was a high watermark for the Wehrmacht advance in Russia. Axis units were standing before the gates of Moscow. With the terri-ble loss of the American fleet in the Pacific, many were now convinced that Hitler would feel free to undertake a new adventure—seize Casablanca, put-ting into peril the West African French port of Dakar.[310]

★ ★ ★

With the coming of war Murphy and the vice-consuls were fair game for Italian OVRA and German security services. Axis agents' reports insistently mentioned the prospects of invasion at a moment when Murphy knew nothing about plans that were going forward in London under Gen. Eisenhower. An extract from a 1941 Italian report shows how closely the OVRA followed Murphy and his men:

> Americans have been advised by their consul to prepare to leave the territory of the Moroccan Protectorate . . . The French General Secretary of the Protectorate, Mr. Monick . . . has relations with American agents and may be preparing an American intervention in Morocco. American agents in Tangier met with General Nogues to discuss an American invasion. American agents are insisting [to the French] that arrivals of members of the German Armistice Commission should be watched and curtailed . . . The former chargé d'affaires to Vichy and now consul, Robert Murphy's, wide, mostly grinning face is set above a fighter's chin. He smiled at any time when he made three trips to Morocco . . . General Nogues is known to be pro-America . . . other American vice-consuls have arrived at Rabat, in French Morocco. Nothing justifies their arrival and they are believed to be Military experts in the guise of consuls; eighteen [sic] new officers are supposed to arrive soon. At the Hotel de France in Tunis, Mr. Jean Borg, an industrialist, gave a banquet in honor of the U.S. Consul, Mr. Springs. At the end of the banquet there were demands for a strong collaboration between France and the United States and a call for the victory of democracy.[311]

THE KING-BÉTHOUART-CANFIELD IMBROGLIO

Just after Pearl Harbor, and with Weygand out of the way, Dave King was secretly approached by an agent of General Marie-Emil-Antoine Béthouart (codenamed "The Black Beast"). Béthouart, a classmate of de Gaulle's, was no Gaullist but had no great love for Vichy, either.[312] He had fought against the Germans in Norway, and was in England in June 1940 when he decided it was his duty to return to France, where Pétain assigned him to Morocco. King was approached by the general's agent and advised that Béthouart wanted to meet in secret with Murphy as soon as a meeting could be arranged.

Potentially, this was a major breakthrough. King knew that behind Béthouart stood a group of pro-American French officers. Secrecy was of capital importance. Murphy was, after all, trying to subvert and recruit a senior French officer sympathetic to the American goals. King informed Murphy by a secret coded telegram to Algiers. (No radio contact was possible at the time.) Murphy replied in code, FOR KING PERSONALLY, and ordered King to set up a time and place for a meeting. Fatefully, Murphy's reply arrived in Casablanca on a day when King was in Tangier.

Vice-consul Franklin Canfield was on duty at the Casablanca Consulate when the message arrived. He decoded it and decided to call at the general's offices himself to arrange the Murphy-Béthouart meeting. Canfield drove to Béthouart's divisional headquarters in a car bearing U.S. Consulate "diplomatic" plates, asked to see the general, and was told the man was absent. Canfield then invited a French officer of very dubious allegiance to lunch with him. (In seeking the limelight, Canfield broke all the rules of clandestine work.)

All this activity was observed by officers loyal to Gen. Béthouart, who reported to him urgently. The general must have feared that this terrible indiscretion by a U.S. vice-consul had also been observed and reported to German agents—and, at the very least, to Marshal Pétain's Vichy intelligence headquarters.

Béthouart panicked. He called for a military plane to stand by on the Casablanca airstrip, ready to fly him to Gibraltar if the worst arrived.

It was a disaster. Béthouart's cooperation might have influenced plans for the Torch invasion; but now, any hope of Murphy establishing a secret working relationship with Gen. Béthouart was thwarted. As it was, Béthouart refused all contact with the "indiscriminate American vice-consuls." Murphy and King were furious. Later, Dave King's efforts to meet with the general failed, until three days before the invasion.[313]

NASTY PERSONNEL PROBLEMS

On the face of it, Murphy seemed to handle the complex business of managing the vice-consuls, the tangled Vichy bureaucracy, the generals, and all the rest.

His letter to his daughter, Catherine, of January 21, 1942 [misdated 1941 and corrected] tells much about his state of mind after Pearl Harbor, and his affection for his daughters. Catherine, the oldest, now twenty and studying at Wellesley College, was called "Katinka." (Rosemary, fifteen, was "Rosemaruschka," and Mildred, the youngest, thirteen, was "Prushy.")

You may . . . deduce that for practically the first time during the past year I have caught up with myself. Largely, I suppose through faulty management on my part I have usually been just about one step behind the parade, sometimes two, puffing along trying to catch up.

After a good many squawks I succeeded with the sympathetic help of the State Department people in obtaining badly needed stenographic assistance. This has helped enormously, even to the point of being able this evening to sit down to write a letter to my neglected Katinka. Needless to say I would much prefer to sit down to dinner with you and talk about everything; letter writing is never satisfactory. Also fathers like to impress their daughters and that can be done so much more satisfactorily across the dinner table.

I did regret Christmas and New Year's away [from you all]. In November things looked very promising and I had received a wire telling me that I was to return for a short stay, which I imagined would include Christmas, when other things began to happen which I shall explain someday, and the word was, stay on. It bothers me a lot to be so out of touch with you . . .

It is unfortunately necessary to develop a war philosophy—always knowing that so many others are the victims of far greater hardships and privations, to say nothing of tragedy and misery.

You have asked me for information about my work and probably feel that I have just neglected telling you about it. Unfortunately, that is partially true but then again there was not much that I could tell you for reasons that must be pretty obvious to you . . .

You will be surprised to learn that I have with me here in Algeria both Gofio—who has been clipped and looks much better for it, in fact looks almost like a blooded dog with a long pedigree—and the good old Buick . . . [It was the same car Murphy had driven in Paris—and it would play a role in the Torch operations.] I wonder what your reaction to our entry into the war was? Imagine—I haven't yet seen any American newspapers published after our entry . . .

After the Canfield mess, Murphy turned to a nasty and delicate personnel problem that had been lurking in the background for weeks. Thirty-six-year-old Sidney Bartlett had arrived late in Casablanca, traveling by tanker, which had been delayed when the ship was seized by British naval forces. He had arrived for work in late June, and was judged by Consul General H. Earle Russell, in Casablanca in October 1941, to be "possessed with suavity and courtesy that is exaggerated almost to the point of eccentricity." The divorced Bartlett, Russell added, "has recently become engaged to a charming young French lady, whose father, a captain in the French Army, has just returned from Germany as a prisoner of war." Still, Russell thought him a good worker with experience in petroleum imports. Seven months later, Robert Murphy wrote that Bartlett "was conscientious, dependable and industrious; there is a marked improvement in his discretion and judgment." But in July three months later, Russell was to write, "His work has been falling off sadly." He refers the reader of this report to a "cipher cable and dispatches from Robert Murphy"—all strictly secret. It is typical mysterious Foreign Service double-talk for "Trouble" with a capital "T."

In a polite letter dated Algiers, June 29, 1942, Murphy thanked Bartlett for his work but advised him that he was to be returned to Washington with the limp excuse that the State Department was making personnel changes. It would be a month later that a nameless Washington personnel officer would reveal to Bartlett that he had been recalled upon the recommendation of Mr. Murphy. The reason: reports concerning alleged Axis associations on the part of his fiancée, Mme. Escarment. A State Department memo adds that Murphy did not tell Bartlett of the real reason for his abrupt dismissal because Murphy "feared that such action might lead to some embarrassment of the Government activities in French Morocco [sic]."[314]

Additional light is shed by Kenneth Pendar:

"One of us," he writes, "fell madly in love with a singularly flamboyant young French woman who passed herself off as an innocent young girl. He proposed to marry her on the spot, over the articulate protests of every American in sight. It was revealed, at the last moment, that the lady not only had some connections with members of the German Armistice Commission, but was already married to a Frenchman at Dakar, who arrived in the nick of time to save her from bigamy."[315]

It sounded very much like the German Gestapo had made a run at Bartlett, and he had almost swallowed the bait.

STAFF'S OUTHOUSE: REID GETS A NEW TOY

"One morning in December 1941," Staff Reid writes in his memoirs, "King and I were called to the office of Mr. Russell, American consul general in Casablanca, and were presented to a person attired in civilian clothes who had just arrived from the states via Tangier. It was Colonel Eddy. He explained that he had been appointed Naval Attaché at Tangier to coordinate the work initiated by the vice-consuls, and to prepare for an invasion that might take place in the year 1942 or perhaps 1943. He asked King and me to pouch our reports to him in Tangier, which would then be the central coordinating base. From this point he, Colonel Eddy, would collect intelligence information which covered the entire front of North Africa from Agadir to Tunis."

Eddy was of course a very tough marine, though he masked an inner torment with a "happy face." He had no easy job laid out before him, and was rarely an easygoing taskmaster.

Donovan thought Eddy was in the mold of Lawrence of Arabia: a man of action who relished Arab life and who drank heavily, probably to ease the pain caused by his wooden leg; who had pronounced dislikes, trusts, and distrusts. But Eddy's Torch crew admired and worked well under him. They would include at various times King, Reid, and later L. Pittman Springs; Carleton Coon and Gordon Browne in Tangier and Morocco, who along with King, would handle the special operations' hit-and-run jobs too dirty and too risky for the vice-consuls under diplomatic cover; and John Knox and John Boyd (who would deal with the Polish Slowikowski network) in Algiers. Under Eddy's leadership, all would eventually carry out the clandestine operations to support Murphy's political gambits.[316]

Eddy set up shop in the international zone at Tangier at the U.S. Legation offices housed in a magnificent Arab palace in the town's walled medina area.[317] (Tangier and its environs had been seized by Spain in 1940. The city was since run by Spanish military.)

From Tangier, Eddy went to work recruiting agents, running operations, and establishing wireless links to the vice-consuls at Algiers, Casablanca,

Oran, and Tunis, incorporating what already existed into a network that would eventually link key posts with Tangier and Gibraltar. Only later would Eddy learn that his operation had been penetrated by a beautiful Spanish agent serving the Germans in the guise of "the loveliest and most amorous charwoman in World War II." Daily, the lady would rifle through filing cabinets and wastepaper baskets—until she was detected by a special OSS counterespionage unit.[318]

Using Murphy's vice-consuls, Eddy financed and augmented the resistance cells already in existence in North Africa; and he set about completing the communications network. Both he and Murphy recommended that Washington furnish arms and demolition materials to the guerrilla groups, including the Lemaigre Dubreuil Group of Five organizations in Algiers and Oran. He specifically asked that d'Astier de la Vigerie's group (*Chantiers de la Jeunesse*) be supplied with enough infantry small arms to equip 15,000 Jeunesse in Algeria. (None of his requests would ever be fulfilled, despite orders to British SI and SO in London to do so.)[319]

Donovan's man had a sleeve full of projects to destabilize the Vichy French. When he informed Murphy of one of his pet "capers," Murphy realized he was dealing with a "one of a kind unique man (and we could have used a hundred like him)." But the "straight-laced" Murphy was "shocked" when Eddy enthusiastically outlined how he was going to "purchase" a pro-Allied native ruler—and floored by "the amount of money" involved. "Nothing would have enraged our French colleagues more than this kind of monkey business, or been more ruinous to our chances of obtaining support of French military forces. As for fifty thousand dollars! Our whole operation in Africa had not cost that much over a period of many months."[320]

Still, Murphy insisted to everyone that "no American (present) knew more about Arabs or about power politics in Africa," than Eddy.[321]

Staff Reid tells how "We worked closely with Eddy and Major Bentley—a newly arrived air attaché at the American Legation at Tangier. Bentley made frequent trips disguised in civilian attire (as a consular diplomat) and was able to enter French Moroccan territory. Bentley had King and I and Teddy Culbert, whose technical knowledge acquired at Annapolis was invaluable, locate potential airfields in French Morocco. We would pace the fields off, orient and minutely sketch the potential terrain; our maps were pouched to Bentley at Tangier, where, in his small pigeonhole office at the Legation, Bentley summarized the material . . . and sent it on to Air Force Command in Washington."

By the early months of 1942, Bill Eddy needed reliable and instant communications with Gibraltar, Malta, London, and the other North African posts. He summoned Staff Reid to Tangier in the late winter. Once there, Reid was given a small, cigar-shaped box in which a compact wireless transmitter was set. Eddy explained that it was a British transmitter called a *Paracette* that he had gotten from Gibraltar.

"I was to take it down to Casablanca concealed in the pouch, and try to look around for a suitable place to set up a station for initial contact with Tangier—and find a reliable operator. Unfortunately I can't give you any American [operator] to help . . . as we have no means of infiltrating one under suitable cover; nor are there any available from London."

Thus began Staff Reid's venture into setting up a sophisticated wireless network that would become essential for the Torch operation.

Reid had made contact with an agent nicknamed "Ajax." He was trusted because he had done some work on behalf of vice-consuls John Knox, John Boyd in Algiers, and Dave King in Casablanca. Ajax had been a wireless operator with the French Merchant Marine and had qualified to take and transmit high-speed messages.

"I cautioned Ajax about the nature of the work and that considerable risk [was involved]," says Reid.[322]

Later, Reid and Ajax dressed in factory work coats with black visor caps, disguised as metallurgical workers. They bicycled in the drizzling rain to a French wine bottling plant. They were able to enter the disused section of a wine mill and in the rear, found two old wine vats where they could hide their transmission equipment. They also discovered a deserted loft connected to the ground floor vats by a stepladder. They threaded a fine wire to serve as an antenna, along the outside roof and down the rough stone sidewalls to the interior of the loft. The place had all the advantages for a temporary wireless tryout station, with the added bonus of giving out onto an important military airfield. Through cracks in the mortar Reid and Ajax had a clear view of the landing strip some fifty yards away. Next door to the wine shed were large German Heinkles (WWII bomber aircraft) and French military aviation repair sheds.

On this visit the two men observed German planes landing, and watched while the crew left the aircraft. The next day, Ajax, in overalls and wooden shoes, was able to get enrolled on the payroll of the wine factory with the help of friends. And on alternative evenings, his insider friends put him to work as a night watchman—allowing him to come and go without attracting undue attention on the part of French authorities.

For the next month and a half, Reid and Ajax were only able to exchange contact signals. A magnetic field, generated from constant night testing by the Germans of aviation motors nearby, was interfering with their transmissions.

Ajax kept busy by giving Reid useful reports as to the movements of German personnel, sketching French defense works around the airfield, and mapping the emplacements of ack-ack (antiaircraft) batteries and the hidden emplacements of French fighter planes. Still, communications were unsatisfactory. Reid wrote about what happened next:

> A bold move was essential. I approached the American Consul General, Earle Russell. [I told him], ". . . in the cellar of the Consulate there is an old water closet . . . I would like to remove the toilet and install a small space to accommodate a table, chair, and a rug . . . set up a wireless communication transmission center between Casablanca and Tangier there. No one needs to know about it . . . we will brick up the enclosure for our equipment, remove the toilet at night . . . and hide the antenna wire.

Consul General Russell was worried that somehow Vichy or Gestapo agents would learn about the transmitter; but he finally agreed with the caveat, ". . . if we [are] caught, it [will] mean our expulsion from North Africa . . . and serious repercussions on a high level involving diplomatic inquiries between Washington and Vichy for abuse of Consular privileges."

A few nights later, Reid, Ajax, and a trusted plumber prepared the code room.

Reid's account continues:

> Ajax fastened the antenna wire across the sides with heavy hooks used to hang tires in a garage . . . we bartered for the hooks with tobacco. At 2:00 a.m. one morning Ajax and I hammered these hooks through hard concrete into the roof, and stretched the lead wire from side to side . . . we beamed the wire for wavelength and direction to the Tangier station [using] signals with Colonel Eddy's operator at Tangier. At 5 o'clock in the morning of 21 March 1942 our message was accepted . . . Later we were able to contact London.

To cover the operation, Reid bought on the open market a Swiss radio out of Special Funds. In broad daylight, he rang the front gate of the consulate and delivered the heavy radio to the porter, asking him to place the radio on the desk of the consulate receptionist. He then told the receptionist he was going to install the radio in the cellar to receive daily war news from BBC.

When Russell learned of Reid's ruse, he congratulated him. "We have so many wagging ears and tongues in this establishment, [so] let each person think they are in on a new secret . . . Staff, you are going to have [to issue] a 'daily bulletin news service' to justify your frequent trips to the cellar."

Reid then had Ajax fired from his job at the wine press establishment. Ajax then went on the "payroll" of the consulate as "interpreter" of the BBC broadcasts.

But Reid's troubles had just begun: "During that time I coded and decoded approximately 350 messages. With the help of [Gordon] Browne [a new OSS agent] and [Donald] Coster, I didn't leave the code room before 3:30 in the morning. Then Browne was ordered to Tangier to work with Eddy (head of OSS there) and Coster returned to the United States."[323]

Staff ran into more trouble when the French banned the sale of batteries. All the garages were then ordered to note all batteries brought in for charging, giving the name of the owner of the automobile, the battery number, and date of the last recharge.

The Vichy French police and Gestapo were tightening up, Staff remembers: "We had to go off the air several times for two or three nights consecutively when the French army came out with a small fleet of 'Gonio cars' (radio detectors) [that patrolled] Casablanca. This happened when our traffic increased and we were drawing heavily on the current . . . We fumbled around for a few weeks, carting charged batteries from Tangier, 270 miles from Casablanca, and leaving the old ones. Finally, the British lent use of a foot-pedal charger; and later we installed a special dynamo charger which operated from an automobile engine."[324]

Stafford Reid, the erstwhile Yale preppie, WWI infantry officer, and New York real estate mogul, was fast becoming Eddy's clandestine communications expert.

ALGIERS, WINTER–SUMMER 1942: MURPHY'S DILEMMA

After Pearl Harbor, Henri d'Astier de la Vigerie and Abbé Cordier left Oran for Algiers, where Murphy would work closely with Jacques Lemaigre Dubreuil and his partners in the Group of Five—let us call them conspirators—who had now agreed to work together to recruit others to their cause. They would build resistance cells and maintain contact with the Allies (Murphy and eventually, the British SOE). Lemaigre Dubreuil pressed Murphy for a supply of arms for their growing insurgent groups.

Murphy was impressed with d'Astier—and even more impressed when Lemaigre Dubreuil threatened to work with British Special Operations Executive (SOE) if America would not advance his cause. Robert Murphy duly alerted Washington to this new event. Soon the whole business would become Murphy's "dilemma."[325]

In Oran, Father Théry became the key man in Knight's and Rounds's growing network of conspirators: "Through Father Théry's unswerving convictions, deep faith and eloquence, we were able to convince several other officers that their real duty lay elsewhere than in respecting an oath given to a chief of state . . . a prisoner of the Germans. Their oaths . . . given under duress . . . were worthless. Their real duty was to carry on the struggle against *les Boches*, and to do so without qualms or twinges of their conscience."[326]

Knight, Rounds, and Father Théry produced a tentative plan for paralyzing Oran's defenses: When the first (Torch) landings were confirmed, Théry's clandestine groups (made up of anti-Vichy former soldiers and Jeunesse) would swing into action. A certain Col. Tostain, close to Father Théry, agreed to seize his commanding general in Oran, General Boissau, with the help of fellow conspirators. He would then issue orders to all units under the general's name to welcome the Americans as friends and liberators. The plan then called for the capture of the key Oran naval headquarters with a native Zouave battalion under another conspirator, a Major Vial.

Simultaneously, it was planned that civilian groups would rise up, arm themselves from the divisional armory, which Col. Tostain agreed to open, and use antiquated Lebel rifles and other equipment of WWI vintage to assist the Allied invaders by holding key locations in and around Oran. (Knight and Rounds had received assurances through Murphy that Eddy had arranged to supply the civilian and Jeunesse groups with modern light weapons, delivered by boat from Gibraltar. As we shall see, and despite orders from Allied high command, the arms never arrived. An attempt to land arms at Oran beaches was foiled by French navy patrols, operating too close to the proposed landing site.)[327]

America's entry into the war provoked Vichy counterespionage agents and German security units to give more attention to tracking suspected anglophiles and Gaullists believed to be involved with Murphy, his vice-consuls, and secret British agents operating from Gibraltar and Tangier. Likewise, America's entry into the war inspired countless anti-Vichy and anti-German groups in Algiers, Oran, and Morocco to seek American aid.

Through the winter and summer, in both informal and official correspondence with the White House and State Department, Murphy repeatedly pleaded, separately from Eddy in Tangier, for aid to those "who offer resistance to Axis aggression."

Despite all he knew about his political aims, Murphy was determined to advance the cause of Lemaigre Dubreuil and his Group of Five—insisting that "nobody else could provide the kind of support he gave to our African project; nobody else combined his important contacts with his inspired daring."[328]

Indeed, Murphy had little choice. The search was on for a substitute for the dismissed Gen. Weygand—a man who would be acceptable to London and Washington. And during the spring Murphy forwarded a number of concrete proposals from the Lemaigre Dubreuil group and others to Washington, asking for comment. Instead of guidance, all Murphy received was assurance that the Murphy-Weygand Agreement had been revived: ships—now loaded with supplies and waiting in New York ports—were said to be about to sail.[329]

MURPHY MEETS RYGOR

Over the winter and spring, John Knox and John Boyd had been taking pouches from Rygor Slowikowski and sending them to Tangier via diplomatic courier; and Knox had helped Rygor collect funds transferred from London. A typical pouch might have contained, for example, documents elaborating on the spy network wireless reports. The list below contains some of the more interesting items (numbers refer to Slowikowski logs):

> Coastal defenses of Cap Falcone—two 75mm guns (193); Effectiveness of maneuvers of Moroccan Army (197); SS *Djebel Amour* leaves port Philippeville via Bone, sails to Marseilles with cargo 20 tons of rubber (198); Tanker SS *Norrait* Algiers-Tunis with 500

tons alcohol (216); Shipment of cobalt from Nemours to France on 19th (217); German U-boats supplied with 600 tons diesel oil in ports of Algiers, Arzew and Philippeville (218); Arab reserve NCOs have received call-up papers to be ready for mobilization (219); Salines airfield outside Bone, 3 new Italian Hunter aircraft in service (221); the battleship *Jean Bart* is ready for action, has received ammunition for all guns, while in port surrounded by protective steel nets (228); railway connection between Tenes-Orleansville in Algiers being dismantled, rails will be transported to Kennasa (230); German Colonel Boehm, member of the Armistice Commission from Wiesbaden, not satisfied with his inspection of coastal defenses of Morocco, possible use of Wehrmacht . . . (232).

Now Murphy believed he could meet Rygor Slowikowski. It was mid-April when Slowikowski slipped into the Consulate General's offices in Algiers. King was waiting and took Rygor immediately to an office where Rygor found to his surprise U.S. consul general Felix Cole and Robert Murphy waiting.

Rygor recalls his impressions of the meeting: "Mr. Cole was an elderly gentleman who was almost prepossessingly polite. He expressed his appreciation of my work in North Africa and told me that if I ever found myself in difficulties I should turn immediately to him."

Rygor found Robert Murphy "friendly and sympathetic . . . with a simple and unaffected manner—the best type of American. After greeting me warmly, Murphy said that he already knew something of my work.[330] He admired my achievements and expressed his pleasure at my cooperation with his vice-consuls and hoped that we would continue to work closely together. I protested that he was praising me too much; I had an Intelligence network behind me to which I owed my success and would always be pleased to pass on information and news. After all, we were Allies."

But Rygor couldn't stifle a cynical comment: "Mr. Murphy, you must be well aware, I [am] giving [your] vice-consuls the fruits of our Intelligence labours [sic] and in an unsealed pouch . . . They could draw on an unlimited supply of information as required by Washington. I had no objection to that, provided that they were informed that their source was Intelligence Service Agency Africa of the Polish Army in North Africa."

Murphy replied with "an enigmatic smile and said, 'Naturally it is understood that this is part of our gentlemen's agreement!' We parted on excellent terms."[331]

EGYPT THREATENED

In the last week of June 1942 calamity struck; newspapers around the world announced in banner headlines: TOBRUK FALLS, AXIS CLAIMS 25,000 PRISONERS; GERMANS DRIVE WEDGE INTO SEVASTOPOL LINES; JAPANESE ASHORE AT KISKA IN THE ALEUTIANS.[332]

The news was devastating, for the loss of the Libyan port was a disaster and a blow to morale. Murphy must have been aghast to learn how desperate things had become, reading NAZIS NEAR EGYPT, BRITISH ARE ON BORDER AS ROMMEL PRESSES ON AFTER VICTORY.[333]

Winston Churchill heard the news just as he'd arrived in Washington for a second round of talks with FDR. And it put a damper on the so-called "second-front speculation" that surrounded their meetings. Covered in utter secrecy, the public knew only (and Murphy knew even less) that the president and prime minister with the chiefs of staff of the United States and Britain, Gen. Marshall and Field Marshal Alan Brooke "continued their exchange of information and their planning for the future."[334] In fact, when the meetings ended, the Allies had approved an invasion of North Africa. Now the final planning could go forward in London.

But a disheartened Bob Murphy knew nothing of this. He could only encourage Lemaigre Dubreuil and company to sit tight and wait for action from Washington about their requests for arms and word about America's plans for an invasion.[335] The search for a leader who would galvanize French military leaders in Algeria, Morocco, and Tunisia to support an American invasion haunted Murphy. He had traveled around North Africa discreetly trying to find such a man. The generals and admirals with whom he talked all backed, to a man, the Vichy leader, Marshal Pétain.

Then Lemaigre Dubreuil and French general Charles E. Mast (who was already cooperating with Eddy, supplying valuable intelligence about French force dispositions) "in desperation" hit upon General Henri Giraud[336] to be the future "noble puppet" to lead French forces in the liberation of North Africa.

It wasn't long before the White House agreed to clandestine communications with Giraud in mainland France and through Murphy—with Gen. Mast (who was now Giraud's representative in Algiers). Though it would take weeks of on-and-off negotiations with Giraud and Mast—and with Eisenhower in London—the pieces were coming together. The scene was set for a momentous secret meeting between Eisenhower's representatives from London, Gen. Mark W. Clark, Gen. Mast, and Murphy on French soil.

To add to Murphy's dilemma: At the same moment as the Giraud-Mast combination began to gel, Adm. Fenard—Adm. Jean-François Darlan's representative in Algiers—made "new and encouraging" overtures to Murphy about the "North African campaign." In fact, Murphy believed in October that Darlan was ready "to climb aboard [the American] bandwagon."[337] When Eisenhower in London was informed of Darlan's advances, he sought approval in London and Washington to marry Darlan and Giraud as a team that would share the top French command between them. And time was running out.

At the time, Churchill responded, "If I could meet Darlan, much as I hate him, I would cheerfully crawl on my hands and knees for a mile if, by doing so, I could get him to bring that fleet of his into the circle of Allied forces."[338] Thus, Murphy had good reason to believe that a deal with Darlan was acceptable in Washington and in London. And he was too astute a politician not to see, despite the assurances of Lemaigre Dubreuil and Gen. Mast, that Darlan was by far more acceptable to French bureaucrats and officers than Giraud could ever become.[339]

The great stage of Anglo-American-French politics in World War II was now set for a sea of trouble—one of the great imbroglios of the war, and an uproar that would bring lightening, thunder, and brimstone down upon the heads of Eisenhower and Murphy.

But first, Robert Murphy would have to return home.

8

WHY, BOB!
WHAT ARE YOU DOING HERE?

A SICK AND OVERWORKED Bob Murphy was called to the consulate early Sunday, August 9, 1942, to hear he had been summoned home. Roosevelt and Churchill had secretly ordered the Torch landings.[340]

The summons didn't surprise Murphy. Bill Eddy had just then returned to Algiers after meeting with Gen. Dwight D. Eisenhower at his Torch command headquarters in London. Eddy had been brought home by Gen. William Donovan to brief America's and Britain's top soldiers and sailors about the state of affairs in North Africa.[341]

High on Eddy's agenda was the fate of a one-legged hero of World War I, Murphy's candidate to lead a coup d'état in North Africa: Gen. Henri Honoré Giraud.[342] Eddy also reported to Ike's staff on the readiness of French Resistance groups to fight, and his fear that French armed forces would resist the American landings.

When marine corps colonel Bill Eddy briefed Murphy upon his return to Algiers, Eddy must have stressed to Murphy, who was "appallingly ignorant of military matters," how the game had changed. From now on operations in North Africa were going to come under the thumb of soldiers—men who Murphy knew nothing about.[343]

Murphy had plenty to worry about as he prepared to leave for Washington, via Casablanca and Lisbon. How would Lemaigre Dubreuil's Group of Five and their paramilitary resistance fighters, now led by Captain d'Astier de la Vigerie, fit in with Gen. Giraud and Adm. Darlan? Murphy had just learned that French inspector André Achiary, his close friend and agent, had been banished from Algiers. Sent to Sétif near the Tunisian border, Achiary barely escaped dismissal due to suspected anti-Vichy activities. Before leaving Algiers, Achiary had warned Daphne Joan Fry Tuyl that the Vichy counterintelligence agents who were after him also suspected that she was a Gaullist agent as well. Soon, an alarmed John Knox asked Murphy to intervene to save Daphne—the woman he loved. (Knox warned that his beautiful, blonde, British spy was about to be arrested and deported to Vichy. Murphy hurriedly met with Adm. Fenard, Darlan's agent in Algiers, and asked him to quash the matter. Daphne was told to lay low.)

Arriving in Casablanca to catch an Air France flight to Lisbon, Murphy fell ill. But he did talk with Rygor Slowikowski. The man brought grim news: the Vichy counterintelligence operatives had struck again, and penetrated the King-Eddy underground in Morocco. Three hundred of their agents were arrested in a week.

It looked to Murphy that things were closing in.

Indeed, Murphy was stretched. Gen. Charles E. Mast now knew an invasion was more than a rumor. He was pressing Murphy and Eddy for information they didn't have: force size, dates, and details of the Torch operation. Mast insisted on knowing what had become of OSS Col. Robert Solborg's mission in June. He knew that Solborg, allegedly acting as Gen. Donovan's spokesman, had secretly come from Lisbon to meet with Murphy, Lemaigre Dubreuil's Group of Five, and Rygor Slowikowski in Algiers and in Casablanca. Solborg, who spoke fluent French and Russian, had reviewed the group's "grandiose plans." He then returned to Washington with a detailed memorandum: an agreement covering the Group of Five's plans for a coup d'état backed by the U.S., and the eventual roles that generals Mast and Giraud would play. Meanwhile, Jacques Lemaigre Dubreuil had gone to France to hand Giraud a copy of the agreement.

And then, silence . . . nothing unusual, until Murphy learned from Eddy that Solborg had been dropped from the OSS.[344]

Murphy couldn't tell Mast about Solborg's dismissal. He was in a quandary. He had every reason to believe that Solborg's meetings in Casablanca and Algiers were sanctioned by the State Department. Earlier, Murphy had cabled Sumner Welles, the number-two man in the U.S. State Department:

> May I respectfully urge that you give me a directive . . . Do you
> wish me to continue these conversations [with the Group of Five]
> or do you want them dropped? Do you wish the conversations
> conducted by someone else? (Colonel Solborg, for instance.) The
> time has arrived for you to give me a directive.

But Murphy would soon learn why he had lived so long on scraps of information from his masters. His predicament lay in a purposeful disconnect
between the White House and the State Department. President Roosevelt
was determined to hide his intentions and plans from Cordell Hull, his secretary of state. American diplomats were kept totally in the dark about the
existence of Torch. As incredible as it may seem in light of today's policies,
no one in the U.S. government outside the military knew about the upcom-
ing landings.[345]

Indeed, Robert Murphy had no idea what awaited him when he boarded
an Air France plane in Casablanca at the end of August.

HYDE PARK

It was a scorching hot September day when Murphy finally entered FDR's
Hyde Park home to find the president and his aide, Harry Hopkins, seated
in the library—both in shirtsleeves.[346]

It was a very hush-hush operation masterminded by Adm. William
Leahy, Roosevelt's chief of staff. Murphy had been whisked unnoticed from
his home in Chevy Chase, Maryland, early on September 4, put on a small
Air Force plane, and unaccompanied, delivered to "Springwood," FDR's
summer White House.[347] Bob's dilemma was over. The saloonkeeper's son
from Milwaukee was about to become part of Roosevelt's great deception: the
best-kept secret of the war to date.

On that abominably sticky-hot Friday morning, Bob Murphy learned
what Roosevelt and the Joint Chiefs of Staff had revealed to only a handful
of trusted advisers: the approximate D-Day for the invasion of North Africa.
As FDR briefly described how he and Churchill had designed Torch, Murphy learned that even as they spoke, Gen. Dwight D. Eisenhower and his
staff in London were drafting a final invasion plan.[348] Roosevelt and Hopkins warned Murphy: "You are . . . not to tell anyone in the State Department about this. That place is a sieve." When Murphy suggested that those

instructions might put him in an awkward position, the president replied, "Don't worry about Cordell [Hull, U.S. secretary of state]. I'll take care of him; I'll tell him our plans a day or so before the landings."[349]

It was straight from the mouth of the commander in chief.

Then it was back to the capital and an all-too-short weekend at Chevy Chase with his family. Earlier, Murphy had prowled about Washington, hoping to avoid notice by newsmen who were bound to wonder why Roosevelt's man in North Africa was in town.

In back-door meetings at the State and War departments, Gen. George C. Marshall told Murphy he opposed a North African venture. Adm. Leahy (still FDR's ambassador at Vichy, in absentia) warned they could not trust French general Alphonse Juin, the commander of all French forces in North Africa, or Gen. Auguste Paul Nogues, resident general in Morocco. Leahy believed they would resist the landings; but he thought that Admiral Jean-Pierre Esteva, France's resident general in Tunisia, General Jean-Joseph-Guillaume Barrau, in Dakar, and Vice Admiral François Michelier, commander in chief at Casablanca, might be friendly to an American effort. Murphy agreed, and told Leahy that Gen. Mast in Algiers had assured him that if Giraud could be brought into a coup plot, then French forces might not resist an American invasion.

When the talk turned to the subject of Adm. Darlan, who still held immense power as the Vichy chief of all armed forces, despite the return of Pierre Laval to the Pétain government, Leahy reminded Murphy that Darlan had said in a private conversation, "if the Allies arrived in North Africa with sufficient forces to be successful against the Nazis, [Darlan] would not oppose us." Then Leahy made it clear that Gen. de Gaulle and his Free French forces would be excluded from all knowledge of the Torch planning and landings.[350]

Murphy was assured that the War Department now had a complete picture of political, economic, social, military, and naval matters in North Africa. Thanks to the work of Murphy's vice-consuls and Bill Eddy, the war planners in Washington and London knew the dispositions of the French land, sea, and air forces stationed in every corner of Algeria, Morocco, and Tunisia. They had an estimate of what resistance might be expected from the French, German, and Italian forces; and they knew something about the capability of pro-American resistance forces if it came to a shooting war.

LT. COL. MACGOWAN GOES TO LONDON

It was time for Murphy to make a secret visit to London to meet with Gen. Eisenhower and his staff. Marshall suggested Murphy should cross the Atlantic bearing the credentials and wearing the uniform of a U.S. Army officer with the fictitious name, "Lieutenant Colonel MacGowan." Marshall declared that "nobody pays any attention to a lieutenant colonel." The one glitch was that Ruth Shipley, the notoriously strict chief of the passport division of the U.S. Department of State, could not be persuaded to issue Murphy a passport under a false name.

On a balmy Tuesday evening, four days after seeing the president, Murphy boarded a Flying Fortress bound for an airdrome in Scotland and delivered by the U.S. Ferry Command. He wore an ill-fitting uniform and carried no identification. The trip was a rude shock for Murphy; it was his first experience aboard a bare-bones unarmed Fortress that lacked any amenities, save for limp ham sandwiches and coffee that tasted like boiled shoe leather. Despite wrapping numerous army blankets around his considerable frame, Murphy nearly froze flying in the dizzying heights above the Atlantic.

It was a very shaky Bob Murphy, aka Lt. Col. MacGowan, who staggered out of the Fortress's hold at the airport in Prestwick, Scotland, early on Wednesday morning, September 16. It was then that he heard a voice cry out in the background, "Why, Bob! What are you doing here?"

Murphy had a retinue of officials and military police officers waiting to take him in hand. Suddenly, the lone greeter who shouted his name was surrounded by burly policemen and whisked away. It turns out that the transgressor was none other than U.S. vice-consul Donald Coster. He was immediately put under arrest and kept incommunicado until after the landings. (This, at least, is Murphy's dramatic version of events.)[351]

Eisenhower's chief of staff, General Walter Bedell "Beetle" Smith, and Murphy's former U.S. Foreign Service colleague, Julius Holmes, now on Ike's staff as a full army colonel, escorted Murphy to Ike's secret hideaway at Telegraph Cottage outside London. Presumably the two old friends joked about how Colonel Holmes now outranked Murphy. Hopefully, Murphy got some sleep.

Knowing "MacGowan" had landed, it took Gen. Eisenhower some forty minutes to reach his country hideaway from his offices at Grosvenor Square, London. His Irish chauffeur, the attractive, willowy Kay Summersby, a former fashion model, later remarked that the tension in Ike's olive-drab Buick sedan, and later at the cottage, was palpable. Who was this mysterious visitor? What was so important that it could make the commander of Torch rush home? Summersby admits that she and the army household staff spied on their boss from a cottage kitchen window. They were intrigued by how the oversized "MacGowan," clad in a wrinkled uniform, got down to business with Eisenhower in the latter's English garden.

Ike listened with "horrified intentness" as Murphy described the tangled state of French politics in North Africa, the complicated loyalties of military leaders, and the complications the U.S. faced in trying to recruit a French leader who would back a coup d'état and an American invasion. But Murphy assured him that Gen. Henri Giraud, the sixty-three-year-old hero of World War I, was favorably known to senior French officers in North Africa. (Giraud had lost a leg fighting in WWI, had escaped from a German camp, and had been a senior officer in Morocco for ten years. Before the occupation of France he had again been captured and again escaped, returning home in May 1942.)

Murphy thought he was their man. The general was under Vichy surveillance in unoccupied France, but Jacques Lemaigre Dubreuil had visited him. Lemaigre Dubreuil reported to Murphy that the general had a plan and wanted to lead a combined U.S.-French force in simultaneous invasions of southern France and North Africa. Ike listened in amused silence. He understood that despite the general's grandiose plan, the potential gain from collaborating with Giraud was immeasurable if indeed he could swing French forces in Africa to the U.S. side. Although the French army in Africa lacked modern equipment, it did have 120,000 men under arms (55,000 in Morocco, 50,000 in Algeria, and 15,000 in Tunisia).[352]

Murphy emphasized that his contacts in Algiers, along with the French major general Mast, had assured him the army would obey Giraud if he showed up with an American force behind him. Murphy went to pains to assure Ike that with Mast aboard, the conspirators (Lemaigre Dubreuil and the Group of Five) would work matters out for a successful military and civilian coup d'état—and obtain French military cooperation once the invasion began.[353]

The only red flag that Murphy raised with Ike was that Giraud wanted to be the supreme commander of a two-pronged invasion force.

This startled Eisenhower. In turn, he told Murphy that the question of command would come later, assuring Murphy, however, that the French

From left: General Eisenhower, Admiral Darlan, General Clark, Robert Murphy. *(Photo courtesy of National Archives.)*

Robert Murphy with his three queens in Pontrezina, Switzerland, circa 1936. *(Photo courtesy of Mrs. Mildred Murphy Pond.)*

Robert Murphy and Felix Cole, U.S. Consul General in Algiers, sometime in 1941–1942. *(Photo courtesy of Mrs. Mildred Murphy Pond.)*

John H. Boyd, the slow but sure Mississippian, seen here (front row, fourth from left) posing with his freshman class of 1913 at Millsaps College, Mississippi. Boyd cemented a close friendship with his partner in Algiers, John Knox. The two men tapped into a dynamic Polish/British spy ring. *(Photo courtesy of Millsaps College.)*

French scholar Franklin O. Canfield, alumnus of St. Paul's, Harvard (magna cum laude), and Columbia University Law School, traveled throughout Morocco in 1941 gathering intelligence until he had a run-in with Robert Murphy. He returned to America to join the OSS, where he rose to the rank of colonel. *(Photo courtesy of Harvard University Archives, Call # HUD 332.04.)*

Carleton Stevens Coon, seen here in the *Harvard 25th Anniversary Report*, was a man of many talents and disguises as an OSS officer in North Africa working with Murphy's vice consuls to prepare the Torch landings. His involvement in the Darlan assassination remains a mystery. He later emerged as a pioneer in social anthropology. *(Photo by Bachrach Studios, courtesy of Harvard University Archives, Call # HUD 325.04.)*

Donald Quested Coster, Princeton Class of 1929, served in Tangier as Col. Eddy's assistant. The two men never clicked; Coster left to work for the OSS under the cover of an advertising executive for J. Walter Thompson Company. Coster later held important government posts in WWII. *(Photo courtesy of Princeton University Library.)*

Frederic Paul "Teddy" Culbert, Harvard class of 1914, seen here as an Annapolis midshipman (class of 1915). A hero in WWI, he joined Murphy in Casablanca as an expert on naval affairs. Culbert was highly decorated for his work before and during the Torch landings. *(Photo courtesy of Harvard University Archives, Call # HUD 314.25.)*

William "Bill" Alfred Eddy, Princeton class of 1917, was a U.S. Marine Corps hero twice wounded in France in 1918. Donovan appointed Eddy to be head of the OSS operation, headquartered in Tangier, from where he and Murphy worked on the Torch landings. *(Photo courtesy of Princeton University Library.)*

David Wooster King, a true American hero of WWI and WWII, left Harvard to fight with the French Foreign Legion in battles on the Western front in France from 1914-1917. King was the driving force for espionage, sabotage, and dirty tricks before and during the Torch landings. *(Photo courtesy of Harvard University Archives, Call # HUD 316.04.)*

Ridgway Brewster Knight, seen here being decorated with the U.S. Medal of Merit by General Mark Clark, was from a patrician family of painters. He became a vice consul in Oran, Algeria in 1941, and played an important role in the famous Cherchel conference. He retired from the U.S. Military as a colonel to join the U.S. Foreign Service, where he rose to ambassador. *(Photo courtesy of Mrs. Christine R. Knight.)*

John Crawford Knox joined the French Foreign Legion and was wounded twice in the 1930's Riff battles in Morocco. Seen here, center, in civilian clothes, aboard the command ship HMS *Bulolo* before the Torch landings. Knox was at Murphy's side during the negotiations to appoint Admiral Darlan to head the French government in North Africa. *(Photo courtesy of A. Derek Knox and Alexandra Curley, children of Daphne and John Knox.)*

John Knox, about 1923 in dress uniform, French military academy Saint Cyr—France's West Point —before going to Morocco as a Legionnaire officer. *(Photo courtesy of A. Derek Knox and Alexandra Curley, children of Daphne and John Knox.)*

From left: John C.
Knox, Marshal Juin,
and Daphne Joan Fry
Tuyl around 1944.
*(Photo courtesy of A.
Derek Knox.)*

The beautiful British spy Daphne Joan Fry
Tuyl, whose first husband was murdered
by the German Gestapo in Holland.
Daphne worked with American, British,
and French undercover agents to help
make the Torch operation a success. *(Photo
courtesy of A. Derek Knox and Alexandra
Curley, children of Daphne and John Knox.)*

Kenneth Pendar, alumnus of St. Paul's
and Harvard, worked from a luxurious
villa in Marrakech, Morocco to spy
on Vichy French officials. He and
Canfield served "cocktails" to Moslem
Arabs in north Morocco and earned
the ill will of French officials. Pendar
served with Murphy in the desperate
hours of the Torch invasion. *(Photo
courtesy of Cassell PLC London.)*

W. Stafford "Staff" Reid, Yale 1915, Lieutenant U.S. Army in France 1917–1919. Reid played a key role with Dave King in Casablanca in the preparation of the Torch operation. He served with great distinction in the North African Theatre and later as an OSS agent with the U.S. military mission to Marshall Tito in Yugoslavia. *(Photo courtesy of Stafford Reid's niece, Donna Reid, PhD.)*

Major Stafford Reid being decorated with the U.S. Medal of Merit, the highest U.S. civilian award (equal to the U.S. Army Distinguished Service Cross) by Under-Secretary of State Dean Acheson in 1946. Twelve of Murphy's pre-Torch team were awarded this honor. *(Photo courtesy of Stafford Reid's niece, Donna Reid, PhD.)*

Leland Lasell Rounds (Lieutenant, Lafayette Flying Corps, France 1917–1919) was the rotund "Boche"-hating partner of Ridgway Knight in Oran, Algeria. Rounds shared an apartment with Ridgway in a hotel that also housed Italian and German security and Gestapo agents. He slept with a .45-caliber automatic under his pillow. *(Photo courtesy of The Montclair Kimberley Academy, Montclair, NJ.)*

John Ellrington Utter, Harvard 1925, was assigned to Tunis, Tunisia to spy on Italian forces working for the Joint French-German Armistice Commission. Kenneth Pendar thought him the bravest of all the vice consuls. Utter later joined the U.S. Foreign Service, retiring to become secretary to the Duke of Windsor and later to the Duchess. *(Photo by Bachrach Studios, courtesy of Harvard University Archives, Call # HUD 325.04.)*

Carleton S. Coon (left) and Gordon Browne, Harvard graduates, served as spies in Tangier on Eddy's original OSS team. Both men spoke Arabic and worked among the Arab and Berber peoples in the Moroccan Riff. Browne and Coon were trained in espionage, communications, and explosives. *(Photo courtesy of Mrs. Joan Bourgoin.)*

Jacques Lemaigre Dubreuil: Passionate French patriot, the forty-six-year-old industrialist played a controversial role in North African politics. Lemaigre Dubreuil was castigated in Gaullist propaganda as pro-Nazi. Counter-terrorists gunned him down in Casablanca in 1955. The place of his murder was renamed in his honor. *(Photo courtesy of Collection of Roger Viollet.)*

U.S. troops shoot at snipers after taking Algiers, 1942. *(Photo courtesy of Corbis.)*

General Henri Giraud (left) was on hand to greet fighting French General Charles de Gaulle when he arrived in North Africa on May 30, 1942. *(Photo courtesy of Corbis.)*

Robert D. Murphy in 1942: a diplomat among warriors. *(Press Association photograph.)*

On the streets of Algiers, liberated French men, women, and children cheer American GI's with V for Victory signs—the World War II signal for hope; but there was still a long road ahead to defeat the Nazi Germans. *(Photo courtesy of Hachette.)*

Under-Secretary of State Dean Acheson pins a medal on six of Murphy's vice consuls at a State Department ceremony on March 13, 1946. From left: W. Stafford Reid, Kenneth Pendar, David W. King, Dean Acheson, Leland L. Rounds, Frederic Culbert, Harry A. Woodruff. Ridgway Knight, John Knox, and John Utter received their awards while overseas. *(Photo courtesy of Mrs. Edith Kunhardt, daughter of Harry Woodruff.)*

would get modern arms and equipment. He wanted the French to be in charge of their own army, but only under his supreme command.

Then, an uninitiated Murphy listened as Ike described how he would lead a combined U.S.-British invasion force of nearly a half-million men. How could an unknown French general really think he would be allowed to command an American and British land, sea, and air force? (The stage was set for weeks of misunderstandings on all sides, and a frustrating loss of time that would bring sinister characters on the scene in Algiers.)

It was agreed that because of French sensitivity (and outright hatred by French naval officers of the British), no mention would be made of the British participation in the invasion.

Over the next thirty-six hours, Murphy, who by now must have been close to burnout, did his best to brief Eisenhower and a select group of military officers and civilians: generals Mark Clark, chief of staff, and "Beetle" Smith, Ike's civil affairs officer; and aides Julius Holmes and Captain Harry Butcher. The civilians included W. Averell Harriman, a special envoy of President Roosevelt's, Ambassador John Winant, and Freeman Matthews, a former diplomat and now civil affairs adviser to Eisenhower. British brigadier Eric Edward Mockler-Ferryman, head of Torch intelligence, was the only British officer present.

Murphy repeated his trust in the Group of Five, his hope that Giraud, as the "heroic French leader," would come aboard; and how five-star Adm. Darlan, through his son Alain and Adm. Fenard, had intimated he might be willing to come to Algiers if backed by the United States, possibly bringing the French fleet to North African ports under his command. Murphy emphasized that Darlan would be able to swing both army and naval forces to cooperate with the United States in Algeria, Morocco, and Tunisia. No eyebrows were raised, and the Darlan connection went without comment.[354]

No one seemed to know about the protocols outlining the details of U.S. cooperation with the Group of Five that Col. Solborg had initiated in Algiers and carried to Washington in July. Yet, these crucial stipulations for Franco-American cooperation in North Africa, and the position of Giraud in a coup d'état, were just then being communicated to Giraud by Jacques Lemaigre Dubreuil in France.[355]

At Telegraph Cottage, Murphy conveyed to Eisenhower and his staff a mastery of Vichy French politics and a conviction that Gen. Giraud and the local French administrations would control the native Arab and Berber populations of North Africa after the Allied landings. The last thing an occupying force needed was to have to keep order.

Bob Murphy's cockiness, disarming, warm personality, and eternal smile reassured Eisenhower. And as President Roosevelt's personal representative in North Africa, Murphy's views were decisive. Robert Murphy, the worldly diplomat, had been equally impressed with Eisenhower.[356]

By breakfast on Thursday, Murphy and Eisenhower had ranged over a number of crucial matters. Proclamations to the French were needed; and ways had to be found to impress upon the French, just in case, that the very size and power of the invading force would make resistance hopeless. Over coffee Eisenhower again emphasized how the chain of command was to work: he was the boss, and he "wouldn't have a bunch of freelancers dashing about . . ." Eisenhower stressed that he wanted to present the French with "a clear-cut and single authority" and that all matters in his theater of operations "must rest with me."[357] Finally, Murphy suggested that Eisenhower secretly send one of his high-ranking officers to Algeria, possibly by submarine. Murphy wanted an army officer to meet and confer with his French army contacts and to delve into various tactical problems related to the landings. Ike's first reaction was positive, but he considered the danger: If a high-ranking American were discovered in Algeria, it could tip off the French that an operation was being planned. Nevertheless, the idea appealed to him.[358]

On Thursday afternoon Captain Harry Butcher, Ike's aide, drove "Lt. Col. MacGowan" to a nearby British airfield, where a waiting plane carried him to Prestwick. From there, Murphy boarded a TWA Stratoliner bound for Washington.

What followed was a blessed but brief rest: a weekend at home for Murphy at his Chevy Chase house. He had somehow found time to buy a radio for his "Katinka"—Catherine, the eldest daughter, who was now twenty. Murphy's three queens had grown up in their father's absence; now they wore "nylons," high heels, and lipstick. Gofio, the Maltese terrier that had shared the Murphys' life in Paris and played in Felix Cole's garden in Algiers, was there, too. He had been sent home some months before with Amalie, one of Cole's housekeepers.

In a rare personal aside, Murphy would say that for those few hours at home, "the war seemed unreal" to him.[359]

A few days later Eisenhower cabled Gen. Marshall in Washington:

I have the most confidence in his [Murphy's] discretion and judgment and I know that I will be able to work with him in perfect
harmony . . . I am sure that Murphy will agree with [the revisions
to the directive appointing Murphy as political adviser to Eisenhower and obliging Murphy to communicate through Eisen-
hower] and with the necessity of presenting the French with a
clear-cut and single authority.[360]

After their first meeting at Telegraph Cottage, Harry Butcher penned
what he thought of Murphy: "Tall, stooped-shouldered and talked more
like an American businessman canvassing the ins and outs of a prospective
merger than either a diplomat or a soldier . . . All of us sat on the lawn for
a couple of hours, enjoying the sun and hearing from Murphy detailed information on the situation in Algeria and French Morocco and the plans
for French cooperation. Murphy impressed all of us as an honest reporter
who delivered his story objectively. If all he anticipates in the way of
French cooperation comes to pass, many of our worries will have been
needless."[361]

THE MALEVERGNE SNATCH

While Murphy stole a few minutes with his "queens," David King back in
Casablanca was hard at work again in the business of dirty tricks.

It began late one night with a knock at the door of the villa he shared with
Staff Reid. Reid was away at the wine distillery, busy with his radio work.
King went to the door, a loaded .42 automatic in hand. Outside, a young
woman who King recognized as a member of his underground greeted him.
He ushered her and her three companions inside. It turned out that one of
them was the nephew of Gen. Charles de Gaulle; all four pleaded with King
to smuggle them out so that they could join the Free French in London. German security officers were now policing the comings and goings at Casa port,
so King had to use an elaborate ruse to get the four (and some others who
needed to escape Casablanca) onto a friendly ship sailing under a neutral
South American flag. De Gaulle's nephew finally joined his uncle in London.
(At the same moment in Paris, his sister, de Gaulle's niece, Geneviève, was arrested by the Gestapo and deported to Ravensbruck.)

Dave King's next job was infinitely more complicated.

Eddy had just received a request at Tangier from the OSS in Washington that the U.S. Navy was desperate to find a marine pilot to guide Allied convoys to Moroccan beaches. King knew of such a man: René Malevergne, the chief pilot of Port Lyautey, located on Morocco's Atlantic coast. King was ordered to arrange the exfiltration of the man to Gibraltar.

René Malevergne had been expelled from France for anti-German activities. He was an ardent anti-Nazi, tickled at the idea of helping the Americans and eager to get into the war—more than willing to be evacuated from Morocco. But how to get him past the French and Spanish border guards and into Tangier?

It happened that Tangier-based OSS agents Gordon Browne and Franklin P. Holcomb were in Casablanca on other business. Browne had a "special" U.S. passport, but Holcomb conveniently carried a U.S. diplomatic passport that would facilitate King's plan to sneak the French pilot across the border.

Dave King proposed that Browne and Holcomb hide Malevergne in the baggage compartment of their consulate Chevrolet sedan and drive their cargo across the border while King followed in another car. Alas, it was too small to fit Malevergne's bulky frame, and King thought it too easily opened for inspection. King then proposed to use a trailer attached to the sedan and filled with fuel drums. Holcomb had misgivings and an argument began about logistics.

The no-nonsense Gordon Browne cut it short. "Do they want the man badly?"

"You're goddamned right they do," replied King.

Whereupon Browne snapped, "Then what the hell is the argument? Let's go!"[362]

At Port Lyautey, Malevergne was hidden among fuel drums, covered with gunnysacks and a Moroccan rug, over which was lashed a heavy canvas cover—leaving enough slack so Malevergne could breathe.

It was a long journey from Casablanca to Tangier, and the roads were rough. Browne and Holcomb knew that their passenger was taking a terrible beating, but what they worried about most were monoxide fumes from the gasoline drums and the exhaust in the rear. They stopped as often as possible to be sure that the plucky Malevergne was still conscious.

The trio reached the border control post just at dusk where King had arranged a *baksheesh* payoff for the French guards. Ultimately, it was only the Spanish check-post that was potentially dangerous. The two OSS agents put on big smiles as they rolled across the border and presented their passports to the Spanish police. Minutes later a hunting spaniel approached the car and began to look suspiciously at the trailer. Had he smelled something despite the gas fumes?

Browne was a man of great resources. He sacrificed a tin of Hormel ham he had brought along for the trip and fed the contented hound from the can to the amazement of the border guards. He was equally generous with the Spaniards; more *baksheesh,* and the border gate was raised.

Barely a half-hour later the Chevrolet sedan towed an exhausted, nearly asphyxiated marine pilot into the International Zone of Tangier and then directly to Holcomb's house, high over the city. Malevergne got out of the trailer, dizzy from fatigue, to be greeted by Dave King who had followed the caravan every inch of the way. Later, as he prepared to be smuggled to Gibraltar and on to London, Malevergne remarked to the young Frank Holcomb, "I like King. He looks like a diplomatic gangster."[363]

The Eddy-King snatch job did not go unnoticed at Eisenhower's headquarters or in Washington, where Gen. Marshall demanded to know how Malevergne had been taken out of Port Lyautey under the nose of the Germans. Ike had already turned down one of Eddy's bloodthirsty D-Day plans (though Mark Clark had approved the deed): the assassination of members of the German Armistice Commission in their Casablanca and Oran hotel beds.[364]

The Eddy-King-Malevergne operation was too much for Ike. When he learned that Wild Bill Donovan had ordered the job to please the U.S. Navy and no one in the army knew about it, he was furious. He worried that such an act of bravado could expose, and might compromise, the Moroccan landings.[365]

It was up to Dave King to find a plausible way of covering the Malevergne job—and he did. He got Malevergne's wife to leak to French authorities that her husband had abandoned her and her two infant children and had fled Morocco with a young Spanish girl.

(A few weeks later, we will meet Captain René Malevergne, codename, "Shark," again, aboard a 1920 vintage "four-piper" American destroyer, the USS *Dallas.*)

BACK AMONG PAPER PUSHERS

It took Murphy two crucial weeks to start the long journey back to Algiers. He spent the wasted time mired in useless negotiations with Washington officials at the U.S. Office of Economic Warfare. He did manage to get the release of ships to carry nonstrategic goods to North Africa; even in war, the bureaucracy could be frightful and impossible. (Unfortunately, the urgent material would arrive after the Torch landings.)

Finally, Murphy managed to fly to New York, get a night's sleep, and on Sunday October 4, board a Pan Am Clipper for the return flight to Lisbon-Casablanca-Algiers—a trip he had now made almost a dozen times. He carried with him a gift from Donovan: five lightweight radio transmitter/receivers sealed in diplomatic pouches. The radios had been found among OSS supplies. The army and State Department had no suitable equipment.

A SECRET AGENT FOR IKE

Murphy also carried in his pocket a directive from President Roosevelt, relieving him of all responsibility to the State Department. It confirmed his verbal instruction to "communicate through channels as General Eisenhower and you may arrange." Murphy for the time being wore two hats: he was the president's "personal representative" prior to the arrival of military forces in French North Africa, and thereafter "the Operating Executive Head of Civil Affairs Section and Adviser for Civil Affairs under General Eisenhower."[366]

Unknown to Murphy, though, Eisenhower was unhappy with the directive. He told Gen. Marshall that it was "essential that final authority in all matters in that theater of operations [North Africa] rest with me." Unless Murphy was clearly under him, Eisenhower said, there was a possibility that the French might think there was a division of authority between the American civil and military officials. Marshall now made this plain to Roosevelt, and the president amended his earlier directive, making it clear that Murphy was to operate under Eisenhower.

Finally, Eisenhower refused to allow Murphy to reveal the exact time of the Allied landings. Indeed, at this point in time, Ike did not know himself the exact date and hour of D-Day. The operation was planned for three separate landings, with one of the forces sailing from the United States and the other two from Great Britain. The complexities of loading and coordinating the arrival of supplies from American sources and the shipping of tons of supplies to Britain to be loaded at ports were mind-boggling. But Ike knew Torch could not go off before November 4.

Murphy wrote years later, "I had become a secret agent for Eisenhower . . . a diplomat among warriors . . . and subject to Eisenhower's powers."[367]

D-DAY MINUS 30

On Friday, October 9, after almost five days of weary travel and less than thirty days before Torch, Murphy arrived at Casablanca. Dave King, Leland Rounds, and Jacques Lemaigre Dubreuil were all eager to confer with him— and key Frenchmen were standing by for meetings. He could give his men only a bare-bones briefing; the details would have to come later. But he did tell Rounds to stand by to go to Lisbon. (A week later, Knox and Rounds would receive secret orders to proceed to Tangier for transfer to London.)

Knowing that the principal American landing would take place around Casablanca and Port Lyautey, Murphy rushed to meet five-star Gen. Auguste Nogues at Rabat—the man who ran Morocco as resident general. Murphy could only hint to the general, whom he admired and knew well, something like: If the United States could send a half-million men with guns, warships, planes, and tanks to North Africa . . . would the general be interested?

Nogues didn't hesitate. He cried out, "Don't try that! If you do I will meet you with all the firepower I possess. It is too late for France to participate in the war now. We will do better to stay out. If Morocco becomes a battle-ground, it will be lost to France."[368]

This abrupt reply from an anti-Nazi French patriot must have shocked Murphy. Where did that leave Mast's assurance that Giraud could rally French forces? Murphy now crossed Nogues off his list and cabled London and Washington with the news. He must have wondered how Béthouart— the Black Beast and head of the military at Casablanca—would be counted.

Returning to Casablanca on Sunday, Murphy found (and perhaps not by accident) Jacques Lemaigre Dubreuil waiting at the Casablanca airport. Later, on the plane to Algiers, the seats were filled with Germans, and there was no question of talking. Upon landing at Algiers, Murphy did tell his friend, cryptically, that they could expect good things to happen soon. A full briefing of the Group of Five would come later.

FDR's man had now been away for almost two months. After a short rest, Murphy set about organizing the secret departures of Knox, Rounds, and Culbert, who would be needed as liaison officers with Eisenhower's command and as guides for the landings.

Daphne tells about John Knox's leaving Algiers for a secret final destination:

Early in September 1942, John received orders to leave for Lisbon. . . . I had begun to realize how much he had become part of my life. I missed him more and more . . . Apart from his protection and sympathy, with all our problems, apart from his share and interest in work, he had become something else: a member of our family. The boys knew and loved him, as did we all. When John asked me to wait for him it seemed the most natural thing in the world. I do not think until then I had realized how subconsciously I regarded him as permanent. I could not envisage life without him. His love and affection had helped me through for so long without my having realized how much I had been relying on him; it was as if I had always known he was meant to be with us.

When we told the other members of the consulate that we were going to get married as soon as possible, they showed no surprise at all. In fact, it seemed that they had seen it coming for months . . . one of them [said it was] 'a heavenly arrangement, a ready-made family for John without any of the trouble.'

I suspected where John was really bound for, and prayed we should not be kept in suspense too long. So he left and I had no news of his whereabouts for two long months. Letters to or from me to him were automatically stopped for security reasons. Not until the landings took place did I know where he was for certain. Meantime, to everyone who asked me where he had gone, I answered, 'Hush, it is very secret, but I think it may be Madrid.' If they mentioned Madrid first, I denied it categorically, hoping I would be disbelieved for my very vehemence. I know that I was successful in this, for after the landings people said that he had been there and were surprised to see him in Algiers. I hope the Gestapo looked for him there.

Thus Daphne waited and waited. "I was relatively inactive, which tried my nerves to the breaking point. I realized that I had to be careful not only for my own sake, but for the success of the whole operation. This was the time to play the part of a devoted mother of a family and keep out of the public eye." Daphne says she "watched the weather, day by day. Usually there is a storm at the end of the summer and the rains wash the dust away. Then the weather settles again for a couple of months. But this year in Algiers nothing happened. The sea shone like opalescent glass and the earth started to crack with dryness. I was afraid that when and if the landings took place, the weather might break at the wrong moment. On October 27, I noted in my diary:

The air is full of red brown dust and the sky is thick with it. This heat and sirocco, after years in the Sahara, bring back the nausea and fear with which I watched it there. Over the town the sky is darker than the houses—white houses, green trees, leaden earth and red air.

A few days later, "The sirocco passed over and the sea remained calm. To me it was ominous. The hope of a new era where we could be free to talk and think without threat of prison or death seemed too dazzling to believe. What if a storm spoiled the success of the landings?"[369]

★ ★ ★

SOMETIME IN MID-OCTOBER, Murphy warned Boyd, Pendar, and Knight that an invasion was imminent. They were elated. Murphy ordered Bill Eddy to alert King, Reid, and his OSS crew of impending action. Then he told Springs, Utter, and Woodruff to stand by, as they might have to evacuate Tunis.

Shortly after, L. Pittman Springs and Harry Woodruff were ordered to report to Algiers, where they would work alongside John Boyd.

Woodruff wrote home to his wife that a courier was just leaving for Casablanca, and worried about future correspondence. "It may be hard to get anything off after this for some time . . . so here goes. My affectation seems to be Algiers until further notice. I'm mixed between being glad to be more in the center of things and regrets [sic] to be out of touch with the friends I have made at the other end [alluding to John Utter in Tunis]. It's Bob's [Robert Murphy's] decision, however, and he certainly has a reason. He needs people here, naturally, and will need more."

Woodruff went on. "These days are a mixture of adventure, detective story, fiction and much more, including history making. Enough to fill a few volumes and yet I can take no notes, it's maddening [sic]. By the time I can, all the ups and downs, hopes, anxieties and episodes which have made this period will probably have lost their edges. Afterthought never has the vitality and truth of day-to-day notes. It's a shame."

He told his wife, "I'm glad we decided I should come. It's been more than interesting and in my small way, I have been able to do my share towards our ends. One always wishes to be even more in the thick of things and have a more important role to play . . . collaborating on anything [so] thoroughly fascinating as a chapter of history than what has been going on."[370]

In Murphy's absence, the Group of Five had not been idle. Captain Henri d'Astier, with Abbé Cordier at his side, was busy organizing and training underground units in the Algiers area—part of Colonel Van Hecke's *Chantiers de la Jeunesse* paramilitary force. They were ready to take to the streets and seize strategic locations throughout the city of Algiers. By all accounts, Abbé Cordier ("Necktie") worshipped Henri d'Astier. D'Astier could do no wrong, and the priest faithfully served the d'Astier family—a family apart—drenched in an "all-encompassing aim of vanquishing the Nazis."[371]

All by himself in his Oran hotel room, sleep did not come easily for Ridgway Knight. He was fearful that "I might not have the chance to defend myself if my German or Italian neighbors tried to seize me. I could not help but think that, should the Germans have an inkling of what was in the offing, I might well wake up to find myself in German hands, with a special thought for Major Beck and his inseparable blond German companion."

Due to a childhood illness Ridgway had lost the hearing in his right ear, and this added to his anxiety. He wedged chairs beneath the handles of the inside doors, bolted the room shutters, and placed a glass-covered table in front of the window "so that the shattering glass would awaken me if someone tried to climb in from the street." His final precaution was "to place fully loaded pistols, with cartridges in the chambers, each one on a chair within easy reach . . . In case I did not awaken quick enough to grab one of these revolvers, I kept a third small automatic (a present from Henri d'Astier) under my pillow. I could go for it without showing that I was awake."

Still, he says, "I eventually slept, fretfully turning over in my mind what the days ahead might hold."[372]

There was also little sleep for Bob Murphy.

Hours after his arrival, Adm. Fenard arranged for Murphy to secretly meet outside the city, away from Vichy surveillance, with one of Adm. Darlan's agents, Col. Jean Chrétien, head of the Vichy army's intelligence office (G-2). Chrétien had just returned to Algiers after meeting with Darlan at Vichy. He knew from his spies all about the Group of Five's conspiracy. And he had astonishing news, coming as it did to Murphy at this critical hour. Chrétien said that he was commissioned by Darlan to tell Murphy that he might be willing to move his base of operations to North Africa and bring the French fleet with him, providing the United States was willing to bring assistance.

This was the message that Adm. Leahy had received from Darlan in Vichy months earlier; but coming now, it stunned Murphy.[373] He immediately cabled Washington and London with a summary of the conversation, asking for instructions, and urging that approval be given for him to encourage Darlan's agents. He stated that Darlan and Giraud might agree to work together. (Darlan was touring North and West Africa at the time. He saw Gen. Alphonse Juin, who commanded the Algiers region in Morocco and may have informed him of the Chrétien mission.)

It could not have been a coincidence, then, that the next day Murphy met secretly with Gen. Juin's aide, Major André Dorange. The man was clearly on a fishing expedition: if the *Germans attacked* North Africa [author's italics], could Juin depend on American intervention? Murphy was evasive and said nothing about the U.S. plan. He was worried about leaks, worried about how Giraud fitted in to all this, and realized that in Adm. Darlan he was stalking far bigger game.

Simultaneously, Adm. Leahy, acting on President Roosevelt's instructions, cabled Murphy on October 17, authorizing Murphy to "initiate any arrangement with Darlan which in [Murphy's] judgment, might assist the military operations." Knowing this, Eisenhower, in London, immediately "devised a formula which he hoped might induce General Giraud and Admiral Darlan to work as a team."

According to Murphy, it was "unofficially approved that the two men would divide the top French command between them. The stage was set for a 'Darlan deal.' "[374] It was D-Day minus 24.

★ ★ ★

TENSIONS IN ALGIERS, Casablanca, and Tunis ran high among the American watchers. It was clear something big was about to happen.

Was it Murphy's long absence from Algiers? Vichy and German agents certainly reported on Murphy's movements to and from Washington, Casablanca, and Lisbon. Vichy and German agents also noticed how the lights were now burning all night long at the American consulates, and that there was a threefold increase in the number of diplomatic pouches coming and going. Spies are paid to report such things!

Wild rumors again spread of a German invasion of Morocco; and bets were laid that the Americans would force a landing at Dakar port in French West Africa.[375]

THE COSTER CAPER

Indeed, it was vice-consul Donald Quested Coster who, many weeks earlier, before seeing Murphy at Prestwick Airport, was the source of the Dakar rumors during Murphy's absence.

Dakar is a principal Atlantic port and a credible strategic target for U.S. landings. A British-de Gaulle force had tried to land there in 1941 and had been repulsed by Governor General Boissau on Pétain's orders. Because Dakar was miles away from where Eisenhower planned the Torch Atlantic landings, it occurred to Eddy's fertile mind to spread the rumor of an American landing at Dakar port as a diversion.

Husky, immaculately dressed Donald Coster, Harvard graduate—and Eddy's problem child—had met two adventurous Frenchmen: friends of a friend in London. The "couple" had been in the French Foreign Legion and had fought in the Loyalist army in Spain. Coster knew them as "Freddie," a French blond romantic movie actor, and Walter, a smooth, dark, muscular, former middleweight boxing champion of Austria. Coster ran into the two men by accident in a Casa café and decided he could use them when he heard that Freddie was a good friend of the German diplomat, Theodore "Teddie" Auer, chief of the Casablanca German Armistice Commission. Freddie had met Auer before the war in the salons of Paris when Auer had been a military attaché at the German Embassy there. (And coincidently, Auer was an old Paris friend of Robert Murphy's.)

Coster cultivated the two men and proposed to Eddy that they be "hired." Eddy immediately agreed, whereupon he devised the Coster caper.

Acting under Eddy's instructions, Coster recruited the two men, suggesting they propose to Auer their services as German agents. They were to convince Freddie's old friend Auer that Coster was a weak and easy target.

Auer was delighted at the proposal. He promised to pay Freddie and Walter handsomely for details of what went on at the American Consulate, along with any information on Coster that Auer could use in a blackmail operation.

So Coster began feeding the two men tidbits of disinformation: the numbers of the American agents' license plates and the dates when Eddy or Murphy would be in Casablanca.

It worked—and Freddie and Walter lived well on Auer's money.

At this stage, Eddy's tradecraft was crude: when Freddie had information or questions, he needed only to telephone Coster at the consulate, saying, "Your friend is in the hospital." When the pair had information for Coster, they would deliver it to him at the always-crowded Café de la Gare.

Auer, however, became suspicious when it was reported to him that Coster, and his agents, Freddie and Walter, were seen too often at the café in animated and friendly conversation with each other.

It was time to put on a show for the Germans.

Coster, Freddie, and Walter were next seen at the café when Auer was dining there with his German Armistice Commission colleagues. Coster and his agents took great pains to order black-market steaks and quantities of wine. They were obviously drinking too much, loudly slapping each other's backs, and enjoying a "wild" evening together. (Coster later admitted that he "got fried that night . . .")[376]

The next day, Freddie presented Auer with the café bill, and told the German in elaborate detail how they had gotten Coster drunk. Auer happily handed over the money and asked for more information.

Eddy judged it was now time to get the hook in.

Coster ordered Freddie and Walter to tell Auer that while drunk again, the vice-consul had confided in his pals that American and British troops would land at Dakar sometime in the coming autumn, and Eddy supplied enough detail to Freddie to make the account appear credible to Auer.

It seemed to work. At a secret meeting, Freddie reported to Coster that Auer had swallowed the bait and was delighted with the news. He paid Freddie handsomely. Freddie reported that Auer would be sending a special message to German headquarters at Wiesbaden, giving Dakar as the American target in late October or early November.

And it is a fact that just before the Allied landings at Morocco, German warships, a cruiser, airplane carrier, and transports were seen off the coast of Dakar.[377]

★ ★ ★

TIME WAS RUNNING OUT. To the dismay of Ridgway Knight and to Daphne Joan Fry Tuyl, Rounds, Knox, and Culbert had left. They traveled inconspicuously to Tangier and Gibraltar, and then hopped a flight to London.

Nonetheless, there were those in the OSS, along with some of the vice-consuls in Algeria, Morocco, and Tunisia, who were kept in the dark about the when and where of military operations.

In Casablanca and Algiers, a limited number of arms had been brought from Tangier to boost the flagging morale of King's and d'Astier's action groups of impatient young insurgents. Unbeknownst to Murphy, after a number of tries the British had failed to land clandestine arms supplies and munitions near Algiers and Oran because of bad weather and other misfortunes. Eddy and the vice-consuls still believed deliveries of significant arms were still possible in the remaining days. Alas, bad weather prevailed.

At Oran, Ridgway Knight made arrangements for his underground agents and pro-American French officers to seize arms from French depots.[378]

Still, outside Eisenhower's closely held group, no one yet knew the exact date of the landings or their precise North African locations. And, purposefully, the French conspirators who were to lead a coup d'état were made to believe that the operation was many weeks away, while U.S. diplomats at their consulates—which Eddy called "snake pits"—were totally ignorant. They would stay that way until D-Day, when they would wake to the sound of gunfire.

After the unfortunate Franklin Canfield incident in Casablanca, David King had now managed to regain the confidence of Gen. Béthouart, the Black Beast. Acting as Murphy's liaison officer, King now met with Béthouart and revealed that the Americans were coming and that landings were probable in his area of command. They worked out how Béthouart would cooperate. He was asked to stand by for details; but he was not told that armed French insurgents, under OSS orders, would take up posts at key locations around Casablanca and Algiers on the eve of D-Day.

Shortly thereafter, the vice-consuls, some agents, and Béthouart (through Dave King) were told they might begin listening to the BBC: listening for the words that would proclaim an invasion was imminent . . . or delayed: "Robert is on time; Robert will be with you soon; or Robert is delayed."

In Algiers, Mast, Giraud's agent on the ground in North Africa, was now demanding that a secret military staff meeting be called that he would arrange near Algiers. Mast realized that Murphy was uninitiated when it came to military matters, and imagined him to be uninformed. The general wanted to confer with senior American military officers familiar with the Torch operations. Murphy agreed, and cabled specific instructions for a meeting to Eisenhower.

(Murphy was, of course, forbidden to reveal to Mast or the other conspirators Eisenhower's attack plan—of which he had only sketchy details—and the date of the Torch landings.)

At the same time, Jacques Lemaigre Dubreuil (who had had his own agents in Lyon conferring with Giraud) met with Murphy to draw up what would become the Murphy-Giraud Agreement: three letters which confirmed the political, economic, and financial arrangements that would govern North Africa and prevail after the landings. The agreement was founded on the principle that France was a valued ally of the United States and that the French nation's integrity would be respected; and on the protocols that Col. Solborg had negotiated with Murphy and the Group of Five in Algiers in June.[379] The document had then been taken by Solborg to Washington before his dismissal from the OSS. It was time for Murphy to raise the delicate question with Mast and Lemaigre Dubreuil concerning cooperation with Adm. Darlan. Both men were resolute. Mast coldly rejected the idea, and ventured that Darlan could not be trusted, declaring, "The Army is loyal to Gen. Giraud. The Navy will fall in line with the Army." (This was a critical assumption in view of what was to come. Murphy promptly reported it to Washington and London.)

And still the matter of Giraud's position in Eisenhower's chain of command remained up in the air.[380]

9

DESPERATE VENTURE AT CHERCHEL [381]

NOW BEGINS THE SAGA of Cherchel—one of the strangest chapters in the political and military history of America's North African adventure.

It began at about ten o'clock on Sunday morning, October 18, at Eisenhower's headquarters on Grosvenor Square in London. In a London annex, a red telephone (offering a direct, scrambled line to Eisenhower) rang on Gen. Mark Clark's desk. Clark picked it up and heard Ike's voice on the line: "Come up," Ike said crisply. "Come right up!"

It took Clark barely a half-hour to reach his boss at Grosvenor Square. On the ride over, Clark had a chance to review a cable from Gen. Marshall in Washington, repeating Robert Murphy's request for an urgent, secret rendezvous with the French commander at Algiers, Gen. Charles Emmanuel Mast. Mast proposed that he and his staff meet with an American delegation near Algiers at a place called Cherchel to discuss Allied operations in North Africa.

Marshall approved. Winston Churchill would have to be consulted. And Ike was certainly agreeable to an on-the-spot meeting with French military leaders—anything to give Torch a chance of quick success.

When Clark walked into Ike's office, the first words out of his mouth were, "When do I go?" [382]

★ ★ ★

As Mark Clark made preparations to fly to Gibraltar, the stepping-stone to Cherchel, Ridgway Knight in Oran began the Cherchel adventure with a phone call from Bob Murphy, early Saturday morning, October 17, 1942.

Ridgway remembers: "Bob's ever, and sometimes fatiguing, cheery voice was on the other end . . . asking me to come to Algiers by car—intriguing!"[383]

Knight arrived at Felix Cole's house in Algiers (where Bob Murphy continued to live) late that same afternoon. As soon as Lutzina, the maid, opened the door, Ridgway sensed that something was up. "Her first words were that Mr. Murphy wanted to see me and had given orders that he be immediately informed of my arrival." Murphy greeted Knight "somewhat less smiling than was his wont. Bob was tense and said that I was to participate in an event which could have untold consequences for good or bad, depending on the outcome."

Murphy explained to Ridgway that a secret meeting was planned at a seaside villa. It would bring Mark Clark and several of his U.S. staff officers in London together with Charles Emmanuel Mast, chief of staff of the French XIX Corps at Algiers, and other key Frenchmen. Clark and party were to travel from London to the "Gib" by Flying Fortress (where they would make a hazardous first landing of a Fortress at the Gibraltar airstrip). From "the Rock," they would take a submarine to a Mediterranean seaside cove in front of a farmhouse at Cherchel, west of Algiers, on the night of Tuesday, October 20–21. If Clark's party were delayed, they would have to wait in the submarine until the night of October 22–23. A Moslem feast holiday was being celebrated in the neighboring village of Gourraya on the night of the 21st, and it was feared that the nearby festivities could endanger Clark's landing on a beach that fronted the lonely farmhouse.

The farmhouse had been arranged through twenty-year-old Jacques Teissier, a friend of Henri d'Astier's and Lemaigre Dubreuil's. It was situated between two streams, 150 yards back from the beach where the coastal mountain range meets the sea. Here the rock-strewn beach that fronted the farmhouse was ideal for a secret landing—hidden from the highway by scrub bushes and knotty olive trees atop a sharp drop in the land down to the sea. To the west was Algiers, 60 miles away by a departmental highway; to the east lay Oran, 180 miles away. Ridgway had used this route often to get from his base at Oran to Algiers and Murphy at Felix Cole's house.

Gen. Mast would be accompanied by Colonel Germain Jousse, his chief of staff and commander of the Algiers garrison; Major Dartois, an air force officer (who would be killed a few weeks later in Tunisia), and Captain (later

Admiral) Barjot of the French navy. The civilians present were representatives of the Group of Five and resistance conspirators—Henri d'Astier de la Vigerie, Bernard Karsenty, Jean Rigault, Lemaigre Dubreuil's "Man Friday," and Col. Van Hecke, the "Robin Hood" commander of the *Chantiers de la Jeunesse*. (Lemaigre Dubreuil, who Mast had excluded from the Cherchel meeting, was standing by in Algiers to fly to Lyon, brief Giraud, and urge his participation.) Murphy's friend, French ambassador Jacques Tarbé de Saint-Hardouin, who had joined the conspiracy, would also attend.

D'Astier arranged for Jacques Teissier and a number of young men to join the group and to patrol the surrounding area while the generals and staff conferred—a so-called strong-arm squad.

Murphy explained that Ridgway had been chosen to manage the logistics of the operation and to act as a second interpreter. (Ridgway speculated that he had been selected because of his age, physical fitness, and because he was at home in the water and familiar with small boats. Knight was also the only completely bilingual member of Murphy's remaining vice-consuls.)

John Boyd, Ken Pendar (who was now living in Cole's villa, too), and Ridgway devoted the day of the 19th to making preparations for the meeting and to getting all parties to the farmhouse in the early morning of the 20th. Everyone was ordered to travel by private automobile and to leave at different times, two by two, to avoid attention.

Meanwhile, once at Gibraltar, Gen. Clark and party would board a British submarine—the 700-ton HMS *Seraph* (U-219)—commanded by Lt. Norman L. A. Jewell, RN. Jewell was an expert at bringing submarines close to shore for clandestine deliveries in the region.[384]

At the farmhouse, an electric light bulb would be hung far back inside an upper bedroom so that it would only be visible from a narrow angle at sea, while invisible from either side on land.

★　★　★

WITH CLARK'S PARTY CRAMMED aboard the crowded submarine, the *Seraph* sped on the surface in order to make the best possible time toward the Algerian coast.

Bob Murphy and Ridgway Knight drove west along the winding Algiers-Cherchel road in Knight's official gray Studebaker coupe, headed for the *Chenoua Plage*, a beach resort near the Cherchel farmhouse.

At the resort, they sat down to a black-market dinner and two bottles of Algerian white wine—making a fuss about enjoying themselves and referring loudly, within earshot of the waiters, to the ladies who would be joining them later. (Some of the wine was poured discreetly into the wine cooler.)

They reached the farmhouse on the Oued Messelmoun shortly after 9:30 in the evening to find a typical pleasant 1900 French colonial villa with vines covering most of the gray stucco walls. The living room and dining room, however, were decorated with cheap furniture covered in velvet with attached tassels. The tables, desks, sideboards, and shelves were solidly covered with an oddball collection of curios and dolls that someone had won at a county fair. Loud yellow wallpaper covered with large flowers was peeling from the walls, coming unstuck from the humid sea air. So much for the setting of a historic WWII meeting place.

Jacques Teissier and his young men were at the house. They soon hung the signal lamp in the upper bedroom. Then everyone tried to compose himself for a long wait . . . occasionally going outside for a breath of fresh air, while each in turn stood watch on the beach below the house. With dawn, it became clear that something had gone wrong.

Something had gone wrong—*Seraph* was late. Now the French "delegates" were arriving and Murphy was apologizing and sending them back home with resigned expressions of "see you the day after tomorrow." Murphy and Ridgway returned to Algiers a little later—Murphy to Felix Cole's house, and Ridgway to the Hotel Aletti, where he fell into a deep sleep. Two hours later he woke to an insistent telephone ringing in his ear; and Bob Murphy's angry greeting, "What the hell are you doing, Ridgway my boy, sleeping, when we need you at the office? I didn't ask you over from Oran just to have fun."[385]

At the Consulate General, on rue Michelet, Ridgway found an impatient, furious Bob Murphy. The *Seraph* had radioed that she had been offshore just at the break of daylight and had to retire to sea for fear of being spotted. Clark's message made it very clear that the meeting had to be held that night—Tuesday–Wednesday, October 21–22—despite the Moslem feast.

Murphy and Knight rushed to visit Mast and the other key military officers while d'Astier got the word to his group that a beautifully planned leisurely schedule of arrivals had gone up in smoke. There wouldn't be another dinner at *Chenoua Plage*.

After alerting the French, Murphy and Knight drove straight to the farmhouse to warn Teissier of the new plan. Nervous and irritated, the confused

Frenchman had to scrap all his precautions for a secret meeting and was forced to tell his Moslem laborers that they could have two nights free. (One of the laborers would boast at a local coffeehouse, that very evening, of his employer's generosity. It did not go unnoticed. A local cop paid to report even crumbs of gossip to the Cherchel police commissioner did not fail in his duty.)

Meanwhile, at the farmhouse, Knight had drawn the first watch. The signal light in the upstairs bedroom was turned on and Ridgway stood behind a bush at the edge of the beach, desperately trying to keep warm and stay awake.

It was nearly 10:00 P.M., under a half-moon, with a feathery sea rolling in on the rocky beach when Ridgway saw the dim outline of a narrow, cigar-shaped craft come through the waves, at first silently, until it crunched against the surf-worn rocks, pebbles, and sand. He watched in amazement as two men made it out of a canoe and onto the beach.

Half terrified, Ridgway challenged, "Who goes there?"

"Colonel Julius Holmes, United States Army—and who are you?" came an angry reply. (Holmes and Knight would later claim that they nearly shot at each other.) Then a British boatman in battle dress, the other occupant of the canoe, gave the signal *K* seaward with a flashlight—the all-clear signal to *Seraph*.

Ridgway raced up the stone stairs to the farmhouse to tell Murphy.

Minutes later, three more British "Folboats" (canvas canoes) made it through the moderate surf and crunched to a halt on the beach. A slightly wet Gen. Mark W. Clark (called Wayne, his middle name, by his friends and "The American Eagle" by Churchill) was then eagerly greeted with a cheerful, "Welcome to North Africa," from Bob Murphy.[386]

Mark Clark left no doubt as to who was in charge. He ordered the three boatmen-like coxswains from the British SBS (Special Boat Section in Gibraltar) to store the boats below the farmhouse. Then the tomahawk-faced, lean, rangy Clark skipped up the steep and stony path, gruffly saying to the trailing Murphy, "I'm damn glad we made it." His companions followed: Brigadier General Lyman Lemnitzer, Captain Jerauld Wright, USN, U.S. Army Col. Julius Holmes, and Lt. Col. Hamblin. The three boatmen tagged behind them.[387] They would now wait an anxious five hours for Mast and his French officers to arrive from Algiers.[388]

Clark, despite his imposing bearing and touch of loftiness, was shown to Teissier's messy bedroom, where he slept for three hours between "sheets that had already been slept in, and apparently by more than one person." Murphy and the others slept fitfully in makeshift accommodations while Ridgway Knight curled up on a rug on the floor of the main room.

At sea, Lieutenant Jewell kept the *Seraph* submerged offshore, resting on the shallow seabed. In case of need, the boatmen could talk to Jewell by a walkie-talkie radio.

It was after 5:00 A.M. when Mark Clark was called: Mast had arrived.

As the French changed from civilian clothes to their uniforms, Teissier laid out a breakfast for the generals and their staff. They had what Clark called a typical French *petit déjeuner*: coffee, bread, jam, and—unusual even for the French in Algeria—sardines!

A half-hour later, Clark and Mast got down to the business of "substantive talks."

Clark, Murphy, and staff had agreed to hide the fact that Torch was well past the planning stage. Indeed, the French could not know that the convoys were already at sea. Clark and Murphy took Mast aside and parried with the French general, asking, "With reference to a hypothetical landing, how would you do it?" Mast, who spoke good English, gave a detailed reply that matched closely the Torch plan—except the French general insisted that the North African landings should be coordinated with landings in southern France. The big questions of how, when, and where were sidestepped—leaving Mast with the impression that an American operation was some time off.

Meanwhile, nearby, American and French staffs met to talk about French requirements for arms supplies and logistics.

Clark then briefed Mast, his officers, and the Group of Five envoys on force size. He told a wide-eyed group that the American landing force would include: "a half a million Allied troops coming in; 2,000 planes could be put into the air and the U.S. Navy was ready to put a major fleet into action." The French were impressed. But later they all agreed they didn't believe half of what Clark said. (The force that landed was 112,000 U.S. and British troops ashore in the first days of the operation.)

Gen. Mast, citing Gen. Giraud, again pleaded for a mainland bridgehead in France simultaneously or, at the latest, soon after the North African landings had been consolidated. Mast insisted that this was a condition for Giraud's participation. Foretelling grave problems ahead, Mast returned to the unsettled question of command. Giraud, he emphasized, as the senior French officer on French soil, must be appointed commander in chief of all the Allied forces in North Africa; otherwise, his cooperation was out of the question.

And Mast made no bones about Adm. Darlan. He was unacceptable. Jean Rigault, Lemaigre Dubreuil's man, was present and taking notes; he had met Giraud at Lyon, and knew the general's mind. He confirmed Giraud's position to Murphy.

Clark then pointedly asked Mast if Giraud had the power to rally French forces. The general's answer was unequivocal: "The Army is loyal to General Giraud . . . the Navy will fall into line . . ."[389] Clark pressed Mast: And if Giraud failed to arrive in time? A confident (and ambitious) Mast replied, "I will assume command."[390]

Mast and his men then presented an imposing list of French requirements for armaments and war materiel needed to rearm eight French divisions with up-to-date equipment, and small arms so the Group of Five's insurrectionist fighters could hold Algiers. Mast insisted that American liaison officers would have to be sent to various French commands before the landings. To all this, Clark assured the French that arrangements would be made.

Before Clark could swallow all the French demands, lunch was announced. Without waiting, Mast rushed back to Algiers to prepare his Algiers Division for an imminent visit by Adm. Darlan, who was to inspect the Algiers garrison. (One wonders if Murphy questioned Mast's ambitions and the man's ability to rally the French. Did he share his reservations with Clark? Did he probe with Clark the devious labyrinths of French political ambitions? Had anyone bothered to consult Churchill's chief of staff, Field Marshal Alan Brooke, who believed Giraud to be "one of those queer personalities that fortune occasionally throws forward into positions of responsibility which they are totally unfitted for"?[391]

It was shortly after noon when the remaining group sat down to Teissier's makeshift lunch, replete with plenty of his Algerian wine made on his farm. Lunch and wine seemed to relax everyone, until a scrawny chicken, served in a very hot sauce, made Gen. Clark wince.

After the meal, a work session with Clark, his staff, and Mast's officers provided the Americans with a wealth of information and intelligence, including a detailed and invaluable French plan for American landings: the locations of airfields, air force depots, and suggested paratrooper drop zones, locations of shore batteries and ammunition stores, the numbers and disposition of ground and naval forces, harbor defense plans, and countermeasures. (This was truly an up-to-date confirmation of the vice-consuls' intelligence gathering.)

Ultimately, Clark was "very impressed" by Mast's sincerity. Eisenhower's planners in London would say that "the completeness and terrific value of the [Mast staff] material was astounding."[392]

It was now nearly 6:00 P.M.

Suddenly, one of the guards dashed into the room. The breathless man gestured up the road and announced that the police chief of Gourraya, the nearby town, accompanied by a squad of soldiers, was marching toward the villa.

Ridgway describes the chaotic and helter-skelter transformation at the farmhouse: "It was sheer pandemonium. In seconds the French changed into civilian clothes, ran for their cars and took off for Algiers."[393] (Gen. Clark swore that some had jumped from the windows.)

Clark, Murphy, and Knight were now prepared for the worst.

The boatman with the walkie-talkie raced from the farmhouse to the beach and radioed *Seraph* commander Jewell to tell of the danger. He then hid in the brush.

Gen. Clark, his four officers, and two of the British Folboat crew needed no urging to disappear into the musty, cobwebbed wine cellar built under the living room and hidden by a rug.

With the trapdoor closed on the seven men, Teissier pulled the rug into place, hiding the trap. He placed a table on the rug and, with Murphy and Ridgway, laid chairs around a table. Together with another Frenchman they gathered around the table, emptied their wallets of loose change, and started a poker game.

In a few minutes, another of Teissier's guards knocked loudly on the farmhouse door. Without waiting, he sheepishly entered to say that the Gourraya police chief wanted to speak to someone in authority. Ridgway Knight was chosen to fence with the man: "The police commissioner apologized for disturbing me, said that some of the workers on the Teissier estate claimed something unusual was taking place here; explained that British and the Polish agents had been landing in secluded spots along the coast; and there had been smuggling operations in the neighborhood. A bit embarrassed at first, the official wanted to investigate."

In the dark cellar below, Clark sat listening to snatches of noise from above and grasped his loaded .30 caliber standard-issue carbine. He later declared, "All of us were prepared to shoot our way out if necessary."[394]

To add to the underground drama, "Gruff" Courtney, an oversized boatman that the Americans called "Jumbo," started to cough. Clark took a piece of chewing gum from his mouth and stuffed it between the man's lips. (Later, "Gruff" remarked that American chewing gum had no taste. Clark is supposed to have replied with his casual dry humor: "That's normal; I have been chewing on it for the last hour.")

Finally, Teissier took the police chief aside and explained that Robert Murphy was the American consul general in Algiers, that they were at the farmhouse for a few days of "relaxation," and that there were ladies in the upstairs bedroom. The policeman graciously relented, and took his men back up the road to everyone's relief.

Clark realized that the intruders had left. He heard Murphy move the table and rug; the trapdoor opened and a hoarse Murphy whispered: "This is Bob. They have gone but they'll be back."[395]

By now everyone was tense but took great pains to appear calm. It became unbearable as Teissier, wringing his hands, pleaded with Clark to get out of the house. (The Frenchman risked several years in prison and perhaps death in this venture.)

With soldierly bravado, Clark declared that he would never allow himself to be captured alive. He ventured that his people should take to the nearby hills and hide there until D-Day; or drive to Cherchel after nightfall, commandeer a fishing boat, and go to sea to find the submarine.

Finally, despite the danger, everyone calmed down. It was now growing dark. The wind had risen strongly and waves were rolling in on the beach. Nevertheless, Clark and the experienced boatman, "Gruff" Courtney, decided they had to try to launch a canoe.

Mark Clark knew "I was going to be soaked, so I stripped to shorts and shirt. It was cold paddling around in the water. I put my money belt—containing several hundred dollars—in my rolled-up trousers, not wishing to be weighed down in a turbulent surf and heavy undertow." He and Gruff then tried to float the boat while standing waist-deep in water with the undertow tearing at their legs. "We managed somehow to advance, and at a favorable moment made a dash for it—just as we were almost clear, a wave turned up! The boat reared up almost vertically as the wave crashed down on us. The canoe rolled over and in an instant we were struggling to free ourselves in the boiling foam. As the water receded I managed to get a grip, trying to avoid being drawn back by the powerful undertow and at the same time to rescue the waterlogged boat."

Someone then yelled, "Never mind the General—for heaven's sake, get the paddles!"[396]

The money belt was lost. (The trousers would be picked up later by Murphy.)

For several suspenseful hours, Clark's officers, Murphy, Knight, and an ever more nervous Teissier sat in the house. Every once in a while, they gazed at the sea below, their ears attuned to the noise of the wind.

About 9:00 P.M. another attempt was made. It failed. The canoes were again hauled back up the hill, through thorn bush and over stone—their bare feet, already sore, were now being cut as they hid the canoes in the thick scrub.

Teissier now managed to feed the group with bread and wine and to distribute a few dry sweaters. Then the guard arrived again to announce that the police were coming back.

Still barefoot, his feet cut on the pebbles and sand of the beach, Clark leaped from the farmhouse, jumped over the seawall and plunged down the path to the beach. Everyone got out of the farmhouse and huddled, shivering with cold, in the bush bordering the beach.

It was now midnight. Ridgway Knight insisted on trying to launch a canoe. He and a Lieutenant Le Hen, one of Teissier's strong men, stripped naked, entered the water, and tried to lift the bows of the canoes to get through the waves. They got farther out . . . but still couldn't get through the strong surf tumbling in front of them, wrestling the canoes from their sore hands. Ridgway says, "I was so high-strung that I felt no pain, noticed nothing, as we trudged through the thorn bushes. Neither did I feel the wind on my naked body."

Meanwhile, an anxious Bob Murphy watched all this—his coat collar turned-up, his hands deep in his pockets.

It was close to 4:30 A.M. Daylight would break in minutes. Clark claimed that the wind had dropped. He called for a last try. "Gruff" Courtney recalled that Gold Coast natives launched their canoes in surf by carrying them high over their heads and out beyond the breakers. Now a shore group formed up: Murphy, stripped, and with Knight, Teissier, and his strong-arm men they waded into the frigid water holding the canoes steady above their heads. There was a miraculous lull in the breakers—the wind had dropped. Clark's men climbed into their boats and were shoved off by eager hands. Two of the boats capsized, were righted; the men got back in and paddled furiously.

It seemed like ages. But paddling away with aching arms and blistered hands Clark and his men finally reached the *Seraph*.

As Holmes's canoe came alongside *Seraph*, a wave swamped the boat. Holmes and his boatman managed to grab a line from the submarine; but the precious *musette* bag he carried, containing secret letters from Murphy and more gold coins, was lost in the sea.

Soaked, chilled to the bone, and exhausted, Clark and his men climbed silently below decks.

In the warmth of the operations compartment, Clark spoke to Lieutenant Jewell: "Haven't I heard somewhere about the British Navy having a rum ration, even on submarines?"

"Yes sir, but on submarines only in an emergency."

"Well," said Clark, "I think this is an emergency. What about a double rum ration?"

"If an officer of sufficient rank will sign the order—okay, sir."

"Will I do?"

Clark put his name to a formal written order for a double rum ration for the passengers and crew of the U-219.

Later, aboard the *Seraph* and at the farmhouse, everyone worried about what would happen if pieces of uniform, documents, Holmes's *musette* bag, and Clark's money belt, all lost in the sea, were to wash ashore. What if the coast guards found them?

At first light, Murphy and Ridgway walked the farmhouse beach, picking up everything their visitors had cast off to lighten the canoes. They found trousers, field jackets, and weapons: three army carbines and five automatic pistols. They swept the beach with tree branches, then loaded the Studebaker's trunk with the uniforms and arms. A weary Ridgway drove Murphy to Algiers. Neither man had slept for two nights. Ridgway feared falling asleep at the wheel, and he claimed that to stay awake he stubbed a lighted cigarette into his hand every few minutes.[397]

Knight records Murphy as saying on the road back to Algiers, "I don't know how you feel, Ridgway, but I am not accustomed to this sort of thing . . . I wish I had a little more experience in planning revolutions and overthrowing governments . . ."[398]

Meanwhile, aboard the *Seraph*, Clark radioed a detailed report of the Cherchel meeting to London. The next day he and his party were transferred at sea to a Catalina flying boat. They returned immediately to London to be greeted on Sunday evening, October 25, by an anxious and jubilant Eisenhower.

★ ★ ★

LATER, MARK CLARK made great sport of the Cherchel meeting, particularly telling an international press corps in Algiers about the wine cellar incident. He got a good laugh at the "chewing-gum" episode and thus managed to deflect some very serious questions about the entire adventure. Despite Clark's attempt at comical drama, Cherchel was no lark. Clark, Murphy, and their staffs as well as the French officers had narrowly avoided disaster. The consequences of Clark's and his officers' capture are almost unimaginable. Mast and his men probably would have faced a firing squad. But Torch, with the convoys already at sea, might have been compromised. The French Vichy pretense of neutrality was a sham. The Germans would certainly have learned the Torch secret. And it was only thanks to bad weather that *Seraph* was not spotted and sunk by patrol boats or reconnaissance aircraft.

Clark and Murphy had pulled off one of the great deceptions of World War II; but the Cherchel bravado left a bad taste in some mouths. The French were bitter about being deceived.

André Beaufre wrote that Clark "paraded, bluffed with the innocent duplicity most of our American friends deploy under such circumstances. It was not a matter of informing the French, but of taking them in . . . It was a frightful comedy which the prodigious general played before Frenchmen who risked not only their honor and lives, but French interests as well."[399]

Murphy's friend, Jacques Tarbé de Saint-Hardouin, feared that the confrontation had done more harm than good. Clark's reported flippant remark at the Cherchel farmhouse was a symbol of the entire Franco-American relationship: "I had my carbine in one hand and fifteen thousand francs in the other, without knowing which I might use if someone showed up." To Saint-Hardouin, this conjured up a vision only too symptomatic of the American attitude—that cooperation could be obtained only through bribery or threats.[400]

Meanwhile, on Friday, October 23, without seeing Murphy, Lemaigre Dubreuil took an Air France plane to meet Giraud in Lyon. He carried only Jean Rigault's brief notes of the Cherchel meeting and a copy of a draft of the so-called Murphy-Giraud Agreement—a document whose contents would soon be overtaken by events.

In the desperate days that followed, the deceit and bravado of the Cherchel meeting would color events and lead to a series of disasters at Algiers, Oran,

Casablanca, and Tunis. Some called the American (Murphy's) duplicity "a virtual double cross by the Americans." (London and Washington truly feared that the French would betray Torch if they had known the D-Day time and date, force size, and landing sites.)

Fourteen days before D-Day, Murphy managed through Lemaigre Dubreuil to entice Giraud to cooperate with the Allies and to come to Algiers—though the caveats remained about how and when Giraud would be named supreme commander of the operation. And Lemaigre Dubreuil and Giraud still remained under the impression they had a month or more of preparation before the American landings.[401]

After receiving a coded message from Lemaigre Dubreuil in France that Giraud seemed to be ready to cooperate, Murphy cabled Eisenhower:

> Messenger sent to France [Lemaigre Dubreuil] after Flagpole's [Mast's] meeting with Clark reports that Kingpin [Giraud] agrees to participate in our proposition. He asks that we continue study of his idea of establishing a bridgehead in Southern France. I am also informed under promise that this is for my personal information only and not as yet for communication to you that Kingpin will be willing to come to Africa for the operation.[402]

(Giraud's insistence on command and his caveats were apparently not transmitted.)

Harassed by Vichy agents, Gen. Giraud left Lyon and drove south to visit his brother-in-law, Captain Beaufre (the same man Murphy had met on New Year's Eve, 1941). Giraud hid in Marseilles while Beaufre made secret arrangements through the French Resistance in Marseilles to contact Gibraltar. Two submarines were laid on to fetch Giraud, his family, and staff and bring them to Gibraltar. (Murphy believed Giraud was coming to Algiers.) From a Toulon beach, none other than Captain Jerauld Wright (of Cherchel fame) sailed the *Seraph*, disguised to look "American" so as not to offend the touchy French. The *Seraph* then picked up Gen. Giraud, his son, Bernard, and his now aide, Captain Beaufre, in heavy seas and carried them to a rendezvous with a Catalina flying boat at sea. (Another British submarine, *Sibyl*, picked up Mme. Giraud and some of Giraud's staff off Cros-de-Cagnes near Toulon, and delivered them to Gibraltar.)

Giraud and party landed on "the Rock" on November 7 and into the impatient hands of Dwight D. Eisenhower. It was the eve of D-Day.

It was also the dawn of grave misgivings about Giraud's part in the Torch venture. On both sides—Giraud's and Eisenhower's—there were longstanding political and military misconceptions and misunderstandings. It would all end very badly for the brave Giraud, a simple soldier transformed into a counterpoison and antidote for President Roosevelt's affliction: General Charles de Gaulle.[403]

And earlier on October 27, Murphy was ordered to wait eight more days before notifying Gen. Mast and other trusted conspirators of an approximate landing date. Eisenhower cabled, "You are authorized to notify Kingpin [Giraud] or Flagpole [Mast] on *November 4th* of the assault date [still November 8th] and of the name of the Commander-in-Chief" [author's italics].The cable advised Murphy for the first time that a submarine was on its way to take Giraud from France to Gibraltar.

The next day, a counter order warned Murphy by cable to say only that "the operation was set for early November."[404]

Other than Knight, Murphy's men knew nothing about what had transpired at Cherchel. It was now time to inform the vice-consuls and some OSS officers (but not U.S. diplomatic officers—with the exception of Consul General Felix Cole, who was handling Murphy's cable traffic) of the probable time and place of the Torch landings along with the plan of attack.

It is worth reading in detail what Murphy recounts about the Cherchel meetings:

> That meeting at Cherchell [sic: the French spelling is Cherchel] was one of the oddest conferences of the war, because the French participants in those staff talks were ignorant of the essential details of the Allied plans. Both Clark and I were under instructions to avoid giving the French conferees specific information about the timing of the expedition or the exact locations selected for troop landings. So these discussions inevitably misled our French associates, who assumed they had months in which to prepare for African D-Day, whereas we Americans knew they had only sixteen days. In fact, the first slow convoys of the expedition already

were starting from the United States as we talked. Because of the secrecy imposed upon the American negotiators, the Cherchell meeting failed to clarify the status of French commanders either in military or political affairs. For example, Giraud's representatives requested from Clark positive assurances that Giraud would have overall command of the Allied forces, American as well as French. Clark explained that this was impractical during the preliminary operations, but he agreed that Giraud would be given over-all command "as soon as possible"—a purposely vague phrase. The question of Darlan's participation also was discussed at Cherchell. Clark outlined the Giraud-Darlan formula devised by Eisenhower, but Mast objected vigorously to the inclusion of Darlan. He declared that the Admiral was belatedly trying to climb on the Allied bandwagon, and that the Allies did not need him because Giraud could swing the support of the African Army and Air Force, and the Navy would soon fall in line. So the conference at Cherchell left Darlan's status unresolved.[405]

DECEPTIONS AND PROVIDENCE, PERHAPS

The Clark-Murphy deceptions at Cherchel were not isolated and unintended stratagems. But Gen. George Patton believed "Divine Providence" would save Torch.[406]

Eisenhower was not the man to leave anything to "Providence," however. In London, his staff approved a British Double-Cross disinformation program to make it appear that Allied convoys passing the Strait of Gibraltar were heading toward Malta and Sicily, and that Atlantic convoys were part of a task force to take Dakar. And German U-boat commanders in the Atlantic were also put off by the normal Allied convoy travel between the UK and Sierra Leone in West Africa. As German wolf packs tracked and sunk some of these ships, the German naval command failed to sight the Morocco-bound armada.

The British were masters at deception. With uncommon skill, they wrote and launched false scenarios with a half-dozen double agents under their control. But for pure intelligence, Bletchley Park's ULTRA intercepts of German military traffic told the British, and Eisenhower's staff, what the Germans were believing—or not believing—about the deception programs.[407]

It was all part of the deadly spy game . . . but this time, the Allies were the winners.[408] The German and Italian high command were made to believe that convoys passing Gibraltar were headed for Sicily. Rome Radio interrupted programs to warn listeners of probable landings in Sicily and Calabria. And the high command also feared Allied landings in Libya and Tunisia would catch Rommel's army as it fell back from El Alamein.

PART THREE:
TORCH BURNS BRIGHTLY—FLICKERS

No other operation in World War II surpassed the invasion of North Africa in complexity, daring, risk, or—"the degree of strategic surprise achieved." [409]

10

FURIOUS HOURS:
REBECCAS AND DOMINICAN ROBES

THE FOG OF WAR rolled over the African lands, from Casablanca to Tunis. As the furious last hours before the landings ticked away, disorder ruled. An exhausted Robert Murphy and Ridgway Knight returned to Algiers to face more crises.

Gen. Mast now reacted violently on being told the landings were scheduled for "early in November." When Lemaigre Dubreuil returned to Algiers from seeing Gen. Giraud, he became "apoplectic" when Murphy told him the landings were imminent. But in Marseilles, Giraud, waiting to board a British submarine prudently disguised as a U.S. ship, inevitably realized that D-Day had to be about November 8.

Mast and Lemaigre Dubreuil argued that the unexpected early D-date was an American "ultimatum" that would defeat their efforts to ensure unopposed landings. There just wasn't time to put all the pieces together to prevent French forces from shooting Americans on the beaches. They cajoled and ranted, threatening to break with Murphy—leaving Vichy forces to resist all comers. Giraud needed time to consolidate resistance and form up the planned coup d'état.[410]

On the evening of November 1, Robert Murphy sat anxiously peering out his office window. Here and there a light twinkled as the headlight of a car swept the nearby walls of the Vichy French Admiralty building. All was quiet except

Murphy's insides; the confident, usually jovial Irishman was suffering a bad case of nerves. Giraud's and Mast's cooperation was threatened—the reality that the French army in North Africa might kill American soldiers and sailors as they landed on the beaches was too much. Torch might fail.[411] Murphy had spent months trying to avoid just such a disaster—and now he cabled Washington and London, asking that the Torch landings be postponed.

One cannot know if Murphy even allowed himself the luxury of consulting his friend, Felix Cole—but the cable was a major blunder: London and Washington were stupefied at Murphy's ridiculous request. The convoys were already on the high seas. Adm. Leahy shot back a negative the next day: "utterly impossible."[412]

The president (and Marshall and Eisenhower) would have none of it. FDR ruled that the operation would be carried out as planned. Murphy was ordered to do his "utmost" to get the French to understand the reasons for American secrecy; a "premature disclosure" of plans would compromise the operation.

In the middle of this, Murphy was hit with yet another complication: on his forty-eighth birthday, Adm. Jean-Francois Darlan arrived in Algiers at the tail end of a tour of Casablanca, Fez, and Oran. And Darlan arrived at a distressing moment: his wife was in Algiers, too, tending to their gravely ill only son—the young naval reserve officer, Alain, who had served as an emissary between Darlan and Murphy. At that very moment Alain lay at Algiers' Maillot hospital, diagnosed with poliomyelitis.

Despite the personal strain, Darlan, impressed with Murphy as Roosevelt's spokesman in Algiers, ordered Col. Jean Chrétien to meet with Murphy to find out what the Americans would do if Germany attacked in North Africa. Then Darlan left the talks in Chrétien's hands and sped to France to arrange to take Alain home for medical care.

Darlan did not then believe there was immediate danger; everyone, even Darlan, seemed to think that if American landings came, they would be at Dakar.[413]

As Allied convoys approached Gibraltar, Murphy (probably at the instigation of Darlan or Chrétien) met secretly on the night of November 2 with the ranking foot soldier in Algeria: Gen. Alphonse Juin. Murphy probed to see how Juin might react to an American intervention. The general was unequivocal: He would ask for American aid only if the Germans attacked. Still,

Murphy found Juin clearly more sympathetic to the Allied cause than Gen. Nogues in Casablanca.

But by now arrangements with Giraud had gone too far; Murphy feared that despite Juin's pro-Allied mindset, his loyalty lay with Marshal Pétain. In parting, Murphy imprudently assured the general that the American forces would not land in North Africa without an invitation.

The very next morning the Darlan-Juin emissary, Col. Jean Chrétien, visited Murphy again to say that Juin would be prepared to discuss Franco-American cooperation with an American officer.

Murphy now had in his hands a heaven-sent opportunity to obtain Juin's cooperation, but having moved so far down the Giraud-Dubreuil road, he hesitated to place confidence in Juin. Without revealing that he was in personal touch with Juin, Murphy then talked the problem over with Gen. Mast, who emphatically advised against telling Juin, Mast's superior, anything! Indeed, Mast saw himself on the threshold of supplanting his senior officers: Gen. Juin, Gen. Koeltz, commanding the XIX Corps in Algiers, and Gen. Boisboissel, Koeltz's deputy. He must have calculated that once Giraud had American tanks and guns to back him, Mast would be elevated to top rank and Vichy officers swept out of power. Mast's refusal to bring Juin into the conspiracy was to cause major problems later.[414]

Mast, Lemaigre Dubreuil, and the Group of Five's tenacious and vigorous promotion of Giraud to Clark and Murphy was not unselfish. The group hoped and expected that an Allied military victory would rate them senior posts in a future Giraud government. They had sold Giraud to Murphy and to Clark—and they were "tied to the general."[415]

In that final "frenzied week," a tired, stressed, and lonely Murphy must have been gripped with the enormity of what he was involved in—and what he had in some way created.[416]

On Thursday, November 5, Admiral Fenard summoned Darlan to return to Algiers. His son, Alain, had taken a turn for the worse.[417]

★ ★ ★

POLISH WARNINGS

Ominous signals were coming to Rygor Slowikowski's agents stationed at the four corners of West and North Africa: The Vichy French military and naval high commands were clearly preparing to repel an invasion.

Rygor knew of the Cherchel meetings but he did not know the exact date of the Torch landings. And he was worried. He sent this urgent message to London:

> General Nogues, the Resident Minister of Morocco, informed Vichy that the Americans were looking at landing sites in Morocco. Lighthouses on the coast near Oran were suddenly extinguished. The Franco-German Armistice Commission in Algiers ordered construction of fortifications and shelters at the Maison Blanche Airport; the troops defending it were reinforced. At Casablanca Port, an observation balloon moored over the town was now manned by a German-French crew. The French Admiralty ordered stepped-up submarine patrols and the closing of all ports at night. La Sénia air base at Oran was on an advanced alert. The military was ordered to occupy nighttime defensive positions at certain key ports.[418]

When Slowikowski delivered a pouch to John Boyd at the U.S. Consulate, he passed all this to John, and warned that the Gestapo must surely have the same information. Boyd was dismissive. Then Slowikowski told Boyd that eleven submarines and three destroyers based in Toulon, France, had just landed in various ports along the North African coast. Boyd was flustered. Though Boyd and the Pole agreed that taken together, all this was threatening, Boyd refused to say more—other than that he would rush the pouch to Tangier for delivery to London. (In fact, he opened the pouch and showed Slowikowski's reports to Murphy. Then Boyd sent the pouch by courier to Tangier, where it was forwarded to Gibraltar and London.)

A sense of excitement, expectancy, anxiety, and dread pervaded Algiers. Adding to the tension, and out of the blue, came the announcement that Rommel had been killed and that his Afrika Korps were in full retreat in the Libyan Desert. The British were on their way to Tunis. (Rommel was unhurt and would regroup his forces before being relieved of his desert command.) Col. Germain Jousse, who had attended the Cherchel meeting, now approached one of Slowikowski's agents and announced that he was "the military commander of the resistance movement and known to General Eisenhower."

Frenetic was the only word that could describe the atmosphere in Algiers. Sophie Slowikowski was told by her concierge that the woman's son was going to a rendezvous on the night of November 7–8 to collect arms and to join a rebellion. Rygor, the professional intelligence agent, was appalled. He immediately confronted John Boyd at the U.S. Consulate General about Jousse's bravado. John Boyd then sheepishly admitted to his friend that the landings were imminent and that the largest American sea convoy ever to be assembled was just then approaching the coasts of Morocco and Algeria.

Suddenly, Murphy arrived and joined Boyd and Slowikowski. Almost as an afterthought, Murphy asked Rygor if he would keep his radio transmitter link with London open on the night of November 7–8.

That night, Rygor, Sophie, and young George Slowikowski didn't sleep a wink.[419]

ORAN TO CASABLANCA: D-DAY MINUS SIX

Early on Saturday, the last day of October, Ridgway Knight and Kenneth Pendar left Bob Murphy and his devoted and aptly named secretary, a Miss Hardy, at Cole's villa and drove to Oran. Ridgway was just then getting over a serious ear infection, and his badly infected feet had barely healed after the nocturnal sea-baths at Cherchel. Leaving Ridgway in Oran, Pendar was to fly from Oran to Casablanca where he would begin a secret mission for Murphy. He was charged with giving Dave King and Staff Reid the date of the landings.

King and Reid would be told only on November 2 of the date and warned to tell no one—not even the U.S. consul general at Casablanca.

Ken Pendar was then to accompany Jean Rigault, Lemaigre Dubreuil's man, as he delivered letters from Gen. Giraud to Gen. Béthouart (the Black Beast) and other senior French commanders throughout Morocco who Giraud trusted to join in the coup d'état. Pendar also carried messages from President Roosevelt addressed to the Sultan of Morocco and Gen. Nogues, the resident general there. The letters announced in florid Arabic and French how American forces would liberate North Africa from the Nazi yoke. (FDR's missives were to be held at the Casablanca Consulate General until the morning of November 8, and released to a consular officer for delivery only on Murphy's orders.)

In Casablanca, Pendar realized for the first time that Dave King, Staff Reid, and Gen. Béthouart still believed that the landings would take place at the end of November. These actors in the coup d'état thought they had a month to set in motion their part in the uprising.

At Casablanca, Pendar met secretly with Jean Rigault and drove him in a consular sedan toward Marrakech to deliver the first of Giraud's messages to trusted French officers. On the way Ken Pendar's mind ticked over; he was in a dilemma. Midway, Pendar stopped the car at roadside. The dilemma became a quandary: If he withheld the November 7–8 dates of the Torch landings from Rigault, the Morocco operation might well be compromised. For Pendar knew that Gen. Nogues had threatened Murphy that an overwhelming French army and naval force would shoot the Americans out of the water.

Ken Pendar tells how at that roadside desert stop, he looked Rigault in the eyes and said: "I am afraid you will have to change your plans with these Generals and Béthouart . . . the landing in Morocco is scheduled for the early morning of November 8th."[420]

"My God," exclaimed Rigault, cursing Murphy. "My wife will be caught in France." (Rigault's part in the coup d'état would be known to Vichy; he feared his wife would be arrested.)[421]

Pendar urged Rigault to warn his wife to get out of France, but he wouldn't hear of it. He was afraid to tip off Vichy agents.

"No," Rigault said, "my wife knows the risks involved . . . she will understand."

From Marrakech, Pendar returned to Casablanca with Rigault. It was time to brief King and Reid on the invasion date; and he left the president's messages with Staff Reid for Murphy's release.

In Tunis, John Utter was to deliver similar messages to the Bey of Tunis and Resident Adm. Esteva on Murphy's signal.

When Rigault reached Gen. Béthouart's headquarters, he revealed to a very angry "Black Beast" the imminent date of the landings. (A few hours later, Béthouart would pass the information to one of his subordinates in Rabat, General Martin. The man would get cold feet at the last moment, and on November 7, spill the hour and date of the Morocco landings to Gen. Nogues. The secret was out in Morocco—and probably in Vichy, too.)[422]

Despite Rigault being wanted by Moroccan authorities, he and Pendar drove on to Rabat, Fez, Taza, and to Oujda—a town just before the Moroccan-Algerian border—and then to Oran and Algiers, stopping along the way to deliver the Giraud messages at French garrisons. It was a frantic and dangerous drive over unimaginable roads that curved like serpents up and down the arid mountains and across the hot Moroccan and Algerian plain. Pendar says, "The heat literally made your eyeballs burn."

The two men stopped only to deliver Giraud's letters, have a cup of tea, and carry on day and night, eating from a basket of stale sandwiches.

Fifty miles from Algiers, on a steep mountain descent, they faced disaster. Pendar failed to make a curve and piled the car into a ditch. Shaken, unhurt, and determined, they miraculously heard a train's shrill whistle—and in the distance, saw a village train station. Rigault leaped from the car and caught the train. Pendar followed, telephoning from the station. He was able to have a U.S. consular car come for him.

Ken Pendar spent the rest of that day with Harry Woodruff, whom Murphy had ordered to come to Algiers from Tunis to lend a helping hand. Without so much as a wink of sleep, the two vice-consuls burned document after document at the Consulate General's office and at Cole's house, in improvised metal trash cans adapted for the purpose. Pendar and Murphy then delivered personal letters and private papers kept at Cole's house to their French patriot friend, Nicole de Brignac—head of a Red Cross ambulance unit in Algiers. Nothing was left for Vichy agents or the Germans to find if the worst came; not a scrap bearing the names of the resistance partisans.

Pendar's trip had taken four desperate days. It was now D-Day minus two.[423]

ORAN, D-DAY MINUS FOUR

Ridgway Knight's and Leland Rounds's plans to kick off a partisan uprising at Oran were unraveling.

Ridgway was still nursing an infected ear and feeling the loss of Leland Rounds, who was now working at Clark's headquarters at Norfolk House in London. After Pendar's departure for Casablanca, Knight met with his chief agent at Oran, the Dominican Catholic priest Father Théry, and a group of partisans that included key men: Col. Tostain, whose codename for some reason was "Fifty Cents," and Roger Carcassonne, codenamed "The Duke." (Knight was codenamed "Helmet.")

Present too were Knight's trained radio operators, René Brunel and Emilien Arnaud, and Jean Ducrot, also a trusted agent.

Father Théry, Tostain, and Carcassonne had been handpicked by Henri d'Astier de la Vigerie to lead the Oran resistance movement. Ridgway had every reason to believe they would carry out their assigned roles. Now he described the Cherchel meeting, the attack plans, and generals Giraud's and Mast's roles in the insurrection.

In the middle of Ridgway's briefing, it struck Col. Tostain that planning for insurrection had ended; the critical moment for action had arrived, and he was to lead a group of partisans destined to seize the Admiralty building at Oran. French blood would be shed—and there laid the rub.

Tostain practically squealed, "But this means there will be French lives lost . . . that is asking too much. I must have these orders from General Mast in person."

Father Théry tried to calm the man. "But my son, we have considered that . . . if we seize the Admiralty, many more lives will be saved."

Argument now wandered up the scale of heroics and down the scale of duty, loyalty to Pétain . . . it seemed endless. Ridgway was disgusted. He saw his own work—and the carefully laid plans of Father Théry and Leland Rounds, all of which had taken months—being destroyed by gutless men. The group leaders had no stomach to resist, much less fight, against their own.

A final blow came when Tostain refused to confirm that he would secretly open Oran's divisional armory and issue ancient Lebel rifles stored there to arm the partisans. (The light automatic weapons promised by the British had not arrived.)

The meeting broke up in confusion. But Tostain did agree to contact Mast in Algiers and get confirmation from Mast that he backed an attack at the key Oran naval base.

There was still hope . . . or was there?

Alone, Father Théry lent Ridgway his white Dominican robes. Ridgway, his face hooded in white, slipped out of the priest's apartment and into the gathering darkness. Incognito, he rushed to the nearby apartment of Frenchman René Brunel, his trusted wireless operator and agent. From there, Brunel would send an urgent warning message to Tangier and Gibraltar: the situation was deteriorating.

After returning the Dominican dress to Father Théry, Ridgway returned to the Grand Hotel to find the hall full of members of the Armistice Commission eyeing the girls, lolling in armchairs, and enjoying late after-dinner drinks.

Dr. Beck, the Gestapo major, was there, as was his sidekick, "the overly handsome young man that never left his side." Ridgway was now convinced that the young man doubled as a Gestapo secret radio operator. It sent chills down his spine.

It was late evening, and D-Day neared. No sooner had Ridgway closed the door to his room than the telephone rang.

"Hello, Ridgway," said Bob Murphy from Algiers. "You are slipping badly if you let a charming young lady wait for you in Oujda any longer."

"What?" Ridgway answered briskly, his nerves frayed. "Bob, I am awfully busy just now, getting a dispatch ready for you for tomorrow's courier."

"I am surprised at you, Ridgway. Rebecca has been in Oujda since last evening. The lady is pining for you at the Hotel Terminus. What's happened to your manners? You asked weeks ago to see Rebecca . . . What is the matter with you?"

Then it came to Knight: "Rebecca" was the codename for a radio beacon device meant to guide airborne paratroopers on the night of the landings to a drop zone near Oran. "She" had slipped Ridgway's mind.

"Is Rebecca alone?" he asked.

"No, Gordon Browne knows her well. He'll go back to the Grand Hotel with you and her! I don't know how you do it, Ridgway!"[424]

It was 5:00 A.M., Thursday, November 5, when Ridgway set out for Oujda, almost a hundred miles away, along a fair but sinuous highway and just across the Moroccan border via Tlemcen. The rains had come late that year. It was a hot and dusty trip, up and down mountains and across dusty plains.

At the Hotel Terminus, a sleepy and insolent European-dressed Moroccan clerk told Ridgway that Mr. Browne was lunching in his room with a lady, adding with a smirk that he could disturb them if Ridgway so dared.

Upstairs, Ridgway was greeted by an impatient Gordon Browne (of the OSS), and an attractive young lady, their "Rebecca"—a clerk at the U.S. Consulate at Casablanca. The room was filled with several stuffed gray canvas bags, all sporting the diplomatic seal of the U.S. Legation at Tangier.

Over lunch with a very real and pretty "Rebecca," Browne explained to Ridgway: "This whole thing came as a last-minute surprise for me. Four days ago I did not know that I was going to draw this mission. I can't begin to tell you how relieved and delighted I am. As a matter of fact, I was beginning to fear that the great day would find me stuck high and dry in Tangier, or Gibraltar, like Coon, with nothing else to do but follow the news bulletins." (Ridgway had heard about the famous OSS twins, Browne and Carleton Coon. They both spoke fluent Arabic. Together, some fifteen years before, they had spent time in Morocco living with, and studying, the warlike tribes of the Riff mountains.)[425]

As Knight and Browne drove away, leaving the live Rebecca to return to Casablanca, Browne warned: "For God's sake, take it easy, our cargo is delicate . . . The set is sealed. If it is thrown out of whack, there is nothing we can do about it. I have orders not to let it be captured intact. It is fitted with a self-destruct explosive charge which I can set off at a moment's notice."

Ridgway says he cut the car's speed in half and swallowed hard.[426]

Browne carried a genuine Diplomatic Courier Letter issued by the U.S. Legation in Tangier, and they had no difficulty crossing the border with the pouches: "With a smile, and a few polite sentences over cigarettes, a friendly inspector bid us *bon voyage* and waved us on our way."[427]

Gordon Browne and Knight went over how Rebecca would be deployed. The next day, D-Day, Ridgway was to lead Browne in the official Studebaker to Eljani, a farmhouse Knight and Rounds had arranged to occupy with Gordon following in a spare Renault car loaded with Rebecca. Browne would hide at the farm until it was dark enough for Gordon to manhandle Rebecca to a nearby, predetermined drop zone between the La Sénia commercial airfield and the Tafaraoui military air base.

Then Browne fell asleep, leaving Ridgway wishing that he had let Gordon drive.

Later, Ridgway was to write: "I could not have chosen a more pleasant, calm and courageous partner; Gordon Browne was a studious man that relished action."

It was already dark when the pair cleared the last hills. Ridgway woke his passenger so that the two could look down on a dimly lit Oran city and the expanse of sea beyond. A good breeze was blowing landwards, and suddenly it seemed in these anxious moments that a hot summer had given way to a pleasant and refreshing hint of autumn.

The streets of Oran were crowded as they entered Oran. The entire town was out to see and to be seen—a Spanish custom. Along the narrow town streets the trolleys crisscrossed from square to square—people afoot everywhere. Driving was nerve-racking and Knight wondered out loud: "Leland and I often said what a mess we would have here . . . momentous traffic accidents when the landings take place . . . the narrow streets filled with American tanks and military trucks."

It was 9:00 P.M. when they reached the Grand Hotel. Would the Germans and Italians be hanging out in the lobby?

Ridgway sauntered in and went directly to his room while Kader the porter took Browne and the Rebecca pouch up the service stairs to join Ridgway. It was a delicate maneuver, and for the occasion, Ridgway produced an exceptional wine.

Remembering the name of the wine years later, he says, "We savored one of the few remaining bottles from my private hotel reserve: a Louis Latour Gorton Charlemagne 1929."

Knight needed more than a bottle of Louis Latour champagne when he met for the last time with Father Théry, Col. Tostain, Carcassonne, and other resistance leaders. Carcassonne, "The Duke," was upset and haggard. Father Théry offered a weak, "Welcome, *Monsieur le Consul*" rather than "my son"— a bad omen. Was he sending a message?

Knight's radio operator, René Brunel, a rabid anti-Nazi, had the look of a thundercloud.

Knight got right to the point with Tostain: "*Mon Colonel*, did you not obtain confirmation in Algiers of what I told you on Monday?"

Tostain: "Yes, *Monsieur le Consul*, everything was confirmed with the sole exception . . . General Mast instructed me to cooperate fully with you, but imposed one restriction: my cooperation must stop short of shedding the blood of Frenchmen by other Frenchmen."

René Brunel cut in with a rude, "Tommyrot!" Brunel knew that Col. Tostain's "sole exception" meant he didn't want to fight. Tostain and his people wouldn't protect the naval dry docks and Vichy loyalists would blow them up upon the arrival of Allied forces, while others would flood the port with burning oil—draining the oil storage tanks on docks into the port. To add insult to injury, Tostain was saying that there would be no arms for the some 500 men that existed on paper as resistant fighters.[428] The failure to receive light automatic weapons from the British was telling. Now the last straw: There would be no arms at all! Who was going to attack armed Vichy defenders with bare hands?

Fearing that French or German radio operators might be tracking their radio signals, Brunel had moved the wireless from his apartment to the farmhouse bedroom of Mlle. Jeanne de l'Espee, the strong-willed and courageous head of the Women's Ambulance Corps in Oran—a fearless, Nazi-hating patriot. Emilien Arnaud, a tried and trusted friend, would share de l'Espee's hospitality and act as a messenger and backup radio operator.

Ridgway sped to the de l'Espee farm with Brunel to flash another warning to Tangier and Gibraltar: only a symbolic resistance could be expected. The paratroopers had to be warned. Knight remembers the opening words of his warning: "Cold feet developing everywhere . . ."[429] Col. Tostain's cowardly about-face sealed the death of the resistance movement at Oran.

Night fell on D-Day minus two.

The next morning, the *Echo d'Oran* newspaper reported that convoys were seen passing through the Strait of Gibraltar. Ridgway was becoming restless, as were the vice-consuls everywhere that day. He was charged with Gordon Browne's safety and the delivery of Rebecca at a moment when their carefully laid plans for an insurgent uprising were falling apart—and Ridgway was the only one able to decode the urgent messages that Brunel picked up at Mlle. de l'Espee's farm. Ridgway cursed Leland Rounds's absence.

That moonless night, Oran was blacked out. In the nearly pitch-black darkness, Ridgway rushed to Father Théry's apartment. It turned out that the convoy, previously reported at Gibraltar, was now off the Oranese coast. The French Admiralty had ordered an emergency blackout, the manning of coastal batteries, and an army and naval forces alert. (In fact, the ships, loaded with the Algiers Task Force, were continuing to steam on a northeasterly course, leaving Algiers astern; they would then cut back toward several beaches fifteen to twenty miles west of Algiers. The Oran assault forces were still out to sea.)

From Father Théry, Ridgway learned that Col. Tostain had given his solemn word that he would divulge nothing about the conspiracy or the landings. In effect, he would fall ill. (Ridgway now reasoned that despite the colonel having given vital secret information to aid the vice-consuls in their planning, he and Rounds should have anticipated Tostain's cold feet. It was too much to expect a French army officer to turn his back on his country's legitimate authority.)

In the darkened city Ridgway made his way back to the Grand Hotel entrance. Pushing aside the blackout curtains he stepped into a brilliantly illuminated scene. A party of sorts was going on. Mostly in full uniform, the Germans and Italians were solicitously surrounding twenty-odd, rather bedraggled-looking German sailors. (Kader, the hotel porter, explained they were the survivors of a German U-boat sunk that same day off the Oranese coast near Nemours.) The first shot in "Operation Torch" had been fired in the Oran sector.

Ridgway wrote later, "This was what I had been hoping and working for continuously during the previous 540 days."[430]

Sleep did not come quickly. The doors were wedged shut, the steel shutters drawn, and the revolvers lay within easy reach.

D-DAY, NOVEMBER 7

Ridgway and Gordon Browne woke to a sunny Mediterranean day and breakfast. Bob Murphy was called and the "all is well" code exchanged. With the help of a large-scale map, Ridgway went over with Gordon the spot where Rebecca was to be set up, giving him the compass bearings and the positions for placing the signal flares. When ignited that night, they would help guide the paratrooper aircraft to the jump zone.

Then he and Gordon set out to a meeting at the Eljani farm with Jean Ducrot, an eager member of the resistance group who had agreed to help Browne. (Ducrot and a small group had volunteered to lay the signal flares on Browne's order.)[431] Browne would pass the day at the farm hideout. At dark, he and Ducrot would wrestle Rebecca to near the drop zone, where Browne would lie up until it was time to activate the device. Ducrot and his helpers would, in the meantime, plant the flares to be ignited on Browne's signal.

Ridgway spent the rest of day doing routine chores, trying to keep a normal bearing. At the Eljani farmhouse, Brunel and Arnaud were already operating the secret wireless set, listening for messages. As evening fell, Ridgway arrived at the farmhouse, where he spent the rest of the evening in a state of nerves, moving between the bedroom wireless and the farm terrace, chatting with Jeanne, Brunel, and Arnaud, and peering into the night sky.

The phone rang. Jeanne answered, spoke for a moment, hung up the phone, and turned to Ridgway with a puzzled look. "Mr. Knight, it was for you. He didn't give his name, and merely asked that I should tell you, 'Robert Franklin would arrive on time at the Oran station.' "

The Torch invasion was on.

It was near midnight when Ducrot's helpers, a very mixed group of young royalists, followers of d'Astier de la Vigerie; and a Lieutenant Galindo, with a band of communist comrades, showed up at the farmhouse. The communists were all ex-Republican fighters from the Spanish Civil War. The six royalist young men were to act as guards while Lt. Galindo directed his followers to plant flares.

Ridgway had Lt. Galindo place the men around the house, hidden in the shrubs some distance from the villa. Jeanne and an ambulance driver prepared two ambulances to take the men to help Ducrot to lay flares near where Browne was positioned. The men were armed and eager to fight when American troops showed up.

Brunel and Arnaud stormed downstairs. They had lost contact with both Gibraltar and Tangier. Even Algiers' wireless was unreachable.

Ridgway paints a picture of the patriot partisan Emilien Arnaud—a man who would face death if caught:

> For hours . . . Arnaud, imperturbable, cool, made a striking picture. In a black business suit with a high stiff collar, he looked the exact opposite of what a clandestine radio operator should look like. Intent on his work, distressed that he was not doing a better professional job, he seemed to care about nothing else. Patient, calm, courageous and thorough, he . . . was the kind of Frenchman who did his job quietly and resisted the Nazis in fact rather than in words.

On the farm terrace, Ridgway could see the light of Oran and the naval base. All was quiet. There was no blackout as there had been the night before. Then the gates creaked open and the gravel crunched, startling Ridgway. Jeanne was back after delivering Ducrot, Lt. Galindo, and his Spaniards to their positions near Browne.

Jeanne had run into trouble: On the way out, at a railroad crossing, she had been stopped by armed sentries. She showed her papers and shuddered, fearing the guards would open the doors of the ambulances, which were crammed full of men. (Fortunately, she showed her twenty-four-hour pass and related how she was on her way to pick up soldiers injured in a car wreck. Her story satisfied the officer in charge.)

Ridgway now decided to drive to a hill above the town of Arzew where he could look out over the gulf and observe the delayed landing force come ashore. Knowing the countryside and the people, Ridgway hoped he might be of some assistance to the Allied troopers.

At that moment, and from the hills above Arzew, a powerfully beamed searchlight could have lit up the Allied assault forces lying silently offshore.

At the farmhouse, and still unable to raise Gibraltar, Arnaud left the villa and returned home. The next morning he would try to use his ham radio equipment to jam military broadcasts. No one knew that communications between Algiers, Gibraltar, and the Allied air command in England had failed. The paratrooper air command in England never received Ridgway's warnings that the insurgents had cold feet; that the French were ready to fight at the drop zones, and at Oran, Algiers, and Casablanca.

But Gordon Browne knew nothing of this. He expected to be able to guide the paratrooper air formations to their targets. In darkness, Browne wrestled Rebecca into an open field where he struggled to erect her antenna and wires. He finally switched the lady on. It worked. Rebecca began emitting a signal. Browne now settled in to wait for the sound of approaching American aircraft formations—the first-ever American paratrooper assault on foreign soil. He waited and waited.

At St. Eval and Predannack, England, thirty-nine C-47 transport planes loaded with eager, highly trained but untried airborne paratroopers had delayed a formation takeoff for Algeria. They would be some four hours late if they made it—believing they could deliver their soldiers in daylight without resistance.

The troopers flew from English airfields in the late evening of November 7. Crammed into overloaded C-47 ships, flying at 10,000 feet and for some 1,100 miles across neutral Spain in the dark of night, their loads of freezing men were jammed into bucket seats for almost nine hours. The weather was frightful, their navigation equipment and their running lights were faulty, which interfered with the pilots' ability to maintain contact. In bad weather the formations broke apart. Inexperienced pilots lost their bearings. The C-47s ran low on fuel. Many aborted, landing at Gibraltar, Spanish Morocco (where their troopers were interned), and near Fez in French Morocco.

A few minutes after dawn Browne heard the sound of gunfire echoing in the distance: The Allies must be landing somewhere nearby. But where were the paratroopers? The sound of gunfire grew louder. The French were resisting. Browne dragged Rebecca a few yards into the brush, flipped a switch, ran like hell, and watched the lady blow into pieces.

★ ★ ★

OFF THE BARBARY COAST[432]

Aboard blacked-out Royal Navy (RN) headquarters ships, John Knox and Leland Rounds must have wondered what the morning of November 8 held for them as they slipped silently past the Pillars of Hercules.

Knox, aboard HMS *Bulolo*, had drawn the assignment of guiding U.S. Major General Charles W. Ryder, who was commanding the 34th Infantry Division—and destined to take and hold the city of Algiers. Ryder was a Kansan like Ike, and had been with Eisenhower, now his commander in chief, at West Point. Rounds, aboard HMS *Largs*, was assigned to guide Major General Lloyd R. Fredendall, commanding the Allied Central Task Force destined to take and hold the region around Oran. The two vice-consuls had been together at Norfolk House in England to help with the Torch planning. They were at sea for thirteen days when their ships approached the Algerian coast.

From Hampton Roads, Virginia, vice-consul Frederic P. "Teddy" Culbert boarded the U.S. Task Force flagship USS *Augusta*, where he met Gen. George S. Patton commanding the troops that would attack Casablanca and Fedhala. Culbert was an old seaman, a graduate of Annapolis, and a decorated hero of World War I. He found a home away from home on *Augusta*— and may even have been amused at the discomfort of his new boss, the foul-mouthed Patton. Everywhere around him, Culbert could see and smell the outrage of three weeks at sea in bad weather. The rolling and pitching ship's motion turned many officers' and men's stomachs to jelly, leaving them seasick everywhere, and jammed into the smallest corners of the ship.

Aboard *Augusta*, the lucky Culbert was given flagship quarters and soon became one of Patton's favorite officers.[433]

Like Culbert, Knox was already experienced in combat, fluent in French and the ways of North Africa. Ryder, tough soldier that he was, spoke no French, knew nothing about the politics of Torch, and was happy to have Knox beside him. Knox's official title for this operation was deputy civil administrator to the supreme commander, Gen. Eisenhower. Leland had the same orders: stick close to Fredendall. For the next few days Rounds was to wrestle with the temperamental general, who knew it all and had an ego the size of a warship. Eisenhower would later dismiss him from the field of battle.[434]

Both Knox and Rounds were destined to serve in "Reservist"—a combined U.S.–British forces attack on Algerian coast targets. Knox was with the Algiers assault forces, and Rounds was with the assault forces that attacked at Oran and nearby Arzew.

Mildly seasick, Leland Rounds paced the decks of HMS *Largs*; worrying about Ridgway, about the French Resistance, and how the British-designed "Reservist" would play out. Rounds knew that if the French resisted, and he believed they would, French and American blood would be shed. Unlike the English-based paratrooper air command, Rounds's command knew of Ridgway Knight's warnings.

Rounds went over and over his secret (British: "MOST SECRET") copy No. 13 of the task force's "S. O. Operations Instructions."[435] He had fought in France in World War I, and he knew how bloody the English could be about committing troops. Did he shudder when he realized he was issued Copy No. 13—an unlucky number at the Western Front in 1914–1918?

He did carry, in a pouch strapped to his body, a letter from Allied Headquarters stating that he was a civilian noncombatant and had the right of protection under the Geneva Convention of July 27, 1929. Also stuffed in his pocket was an unpaid HMS *Largs* wardroom mess bill for £4-2: Minerals and Tobacco, £2-2; and Laundry of Sheets, £2-0.[436]

Aboard HMS *Bulolo*, far from Leland Rounds's HMS *Largs*, John Knox approached the Algiers coast on the same trajectory taken by the French when they sailed in 1830 from France to storm Algiers. Knox says even experienced troopers fell ill. The weather and seas had been frightful, the voyage too long and arduous, and it played havoc with one's guts. The untried National Guardsmen from Minnesota, via a cold and wet England, turned a shade of green as they fought off seasickness, crammed in the stinking holds of the bobbing, churning troopships. Some had written home: "The British . . . feed us stuff a hog wouldn't eat." Another: ". . . I hate myself and hate this life and I am sick of it all."[437]

John Knox managed by sipping gin with fellow officers in the officers' mess. It was served in lieu of drinking water.

As H Hour approached, a great red ball of sun rose above the city of Algiers. Knox may have seen the outline of the hills above the city—and discerned the area where Daphne lay asleep.[438]

A few miles away, awake now in her street-level apartment, Daphne made breakfast for her mother and children—and two Scots White Fathers, novice missionaries. They had dropped by a few days earlier to seek her help for an escape to England. Daphne kept them at the house, where they slept on the floor.

It was too late to go anywhere. John Boyd had warned Daphne the day before D-Day to expect the Torch landings at Algiers. This meant that Knox would come home soon. But her little family was prepared for the worst. Before Knox left for England, he arranged a hiding place for "his" family—and gold sovereigns—just in case.

Later, when she became Mrs. John Crawford Knox, Daphne wrote: "Life without him was unthinkable. I must never allow myself the possibility of thinking . . . or I would lose control of myself."

THE ALGIERS RESISTANCE MOVEMENT

The coup d'état in Algiers called for Col. Jousse and Henri d'Astier de la Vigerie to cripple or seize strategic targets and vital nerve centers in Algiers: the telephone and wireless exchanges, the Algiers radio station, police headquarters, and the post office. Their partisans were also assigned to hold senior civilian and army and naval officers, military garrisons, and units that might hinder the Allied invaders.

But they hadn't reckoned on the shortage of fuel and transportation to move their men. More serious still was that the conspirators never learned that the French navy kept a vital link open directly to France—a teletype line to naval headquarters in Vichy.

The most cohesive insurgent group—pro–de Gaulle resistance fighters—was led by a Jewish physician, Dr. Henri Aboulker, and his sons. The family had had the ingenuity to organize 200 Jewish fighters named the "Geo Gras," from the name of the gym in which they exercised.

Dr. Aboulker, his wife Colette, and sons Raphael and Stéphane, along with thirty-six-year-old Captain Alfred Pillafort, were a dedicated anti-Nazi force to be reckoned with. Pillafort could have been cast from a war novel. A graduate of Saint-Cyr, like John Knox he had fought in the Moroccan Riff wars and was decorated with the *Légion d'Honneur*. In 1940 he had seen action as a commando behind German lines on the Belgian border at the outbreak of the Nazi invasion. When France surrendered, he had fled to Algiers and joined the Aboulker partisans. Pillafort would play a heroic and tragic role in the insurrection.

Robert Murphy had been reporting that Col. Jousse and d'Astier de la Vigerie probably commanded around 800 resistance fighters, affiliated in one way or another—including a group from the *Chantiers de la Jeunesse*. Barely 500 would show up on D-Day, mostly from the Aboulker and Pillafort units.

They were inadequately armed. Just as in Oran, none of the promised British light weapons and Bren guns had been delivered. Against this squad of amateur soldiers stood the Algiers garrison of the XIX Division, the Vichy *Gardes Mobiles*—some 11,000 troops—and the police.[439]

TANGIER AND CASABLANCA[440]

Stafford Reid had been briefed by Bill Eddy at Tangier before he left to join the Eisenhower staff at Gibraltar. Eddy assigned Staff a simple—yet arduous and dangerous—job: At all costs Staff was to keep a communications link going between Casablanca and the Rock during combat operations—from the eve of D-Day to relief at Casablanca by U.S. troops. If the landings failed, Reid and King were to destroy their signal equipment and the contents of the consulate safes and try to escape.

Reid's work was of paramount importance. He would flash messages to Tangier and Gibraltar, Eisenhower's headquarters, with news from Gen. Béthouart and the progress of King's resistance groups in seizing strategic locations. He was to be the only link for outgoing and incoming traffic to and from Morocco.

By mid-October, Reid and his loyal operator, "Ajax," had improved transmission quality from the consulate building in Casablanca to Tangier and the Rock. And with new equipment from OSS and Eddy, they had set up emergency transmitters at secret locations. (Ajax was still ignorant of the date for D-Day, but guessed something terribly important was about to happen.)

One transmitter went up thanks to a "fighting patriot Israelite" ready to join up to free his city. It was located above the man's apartment on the roof of his building, inside an abandoned chicken coop—just 200 yards from the main harbor and near the anchorage of the French flagship *Jean Bart*. A second set was put up at a rented house near the Casa rail station.

On the night of November 6, Reid placed one of his trusted agents in front of a conventional shortwave radio set and ordered the man to listen from 6:00 P.M. on to the regular BBC broadcast, or until he heard something like: "Listen Yankee—Midway—Lincoln—Franklin—Pilgrim. Robert Arrives Two Hours Late."

When heard, the man was to rush to the consulate and inform Reid of the message. Ajax, armed with a .45 caliber automatic and two clips of ammunition, a flashlight, and candles, was placed at the roof transmitter at the harbor. He was to expect to receive urgent messages. Two of Reid's most trusted men were standing by on motorcycles to carry messages between Ajax's wireless station and the consulate basement. One, a French patriot, Captain X, was allowed to know that "something very important" would happen soon, when the city would be shut down and all power cut as vice-consul King's agents blew up the city's "power house." Captain X was armed with a .45 and two hand grenades, which he would carry on his motorcycle. He might have to fight his way around a city plunged into darkness.[441]

When Ken Pendar arrived with the letters from President Roosevelt for the Sultan of Morocco and Gen. Nogues, Pendar told Staff that he was to personally deliver the letters the next day. Reid protested: his job was to keep vital radio communications open. Pendar left in a huff. (Later, another consular officer delivered the presidential declarations.)

David King and Staff Reid had never been close. Reid was miffed that King had the "exotic" job, while he was saddled with the routine but tactically important radio assignment. Still, the two vice-consuls agreed on one thing: They would defend the consulate building to the last man. Do or die, they would prevent Vichy forces or the Germans from taking the consulate, the radio transmitters, or getting into the OSS safes.[442]

In the last hours before the Torch landings, Staff Reid stuck to the wireless room at the consulate while Dave King was in and out. No one was getting much sleep. King was acting as the link with Gen. Béthouart, and busy with last-minute "dirty work." His last caper was to arrange for two of his agents to kidnap the pro-Vichy General Lescroux, who Béthouart knew would resist the American landings.

As darkness fell the evening of the 7th, all the blinds of the consulate were drawn. Seen from the outside, the building was enveloped in a complete blackout. Reid and King gathered in the radio room. The windows were open so that any sounds from the streets could be heard. Captain X's messenger arrived with a message from Gibraltar. Reid decoded it and learned that the consulate must be lit up. The flag must be flown.

Three other consular officers had arrived during the evening. They were briefed by Reid about the landings, and they pitched in to place kerosene lanterns at windows around the building. The flag was run up. Then, a consular officer left to deliver President Roosevelt's messages to Rabat, the Moroccan capital. The president's letters would lie around, unopened, unrecognized in the confusion. A little later, Reid remembers,

King had come over from the Consulate annex where he lived. He hardly had time to greet me when I heard a car drive up in front of the building. I recognized the voice of Mr. Russell. He entered the radio room—his face flushed red—in an excited state. "I have just heard from Vice-Consul King, here, of what is going to take place in a few hours . . . you did not inform me! . . . But I know you are a good soldier and obey[ed] orders . . . I want to be of assistance in these tragic hours . . . have you all had supper?"

The group had not eaten for hours. Reid continues: "Mr. Russell went back to his villa some 200 yards from the consulate, and got his wife to prepare sandwiches. Mrs. Russell then arrived carrying a large basket with sandwiches, two Thermos flasks of hot coffee and apples and oranges."

Consul General Russell had taken off his coat and was having a sandwich when a new face appeared in the doorway. It was U.S. consul Jimmie Brooks—incredulous at the scene, "dressed in a dinner coat—a prized expression on his face . . . he burst out, 'What in the hell kind of a midnight party is this? Mr. Russell, I am surprised to see you and your wife engaged in this nocturnal spree. Why the candles? Why the sidearms, and all my desk-pencils with the points broken?'

" 'Sit down, Brooks,' Russell ordered, 'You are about to witness something that you will never experience again in your lifetime. In a few hours from now the shutters of this building will be rattling from bomb explosions. The Americans are coming at daybreak.' "

Brooks, according to Staff Reid, needed a large slug of whiskey. "And we held him in a chair because he wanted to rush to his wife and tell her the news. [Mrs. Brooks] was French, a woman who talked much too freely. We refused to allow the Consul to leave the building."[443]

At home, Reid's unnamed agent never left his radio. He sat, listening intently for the BBC broadcast message. After many cups of black coffee it finally came through—a bit wobbly, fading in and out—but no mistake, there it was, the gravelly voice from London: Robert would arrive.

The man knew somehow it was terribly important. He rushed to Reid's "battle-order room" and blurted out the news.

It was indeed important, and Reid dispatched his messenger with a coded signal for Ajax to transmit to Bill Eddy on the Rock: the BBC message had been heard in Casa. (Reid was ultracautious about his agents. Because the Frenchmen lived in and had families in Casablanca, even years later, Reid would not reveal their identities.)

It was just after midnight, Sunday the 8th of November. Suddenly an agitated and white-faced Captain X rushed to the consulate to announce: "French fascists" were planning to raid the American Consulate within the hour. A few hours later, another desperate messenger stormed into the consulate. He had broken away from Gen. Béthouart's headquarters: planes had strafed military targets and airfields at Rabat, Casablanca, Salé, and Port Lyautey. Ground troops were reported landing at Fedhala and Safi beaches. The general and his immediate staff had been arrested. The messenger believed Béthouart and his men were imprisoned at Meknès. He had heard that Gen. Nogues threatened to shoot Béthouart for treason.

Indeed, the Black Beast had again imprudently contacted Nogues in Rabat and announced that the Allies were about to land. He actually invited his boss to join "the party" and take a lead in the insurrection. Nogues wouldn't hear of it. He telephoned Vice Adm. Michelier at Casablanca and ordered Béthouart and his staff arrested.

Then, the messenger revealed that Gen. Lescroux, whom King had kidnapped, was back on the job. It looked grim. The police were looking for David King, who had been seen with Béthouart. (King was not protected by diplomatic immunity.)

Within minutes, a unit of the French *Gardes Mobiles* took up post in front of the consulate gates. King had brought hand grenades, flares, .45 caliber automatics, and ammunition from the OSS annex to arm the staff. Reid and King were determined to resist. If French police or military forces tried to break through the gates, they would be greeted by hand grenades and burning flares thrown into their midst. The American consular officers were assigned to defensive positions: to windows, the main entrance, and to guard the safes.[444] A few minutes later wireless reception with Tangier and Gibraltar ceased.

Consul General Russell got wind of what Murphy's men were up to. In the midst of the commotion he confronted King and Reid: "Sure we're in a tight spot if the French decide to violate the sovereign property of a United States Government Consulate," he admitted. But Russell insisted he would not allow the building to be turned into a fort. "As commander in chief of this post, I alone will issue orders affecting the safety of Consulate personnel. If we are stormed and resist, none of us, of course, would be alive more than a short time, outnumbered as we would be a thousand to one; our government would then be placed in a very difficult position to prefer charges later if the French could prove that the Consulate was at the same time, an arsenal."[445] Russell ruled that the staff would have to accept capture rather than fire on the French.[446]

Crowds of unruly fascist paramilitary youth began to gather in front of the building mixing with French troopers. Ajax, who was then at the consulate, slipped out of the building via a secret exit to return to the radio transmitter. When he arrived at the harbor he realized that they had been betrayed. The police were everywhere. He slipped away into the night.

It was 4:30 A.M. on D-Day. The hour advanced for Torch forces to hit Casablanca. Nothing seemed to happen.

Some fifteen miles up the coast from the U.S. Consulate in the surf off of Fedhala beach, troopers of the 30th U.S. Infantry Regiment, wearing herringbone twill fatigues with U.S. flag armbands, heavily laden with everything from gas masks to MI rifles and ammo pouches, were meeting disaster as their landing craft struck hidden reefs in the surf. Only a handful of these poorly trained National Guard troopers from small Midwestern towns would ever see home again.[447]

GIBRALTAR: EXCRUCIATING HOURS FOR IKE

Gen. Henri Honoré Giraud, now acting the part of the frustrated noble puppet, arrived on the Rock on November 7. He soon turned into an exasperating dogmatist and thorn in Eisenhower's side as he insisted stiffly to Ike and Mark Clark that he was to become "supreme Allied commander in North Africa" immediately after the Torch landings.

Hearing this, Clark "gasped," and "thought that Ike had never been so shocked and showed it so little. It was rather like a bomb explosion," Clark later wrote. Eisenhower announced he knew nothing about Giraud heading the "Inter-Allied Command." Still, Ike remained friendly and cool, and cautiously told Giraud, ". . . there must be some misunderstanding."[448]

In fact, Eisenhower took an immediate liking to the man and his energy, commitment, and grasp of things. But Giraud hung onto his illusions of grandeur. It took "excruciating" hours of torturous discussion for Ike and Clark, Eisenhower using the carrot and Clark the stick, to convince Giraud how the command of the Allied Expeditionary Force must rest in American hands, and, more specifically, Ike's.

Giraud was angry, Giraud was disinterested, and Giraud was shocked—knowing finally that he had been duped by the clever Lemaigre Dubreuil. (He had been; and often by omissions of the truth from the Frenchman and Robert Murphy.)[449] Eisenhower never intended to turn over the supreme command of Allied troops—even once they were securely on the ground—to Giraud. Ike the shrewd poker player suspected Giraud was bluffing. He would wait the man out but not without some rather frustrated comments to his aide, Harry Butcher: "What I need around here is a good assassin," he said at one point. Ike had no intention of fighting with the heroic Frenchman. He patiently, as only Ike could, convinced Giraud to accept to the role of commander in chief of all French forces and governor of North Africa.

The two men shook hands, but the dispute had delayed Giraud's flight to Algiers, where Lemaigre Dubreuil was anxiously waiting for his man.[450]

The next evening Eisenhower wrote to Marshall in Washington, a prophetic few words of how things stood with the French: "I am so impatient to get eastward and seize the ground in the Tunisia area that I find myself getting absolutely furious with these stupid frogs."[451]

Eisenhower suspected that Robert Murphy—pacing around in Algiers with a "big and little case of the jitters" as he waited for the troops to land—had been mistaken about Gen. Giraud's power with the French high command. It seemed "none of Murphy's elaborate schemes were getting off the ground." He knew by now that at Oran, Tostain had changed his mind and that Béthouart was a prisoner. A lot was going wrong all over North Africa.[452]

11

LANDINGS—DARLAN BECOMES THE U.S. NOBLE PUPPET

IN ALGIERS AS H HOUR of D-Day approached, nothing seemed to be going as planned. Gen. Giraud hadn't shown up and Gen. Mast had disappeared—unreachable when Robert Murphy needed him. Then, only a fraction of the partisan young men expected to fight Vichy forces had answered the call to mobilize.

Murphy and Consul General Felix Cole, together with the leaders of the Group of Five, and vice-consuls Springs, Pendar, Woodruff, and Boyd held a war council at the spacious and central Algiers apartment of Dr. Henri Aboulker—now the headquarters for the uprising. Murphy selected John Boyd to remain at the headquarters permanently and manage the operation as his spokesman. The other vice-consuls were to stand by to go to the landing beaches when the time came. A U.S. wireless set had been installed there a few days earlier by Joe Raichle, an OSS expert now working with Murphy. (Another secret radio transmitter was hidden elsewhere in town.) And present, too, were Henri d'Astier de la Vigerie, Abbé Cordier ("Necktie"), and Col. Jousse, who went about making final arrangements to paralyze the city until the Allies arrived.

A little before midnight, a hapless police officer came to the door of the Aboulker apartment to investigate a tip that something strange was going on. A gun was put to his head and he was locked away for the rest of the evening.

Proudly dressed in full uniform, with decorations, Jousse distributed armbands bearing an official seal for the conspirators to wear, inscribed with the words V.P.—VOLONTAIRES DE LA PLACE. The young partisans were given code words with which to greet their American liberators: for example, *whiskey* should be met with the response, *soda*.

Sometime after midnight Ken Pendar picked up the BBC announcement signaling that the landings were on. He rushed to Robert Murphy's side, "a smile on his cracked lips, the corners of his eyes pink from lack of sleep: 'Bob,' he cleared his throat, 'the BBC says Robert will arrive on time.' "[453]

D'Astier and Cordier now dispatched the leaders of their (shrinking) forces to seize key points in Algiers. Groups of partisans sneaked through tunnels under the city that Barbary pirates had once used. They were equipped with maps showing where to cut vital telephone and cable lines. Suddenly all telephone service in and out of Algiers went dead. Here and there small groups of partisans seized the main post office (which controlled the telegraph lines) and power stations. It was hoped that many of the officials at these locations would rally to the coup d'état; if not, they would be held in custody. A crucial target was the Algiers radio broadcasting station where, if plans had worked out, Gen. Giraud was to broadcast a message to the people of North Africa.

Abbé Cordier left the Aboulker apartment with partisans to cut the lines at the French army telephone exchange, and returned a few minutes later to say that a German shepherd dog and handler were preventing him from accessing the phone lines. Dr. Aboulker gave "Necktie" a dose of poison wrapped in meat. (History does not record if the dog handler joined the partisans.)

Vice-consuls Boyd, Woodruff, and a consular officer, Dick Laroux (who had just arrived in Algiers) led a group of conspirators to the landing beaches. They would act as guides to senior American officers—who again were to be greeted with the code word *whiskey*; answer, *soda*.

Later, Murphy, Jousse, and d'Astier de la Vigerie joined Jacques Lemaigre Dubreuil at a nearby apartment. It was agreed that Murphy must arrange to see Gen. Juin, commander in chief of all Vichy ground forces in North Africa, to convince him to issue a general ceasefire. Col. Jean Chrétien was located and agreed to arrange a meeting for Murphy at Juin's villa.

Lemaigre Dubreuil then prepared to go to the Blida airfield, forty miles from Algiers, where he expected to greet Gen. Giraud who was flying in from Gibraltar. (Unbeknownst to Murphy, Lemaigre Dubreuil would return hours later without Giraud. The general would not arrive for twenty-four hours, and in the middle of the fighting around Algiers. With no fanfare he slipped from the airport unrecognized and hid at Lemaigre Dubreuil's house. He and Lemaigre Dubreuil now understood that Darlan had the upper hand. All the months of work with Robert Murphy had come to naught. And Lemaigre Dubreuil's scheme to become the North African power broker was quashed.)

As nearly 100,000 U.S. and British soldiers, sailors, and marines prepared to hit the beaches of Algeria and Morocco, Bob Murphy sped off with Col. Chrétien in the officer's official limousine, followed by Ken Pendar and a bodyguard supplied by Jousse in Murphy's ever-handy Buick automobile. They reached Gen. Juin's Villa des Oliviers high above the city at El Biar, and were waved through the sentry posts by huge black Senegalese guards. Pendar and the partisans waited in the villa's garden while Murphy and Chrétien bounded up the villa stairs to see Juin.[454]

It was nearing 0100 hours and Murphy had no word of the Allied assault forces, no sounds of battle.

Chrétien did not want to disturb the sleeping Juin. Murphy describes the moment after convincing a servant to wake the general:

"[Juin] came to the drawing room in pink-striped pajamas, tousled and sleepy, but my news snapped him wide awake. I told him, as calmly as I could, that an American expeditionary force of half a million men was about to land all along the coasts of French North Africa. According to my instructions, I multiplied the size of the expedition and made no mention of its British components."

Murphy was to use all his powers of persuasion that night. He continued:

"I wish to tell you about this in advance, because our talks over the years have convinced me that you desire above all else to see the liberation of France, which can come about only through cooperation with the United States."

Juin was taken aback. "What? You mean that the convoys yesterday in the Mediterranean are not going to Malta but will land here? . . . You told me only a week ago that the United States would not attack us!"

It was true. Murphy had deceived the man, a friend of America. But he assured Juin that the American expeditionary force was not coming to attack the French, but was coming at French invitation to cooperate in the liberation of France.

Juin asked, "Who gave this invitation?"

Murphy replied, "General Giraud . . . and we expected him momentarily."

Juin then began to walk agitatedly up and down, stopping now and then to express vehement regrets that he had not been consulted sooner. After a few more minutes of floor pacing, Juin said, "If the matter were entirely in my hands, I would be with you. But, as you know, Darlan is in Algiers. He outranks me and no matter what decision I might make, Darlan could immediately overrule it."

Murphy didn't hesitate, "Very well, let us talk with Darlan."[455]

Bob Murphy then alerted Ken Pendar, who was asleep in his Buick, and asked him to fetch Adm. Darlan.[456]

COMIC OPERA AT THE VILLA DES OLIVIERS

Now began a series of comic missteps:

Adm. Darlan entered the Juin villa with his chief of staff, Adm. Jean-Louis Battet. Jousse's bodyguards, who had accompanied Pendar, had swelled in ranks to include forty young partisans, led by Lt. Bernard Pauphilet. They took over the villa by convincing Juin's Senegalese guards they were relieved of duty.

Inside the villa, this switch went unnoticed for the moment.

Nineteen months had passed since Darlan and Murphy had met face-to-face. The admiral listened intently as Murphy announced the Torch landings and repeated his earlier pleas to Juin. But the Anglophobic Darlan, at sixty-one, a tough, Napoleonic-like character—and about the same size as the former French emperor—became furious. His face became the purple of a ripe eggplant, and he shouted at Murphy: "It is another one of the filthy tricks you Anglo-Saxons have abused us with for two years . . . I have orders from the Marshal! I will execute them! Since you want to fight, we will fight." Darlan turned the screw: "I have known for a long time that the British are stupid, but I have always believed that Americans are more intelligent. Apparently, you have the same genius as the British for making massive blunders."[457]

In fact, the feisty little admiral, whom the Americans called "Popeye," did not know if Murphy was bluffing. Darlan wondered if the Allied action were merely a series of commando raids by British-Gaullist units—which would trigger a massive German response.

Darlan needed time. If this were a serious and massive Allied invasion, what would be the consequence for France? Would the Germans now attack North Africa? Would they seize Pétain and invade the unoccupied zone of southern France? What would become of the French fleet at Toulon?

He stalled, telling Murphy and Juin: "I have given my oath to Pétain . . . I cannot revoke that now. This premature action is not at all what we have been hoping for." Murphy shot back: "French blood will be shed by senseless resistance to the American landings already in progress."[458]

Following this damning statement, Darlan and Juin fell silent. Finally, after whispered consultation, they told Murphy that they could cooperate only with the approval of Marshal Pétain at Vichy. Darlan then drafted a message to be wired to Vichy from the headquarters of the French Admiralty located a few minutes away on the Algiers waterfront. Murphy, tense from the drama and lack of sleep, was beginning to wilt.

At this point, Darlan needed some air, and he stepped out to the villa garden. He was bowled over by what he found: Juin's home was now surrounded by irregular partisans wearing the Jousse VP armbands. He rushed to Murphy inside: "Are we prisoners?"

Murphy was aghast. He knew nothing of Col. Jousse's action or how Lt. Bernard Pauphilet had brought in a platoon of young partisans to take Juin's villa. (Among the young men was a twenty-year-old patriot, Fernand Bonnier de la Chapelle, who would alter history in four weeks' time.)

It was all very upsetting to Murphy. Pauphilet refused to allow anyone but U.S. consular officers to leave the property.

Chrétien now further embarrassed Murphy with, "If these fellows are your friends, they are behaving in a most disgusting way."

Darlan was outraged. He and Murphy paced back and forth across the villa's reception rooms. Murphy insisted that he knew nothing about the seizure of the villa. He again explained the Giraud deal; he persuaded, cajoled, and insisted that this was the moment "to strike an effective blow for the liberation of France; American and French blood must be spared."[459]

The pair must have made a strange if not comic sight: the little admiral puffing on his pipe, fiddling with his tobacco pouch, glancing up at Murphy—barely reaching Murphy's shoulder—and finally agreeing that Ken Pendar could go to the Admiralty to dispatch Darlan's draft cable to Pétain.

Pendar rushed off in Murphy's 1936 Buick. He drove straight to the Aboulker apartment, where Boyd and d'Astier steamed open Darlan's sealed envelope. They were not surprised to read that the wily admiral's handwritten message only assured Pétain that he would defend the Empire. (The message was never delivered to the Admiralty.)

When Ken Pendar returned to the Juin villa, he found Adm. Fenard consulting with Darlan. The sly Fenard suspected that the message had been diverted. He quizzed Ken Pendar about its delivery to the Admiralty. True to form, Pendar told Fenard, "The necessary has been done . . ."

Murphy was beyond being anxious. There was no news of the landings anywhere. It was now 0330 hours.

While Murphy was wringing his hands and hoping to convince Darlan, Juin, and Fenard, at Cape Matifou French cannoneers were firing 7 1/2-inch guns trying to sink Allied warships and transports lying offshore. And since 0200 hours U.S. and British assault teams had been landing on beaches twelve miles east of Algiers. To the west, at Sidi Ferruch, fifteen miles from Murphy and the Juin villa, commando units were moving inland.

But Algiers was not yet to be relieved. In the hours that followed, the assault force became hopelessly lost. Often, tough French troopers and Legionnaires halted the Allied advance on Algiers.

This "orgy of disorder" would rage around Algiers and Oran for the hours to come. And in Morocco the next three days would bring what Gen. George S. Patton called "moments of blood and steel."[460]

Those tense hours, as Murphy desperately waited for some sign that American troops had arrived in force, were engraved in his psyche.

"The hours dragged on . . . and still no word came . . . I had gotten very little sleep [for many days] and I hazily began to wonder if I had made the terrible mistake of starting things a day early . . . something had gone wrong."[461]

Darlan and Murphy spent what was left of the night of Sunday–Monday, November 8–9 together.

"I was becoming more tense . . . Darlan became more relaxed. We sat down and had a dispassionate discussion of the possibilities before us now . . . I told him [Darlan] the entire story of how we had arranged matters with Giraud. [Darlan countered] . . . shook his head, saying positively, 'Giraud is not your man. Politically he is a child. He is just a good divisional commander, nothing more.' Unfortunately, that analysis proved correct."

It was nearing 6:30 A.M. Four hours after H Hour, when American troops were due, suddenly, Murphy recalls, "we heard excited voices outside . . . our underground helpers had been overpowered by a group of state police, *Gardes Mobiles*. I went out into the garden just as fifty *Gardes Mobiles* equipped with submachine guns rushed the place. I was brusquely taken into custody, with a tommy gun poked in my back, and unceremoniously hustled together with Pendar into a small pavilion which served as a guardhouse. It was guarded by Senegalese soldiers and one of them, not doubting that we were to be shot, offered me a *Gitane* cigarette."[462]

(The French soldiers of the *Gardes Mobiles* said later that in the confusion of the moment, they thought that Murphy and Pendar were Germans.)

It must have tickled "Popeye" that now the tables were turned. Darlan ordered a guard to take Ken Pendar to the Admiralty with a new message for Pétain. Then a few minutes later, Darlan and Juin left the villa for a meeting at French military headquarters at Fort Lempereur. Now in command, Darlan would to try to unravel the events of the night.

At dawn, Adm. Fenard had Murphy freed and brought to him. Dejected, worn thin by the comedy and drama, Murphy was unable to unwind. He and Fenard went over and over the embarrassing situation. Finally, Ken Pendar and Harry Woodruff arrived from Felix Cole's villa with a bottle of Scotch whiskey for Murphy, a change of clothes, and a shaving kit.[463]

Over Monday morning's breakfast and a drink, Murphy ventured to Fenard that by now Marshal Pétain must have received the message from President Roosevelt; the BBC must have by now broadcast his voice and a French translation of his message. Murphy revealed to Fenard that leaflets bearing the president's printed words would soon be dropped all over North Africa.

The two men expressed the hope that a positive word would arrive from the old marshal at Vichy. But unbeknownst to Murphy (and to Darlan at the time), a secret message had earlier been sent from Algiers to Vichy, alerting French naval headquarters. Vichy knew hours earlier that an invasion was on. Pétain would soon order French forces to fight.

Earlier that same morning, off "Beer Beach" west of Algiers, HMS *Bulolo* snuck close to shore. Gen. Charles W. Ryder and vice-consul John Knox hauled themselves down a landing net and into a small craft alongside the ship. The navy coxswain headed for the beach, with Knox guiding him to an area where he had been swimming with Daphne and her children just a few weeks before. The sea was calm and the small boat got stuck on a sandbank. Ryder and Knox jumped into the water. They swam and trudged to a beach command post with Ryder's staff in tow.

Suddenly, out of the blue of a splendid Algerian morning, Gen. Charles Mast appeared on the same beach with his staff. Murphy may have failed to find Mast, but the French general had found Ryder and Knox. General Mast immediately informed Ryder, through Knox, that a large and substantial beachhead, under Mast's command, was open to the Americans.

The Beer Beach command post was known to Murphy and to his vice-consuls. A short while later Knox's friend and companion for the past eighteen months, John Boyd, left his command post at the Algiers apartment of Dr. Henri Aboulker. Boyd sought to find American troops at Beer Beach when he ran into Ryder, Mast, and Knox. He bore important news for Gen. Ryder: Adm. Darlan was in Algiers and in command. Shortly, Ken Pendar and Harry Woodruff arrived in a consular car. The four vice-consuls had a quick reunion, and then Knox took his colleagues to Ryder's side.

Pendar ask Ryder pointedly if he would be willing to discuss terms of a ceasefire or a truce. "The General drew up his long, lanky cavalryman's body, almost buckling with fatigue, increased by anxiety: 'Where and with whom?' he asked."[464] Pendar told the general he had come with Murphy's authorization and at the expressed request of Gen. Juin.[465]

In the meantime, HMS *Bulolo* turned around at sea and headed for the port of Algiers. The ship's next mission was to crash the port's protective barriers and land commandos ashore.

★ ★ ★

AT A RAILROAD SIDING near Munich, Adolf Hitler, on his way to a reunion at his old Munich beer-hall haunt, was awakened from a deep and drug-induced sleep on the morning of November 9. The German general staff knew that Allied convoys had slipped through Gibraltar, but Hitler was startled at the news of the landings in North Africa. Despite Rommel's losses that very week, Hitler ordered the general staff to fight to the last man in Tunisia—the "cornerstone of our conduct of the war on the southern flank of Europe."[466] In the coming hours a furious Adolf Hitler would order the occupation of all of southern France and the seizure of the French fleet at Toulon. German forces from Greece and Italy moved into Tunisia to support Rommel's Afrika Korps. With that decision, Hitler condemned over a million Axis and Allied souls to a useless eighteen-month fight in Libya and Tunisia.

★ ★ ★

DARLAN WAS RIGHT to be worried. His freedom restored, the admiral took control.

At French military headquarters and at the Villa des Oliviers, the sounds of war could be heard. French shore batteries had zeroed in on the Allied force transports and the landing assault boats. At Algiers harbor, two Royal Navy destroyers, *Broke* and *Malcolm*, were trying to crash through naval boons and enter the Algiers harbor to land commandos. Darlan and Juin now knew something very big was going on. Reports from Morocco confirmed the extent of the Torch operation. Indeed, by early Monday—a clear and splendid day in Morocco and Algeria—Allied naval, air, and ground forces were gaining footholds at Algiers, Oran, and Arzew. For the next three days in Morocco, American and British soldiers, sailors, and airmen would slug it out with French forces: beefed up legionnaires and native African and Vietnamese troops. From Mehedia-Port Lyautey and Safi on the Atlantic coast to Fedhala and Casablanca on the Mediterranean coast, desperate sea, air, and land battles would rage day and night.

For most of the day Darlan and Juin desperately tried to communicate with Vichy, and in Morocco with Gen. Nogues, Adm. François Michelier, and other commanders. Darlan was able to exchange information in a private code with his trusted friend Adm. Paul Auphan at Vichy. He knew that Pétain, at the very least, wanted a show of resistance, and men around him—the pro-Nazi Pierre Laval, for instance, who waged the future of France on a German victory and would be tried, convicted of treason, and shot when de Gaulle came to power—wanted a German occupation of all North Africa.

By the afternoon, Darlan had made up his mind to arrange a ceasefire. He returned to Juin's villa and requested Murphy to take his official chauffeur-driven automobile, bearing one French flag and one white flag of truce, and drive through the advancing American lines to meet with Gen. Ryder, reported to be on a beach about ten miles west of Algiers.

The prospect for action must have stirred Bob Murphy. He wrote twenty-two years later:

> There was [now] brisk small-arms fire in front of the house [villa].
> I made a quick reconnaissance down the street and saw a platoon
> of American soldiers hugging the wall and firing as they advanced

in our direction. With the white flag prominently displayed on the front fender of our car, we moved cautiously in their direction. They stopped firing and waited. I came up to them, introduced myself, maintained a respectful distance as ordered by the young lieutenant in command, and shouted an explanation . . . The lieutenant asked me to repeat the story slowly. Then, apparently convinced it was not a ruse, he allowed me to walk up to him. I asked his name and he replied, 'Lieutenant Gieser.' I could not help a smile and the remark, 'You are the best-looking Gieser I have seen in a long time!' That seemed to convince him I was a bona fide American. He detailed one of his men to accompany me and we drove down to the landing beach . . . [There] I met Randolph Churchill [Winston Churchill's son] in a Ranger uniform. He seemed to know about me and said something to the effect that the British diplomatic service could use a few like me. I considered that quite a compliment. He took me to General Ryder [and] I explained quickly the situation at Algiers, the decision of Darlan to ask for a local cease-fire . . . I was ready to drive Ryder at once to French headquarters.

Gen. Ryder was short of transport, and he welcomed Murphy's offer of a lift.

Exhausted, Ryder added, "But I must send a message to Gibraltar and get into a fresh uniform."

Murphy begged the man to hurry. Still, Ryder sat down on a rock to dictate the message to his aide.

It must have been comic. Murphy says the general "took forever to dictate a paragraph. He seemed dazed . . . referring vaguely again to his need for a fresh uniform."

Finally, Ryder sensed Murphy's impatience. "You will have to forgive me," he said. "I haven't slept for a week."

Murphy knew how Ryder felt, because he hadn't slept for several days. ". . . I took him by the arm gently but firmly and we were in the car and on our way to [meet the French at] Fort Lempereur. When we arrived at the fort we found about fifty French officers . . . standing . . . in a large room with Darlan and Juin at the head of a table covered with green baize. Just as we entered the room, one of our American planes came over and dropped a stick of bombs at what seemed a distance of perhaps a hundred yards."

As the bombs exploded, an ecstatic smile spread over Ryder's face. "He stood still and exclaimed, 'How wonderful! This is the first time since World War I that I have been under fire.' "

No one, including Murphy, found that very funny. "An icy French silence followed."[467]

Ryder wore the medals he had won in the Great War on his fatigue jacket. Among them were the French War Cross and the Légion d'Honneur. The tough cavalryman reached out to Gen. Juin, who by now had tears streaming down his craggy face, and clasped him to his heart. In that simple emotional gesture, between men at arms, Ryder sealed a Franco-American bond.[468] The two generals signed a preliminary ceasefire treaty. Looking on, an exhausted Murphy and vice-consuls Knox, Pendar, Boyd, and Woodruff breathed sighs of relief and beamed.

With a ceasefire, French buglers announced the news to lay down French arms. Along Algerian byways, cars and trucks wandered the city with blaring loudspeakers, giving the good news. All resistance stopped in the Algiers area.[469]

To the sound of the bugles, U.S. and British troops entered the city of Algiers to be greeted by crowds of French and Arab bystanders, who packed the roads and streets. Here and there, men, women, and children assembled in little groups, holding out their arms in welcome. Hands held high showed the V-for-victory sign made famous by Winston Churchill. And smiling GIs loaded down with gear entered the town with their helmets filled with Algerian wine.

★ ★ ★

MURPHY DROVE WITH Gen. Ryder to Blida airfield, where Gen. Clark was due to arrive without fanfare from Gibraltar.

The Germans decided otherwise. When Clark landed at 5:00 P.M. that Monday, he was greeted by a flight of German Junkers 88 fighter planes attacking Blida airfield. Clark, Ryder, and Murphy watched in fascination as a German formation flew through heavy antiaircraft fire. Then, British Spitfires attacked—one diving under a Junkers's belly. The German plane was hit, its engines trailing dark smoke. The pilot crashed into the sea.

For Clark, it was a dramatic welcome to the city of Algiers. As Murphy and Ryder traveled with Clark to the deluxe Hotel Saint George, they filled

Clark in on the status of their negotiations with Darlan—and how Giraud seemed less the man of the hour.

After sending a message to Eisenhower, Clark and Murphy secretly met with Giraud in an automobile. The general was lethargic and depressed; he had no enthusiasm to take on Darlan, who was clearly the senior officer. (And perhaps Giraud, for the first time, realized that Lemaigre Dubreuil, the kingmaker, had vastly exaggerated the support he, Giraud, had among senior French officers.) Giraud finally told Clark and Murphy that he was overtaken by events, had not realized the complexities of the political situation in North Africa, and wanted only to fight Germans. He said he would be content to serve under Darlan. He proposed that he be appointed as commander in chief of French forces.

Back at the Hotel Saint George, Clark had Murphy schedule a meeting with Darlan and his senior officers for 9:00 Tuesday morning. The general then ordered his sergeant major to let him sleep.

An eerie darkness fell on the city of Algiers. The night of November 9 was calm.

Many believed it had been a memorable day: The highest-ranking French officers in Africa had personally arranged a local ceasefire and had tentatively promised to arrange similar ceasefires throughout French Africa. But in Morocco, battles still raged; and in nearby Oran, units of the French army and navy fought on. Behind Arzew, east of Oran, a 9,000-strong determined French force fought off U.S. 1st Division troopers around the farm town of St. Could.

Robert Murphy did not then "suspect how deceptive was the outward appearance of calm and success . . . [and] how badly some of our [U.S.] plans had misfired. Nor how close Algiers had come to a disastrous bombardment . . . the situation still remained potentially explosive between Frenchmen and Anglo-Americans throughout Africa."[470]

Indeed, as Darlan moved to accommodate the Americans, "Vichy moved toward appeasing Hitler in a desperate gamble to head off occupation of the free [southern] zone of France."[471]

At the U.S. Consulate General, Murphy learned from Felix Cole that the radio facilities at Gibraltar were jammed up. Urgent messages from London and Washington, and between Algiers and Gibraltar, were left unread or were read hours later. Murphy only hoped that Clark's message had reached Eisenhower. Bob Murphy feared, as did generals Clark and Ryder, that a delay on a general ceasefire at Oran and at Morocco would help the Axis's chances of gaining a foothold in Tunisia.

Darlan now had generous terms for peace in all of North Africa—but the wily admiral decided he had to seek Pétain's approval.

Murphy went another night without sleep. The diplomat among warriors would spend the next eighteen hours negotiating the so-called "Darlan Deal," and making independent decisions. Darlan remained awake, too, never far from his radio link with Vichy. Murphy joined the admiral as the two men tensely expected a message from Pétain. And they listened for news of a German movement south—a violation of the Vichy free zone. If the Germans moved south and tried to seize the fleet at Toulon, it would liberate Darlan from Pétain.

As morning dawned and Darlan prepared to meet Gen. Clark for an armistice conference, he received a message in a secret personal code from his friend in Vichy, Adm. Paul Auphan: . . . SITUATION INTERIOR UNCHANGED . . . PROBABLY NO DECISION WILL BE TAKEN . . . UNTIL CHIEF RETURNS . . . EXPECTED THIS AFTERNOON. SIGNED, GABRIEL.[472]

Adm. Darlan was still bound to Pétain.

★ ★ ★

EARLY TUESDAY MORNING, November 10, a weary and nervous Adm. Darlan arrived at the small foyer meeting room at the Hotel Saint George. Clark, Murphy, and Col. Julius Holmes were already in the room when the French delegation led by Darlan and including generals Juin and Giraud arrived in formal military dress.

Clark was impressed.

Outside, Clark had stationed a platoon of U.S. infantrymen to intimidate the French. He and Murphy adapted a formal air, agreeing that they would be very tough despite the pleasant atmosphere created by peaceful gardens filled with flowers and palm trees.[473]

It was immediately apparent that Darlan, not Giraud, led the delegation. (Clark and Murphy had already decided to deal with Darlan. Eisenhower, in Gibraltar, wanted a speedy armistice to get on with the fighting in Tunisia. Moreover, Ike wanted a ceasefire in Morocco and needed French cooperation to ensure public services and inland security throughout North Africa.)

Murphy, speaking in French for Clark, immediately made "forceful and abrupt" demands for a general ceasefire. He threatened that if by 0930 that very morning, an agreement could not be reached, Clark would order U.S. mortar batteries positioned around the city to destroy French installations— and he would put Darlan, Juin, and the others under arrest. Murphy told the French that Clark would then treat with Giraud.

Darlan was astonished. It was a typically eagle-faced Mark Clark throwing "his weight around."[474] The admiral told Clark that he had wired a summary of armistice terms to Vichy and that he was awaiting an answer. Clark snapped back now, through Holmes, bypassing Murphy: "Pétain is nothing, is nothing in our young lives . . ."

Ill at ease, "Popeye" mopped his balding head with an immaculate white handkerchief.

Clark stood, towering over every person in the room. He pounded the table and raged in army barracks' language.

Darlan argued, "I am not certain the troops will obey."

Clark: "Issue an armistice order now!"

Darlan pleaded, "The Germans will occupy southern France."

Clark roared, "You are under domination! Here is an opportunity for all Frenchmen to rally and win the war. Here is your last chance!"

The admiral asked permission to contact Vichy. Clark refused, and then and there, threatened to arrest Darlan.

Gen. Juin took Clark's threat seriously, and believed that the Americans were ready to turn to Giraud. Juin pleaded with Clark to allow a few minutes' recess.

When they were alone, Juin told Darlan that they risked civil war throughout North Africa. Darlan then wrote out a message for Vichy, telling Pétain that he had accepted an armistice on grounds that the Americans would, otherwise, deal with Giraud.

When Clark returned, Murphy read the message to him. Clark refused to have it sent. "I want orders to the troops," he bellowed.

It was over, at least for the moment. Still, Clark would later rage to Eisenhower that anyone that didn't join in fighting against the Germans were "YB-SOBs" —yellow-bellied sons-of-bitches.[475] (Years later, when Juin and Clark had fought many a battle as allies, Mme. Juin would tell Clark that after her husband met him at the Hotel Saint George, "he came home and said he had been dealing with a big American who does nothing but shout and pound the table.")[476]

Murphy now helped Darlan draft a ceasefire to all French commands. Clark allowed him to say that he was assuming authority in North Africa in the name of the marshal. The French administration would remain in place under Darlan's orders. The admiral and his delegation left for their command post at Fort Lempereur to wire the news.

And in a few hours' time, Marshal Pétain in Vichy would repudiate Darlan.

It would take another forty-eight hours of fighting for Gen. Auguste Nogues in Morocco to agree that enough French and American lives had been lost in the name of French honor.

★ ★ ★

DALLAS WINS THROUGH[477]

The USS *Dallas* came out of the Atlantic sea off the Moroccan coast on that morning of November 10. The ancient two-piper destroyer moved offshore at the mouth of the Sebu River off Port Lyautey. She slowed and then stopped to allow a naval detail to cut the inch-and-a-half wire boom cable, allowing *Dallas* to enter the Sebu. The seas were high and breaking; the ship yawed and pitched as she reached the port's jetties.

René Malevergne, the French pilot whom vice-consul David King had earlier "kidnapped," took the wheel and steered *Dallas* up a tight channel under machine-gun fire from Vichy forces on shore. Malevergne had *Dallas* ram another boom at high speed. Under heavy fire from shore batteries, the pilot steered the ship between sunken craft, driving her at full speed, cutting through mud shallows upriver—a task which most navy men thought could not be done.

Now level with the Port Lyautey airport, *Dallas* completed her mission, launching rubber boats for a detachment of seventy-five U.S. raiders to board. The Ranger team then rowed desperately ashore under fire to secure the airport. Malevergne would be awarded the U.S. Navy Cross for his gallantry under fire.[478]

NOGUES HAS TO FIGHT

At 8:00 A.M. on D-Day, Gen. Patton with Fred Culbert and staff tried to leave the *Augusta* for the Fedhala beaches. They started to board a landing craft rigged on davits at the ship's side, when *Augusta*'s monster batteries roared, and roared on, for three hours, nonstop. They were lucky men—the muzzle blast of *Augusta*'s rear turret blew the waiting landing craft to pieces, destroying Patton's baggage. Patton boasted later that all that survived were the clothes on his back and the famous brace of the ivory-handled pistols he wore at his sides.

Patton made it to Fedhala at about 1:30 P.M. after most of the beachhead resistance had been snuffed out by U.S. dive-bombers and overwhelming ship-to-shore fire.[479]

In London, Churchill exulted, and made his famous public statement about "the beginning of the end . . ." But in secret, the British War Cabinet and Churchill's privileged inner circle were worried about how the United States was shaping the political future of the French African colonies and about the competence of Eisenhower's "political advisers" (read: Robert Murphy). They griped that Murphy and others around Ike believed that Britain was "hated and the U.S. loved"; and how Adm. Darlan was "clinging" to the Americans.[480]

Already on D-Day minus one, the British knew that Darlan was to become Eisenhower's and Murphy's man. Churchill fretted at a War Cabinet meeting about how Gen. de Gaulle and his Free French fitted into all that was happening. Churchill's inner circle worked to get Eisenhower to accept new staff: "people well disposed to us" (the British). Churchill would remark on December 21, "If Darlan faded out and Giraud faded in, de Gaulle's position would be overshadowed; de Gaulle should unite with Giraud."[481]

Anthony Eden made no bones about Darlan: "Let [the] French themselves remove him (Darlan)."[482]

In his early-morning vigil from the heights of Arzew, a distraught and discouraged Ridgway Knight may have seen the only C-47 planes that made it over Tafaraoui and La Sénia airfields west of his position. It would have been a cruel sight: French fighter pilots and eager French antiaircraft gunners tried to down the unarmed, unescorted C-47s. Soon the planes were full of wounded troopers as the pilots, some wounded, too, aborted their drops and crash-landed in a nearby dried swamp. The operation was a disaster. "It contributed nothing to the Torch invasion."[483] Gordon Browne learned of the terrible loss only a week later.

KING DOES IT AGAIN

The Consulate General at Casablanca had been locked down—no one entered or left the main building. Consul General H. Earle Russell, David King, Staff Reid, and all consular officers and staff were prisoners of the French.

Reid could not raise Gibraltar or Tangier on the wireless. Telephone lines had been cut. There were sounds of warplanes dropping bombs all around. Then, a friendly French *Garde Mobile* officer warned David King that Gen. Nogues had ordered all American consular officers and their families loaded onto buses and driven to the French military base at Kasba-Tadla—about 120 miles in the interior.

An hour later and under police escort, American staff members were allowed to go home to collect clothes and toilet articles.

The Swiss Consulate now placed seals on the building; American diplomatic matters would no longer be handled by Consul General Russell, but by the neutral Swiss. Mrs. Russell came again to the main building from her residence at the consulate annex with more sandwiches and coffee.

Late in the evening, the friendly guard slipped Dave King a message. King's agents on the outside were setting up an escape for him that evening. Later still, King told Earle Russell that his contacts had arranged an escape at the moment when American staff would board buses for the trip out of Casablanca.

It was near 8:00 P.M.—time for the motorbuses to arrive.

King and others began pacing up and down in front of the consulate. Soon the *Gardes Mobiles* lost interest. When the huge motorbuses arrived, they created enormous confusion as they tried to enter the gates. In an instant, King slipped around the corner of the building into a darkened side street. He jumped into the open door of a waiting automobile. The car sped toward the seaside resort at Fedhala, where the American assault headquarters was located. The drive was perilous. It turned out that all the roads were guarded; some had been mined.

King spent the night and the next day trying to reach Patton's lines only a few miles away. In the afternoon his agents arranged to bring him French clothes. Dressed as a hospital stretcher-bearer, he drove about in a French ambulance, trying desperately to reach an advancing American unit. Overhead, Grumman fighter planes swooped from the sea to bomb and strafe resisting French units.

Hours earlier, at the American Consulate, Staff Reid and his fellow consular officers finished burning the voluminous U.S. files. The U.S. flag was lowered on the building. In a touching ceremony the Swiss consul general, a Mr. Criblez, accepted the key of the Consulate General from H. Earle Russell. Everyone was either too tired or tense to care.

A few minutes later Russell and his wife, along with Reid and other officers and their wives, boarded the French buses. They drove through the night in the direction of the snowcapped Atlas Mountains—and internment at a hotel in Kasba-Tadla. Staff Reid remembers that as Tuesday morning dawned, his bus passed through a French town where groups of women dressed in black were gathered at the town square. They watched silently, clutching handkerchiefs to their eyes as the American convoy passed. (Reid learned later that the women drying their eyes were newly made widows of French sailors killed by American fire the previous day.)[484]

One day later, a ceasefire would be sounded all over Morocco.

NORTH AFRICA SECURED: D-DAY PLUS FOUR

At 0700 on Wednesday, November 11, as U.S. naval and air units prepared to renew the devastation attacks on Casablanca fortifications, Gen. George Patton received a French flag of truce.

Five hours later, U.S. and French commanders—Gen. Patton, Vice Adm. François Michelier, admirals H. Kent Hewitt and John L. Hall, Jr., and other U.S. and French officers—dined together at a French naval mess. U.S. Signal Corps pictures taken at the luncheon-conference at Fedhala on that Wednesday show an animated group laughing as they no doubt traded battle stories.

Michelier ended this bloody chapter in American-French relations when he shook the hand of Admiral Hewitt—the man he had desperately fought for three days and nights. Michelier said, "I had my orders and did my duty, you had yours and did your duty; now that is over, and we are ready to cooperate."[485]

Algeria and Morocco were finally secured. After three days of sharp and bitter combat, "the traditional friendship between American and French fighting forces was restored—the Allied soldiers, sailors and airmen could now make common cause with their French brothers-in-arms against the Axis powers." Nothing was surrendered. The *tricolore* continued to fly over French property, ships, and units. The French retained their arms and munitions. All prisoners were returned.[486]

Eisenhower and Murphy now wisely promoted cooperation with Adm. Darlan, and with the ex-Vichy French administration. Murphy understood that keeping Algeria and Morocco a secure base of operations was crucial to the war effort, and that only a French administration could keep Jews and the Arab and Berber peoples apart and quiet. The goal was to win a war. That meant winning battles against German and Italian forces in Tunisia.

The road ahead would indeed be long and perilous: At Vichy, Pierre Laval had already bypassed Marshal Pétain and ordered that German troops must be permitted to land at Tunisian airdromes and ports; Arabs and Jews were already rioting in the Jewish quarter of Casablanca; reports of Arabs sniping at U.S. troops and cases of Americans being knifed in the casbah were frequent. Meanwhile, German agents were still paying large sums for Arab support of the Axis.

★ ★ ★

For the next six months American, British, and French armies, with other United Nations forces, would engage Gen. Erwin Rommel's German Afrika Korps and Italian armies. Rommel would be recalled, but the battle would rage on in the Libyan Desert, in Tunisia. Finally, by mid-May 1943, North Africa would be cleared of the Axis. Allied sea and air power would be supreme throughout the southern Mediterranean. The routes to Egypt and the Suez Canal would be secured.

Meanwhile, new landing ships—LSTs, LCTs, and LCIs[487]—carrying men and tanks were being assembled along the Barbary Coast. American and British soldiers, sailors, and marines were being trained for amphibious warfare—a dress rehearsal for the invasion of Sicily and the Italian mainland. Indeed, despite the virulent press attacks against Churchill, Roosevelt, Eisenhower, and Murphy for doing a deal with the so-called *fascist* admiral, "It would have been the height of folly to dislocate [French] authority or injure French prestige and so throw the whole native population into our [the U.S.] lap."[488]

12

DARLAN ASSASSINATED — A DARK SECRET

MOMENTOUS EVENTS LIKE the Darlan deal bring strange turns of fate. The man who should have been the head of a liberated North Africa was the leader of the Free French, Charles de Gaulle, and not Jean-Francois Darlan. Indeed as it turned out everyone felt cheated by Darlan's ascension to power. Almost to a man, the vice-consuls resented that the Vichyites, many of them pro-fascist, still ran Algeria and Morocco. While American and British forces turned to fighting Germans and Italians in Tunisia, the French went on squabbling.

By mid-November, Adm. Darlan had taken charge of French North and West Africa under Gen. Eisenhower, with Murphy as Ike's civil affairs-political adviser.

Leland Rounds and Ridgway Knight had finally hooked up at the Arzew headquarters of Gen. Fredendall, and immediately got into an argument with the stubborn general. Despite their knowledge of the language, the people, and the area, the general insisted on "doing things his way." Among many serious errors, he hired pro-fascists—including a man who had been an agent of the (now long gone) Gestapo chief in Oran, Major Beck. Fredendall used the pro-German opportunist to guarantee security in Oran.

Before leaving for the United States to see Betty and the children, Ridgway called on his friends from his early days at Oran, Henri d'Astier de la Vigerie, now an official under Darlan dealing with the police and intelligence matters, and Abbé Cordier, who headed intelligence at Algiers. Their appointments were arranged by Robert Murphy and Gen. Giraud.

Ridgway found both men "noticeably more cheerful. D'Astier, with his devilish and rather perverted sense of humor, was in one of his devil-may-care moods." Ridgway felt "some kind of action, especially dangerous, was imminent."

D'Astier soon asked his friend, and "in a . . . quizzical wondering tone of voice . . . what would you Americans think if the Comte de Paris appeared on the scene to put an end to the intolerable political situation we now have with Darlan?" D'Astier proposed that the Comte (whom he called "Le Prince") would head a government of all political tendencies—becoming a trustee of the nation and "maintaining neutrality until the day comes when the entire French nation can freely decide for itself."

Ridgway was taken aback.

But what Ridgway did not know was that as they spoke, Henri, Comte de Paris, was actually staying in d'Astier's apartment in Algiers after being brought there secretly from his place of exile in Morocco by Abbé Cordier and a French master sergeant named Sabatier—an instructor at an OSS-SOE camp near Algiers. Strange as it may seem, Sabatier's boss was OSS agent Carleton Coon.

Nor did Knight know, then, that d'Astier had already asked Bob Murphy for the Americans' approval of a royalist coup d'état, supposedly backed by the presidents of the three Algerian *conseils generaux*—pseudo-parliamentary bodies representing the departments of Oran, Algiers, and Constantine. These men had recently signed a joint letter to Darlan, inviting the admiral to resign in favor of a constitutional solution.

Ridgway would leave Algiers, uncertain of the future.

Adm. Darlan ignored the letters and their authors.[489]

But what of the other vice-consuls?

John Utter had been jailed in Tunis for five days after the landings, but managed to escape to Algiers. Utter and Harry Woodruff moved into a lovely villa named Dar-el-Saadia: House of Happiness. Both men now worked with John Boyd on Murphy's staff.

Kenneth Pendar was assigned to the Consulate General at Rabat, Morocco, from where he returned to his beloved villa La Saadia, Marrakech, to manage the secret visits of Gen. Marshall, President Roosevelt, and Prime

Minister Churchill. Pendar arranged for the VIPs to live for a few days at the fabulous villa where he and Frank Canfield had spent time entertaining Moroccan Arab leaders. (To his credit, it must have been a monstrous security and catering job.)

Dave King continued in "the great game." When Vichy officials tried to arrest one of King's agents, a pro-Allied French officer, King had Staff Reid hide the man in Reid's new apartment until he could arrange amnesty for him.

John Knox wound up his affairs and spent time looking after Daphne's family; later he would take Daphne and the two children out of Algeria, where she was still wanted for espionage. Fred Culbert stayed in Casablanca at his magnificently modern top-floor apartment, working for Gen. George S. Patton. He was reputed to give "marvelous parties," hosting the very French officials Patton was trying to kill during the Torch landings.[490]

Most of the German and Italian Armistice Commission officers and Gestapo agents—with the exception of a few captured at the Fedhala U.S. landing site—fled, thanks to help from French officials. And the prostitutes at the Hotel Aletti were delighted to greet the hundreds of American officers, billeted around town and at the hotel—ready to spend American dollars.

Gen. Mark Clark and Robert Murphy believed they had successfully arrived at the best possible solution: Darlan would head the civil and political government.[491]

But if the friends of the Allied powers in North Africa, and de Gaulle's Free French, felt cheated by the Darlan deal, the liberal press in England and the United States (and their correspondents in Algiers) went wild. Neither Clark nor Murphy ever imagined that keeping Darlan (and the Vichy governors) in power would cause such a fuss.

Gen. Eisenhower was "excoriated" in the press. Clark and Murphy were accused of at least "naiveté," with Murphy (because of his relations with Lemaigre Dubreuil, Rigault, and the Group of Five) being singled out as pro-fascist.[492]

Jacques Lemaigre Dubreuil and the Frenchmen that made up the Group of Five were all hurt in some way—despite the fact that Murphy arranged for Darlan to have them appointed to minor roles on Giraud's staff. Lemaigre Dubreuil, ever the passionate politician, now became an open adversary of the way things had been sorted out. From being Murphy's privileged French political consultant, Lemaigre Dubreuil became a moving target for rival

Frenchmen long after the Allied landings were over.[493] Still, for a while at least, he would desperately try to get Giraud to oppose Adm. Darlan.

And as the Darlan deal exploded in the American and British press, and President Roosevelt announced that the accord was a "temporary arrangement . . . a temporary expedient, justified solely by the stress of battle," Lemaigre Dubreuil took heart and tried to get Giraud to refuse to be part of Darlan's government.

In the end, Lemaigre Dubreuil had to pin his hopes that a Comte de Paris-d'Astier coup d'état would depose Darlan and bring Giraud, his man, to the top. As originally conceived, a Giraud government would finally raise the Five from their "lackluster positions" to power.[494] But by then Gen. Giraud had lost confidence in Lemaigre Dubreuil and his political adviser's never-ending machinations. He may have now shared Gen. Charles de Gaulle's view that Lemaigre Dubreuil was "a slippery fellow: always looking to have his palm greased!"[495]

As the days slipped by, it became clear that Adm. Darlan was working in concert and harmoniously with Robert Murphy and Gen. Clark. Gen. Giraud became convinced that he had to cooperate fully with the Allies. Lemaigre Dubreuil's star faded . . . and with that his political leverage ended.

On November 15, Darlan appointed Murphy's close friend, French ambassador Jacques Tarbé de Saint-Hardouin, his secretariat of Foreign Affairs—the only one of the original group to hold a meaningful post. Lemaigre Dubreuil's man, the journalist, Jean Rigault, became a political affairs adviser—controlling police, information, and intelligence. And Henri d'Astier de la Vigerie and Abbé Cordier were given their local police and intelligence jobs.

Mistakenly, Gen. Clark was delighted with the appointments, telling Eisenhower that Darlan had accepted "certain friendly elements" into his government, which "should be favorable to our position."[496] Eventually, Giraud sent Lemaigre Dubreuil to Washington on a mission to negotiate rearming French troops that Giraud would command.[497]

★ ★ ★

WILD BILL STRIKES

William Donovan had packed Algiers, Casablanca, and other North African posts with his OSS men. Now William Eddy set about recruiting Murphy's vice-consuls. Eddy brought King, Reid, Rounds, Utter, and Boyd on board Donovan's OSS team. (He failed to recruit Ridgway Knight.) And Eddy had Carleton Coon moved to Algiers—and to a secret assignment with a British SOE unit. Gordon Browne returned to work among the Arabs and Berbers in the Atlas Riff.

Donovan was deeply troubled by Darlan's appointment. He thought Darlan's association with Gen. Eisenhower and American war plans undermined the moral authority of the United States—for Darlan represented the very forces that had brought about the surrender of France.

A memorandum of December 7, 1942, from Donovan[498] expresses how deeply troubled "Wild Bill" was by the Darlan deal—and the grave consequences he believed would ensue. Wild Bill didn't pull punches with President Roosevelt, Gen. Marshall, and the joint chiefs. The memo stated:

> . . . the identification of Darlan with our operations in North Africa presents difficulties, which cannot be ignored. These difficulties are not changed, whether Darlan foisted himself upon us or was forced upon us by someone else, or whether we made a deal with him on our own.
>
> By whatever means we were placed in this position *we have before us the very practical problem of eliminating the political leadership of Darlan* with its attendant consequences to the French people and to our own successful prosecution of the war [author's italics]. Our great influence with the people of France has been due not only to our strength but to our straight dealing . . . We cannot wait too long to find a solution.
>
> While *it is essential to prevent the concentration of power in Darlan, it may be impossible for us at this time to repudiate him at least until Tunisia has been settled* . . . [author's italics][499]

By mid-November, warnings were coming from Algiers (possibly from Slowikowski) to the British Foreign Office that, "No one expects Darlan to be allowed to end his days in peace. There are too many people that want his blood." And from Switzerland, Donovan received information that Darlan's murder was contemplated.[500]

In London, Darlan had become an albatross around the neck of Churchill's government. Anthony Eden, Churchill's foreign secretary, reported that, "a . . .

telegram came through from Eisenhower announcing an agreement with Darlan. Didn't like it a bit . . ." And later, Eden made no bones about his feelings: "I don't like the text of Darlan-Eisenhower agreement . . ." After talking with Churchill, Eden wrote: "I cannot get W. [Winston Churchill] to see the damage Darlan may do to the Allied cause if we don't watch it. He can make rings, diplomatically, round Eisenhower . . ."[501]

Anthony Eden's reflections and Donovan's thoughts to FDR make it certain that a collective political will existed to end the Darlan affair. It is impossible not to conclude that the Allied powers wanted Darlan eliminated from political power. And at this point no one in London, Washington, Berlin, or in Vichy France had to issue an order, push a button, or ring a bell. All that was needed was a wink, a shrug of the shoulders. There were dozens capable and willing to do the deed.

The stage was set; the actors in place: Camera, action . . .

★ ★ ★

ANATOMY OF A MURDER

Ain Taiya, Cape Mafou, Algeria, Monday, December 14, 1942:

At Algiers, Carleton Coon went to work as the senior OSS-SOE liaison officer at the British training camp for Free French recruits and others located around a group of villas at Ain Taiya, some twelve miles from Algiers. Coon ate and slept in the mess and proudly "wore British battle dress with a blue Corps Franc cap; when I went to Algiers [to visit OSS Algiers officers] I wore civilian clothes. I drove my Studebaker with Consulate d'Amerique plates."[502]

Coon loved the work of teaching communications, explosives, and weapons. A few days after his arrival at Ain Taiya, he gave his young men a demonstration on the use of explosives by blowing up a wrecked landing barge on the beach. He had six French instructors assisting him. The chief instructor was Gilbert Sabatier—the same man who drove the Comte de Paris and Abbé Cordier to the d'Astier apartment in Algiers. Sabatier claimed to be a former French army captain, but was in fact a thirty-five-year-old master sergeant and one of d'Astier de la Vigerie's partisans.

Sabatier did odd clandestine jobs for Henri d'Astier. And he commanded a group of young patriots—all in their twenties, all royalists-de Gaullists, and all d'Astier partisans in the insurrection of November 7–8. They included Fernand Eugene Bonnier de la Chapelle; Mario Faivre; Jean-Bernard d'Astier

(Henri's son); and Roger Rosfelder. They were all issued Colt .45 caliber automatic pistols.[503]

On December 18, the Ain Taiya mission group, or their chief, received "a very strong warning that if they offered any assistance to anti-Darlan elements, or Free French–Gaullists, General Eisenhower would order the removal of the mission."[504]

As Christmas and the new year of 1943 approached, Jacques Lemaigre Dubreuil, now a disappointed office seeker, and Henri d'Astier, still the "brilliant but enigmatic *condottiere*,"[505] and other members of the Group of Five[506] had finalized plans to carry out a new coup d'état. Darlan—the man who stood in the way of Gen. Giraud and power for the d'Astier–Lemaigre Dubreuil inner circle—was to be eliminated.

Many of d'Astier's colleagues and many of the young Catholic partisans of November 7–8 were nostalgic royalists. D'Astier had no difficulty drawing Henri, Comte de Paris (the Orléans-Bourbon pretender to the French throne) into his scheme. Over the years, Henri had dreamed of coming to power as a nonpolitical actor to unite the Empire. He had done his best to have Marshal Pétain appoint him as his successor. In the spring of 1941, with British assistance, the Comte issued a manifesto calling on the French to unite under a royalist banner.[507]

No matter how extraordinary it sounded, it all seemed to fit—at least by d'Astier's, Cordier's, and others' designs.

D'Astier had good reason to believe that if successful, Gen. de Gaulle would unite with Giraud to run a Free French union. His brother, General François d'Astier de la Vigerie, one of Charles de Gaulle's right-hand men, had just visited Algiers with the permission of Winston Churchill and Gen. Eisenhower. François had met Eisenhower, Murphy, and perfunctorily, with a cold eye, Darlan and other senior officials, ostensibly to discuss how de Gaulle might cooperate with Gen. Giraud. In fact, he was in Algiers to promote the de Gaulle Free French cause.

Darlan begged Eisenhower to get François d'Astier out of Algiers. And the Gaullist general did fly out of the city on December 23—but not before leaving over forty thousand dollars in cash with his brother, Henri, for distribution to Gaullists.

In his room at the Hotel Aletti, General François d'Astier told his brother Henri, in so many words, that Darlan had to be eliminated—for there was no hope of getting out from under American control with him in power. The homeland French Resistance risked being taken over by communists because Darlan was so hated in France. Indeed, de Gaulle feared that the Germans would be supplanted one day by Soviets.

MURDER AT THE SUMMER PALACE[508]

The day before Christmas dawned bright and blue in Algiers. By noon, the air had lost its winter chill. Still, the Allied soldiers and sailors, the French and the Arabs bustling about doing last-minute Christmas shopping, needed a sweater or a light coat.

It was about noon that Darlan left his summer palace office high above Algiers for lunch. As he drove home, a pale sun lit the gardens and stately palm trees that lined the palace driveway.

Just before noon that 24th day of December 1942, the young partisan Mario Faivre had settled into a seat at the Café Coq Hardi on rue d'Isly, barely a mile and a half from Darlan's elegant offices. For weeks, Mario had felt he was part of the new endeavor, a coup to defeat the Vichy collaborationists.

But that Christmas Eve day Mario was depressed. For the past few days, he and Jean-Bernard—a fellow partisan of the November 7–8 uprising and son of Henri d'Astier de la Vigerie—had anticipated the death of Darlan, and it hadn't happened.

In truth, Mario, Jean-Bernard, and a small group drawn from the partisans of the November 7–8 insurrection had been selected by Henri d'Astier and Abbé Pierre-Marie Cordier to play minor roles in the assassination of Adm. Darlan. These young men desperately wanted to fight Germans; to be part of the French Resistance now going on in the homeland—in Paris, in Lyon, and in other French cities where Frenchman were finally taking their revenge on *les sales Boches* for occupying their country. They believed Darlan to be a vile Vichy fascist.

Part of Mario's gloominess and sense of hopelessness was due to the fact that the Comte de Paris had left Algiers. Mario knew that the "prince" had been living with the d'Astier family at their apartment on the rue La Fayette, where Mme. d'Astier had seen him through a bout of malaria. And presumably, the Comte attended daily mass said by Abbé Cordier, who still lodged with the family. Now Mario feared that at this late hour, the Cordier plan would not be put into effect.

"I had the impression that it was a fine idea that would have no consequence, an Alexandre Dumas–like concept that would not materialize," he said.[509]

As noon approached, Jean-Bernard d'Astier joined Mario and suggested they go on to the Café de Paris, where he knew that his father, Henri d'Astier, and perhaps Cordier would be having lunch. Mario left his 302 (Peugeot automobile) parked opposite the brasserie in the rue Balay, and the two young men walked to the Paris, close by at the corner of the avenue Pasteur and boulevard Lafferrière. It was while walking that Jean-Bernard broke the news: their fellow partisan, Fernand Bonnier de la Chapelle, was at Darlan's office at the Summer Palace. Jean-Bernard had driven Bonnier there in an auto belonging to his father's office.

By the time the two settled in at the Café de Paris, they expected a telephone call (the d'Astier clan was well known by the café's owners) announcing that Darlan was dead.[510]

Nothing happened. Jean-Bernard's father, Henri d'Astier, came to their table and in a voice for all to hear, declared, "My dear Mario, since you have a car handy, could you do . . . a service? . . . There are no turkeys for the midnight celebration; you would help a lot if you could go and get them." Henri then returned to his table.

This seemed very queer to Mario. He told Jean-Bernard he thought that his father looked "preoccupied," and that the turkey story was a way to be sure that he (Mario) and Jean-Bernard would be available. He wondered to his friend what was going on.

After lunch, as Mario and Jean-Bernard were leaving the café, Abbé Cordier got up from Henri d'Astier's table and went toward the double-door exit.

"It's Bonnier," said Jean-Bernard, who could see out to the street from where he stood. Jean-Bernard then ran out after Cordier, had a few words, and returned to Mario's side. Jean-Bernard reported: "Bonnier couldn't do anything. Cordier wants to see you." (Darlan had not come back from lunch as expected.)

Cordier, still outside the café, seemed troubled and confused. He looked at Mario and explained, "Bonnier is going back to the Summer Palace. He recognized your car and wants you to take him there, but he wants to try out his gun first. He's waiting for you and Jean-Bernard by your car."

Mario and Jean-Bernard then walked to the rue Balay. Mario says all his questions were forgotten. He recalls that:

> Bonnier de la Chapelle was waiting, leaning on my car. Bonnier was a tall, handsome fellow, holding an umbrella. We shook

hands as Jean-Bernard introduced us, and Bonnier said he knew me, as well as my 302 [Peugeot automobile] by sight. We opened the doors to climb in. Across rue Michelet, on the terrace of the [Café] Coq Hardi, five or six of our comrades [d'Astier's partisans] saw us and came over. They all wanted to go with us, but I told them there was no room.

Roger [Rosfelder], another partisan and comrade, shook hands with Bonnier and took a seat with him in the back of the Peugeot. Jean-Bernard got in beside me.

Mario says that as they drove away, some sixty people on the terrace of the Coq Hardi must have watched what had transpired. "Most knew or suspected what we were going to do . . . and . . . that included a few policemen, who had been spying on us for several weeks . . ."

As they continued toward the Hydra section of Algiers, Bonnier was absolutely calm—perfectly at ease. Mario says he acted as if "he might have been going to play tennis." They passed the summer palace and headed toward the park at Hydra, then turned down an empty side road bordering the old golf course. (This was not far from Felix Cole's villa.)

When the car stopped, Bonnier lowered his window. He aimed an enormous revolver (most certainly the SOE-issued .45 caliber pistol) and pulled the trigger. "The first shot failed." A second and third shot went off properly. "Bonnier asked if we had a more reliable weapon." Jean-Bernard took out a Rubis 7.65 naval sidearm that Mario had procured for him. He gave it to Bonnier, who fired several shots. The pistol worked perfectly. Without saying a word, Bonnier put the Rubis into his pocket and gave the big revolver to Jean-Bernard, who put it in the glove compartment.

The four men then drove to Mario's house nearby, where he had two full magazines for the Rubis weapon—and the 7.65 caliber magazines were given to Bonnier.

The group then headed back to the summer palace in complete silence. At the little church square at the summer palace's iron gate, heavily guarded by *Gardes Mobiles*, Mario remembered, "Bonnier got out of the car and told us not to park. He said goodbye and moved toward the gate."

It was 3 o'clock in the afternoon when Darlan returned to his Moorish Summer Palace office accompanied by his aide, Commander Hourcade.

In an adjacent waiting room a young man calling himself Morand had been waiting for half an hour. It was Bonnier de la Chapelle, who had arranged an appointment to see the admiral, as incredible as it may sound, for "personal reasons."

As Darlan approached his office door, with Hourcade following, he heard a noise behind him and turned to see the young man. He must have been face-to-face with the barrel of Bonnier's pistol. Darlan took two shots, one directly in the mouth and the following shot lower into the chest cavity. With the shots ringing in his ears, Hourcade rushed forward as Darlan's body slid to the floor. Bonnier ran to dive through an adjacent window but stopped short—the window was barred from the outside. (Had he been purposely, deceptively briefed?) Bonnier then turned on Hourcade, shooting him in the thigh and the ear.

In a nearby office, Adm. Battet and another officer heard the shots. They rushed into the corridor and ran smack into Bonnier. Battet went to Darlan's side while Bonnier surrendered without firing another shot. As Bonnier was led away Darlan was carried to Battet's car by orderlies and rushed to Maillot hospital. He was x-rayed, and a bullet found in his lung. Madame Darlan arrived as a priest was giving Darlan extreme unction. The surgeons tried in vain to extract the bullet, as they knew it was useless.

François Darlan, Admiral of the French Fleet, Commander in Chief of French Armies and High Commissioner of France—and in the end, friend to the Allied cause, died never speaking a word.

Mario recalls what happened after he left Bonnier:

> Our hearts heavy . . . I dropped Jean-Bernard off at the entrance to the rue La Fayette so that he could bring Cordier up to date; then Roger and I went after the turkeys.
>
> The traffic was heavy as I drove my way among the jeeps, the G.M.C.'s, and the carts. We were in a hurry to be done with this ridiculous inconvenience. When we got to [the depot] we found that there were no more turkeys.

Mario then went to the d'Astier apartment, where he joined Mme. d'Astier and her daughters. No sooner had he arrived then the doorbell rang. It was a breathless Alfred Pose, an important member of the d'Astier plotters, who announced, "Darlan is dead!"

Mario says that, "Madame d'Astier asked me to take her and her daughters to Saint-Augustine Church, to pray." The group headed for the church, but after a few blocks, Mario's car tire went flat and the spare tire was unusable. Mme. d'Astier and her daughters would continue on foot as Mario looked for a garage.

It was dark when Mario returned to the rue La Fayette. Jean-Bernard, Henri d'Astier, and Cordier were there with two or three others. The news had just arrived. Bonnier had been unable to escape through an office window as planned. He was now in the hands of the police, heavily guarded by *Gardes Mobiles* and away from André Achiary's possible help. (Bonnier had been recognized by a friend of his father's, a journalist for the *Echo d'Alger*. By 8:00 P.M., the news of his arrest would leak out.)

Mario tells that "Jean-Bernard and I asked Cordier if Darlan was killed immediately. . . . Later, [Cordier] answered, 'probably in the car transporting him to the Maillot Hospital or very soon afterward on the operating table.' "

The young partisan then inquired as to the whereabouts of Henri, Comte de Paris.

It turned out that on that Christmas Eve, Henri, Comte de Paris was in a drawing room at the Hotel Aletti, declaring to Henri d'Astier that he could not accept being "raised to the presidency of a Council of Empire [an interim republican system with the count serving as chief of government based at Algiers] by illegal methods."

That evening, Henri d'Astier and friends went to see Murphy to propose that he act as an arbitrator between Giraud and the Comte de Paris. They believed that only Murphy could establish a new government headed by the Comte, and in time to save Bonnier.

Later that night, Abbé Cordier came to say that Murphy could not make the decision to appoint the Comte de Paris; Gen. Giraud was being recalled from the Tunisian front and would succeed Darlan. Everyone at the d'Astier apartment speculated: Would Giraud agree to save Bonnier? After all, d'Astier and the Group of Five had brought him to power.

Mario then got Cordier to agree to allow him to go immediately to the OSS-SOE camp at Cape Matifou, and there hopefully raise partisans as volunteers for an eventual attack in force to free Bonnier. He had no luck. Most of the old partisans had left there to fight on the Tunisian front. But he learned that Master-Sergeant Sabatier had been arrested along with some of the French instructors who had worked for Carleton Coon. And the American leader himself, Carleton Coon, had disappeared.

On Christmas day at the d'Astier apartment, Mario learned that Giraud had arrived at the Summer Palace.

They all wanted to believe there was hope for Bonnier. Henri d'Astier, Cordier, and others were sure that Giraud would turn out to be the leader they had originally hoped for—and that he could surely save Bonnier.

At 8:00 A.M. on December 26, Mario returned to the d'Astier apartment. In the dining room he found Mme. d'Astier and her daughters weeping. Fernand Bonnier de la Chapelle had been shot by an execution squad that morning. Mario also learned that Abbé Cordier, "Necktie," had heard Bonnier's confession and had given the boy absolution a few hours before the young patriot had gone to Darlan's office to murder the admiral. Mario only learned later that Bonnier had written a confession to French police commissioner Garanacci. He discovered that the commissioner was so shocked when he reviewed the signed confession that he burned the only copy. Later, when Bonnier realized that he had been duped and abandoned by his well-placed friends and that he was to be executed, he sat in his prison cell with the prison chaplain and wrote a short statement on a visiting card he had with him. In a few words he revealed the existence of a monarchist plot. He named those who had aided him, including Abbé Pierre-Marie Cordier. The name printed on the visiting card was Henri d'Astier de la Vigerie, Secretary General of the Police.[511]

THE ANTICLIMAX

In the first weeks of January 1943, Gen. Giraud called for a complete investigation of the Darlan assassination. His death was now a monstrous political scandal. The suspects were many: the U.S. OSS, British intelligence, Vichy agents acting for Marshal Pétain, the various German security services, Le Comte de Paris, and the Group of Five.

Henri d'Astier de la Vigerie, his son Jean-Bernard, Abbé Pierre-Marie Cordier, Mario Faivre, and André Achiary were arrested and jailed—as were most of the partisans who had helped Robert Murphy and his vice-consuls on the night of the insurrection. Even the venerable Dr. Henri Aboulker was hauled away in handcuffs.

But by then, Carleton Coon was miles away . . . his lips forever sealed.

EPILOGUE: MEDALS OF MERIT

IN HIS SYNDICATED COLUMN, Walter Lippmann had a final word to say about the Darlan Deal and all that followed:

> It is now necessary to examine candidly the political muddle in North Africa. It is due to bad judgment based on incorrect information received from our agents in France and North Africa before the expedition landed.
>
> According to their information, General Giraud was held to be capable of rallying the French authorities to our cause and therefore of leaving General Eisenhower free to devote his attention to the military campaign against the Axis. The whole political plan based on this information broke down at the outset.
>
> Thus it was not foreseen that in addition to commanding the United Nations forces, General Eisenhower would have to deal with the subtle and explosive complications of French imperial politics. . . . That is the kind of burden we have placed on this brilliantly promising young American commander.
>
> It was placed there because our political agents misjudged the situation and the men with whom we were preparing to deal. Yet when General Eisenhower was confronted with a political problem, which no one had prepared him for, his chief American adviser was the political agent, Mr. Robert Murphy, *who had misjudged the situation.*[512]

★ ★ ★

IT MUST BE SAID THAT Robert Murphy was thrust into the North African swamp barely equipped to navigate in the political quagmire—and was at all times subject to the whims of Franklin Delano Roosevelt. Murphy—a practicing Catholic—was thought to be acceptable to Gen. Weygand, and he faithfully carried out the president's orders, to attempt to bring Weygand to the side of America and to exclude de Gaulle from obtaining political power in North Africa. As events evolved, however, Weygand proved to be uncooperative and obedient to Marshal Pétain.

Instead of building an anti-Nazi clandestine resistance movement in North Africa—one that might have paved the way for eventual U.S. intervention, and a liberal North African regime—Weygand went along with Pétain's wishes to cooperate with Hitler. At the time, a *Washington Post* columnist thought that "Weygand permitted Pétain, under German influence, to remove democratic officers from the army and replace them with Vichy stooges, royalists, and other fish of the type attractive to Mr. Murphy."[513]

On the other hand, as the world would later learn, Charles de Gaulle proved to be the leader he was born to be, and opposed Vichy, German, and U.S. hegemony in North Africa.

The brave but politically inept General Giraud—a "reactionary" and throwback to other times—was a terrible mistake, and made Eisenhower's appointment of Admiral Darlan inevitable. Again, the *Washington Post* noted: "The truth is that our political preparations in this war have always lagged behind our military preparations."[514]

Indeed, Washington, in general, and the State Department in particular, suffered in 1941–1942 from a chronic dysfunction when American foreign policy was to be decided. (And when the U.S. Congress abrogates its powers in wartime, it licenses the dysfunction.)

In Murphy's defense, it must be said that the man never received proper instructions from the White House. Roosevelt, having no confidence in his secretary of state, Cordell Hull, emasculated the foreign policy apparatus and the communication lines between Washington and a field post—Murphy in Algiers, and other posts in North Africa. The diplomatic game was lost, and Eisenhower was left to pick up the pieces. Once again, the political management of a conflict was left in the care of the military mind.

Even if one discounts the fact that before Darlan, Giraud was unacceptable to the senior leadership in North Africa loyal to Vichy, it is a wonder to read the process that ended in the selection of Giraud as America's noble puppet in North Africa. Giraud possessed neither the authority nor the talent Murphy credited to him, and the political preparations for the invasion blew up in Eisenhower's face. (The miracle that brought Darlan to power and saved thousands of American and British lives is almost too good to believe.)

Was it possible, knowing General Giraud's background (and the State Department did), to believe that Giraud could or would function as the leader of a French provisional government as events mandated in Algiers? Eisenhower saw through his majestic behavior immediately when Giraud arrived on the Rock of Gibraltar.

Professor Arthur Layton Funk rightly judges this aspect of Murphy's stewardship: "Murphy exposed Eisenhower to devastating criticism on the part of Allied correspondents in North Africa, who saw vast populations of underprivileged Arab natives with no political rights; Jews persecuted under Vichy laws, which remained in effect; prisons and concentration camps filled with communists, Jews, and Vichy political prisoners and Spanish Republicans."[515]

The liberal press in the United States and Britain went wild. Gaullists in London "became livid in their denunciation of the Anglo-American follies."[516]Murphy had often been criticized for his attachment to the right; his collaboration in Algiers with Lemaigre Dubreuil, his friendship with French industrialists and royalists and Algiers high society. But Murphy, like most diplomats, could not read the "masses"—the Gaullist sentiment among the enlisted personnel of the armed services, the professionals—and the influential Jewish component of North Africans was ignored or unknown to him.

Was he, as Felix Frankfurter thought, "Grottier than the Grotties?"

Later, internal French divisions were embittered as de Gaulle struggled for Allied recognition. After Torch, the Darlan and Giraud regimes continued Vichy's repressive and anti-Semitic policies, causing divisions and grave concern amongst the Allies. Yves Danan was right when he remarked bitterly that Murphy's choice of leaders "substituted Vichyism under German control for Vichyism under American protection—an unsavory episode in American policy."[517]

★ ★ ★

But nothing can take away from Murphy's bravery, dedication, and dogged perseverance under unbearable pressure. Robert Murphy was decorated with the Distinguished Service Medal for his work in North Africa—a unique distinction for a civilian. The medal was pinned on his suit coat by Dwight D. Eisenhower in Algiers in 1943. His career after Torch was marked with success in various diplomatic and ambassadorial roles. He achieved perhaps the summit of his career goal as "the ranking old-pro" in the State Department—Undersecretary of State for Political Affairs—the number-three spot and usually the highest to which a career officer may aspire.[518]

Medals of Merit went to ten of FDR's Twelve Apostles, and to Gordon Browne of the OSS and U.S. vice-consul L. Pittman Springs—a member of the U.S. Consular Corps since 1920. Here are their citations as written by the U.S. State Department:

JOHN HERVEY [sic] BOYD, Vice-Consul of the United States of America and Technical Adviser at Algiers, Algeria, for exceptionally meritorious conduct in the performance of outstanding services between June 1941 and November 1942. He was instrumental in setting up clandestine radio stations at Algiers in July 1942, which maintained daily contact with Allied Headquarters at Tangier, Gibraltar, and London until November 1942. Throughout this period of eighteen months, Mr. Boyd as Vice-Consul of the United States of America and Technical Adviser, performed secret missions, often at the risk of his life, in obtaining important and valuable military information such as detailed sketches of landing beaches, airfields, ports, orders of battle, movements of French and Axis shipping, etc. Mr. Boyd assisted in organizing and was in charge of the headquarters of more than five hundred French patriots who, on the night of the Allied embarkation in Algiers, took over strategic points and held them until the arrival of the Allied forces. On November 8, at risk to his life, he made his way twice through the French lines of resistance and made contact with the American forces at Guyotville and Sidi Ferruch, furnishing valuable military information to the Allied commander with respect to French resistance.

GORDON H. BROWNE, Vice-Consul, American Consulate, Tangier, Algeria, for exceptionally meritorious acts on the night of November 7–8, 1942. Gordon Browne, a civilian, knowing that only with great difficulty could a member of the armed forces be procured prior to the invasion to install and operate a secret radio location device, himself volunteered to render this service for the landing of the American paratroop force near Tafaraoui, Algeria. Realizing the consequences if apprehended, disregarding his own safety, he remained with the instrument for four hours under fire, and then upon completion of his mission, assisted in its disposal. The heroic and fearless loyalty of Gordon Browne, who voluntarily jeopardized his life for the success of his country's cause in battle, reflects great credit and glory upon the whole nation.

FREDERICK P. CULBERT, Vice-Consul of the United States of America and Technical Adviser at Dakar, French West Africa, and later at Casablanca, Morocco, for exceptionally meritorious conduct in the performance of outstanding services between June 1941 and December 1942. During this period Mr. Culbert, as Vice-Consul of the United States of America and Technical Adviser, obtained from French patriots information which was of inestimable value to the Allied forces. He was instrumental in setting up a clandestine radio station at Casablanca, which maintained contact with Allied Headquarters at Tangier and Gibraltar. In September 1942, Mr. Culbert was called to Washington by the United States Navy as a consultant and returned to North Africa with the Western Task Force.

DAVID WOOSTER KING, Vice-Consul of the United States of America and Technical Adviser at Casablanca, Morocco, for exceptionally meritorious conduct in the performance of outstanding services between June 1941 and November 1942. During this period, Mr. King, as Vice-Consul of the United States of America and Technical Adviser, obtained from French patriots information which was of inestimable value to the Allied troops. He was instrumental in setting up a clandestine radio station at Casablanca which maintained contact with Allied Headquarters at Tangier and Gibraltar. When the American Consulate General and annex were surrounded by French *Gardes Mobiles*, he made his way through the French lines, at great risk to his life, to the Consulate General and before capture warned the consul general to burn all secret War and State Department codes, thus preventing them from falling into other hands.

RIDGWAY B. KNIGHT, Vice-Consul of the United States and Technical Adviser at Oran, Algeria, now a Major AUS [Army of the United States]. For exceptionally meritorious service in the performance of outstanding services in contributing substantially to the success of the United States and Allied landing operations. His intelligence missions carried out during a year and a half prior to the North African assault rendered exceptionally meritorious service to the United States and Allied cause. The highly efficient services rendered by Major Knight under extremely difficult conditions are evidence of his exceptional ability and a high type of leadership.

JOHN CRAWFORD KNOX, Vice-Consul of the United States of America and Technical Adviser at Algiers, Algeria, for exceptionally meritorious conduct in the performance of outstanding services between June 1941 and November 1942. He was instrumental in setting up clandestine radio stations at Algiers, which maintained daily contacts during this period with Allied Headquarters at Tangier, Gibraltar, and London. Throughout this period of eighteen months Mr. Knox, as Vice-Consul of the United States of America and Technical Adviser, performed secret and dangerous missions, often at great risk to his life, and obtained very important and valuable military information such as detailed sketches of all landing beaches and exits, airfields, ports, orders of battle, defensive measures, movements of French and Axis, shipping, etc. In September 1942, Mr. Knox was ordered to London to work with Allied Force Headquarters as a member of General Eisenhower's staff in completing final plans for the landings in North Africa. He was afterwards assigned to the staff of General Charles W. Ryder, General Commanding the Eastern Assault Force, and took an active part in the landing operations at Algiers.

KENNETH W. PENDAR, Vice-Consul of the United States of America and Technical Adviser at Marrekech [sic], Morocco, and later at Algiers, Algeria, for exceptionally meritorious conduct in the performance of outstanding services between June 1941 and November 1942. During this period Mr. Pendar, as Vice-Consul of the United States of America and Technical Adviser, obtained from French patriots information which was of inestimable value to Allied troops. In August 1942, in accordance with instructions, he set up a clandestine radio station at Marrekech [sic] which maintained daily contact with Allied Headquarters at Tangier until November 1942. After his transfer to Algiers in September 1942, to aid in the final preparations for the Allied debarkation at Algiers, Mr. Pendar rendered services of great value to the Allied cause. On the night of debarkation at Algiers, Mr. Pendar at great risk to his life volunteered to carry a message from Admiral Darlan to the French Admiralty Headquarters ordering the French to cease firing. Throughout this period of eighteen months Mr. Pendar performed secret and dangerous missions, often at great risk to his life.

W. STAFFORD REID, Vice-Consul of the United States of America and Technical Adviser at Casablanca, Morocco, for exceptionally meritorious conduct in the performance of outstanding services between June 1941 and November 1942. During this period, Mr. Reid, as Vice-Consul of the United States of America and Technical Adviser at Casablanca, obtained from French patriots information which was of inestimable value to the Allied forces. For one year and a half previous to the Allied debarkation in North Africa, Mr. Reid was engaged in obtaining vital military information for the Allied cause and worked at the risk of his life in opposition to the Axis armistice commission. He was instrumental in setting up a clandestine radio station at Casablanca which maintained contact with Allied Headquarters at Tangier and Gibraltar, thus furnishing valuable military information to the Allied forces.

LELAND L. ROUNDS, Vice-Consul of the United States of America and Technical Adviser at Oran, Algeria, for exceptionally meritorious conduct in the performance of outstanding service between June 1941 and November 1942. He was instrumental in setting up a clandestine radio station at Oran which worked in daily contact with Allied Headquarters at Tangier and Gibraltar from July to November 1942. Throughout a period of eighteen months Mr. Rounds, as Vice-Consul of the United States of America and Technical Adviser, performed secret and dangerous missions, often at the risk of his life. Through his contacts with French patriots he obtained valuable military information such as sketches of landing beaches and ports, movements of Axis vessels, etc. In September 1942, Mr. Rounds was ordered to London to report to Allied Headquarters and as a consultant gave information of great military value to the debarkation forces. He returned to Oran with the first assault forces.

L. PITTMAN SPRINGS, Vice-Consul of the United States of America at Tunis, Tunisia, and later at Algiers, Algeria, for exceptionally meritorious conduct in the performance of outstanding services between August 1941 and November 1942. He was instrumental in setting up clandestine radio stations at Tunis which maintained daily contacts between July 1942 and November 1942 with Allied Headquarters at Malta, Tangier, and Gibraltar. Throughout this period of fifteen months, Mr. Springs, as Vice-Consul of the United States of America, performed secret and dangerous missions. In October 1942, Mr. Springs was ordered to Algiers to assist in the final preparation for the Allied debarkation in North Africa. At the risk of his life, Mr. Springs on the night of November 7–8 went out to meet the first debarkation forces in the vicinity of Guyotville.

JOHN E. UTTER, Vice-Consul of the United States of America and Technical Adviser at Tunis, Tunisia, for exceptionally meritorious conduct in the performance of outstanding services between June 1941 and November 1942. During this period, Mr. Utter, as Vice-Consul of the United States of America and Technical Adviser of Tunis, obtained from French patriots information which was of inestimable value to the Allied troops. He was instrumental in setting up a clandestine radio station at Tunis which maintained contact with Allied Headquarters at Malta and Gibraltar. Throughout this period of eighteen months Mr. Utter performed secret missions, often at risk to his life, in opposition to the German-Italian Armistice Commission.

HARRY A. WOODRUFF, Vice-Consul of the United States of America and Technical Adviser at Tunis, Tunisia, and later at Algiers, Algeria, for exceptionally meritorious conduct in the performance of outstanding services between June 1941 and November 1942. During this period Mr. Woodruff, as Vice-Consul of the United States of America and Technical Adviser at Tunis, Tunisia, obtained from French patriots information which was of inestimable value to Allied troops. He was instrumental in setting up a clandestine radio station at Tunis which maintained contact with Allied Headquarters at Malta and Gibraltar. In October 1942, Mr. Woodruff was called to Algiers to render service to the Allied forces during the debarkation on November 8. At risk to his life, he volunteered to make contact with the first Allied troops landed during the debarkation, thus rendering valuable service.

★ ★ ★

This is the swan's song for FDR's Twelve Apostles. It is perhaps appropriate to end with a remembrance by A. Derek Knox—son of Daphne Joan Fry Tuyl Knox and stepson of John C. Knox. He wrote the author in 2006:

> My mother married John Knox on April 28, 1943. I remember that there had been a lot of anticipation for quite some time and we were really looking forward to the ceremony. It seemed everyone went except me. I was totally devastated and could not understand why my brother could go and I could not. . . .
>
> Late in 1944 John Knox was assigned to the SHAEF Mission in Paris, leaving the rest of the family in Algiers. My mother was determined to join him there, but during wartime and [with] the lack of transportation, it was no easy undertaking—especially with three young children. Somehow she managed to succeed, and off we went.
>
> The plane was small by today's standards, barely the size of a bus, with a wooden bench running the length of each side of the plane and, of course, without seat belts. Looking out the windows I was fascinated by everything we could see . . . over Corsica—the mountains going right into the sea. As we came over the Pyrenees we hit an air pocket and I surprisingly found myself floating weightlessly in the cabin. I couldn't make up my mind whether this was fun or dangerous. The expression on everyone's face indicated the latter. As the plane came out of the pocket we were rudely brought back to gravity, [and were] smacking down on the hard wooden benches or in some cases, on the floor of the cabin. This was my last . . . association with Algeria.

APPENDIX

JACQUES LEMAIGRE DUBREUIL, FRENCH PATRIOT, AND ROBERT MURPHY

Onto the chaotic, political Algerian scene of mid-1941 there appeared "one of the most mysterious and ambiguous men of his time"[519]—a passionate and determined Frenchman, Jacques Lemaigre Dubreuil—who would play a pivotal role in the life of Robert Murphy during the coming eighteen months. He would be the principal link between Murphy, Giraud, and dissident-patriots within the French General Staff and the French colonial administration—many of whom had sworn oaths unto death to Marshal Pétain.

For Robert Murphy, Lemaigre Dubreuil was a hero; to others he was an ambitious fascist politician seeking power. Still to others, he was a traitor to Pétain and a tool of Pierre Laval's.

William Donovan and the OSS agency would be confused about his allegiances. While Murphy was defending him as an idealist and patriot, Donovan's intelligence service would be denouncing him as a ". . . leading French fascist and a member of that segment of French society that, fearing bolshevism to be the only alternative, gave Pétain its blessing and support that fateful day, 10 July 1940—the day on which the constitution of the Third Republic was dissolved and full powers were conferred on Pétain, who promptly abolished the Republican slogan of 'Liberty, Equality, Fraternity' and replaced it with the French fascist slogan of 'Work, Country, Family'"[520]

Murphy always insisted that Lemaigre Dubreuil was not a fascist. Rather, he was devoted to American war aims—the Atlantic Charter and the Four

Freedoms—and was politically ambiguous so that he might circulate more easily in Vichy French and Parisian fascist circles to gather intelligence for the U.S.

On the other hand, Lemaigre Dubreuil's OSS dossier reported that he
was the brother-in-law of Pierre Laguionie, whose family owned the leading
Parisian department store, Le Printemps; and that his wife was Simone
Lesieur, daughter of Georges Lesieur of Huilles Lesieur, France's most important peanut oil producer. It was believed that Lemaigre Dubreuil was sub-
sidized in his fascist activities by these industrialists and had used their
subsidies to create the right-wing French organization named "The League of
Taxpayers." (The league was allegedly affiliated with the *Cagoule*, a secret society formed by the French synarchists to defend France against the Soviet
Communist International operating in France and Europe.)

William Donovan established[521] that during the Popular Front movement
—1936 to 1938—Lemaigre Dubreuil was appointed a regent of the Banque
de France (a citadel of 200 of the most powerful families of France). The
French government in May 1940 claimed that he received German funds for
anti-government propaganda through the Banque Worms et Cie. Donovan
stated in a memorandum to President Roosevelt that Lemaigre Dubreuil had
been the official distributor of Nazi funds in France. Under French law, that
was considered treason in wartime, and Lemaigre Dubreuil was placed on the
arrest list by the Vichy interior minister.

Donovan also established that Lemaigre Dubreuil was closely associated
with the leading right-wing newspapers *Le Matin* and *Le Jour;* had contributed to the *Cagoule's* finances; and was intimate with synarchists within
the French General Staff. It seemed to the OSS analysts that he was more
likely to be a friend of Germany than of America.

Yet there might be some truth in Murphy's assertion that Lemaigre
Dubreuil was really a patriot-democratic sheep in a fascist wolf's clothing. He
had fought against the Germans in World War I as a front-line officer. In
World War II, he had commanded a machine-gun battalion and had fought
with great gallantry until he was taken prisoner by the Germans at Nogent-
sur-Seine during the French surrender. It was not clear whether he had escaped or was released. Escape would be a sign of honor. But release could
mean that his freedom was arranged by one of those leading French industrialists whom the Germans believed would contribute to the economic collaboration so necessary for their plans for the "New Order."

At some point, Donovan accepted Murphy's assurances but warned him that the joint chiefs were extremely vigilant concerning the security of Torch —and that no more than was necessary should be confided to Murphy's French associate.

After the Torch landings, Donovan had Lemaigre Dubreuil investigated. He found:

> Dubreuil, undoubtedly a man of courage and force, is a French oilman and financier who has maintained association with the 'Cagoulards,' a French fascist organization, exported lubricating oils to [the Italian Army at] Tripoli, Libya [the main supply port for Axis operations against the British in Egypt].[522]

After Operation Torch concluded, Lemaigre Dubreuil was sent to Washington by General Giraud and worked on "the Anfa Memorandum" destined for President Roosevelt. (The name was taken from Casablanca's Anfa Hotel, where Roosevelt met Churchill, de Gaulle, and Giraud in January 1943.)[523] He was eventually arrested and tried at a Paris court for collaboration and, if not exonerated, then freed due to Robert Murphy's help. (The two men remained close friends for many years after Torch and the war.)[524] Later still, he was active in post-war French Morocco and owned the liberal newspaper, *Maroc-Presse*.

In June 1955, Jacques Lemaigre Dubreuil was machine-gunned to death in Casablanca by French professional counterterrorists for his stand on Franco-Moroccan solidarity. Many in France thought him an opportunist who was prepared to back any winner in WWII to protect his industrial holdings: the Lesieur oil business in North Africa. Others saw a rabble-rouser, a demagogue, a betrayer of French interests at home and overseas; or a reformer, a patriot, and a hero of the anti-German resistance.[525]

BIBLIOGRAPHY

CORRESPONDENCE AND INTERVIEWS:

Susan Alsbury, Librarian, Longie Dale Hamilton Memorial Library, Wesson, MS

Whitney S. Bagnall, Diamond Law Library, Columbia University, NY

Mrs. Joan Bourgoin

Mrs. Alexandra Curley

Mrs. Carolyn Graham, Wesson, MS

Jacqueline Haun, Archivist, The Bunn Library, The Lawrenceville School, Lawrenceville, NJ

Mr. A. Derek Knox

Mrs. Edith Woodruff Kunhardt

Debra McIntosh, College Archivist, Millsaps-Wilson Library, Millsaps College, Jackson, MS

Phyllis Michaux, Paris, France

Ms. Rosemary Murphy

Prof. J. M. Oughourlian, Chief of Psychiatry at the American Hospital of Paris

Robert H. Parks, Franklin D. Roosevelt Presidential Library and Museum

Judy Polonofsky, Director of External Affairs, Montclair Kimberley Academy, Montclair, NJ

Mrs. Mildred Murphy Pond

Sameer Popat, College Park, MD

Professor Charles Robertson, Smith College

Pamela Susi, St. Paul's School, Concord, NH

Ms. Louise W. King

PUBLICATIONS:

The Biographic Register of the Department of State, Washington, D.C.: 1939, 1940–42, 1944, 1973

Extrait de bulletin statistique (Paris: Generale de la France, Press Universitaires de France, 1947).

The Los Angeles Times

The Nation

The New York Herald Tribune

The New York Times

The Saturday Evening Post

The Times of London

The Washington Post

Time Magazine

VFW Magazine, Anniversary Issue, November 1992

ARTICLES:

Kelly Bell, "Death of a Double Dealer," *World War II* 13.3 (September 1998): 50.

Demarré Bess, "Our Secret Diplomatic Triumph in Africa," *The Saturday Evening Post* (December 26, 1942): 21, 81.

_____ "The Backstage Story of Our African Adventure," *The Saturday Evening Post*, 216.2 (July 10, 1943): 18–90.

_____ "The Backstage Story of Our African Adventure," *The Saturday Evening Post*, 216.3 (July 17, 1943): 20–84.

Arthur L. Funk, "A Document Relating to the Second World War: The Clark-Darlan Agreement, November 22, 1942" (in Documents), *The Journal of Modern History* 25.1 (March 1953): 61–65.

_____, "American Contacts with the Resistance in France, 1940-43," *Military Affairs* 34.1 (February 1970): 15–21.

_____, "Eisenhower, Giraud, and the Command of 'TORCH,' " *Military Affairs* 35.3 (October 1971): 103–108.

_____, "Negotiating the 'Deal with Darlan,' " *Journal of Contemporary History* 8.2 (April 1973): 81–117.

_____, "The 'ANFA Memorandum': An Incident of the Casablanca Conference" (in Notes), *The Journal of Modern History* 26.3 (September 1954): 246–254.

Matthew Gordon, "What the Axis Thinks of the OWI," *Public Opinion Quarterly* 7.1 (Spring 1943): 134–138.

Ellen Hammer, "Hindsight on Vichy," *Political Science Quarterly* 61.2 (June 1946): 175–188.

John Herman, "Agency Africa: Rygor's Franco-Polish Network and Operation Torch," *Journal of Contemporary History*, 22.4, Intelligence Services during the Second World War: Part 2 (October 1987): 681–706.

Robert L. Melka, "Darlan between Britain and Germany 1940–41," *Journal of Contemporary History* 8.2 (1973): 57–80.

Bernard Metz, "The North African Imbroglio," *The American Foreign Service Journal* (November 1943): n.p.

Benjamin Rivlin, "The United States and Moroccan International Status, 1943–1956: A Contributory Factor in Morocco's Reassertion of Independence from France," *The International Journal of African Historical Studies* 15.1 (1982): 64–82.

James R. Robinson, "The Rommel Myth," *Military Review* 77.5 (September/October 1997): 81.

Egya N. Sangmuah, "Sultan Mohammed ben Youssef's American Strategy and the Diplomacy of North African Liberation, 1943–61," *Journal of Contemporary History* 27.1 (January 1992): 129–148.

Richard W. Steele, "Political Aspects of American Military Planning, 1941–1942," *Military Affairs* 35.2 (April 1971): 68–74.

Jesse H. Stiller, "Back Stabbing at State," *Diplomatic History* 20.2 (Spring 1996) n.p.

Martin Thomas, "After Mers-el-Kebir: The Armed Neutrality of the Vichy French Navy, 1940–43," *The English Historical Review* 112.447 (June 1997): 643–670.

David A. Walker, "OSS and Operation Torch," *Journal of Contemporary History* 22.4, Intelligence Services during the Second World War: Part 2 (October 1987): 667–679.

Murray Williamson, "Triumph of Operation Torch," *World War II* 17.4 (November 2002): 44.

David T. Zabecki, "Battlefield North Africa: Rommel's Rise and Fall," *World War II* 11.7 (March 1997): 26.

RADIO:

"Robert Trout aboard a Pan Am Clipper," National Public Radio, *All Things Considered*, Washington, D.C., July 3, 1999.

BOOKS:

Alan Brooke, Field Marshall. *War Diaries 1939–1945* (London: Weidenfeld & Nicolson, 2001).

Ambrose, Steven E. *Ike's Spies* (Jackson, MS: University of Mississippi Press, 1981).

_____. *The Supreme Commander: The War Years of General Dwight D. Eisenhower* (New York: Doubleday, 1969).

Atkinson, Rick. *An Army at Dawn: The War in Africa, 1942–1943, Volume One of the Liberation Trilogy* (New York: Henry Holt & Company, Inc., 2002).

Bankwitz, Philip Charles Farwell. *Maxime Weygand and Civil-Military Relations in Modern France* (Cambridge, MA: Harvard University Press, 1967).

Beaufre, André. *La Revanche de 1945* (Paris: Plon, 1966).

Bender, Marilyn and Selig Altschul. *The Chosen Instrument: Pan Am and Juan Trippe* (New York, Simon & Schuster, 1982).

Black, Conrad. *Franklin Delano Roosevelt: Champion of Freedom* (New York: PublicAffairs, 2003).

Breuer, William B. *Operation Torch: The Allied Gamble to Invade North Africa* (New York: St. Martin's Press, 1985).

Brown, Anthony Cave. *Wild Bill Donovan: The Last Hero* (New York: Times Books, 1982).

_____. *Bodyguard of Lies* (New York: Harper & Row, 1987).

Brownell, Will and Richard Billings. *So Close to Greatness: The Biography of William C. Bullitt* (New York: Macmillan, 1987).

Bullitt, Orville, ed. *For the President, Personal & Secret* (Boston: Houghton Mifflin, 1972).

Bullitt, William C. *Report to the American People* (New York: Houghton Mifflin, 1940).

Canfield, Franklin O. *Memoirs of a Long and Eventful Life* (n.p., n.d.), courtesy of Peter M. F. Sichel.

Clark, Mark W. *Calculated Risk* (New York: Harper and Brothers, 1950).

Cointet, Michele. *De Gaulle et Giraud* (Paris: Perrin, 2005).

Collins, Larry and Dominique Lapierre. *Is Paris Burning?* (New York: Simon & Schuster, 1965).

Cook, Don. *Charles de Gaulle: A Biography* (New York: Putnam, 1983).

Coon, Carleton S. *Adventures and Discoveries: The Autobiography of Carleton S. Coon* (Upper Saddle River, New Jersey: Prentice-Hall, 1981).

_____. *A North African Story: The Anthropologist as OSS Agent 1941–1943* (Ipswich, Mass., Gambit Publications, 1981).

Cowles, Virginia. *Looking for Trouble* (New York: Harper, 1941).

_____. "The Beginning of the End: Flight from Paris: June 1940." In *Reporting World War II: American Journalism: 1938–1944: Volume One* (New York, Library of America, 1995).

Cray, Ed. *General of the Army: George C. Marshall, Soldier and Statesman* (New York: W. W. Norton & Company, 1990.)

Crémieux-Brilhac, Jean-Louis. *La France Libre* I-II (Paris: Gallimard, 1997).

Danan, Yves Maxime. *La vie politique à Alger, de 1940 à 1944* (Paris: L.G.D.J., 1963).

de Gaulle, Philippe. *De Gaulle mon père* (Paris: Editions Plon, 2003).

de Kerillis, Henri. *Francais, Voici la Vérité!* (New York: Editions de la Maison Française, Inc., 1942).

Dunlop, Richard. *Donovan: America's Master Spy* (Skokie, IL: Rand McNally & Company, 1982.)

Eden, Anthony. *The Memoirs of Anthony Eden. Earl of Avon: The Reckoning* (Boston: Houghton Mifflin Company, 1965).

Eisenhower, Dwight D. *Crusade in Europe* (Garden City, New York: Doubleday, 1948).

_____. *The Papers of Dwight D. Eisenhower.* Edited by Louis Galambos and others. (Baltimore: The Johns Hopkins University Press, 1978–1996).

Encyclopedia of Aviation (New York: Charles Scribner's Sons, 1977).

Faivre, Mario. *We Killed Darlan: A Personal Account of the French Resistance in North Africa, 1940–1942* (Manhattan, Kansas: Sunflower University Press, 1999).

Funk, Arthur Layton. *The Politics of TORCH: The Allied Landings and the Algiers Putsch, 1942* (Lawrence, KS: University Press of Kansas 1974).

Furst, Alan. *Kingdom of Shadows* (New York: Random House, 2000).

Garraty, John Arthur and Mark C. Carnes, eds. *American National Biography, Vol. 16* (New York: Oxford University Press, 1999).

Gelb, Norman. *Desperate Venture: The Story of Operation Torch, the Allied Invasion of North Africa* (New York: William Morrow & Co., 1992).

Gosset, Renée. *Conspiracy in Algiers* (New York: The Nation, 1945).

Grose, Peter. *Gentleman Spy: The Life of Allen Dulles* (New York: Houghton Mifflin, 1994).

Guillemot, Pierre-Charles. *Les 12 Vice-Consuls. Afrique du nord 1942* (Paris: Editions Olivier Orban 1977).

Hamilton, Ronald. *Now I Remember* (London: The Hogarth Press, 1984).

Hansen, Arlen. *Gentlemen Volunteers* (New York: Arcade Publishing, 1996).

Hoisington Jr., William A. *The Assassination of Jacques Lemaigre Dubreuil: A Frenchman Between France and North Africa* (Oxford: Routledge, 2005).

Howe, George F. *Northwest Africa: Seizing the Initiative in the West* (Washington, D.C.: Center of Military History, United States Army, 1993).

The International Who's Who 1962–3 (London: Europa Publications Ltd., 1962).

Irving, David. *Churchill's War: Volume 2: Triumph in Adversity* (London: Focus Point Publications, 2001).

Isaacson, Walter and Evan Thomas. *The Wise Men* (New York: Simon & Schuster, 1986).

Jakub, Jay. *Spies and Saboteurs: Anglo-American Collaboration and Rivalry in Human Intelligence Collection and Special Operations, 1940–45* (New York: St. Martin's, 1999).

Jeffreys-Jones, Rhodri. *Cloak and Dollar: A History of American Secret Intelligence* (New Haven, CT: Yale University Press, 2002).

Jenkins, Roy. *Churchill: A Biography* (London: Macmillan, 2001).

Kammerer, Albert. *Du débarquement africain au meurtre de Darlan* (Paris: Flammarion, 1949).

Kaplan, Justin, ed. *Bartlett's Familiar Quotations, Seventeenth Edition* (New York: Little, Brown and Company, 2002).

Kersaudy, Francois. *De Gaulle et Churchill* (Paris: Perrin, 2001).

Klein, Alexander, ed. *Double Dealers: Adventures in Grand Deception* (Philadelphia, Lippincott, 1958).

Knight, Ridgway B. *A Secret Affair* (n.p., n.d.).

———. *Code Name Rebecca: The Memoirs of Ridgway Brewster Knight, 1940–45* (n.p., n.d.).

Knox, John C. *The First 36 Hours of November 8, 1942* (n.p., n.d.).

Langer, William L. *Our Vichy Gamble* (New York: Knopf, 1947).

Laughlin, Clara E. *So You're Going to the Mediterranean* (London: Methuen, 1935).

Leahy, William D. *I Was There* (New York: McGraw-Hill Book Company, Inc., 1950).

Liebling, A. J. "Paris Postscript: Paris Before the Fall: May–June 1940." In *Reporting World War II: American Journalism: 1938–1944: Volume One* (New York, Library of America, 1995).

Lottman, Herbert R. *The Fall of Paris: June 1940* (New York: Harper-Collins, 1992).

Mason, F. K. and M. C. Windrow. *Know Aviation* (London: George Philip & Son Ltd., 1973).

Maugham, W. Somerset. *Ashenden* (Salem, NH: Ayer Co. Pub., 1928).

Melton, George E. *Darlan* (Westport, CT: Praeger, 1998).

Morison, Samuel Eliot. *Operations in North African Waters: October 1942–June 1943* (Edison, NJ: Castle Books, 1947).

Morse, Edwin T. *The Vanguard of American Volunteers in the Fighting Lines and in Humanitarian Service, August 1914–April 1917* (New York: Charles Scribner's Sons, 1919).

Murphy, Robert Daniel. *Diplomat Among Warriors* (New York: Doubleday, 1964).

Nossiter, Adam. *The Algeria Hotel: France, Memory, and the Second World War* (New York: Houghton Mifflin, 2001).

O'Donnell, Patrick K. *Operatives, Spies, and Saboteurs: The Unknown Story of the Men and Women of WWII's OSS* (New York: Free Press, 2004).

Ousby, Ian. *Occupation: The Ordeal of France 1940–1944* (London: Pimlico, 1999).

Paxton, Robert O. *L'Armee de Vichy* (Paris: Tallandier, 2004).

_____. *Vichy France: Old Guard and New Order 1940–1944* (New York: Columbia University Press, 1982).

Pendar, Kenneth. *Adventure in Diplomacy* (New York: Dodd, Mead & Co., 1945).

Persico, Joseph. *Roosevelt's Secret War* (New York: Random House, 2001).

Podell, Janet, ed. *The Annual Obituary: 1981* (New York: St. Martin's Press, 1982).

Richards, Brooks. *Secret Flotillas: Clandestine Sea Lines to France and French North Africa 1940–1944* (London: HMSO, 1996).

Roosevelt, Pres. Franklin Delano. *The Public Papers and Addresses of Franklin Delano Roosevelt, 1942, Humanity on the Defensive* (New York: Harper and Brothers Publishers, 1950).

Singh, Simon. *The Code Book: The Science of Secrecy From Ancient Egypt to Quantum Cryptography* (London: Fourth Estate, 1999).

Slowikowski, Major General Rygor. *In the Secret Service: The Lighting of the Torch* (London: The Windrush Press, 1988).

Smith, Bradley F. *The Shadow Warriors: OSS and the Origins of the CIA* (New York: Basic Books, Inc., 1983).

Smith, R. Harris. *OSS: the Secret History of America's First Central Intelligence Agency* (London: University of California Press, 1972).

Stevenson, William. *A Man Called Intrepid* (New York: Harcourt Brace Jovanovich, 1976).

Tute, Warren. *The Reluctant Enemies: The Story of the Last War Between Britain and France, 1940–1942* (London: HarperCollins, 1990).

Tuyl Knox, Daphne Joan Fry. *How Long Till Dawn* (n.p., n.d.).

U.S. Department of State, *Foreign Relations of the United States, 1941: Volume III* (Washington, DC: U.S. G.P.O.), 1959.

_____. *Foreign Relations of the United States, 1942: Volume II* (Washington, D.C.: U.S. G.P.O.), 1962.

Verrier, Anthony. *Assassination in Algiers: Churchill, Roosevelt, De Gaulle and the Murder of Admiral Darlan* (New York: Norton, 1990).

Voituriez, Albert Jean. *L'Affaire Darlan, instruction judiciaire* (Paris: J. C. Lattés, 1980).

Waller, John H. *The Unseen War in Europe* (New York: Random House, 1996).

Walter, Xavier. *Un Roi Pour La France* (Paris: Francois-Xavier de Guibert, 2002).

Weygand, Maxime. *Rappele au Service* (Paris: Flammarion, 1950).

Who's Who in America, 39th Edition, Volume 1, 1976 (Skokie, IL: Rand McNally and Co., 1976).

Williams, Charles. *The Last Great Frenchman* (London: ABACUS, 1995).

ARCHIVES:

Archivio Centrale dello Stato, Rome, Italy

The Papers of William Alfred Eddy, Seeley G. Mudd Manuscript Library, Princeton University, Princeton, New Jersey

The Papers of Robert D. Murphy, Hoover Institution Archives, Stanford, California

The U.S. Department of State Personnel Files

Harvard University Archives, Cambridge, MA

Princeton University, Seeley G. Mudd Manuscript Library, Princeton, NJ

The Papers of Arnold Wesker, Harry Ransom Humanities Research Center at the University of Texas at Austin

The Papers of Leland L. Rounds, Hoover Institution Archives, Stanford, California

The Papers of Sumner Welles, FDR Library, Hyde Park, NY

National Archives at College Park, College Park, MD

NARA Record Group 226, Box 119

NARA Record Group 226, Box 294

NARA Record Group 226, Box 5, Folder 80

NARA Record Group 226, Entry 92A, Box 1, Folder 6

NARA Record Group 226, Entry 92A, Folder 22

NARA Record Group 226, Entry 92A, Folder 25

NARA Record Group 226, Entry 92A, Folder 39

NARA Record Group 226, Entry 92A, Folder 82

NARA Record Group 226, Entry 97, Box 5

NARA Record Group 226, Entry 99, Box 43

NARA Record Group 226, Entry 99, Box 49

ENDNOTES

PART ONE

1   *Bartlett's Familiar Quotations, Seventeenth Edition* (New York: Little, Brown and Company, 2002), 587–9.

CHAPTER I ENDNOTES

2   The smoke in Paris came from burning petrol depots in the suburbs. The charred matter was the remnants of burned documents and codebooks from embassy and government files. Walter Kerr, *The New York Herald Tribune*'s Paris correspondent, describes how on June 11, 1940, Paris was covered in a dark fog: "At 9:00 A.M., from the Rond-Point on the Champs Elysées, it was so smoky you couldn't see the obelisk on the Place de la Concorde or the Arc de Triomphe." Herbert Lottman, *The Fall of Paris: June 1940* (New York: HarperCollins, 1992), 282.

3   By May 20, 1940, Wayne Taylor of the American Red Cross in Paris told U.S. Ambassador William C. Bullitt that at least five million persons were fleeing on French roads. In fact, the number was fourteen million, and a vast number would die of starvation and illness unless they could be cared for. Orville Bullitt, ed., *For the President, Personal & Secret* (Boston: Houghton Mifflin, 1972), 429; and Robert Murphy, *Diplomat Among Warriors* (New York: Doubleday, 1964), 40.

4   Virginia Cowles, "Flight From Paris: June 1940: The Beginning of the End" In *Reporting World War II, American Journalism 1938–1946* (New York: Library of America, 1995).

5   Will Brownell and Richard Billings, *So Close to Greatness: The Biography of William C. Bullitt* (New York: Macmillan, 1987), 258–259; and Murphy, 40–41.

6   Minutes earlier, Murphy had accidentally bumped into the Grand Rabbi of Paris, Julian Weill. With his wife and two friends, Weill had just set out from his apartment to locate an American official who might help them all escape Paris. He had realized only a few hours earlier that the French government had fled the city for Bordeaux. Weill's

little group made their way along the empty, blacked-out Faubourg Saint-Honoré, past the Hotel Bristol—full of Americans seeking U.S. protection—past the Elysée Palace and beyond U.S. ambassador William Bullitt's residence. (The ambassador's home was also crammed with Americans who feared the invading Germans.) On the avenue Gabriel, at the gate of the American Embassy, Rabbi Weill practically bumped into the man he sought as a savior: the U.S. Embassy Counselor, Robert Murphy. Then and there, standing on the sidewalk, Rabbi Weill and his wife pleaded with Murphy for seats in an embassy automobile going to Bordeaux. Murphy had to tell the group that Paris was surrounded by German armored divisions. But the rabbi was so distressed that Murphy summoned a chauffeur from the guarded embassy compound and instructed him to drive the party to the outskirts of Paris. There, the Germans turned the group back; Grand Rabbi Weill had waited too long. Murphy, 42.

7   Murphy, 41.

8   Vincent Banville in *Kingdom of Shadows*, Alan Furst (New York: Random House, 2000), front matter.

9   *New York Herald Tribune* correspondent Walter Kerr to Virginia Cowles on June 14, 1940, in Lottman, 323.

10   Confirmed in a telephone interview on October 4, 2004, with Rosemary Murphy in New York City; and in a letter to the author from Mildred (Murphy) Pond, dated October 20, 2004. According to Prof. J. M. Oughourlian, chief of psychiatry at the American Hospital of Paris, treatment for manic depression in 1940 was limited. Sufferers were subjected to cold showers and eventually, electroshock therapy. Author's conversation with Dr. Oughourlian on October 4, 2004.

11   Lottman, 359.

12   Murphy, 39.

13   Lottman, 361.

14   Murphy, 44.

15   Murphy, 44.

16   In *For the President*, Orville Bullitt's compilation of Ambassador Bullitt's correspondence, there is a startling omission. On page 469, Orville Bullitt states that Adm. Roscoe H. Hillenkoetter (naval attaché at the time in Paris) "has kindly written to me the following account of the German occupation of [Paris]." Then Orville Bullitt gives Hillenkoetter's account about the Hotel Crillon meeting with von Studnitz. But there is no mention of Ambassador Bullitt having ordered Robert Murphy to call on von Studnitz with the U.S. military and naval attachés. In fact, Murphy's name is never mentioned in the Hillenkoetter account; it's as if he never existed. This omission is odd for several reasons. Hillenkoetter had been a close friend of Murphy's. There's no doubt that he and Orville Bullitt had read Murphy's account of the incident in Murphy's 1964 biography, *Diplomat Among Warriors*—at least by the time Orville Bullitt's book was released in 1972.

17   UP dispatch datelined Paris, June 16, 1940, via Berlin and Bern, Switzerland: Delayed. No byline given.

18 Lottman, 361. Murphy does not mention the incident in his memoirs. Kerr's piece may never have reached New York because it had to be sent via Berlin.

19 UP dispatch dated June 16, 1940.

20 Lottman, 378.

21 This story may be due more to Ambassador Bullitt's imagination and love of a good tale for FDR in Washington, than the truth. Orville Bullitt, 434.

22 In his memoirs, Murphy refers to him as "M. Jacques-Simon."

23 Murphy, 54.

24 Brownell and Billings, 256–260; and from Bullitt's cable to FDR, June 9, 1940, and FDR's cable to Bullitt, June 9, 1940, as cited in Orville Bullitt, 457–458.

25 Conrad Black, *Franklin Delano Roosevelt: Champion of Freedom* (New York: Public-Affairs, 2003), 557; and Charles Williams, *The Last Great Frenchman* (London: ABACUS, 1995), 103–104.

26 There is ample evidence that Marshal Pétain was part of a powerful French right-wing political clique that was under Nazi influence. Henri de Kerillis, *Francais, Voici la Vérité!* (New York: Editions de la Maison Française, Inc., 1942).

27 Bullitt cabled FDR on June 4, 1940, that Pétain would never agree to any Churchill proposal. The marshal believed that Britain had betrayed France by withholding its air force and reserve divisions in the fight for France. Orville Bullitt, 449–451.

28 For England, it was a day of glory when Henry V became regent and heir of France, marrying into the bargain Catherine, the daughter of France's Charles VI. Henry died of dysentery seven years later. Ronald Hamilton, *Now I Remember* (London: The Hogarth Press, 1984), 80.

29 Williams, 104.

30 "London v. Bordeaux," *Time* Magazine, 1 July 1940: 25.

31 Georges Mandel, one of those deputies who fled to Morocco, was later deported by the Germans to Buchenwald. In July 1944, he was returned to the Santé prison in Paris and executed by Pétain's police, the *Milice*, in the forest of Fontainebleau. Robert O. Paxton, *Vichy France: Old Guard and New Order 1940–1944* (New York: Columbia University Press, 2001), 175.

32 Murphy, 40–41; and Don Cook, *Charles de Gaulle: A Biography* (New York: Putnam, 1983), 9.

33 Perhaps Bullitt's decision to stay in Paris was inspired by the tradition of his predecessors. U.S. ambassadors Elihu Benjamin Washburne and Myron T. Herrick remained in Paris during the Franco-Prussian war of 1870–71, when Paris was under siege, and again during the battle of the Marne in 1914. Murphy defended Bullitt's decision to stay in Paris until the end of June. "The Germans were not only willing but eager to talk and . . . we easily arranged meetings with high-ranking German officers; and the information we obtained was transmitted to Washington immediately after we left Paris and thence relayed to London. Paris proved to be one of the best

intelligence centers in Europe." But in his memoirs, Murphy's idea of "immediate" proved to be three weeks later, which is when the "information" was actually transmitted from Vichy. Murphy, 40–41; and Cook, 93.

34 Murphy, 48.

35 Murphy, 45.

36 In fact, Bullitt wanted to return to Washington and the post of secretary of the navy that he had hoped FDR would give him. From Vichy, Bullitt cabled a report to FDR after the meetings with Pétain that American diplomat and historian George F. Kennan later described as a "uniquely authentic portrayal of the mentality and calculations of the Vichy leaders." Orville Bullitt, 441; Brownell and Billings, 261; and Murphy, 53.

37 Lottman, 382.

38 The U.S. would not have a fully staffed diplomatic presence in Paris again until the city was liberated of Nazi power in August 1944.

39 Murphy, 5.

40 Murphy, 5.

41 Murphy, 5.

42 Murphy, 6.

43 W. Somerset Maugham. *Ashenden* (Salem, NH: Ayer Co. Pub., 1928), 111.

44 The Black Chamber was the German nerve center for deciphering messages and collecting intelligence. Simon Singh, *The Code Book: The Science of Secrecy From Ancient Egypt to Quantum Cryptography* (London: Fourth Estate, 1999), 59–63.

45 Dulles would return to Bern in 1942 as a senior OSS officer and station chief of the U.S. spy organization in charge of occupied Europe. In 1953, he would head a giant CIA high-tech spy house with a multibillion-dollar budget. Murphy, 1–26; "Robert Murphy, Diplomat, Dies," *The New York Times*, 10 Jan. 1978: 1; and Peter Grose, *Gentleman Spy: The Life of Allen Dulles* (New York: Houghton Mifflin, 1994), 30–31.

46 Murphy, 1–26.

47 Murphy, 13.

48 Letters to author from Mildred Murphy Pond, dated October 20 and 27, 2004.

49 Murphy, 10–12.

50 Letter dated January 2, 1919, from W. Carr, Director of Consular Services, U.S. Department of State, Washington, D.C.

51 Cable from Stovall to Washington, D.C. dated May 5, 1919; and from Murphy to W. Carr, May 15, 1919.

52 Murphy, 12.

53 Moving around Europe, traveling to and from the United States, long separations from her husband, and the political tensions of the time all took a toll on Mildred's emotional stability and on the Murphy children. Bob would try to shield his wife from the rounds of receptions, cocktail parties, and dinners. Still, the family was con-

strained by matters of protocol and the code of etiquette when daughters Catherine, Rosemary, and Mildred were growing up. Letters to author from Mildred Murphy Pond, dated October 20 and 27, 2004.

54 U.S. Foreign Service Report dated Munich, April 25, 1922.

55 U.S. Foreign Service Annual Efficiency Report dated Munich, April 17, 1924.

56 Murphy, 25.

57 Murphy, 13–26; and "Robert Murphy, Diplomat, Dies," *The New York Times*, 10 January 1978: 1.

58 "Consul Defends Wife," *The New York Times*, 4 August 1925: 2.

59 Mildred's disability might have hindered her husband's career if Ambassador William C. Bullitt—a powerful friend of President Franklin Delano Roosevelt's—hadn't later protected him. (One Foreign Service inspector did report from Seville in 1926 that "They [the Murphys and their girls] have lived very quietly because of Mrs. Murphy's ill health, which has been a source of considerable worry to her husband . . . Murphy's usefulness may be affected in the future through the ill-health of his wife.") U.S. Foreign Service Inspector's reports, 1926.

60 Murphy cites 30,000 American residents living in Paris during the Depression years, but Professor Charles Robertson of Smith College puts the number closer to 10,000. *Extrait de bulletin statistique*, 1947; and Murphy, 30.

61 Murphy, 36.

62 Conrad Black, 385.

63 Franklin D. Roosevelt's "Quarantine" Speech, Chicago, October 5, 1937.

64 Black, 427.

65 Black, 403.

66 Neville Chamberlain after the Munich conference, September 30, 1938.

67 Kenneth Pendar, *Adventure in Diplomacy* (New York: Dodd, Mead & Co., 1945), 20.

68 Bullitt's letter to G. Howland Shaw, U.S. Department of State, May 6, 1940; and Lottman, 24–25.

69 Bullitt cabled FDR on May 16, 1940 that ". . . the French Army will be crushed utterly." Orville Bullitt, 427.

70 Letter to the author from Mildred Murphy Pond, dated October 20, 2004.

71 At the last count, Vichy was responsible for 50,000 acts of Aryanizing and appropriation of Jewish property, forbidding 2,000 Jews to exercise their profession, and deporting more than 75,000 Jewish men, women, and children to Nazi extermination camps. *LeMonde*, June 2, 2006; and Paxton, *Vichy France and the Jews*, 103.

72 Murphy, 37–41; Ian Ousby, *Occupation: The Ordeal of France 1940–1944* (London: Pimlico, 1999), 40–41; Roy Jenkins, *Churchill: A Biography* (London: Macmillan, 2001), 619; and Atkinson, 31.

73 The acronym, "OVRA" may mean *Opera Volontaria di Repressione Antifascista* or

Organo di Vigilanza dei Reati Antistatali. Some scholars have suggested that the acronym for the Italian political police called to mind the *piovra*, the Italian word for the giant squid and its many tentacles. As we shall see, OVRA agents under their chief, Guido Leto, would track Murphy and the twelve vice-consuls throughout their work in North Africa.

74 Orville Bullitt, 431.

75 They had reason to fear: Gen. Erwin Rommel, later dubbed the Desert Fox, would arrive in Tripoli, Libya, in February 1941 to lead the Afrika Korps—German and Italian infantry and armored divisions—against British forces. Some seventeen million French, Arabs, and Berbers—a heterogeneous mix of Christians, Muslims, and Jews—lived in Algeria, Morocco, and Tunisia under French colonial rule. Their land was spread over a million square miles stretching from the Libyan Desert to the Atlantic coast at the Strait of Gibraltar—the sea route from the Atlantic Ocean to the Mediterranean Sea. At its closest point, Tunisia was hardly 200 nautical miles from Catania in Sicily. Murphy, 37–41; Ousby, 40–41; Jenkins, 619; and Atkinson, 6.

76 Murphy was chargé d'affaires at Vichy as of July 3, 1940, when the British suddenly threatened and then attacked the French fleet in British and Mediterranean ports. But in his book, Orville Bullitt writes that Ambassador Bullitt saw Marshal Pétain the day after the attack at Mers-el-Kebir. They likely met in an unofficial capacity, because William Bullitt and Murphy did not want to officially celebrate Independence Day at Vichy in 1940 when the mission would have had to invite the German and Italian delegates. By July 5, 1940, Bullitt was calling himself "The Ambassador in France." He cabled Roosevelt from Madrid on July 12, giving the Vichy reaction to the British attack on the French fleet. Orville Bullitt, 480–490; and Murphy, 53.

77 The French warship *Dunkerque* was run aground, the *Bretagne* blown up, the *Provence* beached, and minor ships immobilized. On hearing the news, a British senior general said, ". . . two nations who were fighting for civilization turned and rent each other while the Barbarians sat back and laughed."

One could hardly have expected the proud French navy to drop to their knees and surrender when threatened by an ally, despite the British rationale. The British destruction of the French fleet at Mers-el-Kebir was certainly a low point in Anglo-French relations; indeed, it was "the last war between Britain and France." Murphy, ever the keen political observer, sided with Charles de Gaulle, who called the event "lamentable." Murphy said that the attack was unnecessary and "perhaps the most serious British mistake in the war." Despite Churchill's belief at the time that the fleet was an "imminent menace" to British interests, Murphy contended that the shocking attack by the British fleet on a proven "ally" cost much more than it gained. It undermined the influence of pro-British moderates in Vichy and de Gaulle in London, whose efforts to organize French resistance was abruptly checked.

After the attack, French military officers, former allies of the British, turned bitterly anti-English. Many of them remained so for the rest of their lives. The British blockade of French ports was salt in French wounds. Adm. William D. Leahy, the U.S. ambassador to Vichy, said he was unable to understand why the British (and some

Americans, too) wanted to maintain "the ill will of the French people by forcing them onto starvation rations"—a fact of life in France between German forced rationing and the British blockade. The French, of course, riposted: Vichy French warplanes bombed British airfields on Gibraltar, and Vichy-controlled forces repelled an Anglo-Gaullist attempt to take Dakar in French West Africa.

For years afterward, French officers distrusted the British and bore a special grudge against their former allies, hindering de Gaulle's work to establish a Free French resistance in Europe. Rhodri Jeffreys-Jones, *Cloak and Dollar: A History of American Secret Intelligence* (New Haven, CT: Yale University Press, 2002), 148; William D. Leahy, *I Was There* (New York: McGraw-Hill Book Company, Inc., 1950), 7–9; Warren Tute, *The Reluctant Enemies: The Story of the Last War Between Britain and France, 1940–1942* (London: HarperCollins, 1990), 27–39; and George E. Melton, *Darlan* (Westport, CT: Praeger, 1998), 86–87, 107.

[78] Murphy, 55.

[79] Murphy, 55.

[80] Murphy, 56.

[81] Murphy, 56–57.

[82] Murphy, 55–57.

[83] Murphy, 55–57.

[84] Renée Gosset, *Conspiracy in Algiers* (New York: The Nation, 1945), 204.

[85] Letter to the author from Mildred Murphy Pond, dated November 23, 2004.

[86] As a Vichy minister, Pucheu sought Murphy's favor by pushing the U.S. program to offer economic aid to French North Africa among the ministers in Marshal Pétain's Vichy cabinet. He promoted the plan to senior ministers Pierre Laval and Adm. Darlan. Fascist that he was, Pucheu even tried later to convince Adm. William Leahy to get President Roosevelt to work with Pope Pius XII and arrange a peace compromise with the Nazis. Gosset, 204; Leahy, 47 and 466–467; Melton, 105; Pendar, 211; and Xavier Walter, *Un Roi Pour La France* (Paris: Francois-Xavier de Guibert, 2002), 490.

[87] Historians hold that Banque Worms and a group of businessmen and their German friends formed a prewar financial-industrial establishment to subsidize right-wing movements, and in the 1930s formed a fascist organization, the synarchy, to advance their capitalist interests. Pucheu was eventually banished from Vichy for treachery. (In March 1941 he would be tried for treason, convicted, and shot in Algiers when de Gaulle came to power. To the French monarchists Pucheu's execution was billed as the murder of a patriot; for the Gaullists and communists it was the execution of a traitor.) Gen. Charles de Gaulle would condemn Murphy's association with Pucheu and the so-called Franco-German Parisian high-society refugees in Vichy and in North Africa. Philippe de Gaulle, *De Gaulle mon père* (Paris: Editions Plon, 2003), 266, 282–288.

[88] William A. Hoisington Jr., *The Assassination of Jacques Lemaigre Dubreuil: A French-man Between France and North Africa* (Oxford: Routledge, 2005), 17, 34–36; Melton,

FDR'S 12 APOSTLES

105; and Arthur Layton Funk, *The Politics of TORCH: The Allied Landings and the Algiers Putsch, 1942* (Lawrence, KS: University Press of Kansas, 1974), 29.

89 C. L. Sulzberger, "Up Front With Robert Murphy," *The New York Times*, 23 February 1964: BR1.

90 Adam Nossiter, *The Algeria Hotel: France, Memory, and the Second World War* (New York: Houghton Mifflin, 2001), 208–210.

91 Paxton, *Vichy France, Old Guard and New Order*, 261.

92 Letter to the author from Mildred Murphy Pond, dated November 23, 2004.

93 Albert Kammerer, *Du débarquement africain au meurtre de Darlan* (Paris: Flammarion, 1949), 62.

94 Ousby, 40.

CHAPTER 2 ENDNOTES

95 Demarre Bess, "Our Diplomatic Triumph in North Africa," *The Saturday Evening Post*, 24 December 1942: 21 and 81.

96 Edward Grey, British Foreign Secretary, 1914.

97 Larry Collins and Dominique LaPierre, *Is Paris Burning?* (New York: Simon & Schuster, 1965), 63; and "Robert Trout aboard a Pan Am Clipper," NPR broadcast, July 3, 1999.

98 Hélène de Portès (spelled "des Portes" in Murphy's autobiography) was something of an enigma, and no one in Paris could understand why Reynaud was hypnotized by her. She was not terribly attractive, with a sallow complexion, a big mouth, untidy in dress, and loquacious. In short, she was in the words of one observer, "a dark, homely, talkative little woman." Apparently, though, she made the small-statured Reynaud feel "tall, grand, and powerful." It was later said that "had the Prime Minister been a few inches taller, the world might have been changed." Williams, 95.

99 Murphy, 52.

100 William C. Bullitt, *Report to the American People, 1940* (New York: Houghton Mifflin, 1940).

101 "Diplomat Praises New French Envoy," *The New York Times*, 6 September 1940: 7.

102 Ambassador Henry-Haye would be locked out of the Vichy French Embassy in Washington by the FBI and sent home on November 9, 1942, coinciding with the North African invasion that day. British agents had penetrated the Vichy Embassy in Washington and found a telegram, No. 4093, from Vichy requesting the embassy to transmit "German intelligence information on the movement of British warships undergoing repairs in the United States." Among the other papers found was report 1236-1237, dated July 15, 1941, from the French naval attaché in Washington, reporting to Vichy the status of the British warships: "Illustrious at Norfolk, Repulse at Philadelphia and British cruisers in New York Harbor—all ships under repair and immobilized for months." The report was signed by Ambassador Henry-Haye. And at a Pan Am Clipper stopover in Bermuda, British agents found that Mme. de Chambrun

268

was using her diplomatic status as the wife of a member of the Vichy Embassy in Washington to act as a courier between Nazi-occupied France and the United States. The agents discovered that she was carrying confidential papers promoting a fascist union for Europe, along with plans to launch financial and business arrangements between German cartels, French industry, and the United States. Josée was also found carrying a letter from Jean-Louis Musa to SS-Standartenführer Otto Abetz, the Nazi ambassador to France. (Musa was a Nazi propagandist. Abetz was later involved in the deportation of French Jews from France. Josée's husband, René de Chambrun, did later claim that his mission in the United States was to convince Americans that Britain would hold; and Britain's Lord Halifax did thank him for his efforts in this respect.) Even more damning, British intelligence claimed that René de Chambrun, who held American citizenship under the laws of the State of Maryland as a direct descendant of the Marquis de Lafayette, had created a "French Gestapo" with links to Canada. William Stevenson, *A Man Called Intrepid* (New York: Harcourt Brace Jovanovich, 1976), 308–309; and "French Envoy Held 'Prisoner': Henry-Haye Not Permitted to Leave Embassy and All Visitors Barred," *Los Angeles Times*, 10 November 1942: 2.

[103] Black, 565.

[104] Later, that number would diminish to 50 percent and then shift between 60 to 40 percent, in favor of helping Britain. Black, 577.

[105] As the French government proclaimed a day of mourning, Hitler declared, "In humility we thank God for his blessing. I order the beflagging [sic] of the Reich for ten days, the ringing of bells for seven days." Reichstag speech, June 25, 1940.

[106] Knight, *A Secret Affair*, 41. The author was a friend of Ambassador Knight's, and worked under him at the U.S. Embassy in Karachi, Pakistan from 1958 to 1959. Before his death in 1999, Ambassador Knight confided his two unpublished memoirs, *Code Name Rebecca* and *A Secret Affair* to the author. All references in this work are to the latter manuscript.

[107] Knight, 41.

[108] Biographer Conrad Black describes FDR's personality as "overpoweringly regal; his advisers constituted a court rather than a cabinet." His closest supporters "complained that he deliberately concealed the process of his mind," and he never talked "frankly even with the people who were loyal to him." Indeed, FDR was a mass of conflicting characteristics not so much ill balanced as constantly shifting. Like the agile predator, FDR knew when to emerge, reveal his design, and execute it. Once he was determined to lead opinion and implement a policy, he was unflappable, devious, utterly determined, and usually inspiring, yet cold and distant behind the apparent warmth of personality with which he could overwhelm even the most hardened visitor. Black, 504–505.

[109] Black, 504–505.

[110] Hillenkoetter was well regarded in Washington intelligence circles. The U.S. Navy had been involved in counterinsurgency in Central America, and Hillenkoetter had helped to organize elections in Nicaragua in 1928. Jeffreys-Jones, 128.

[111] Murphy, 55, 67; Tute, 62–63; *Time* Magazine, 24 June 1940; Williams, 119; and John H. Waller, *The Unseen War in Europe* (New York: Random House, 1996), 152–153.

[112] France had the second-largest fleet in Europe; French colonies were strategically important for their military bases and as a source of raw materials—France was a major supplier of aluminum for aircraft production. The bulk of the country's gold reserves—some $150 billion in 1975 terms—was stowed on the island of Martinique. Thus, French power and influence thrown into the German side, its industry geared to the Ruhr's war machine, would have been a disaster for Great Britain and a blow to the United States. Stevenson, 309.

[113] Black, 823.

[114] Brownell and Billings, 294–298.

[115] Murphy, 67–69.

[116] The president and the State Department were mistaken in believing that men like Gen. Weygand would be willing to help the Allied cause. The general had an extraordinary personality; had entered the French military academy Saint-Cyr as someone of "unknown parentage," and was rumored to be of "royal foreign birth." He was anti-Nazi, but he believed the war had been lost and France needed the stability offered by a Pétain government. Paxton, *Vichy France*, 13, 41, 59; and Pendar, 65. As commander in chief of the French Army, Weygand pressed for an armistice with Germany and convinced Gen. Auguste Nogues, the French commander in Morocco, to give up any idea of resisting in North Africa. He brought all governor-generals in North Africa, "into line for the armistice." Later, as the seventy-four-year old delegate-general for North Africa, Weygand personally oversaw the checkmating of Gaullist infiltration in all French Africa.

[117] Murphy, 67–69.

[118] Murphy, 69.

[119] With the help of British naval units, de Gaulle convinced Churchill to send a small Free French and British force to take over Dakar in West Africa. An attempt during September 23–25, 1941 failed when the French governor general, who was supposed to follow de Gaulle, resisted. The effort was seen in London and Washington as "an outrage and a disaster—a clumsy, amateur effort at subversion between Frenchmen that would have given the Germans a pretext to occupy all of France and seize the French fleet at Toulon. It almost ruined de Gaulle." Murphy, 76.

[120] Catherine Murphy suffered from emotional problems as well. In a telephone conversation between Rosemary Murphy (in New York) and the author (in Paris), Ms. Murphy said she thought her sister's battle with mental illness was partly due to the terrible pressure Catherine was under as a twelve-year-old, responsible for her younger sisters when their mother was ill and their father so often absent. Catherine Murphy committed suicide at the Murphy home in Maryland in 1957, when she was thirty-seven years old. Telecom: October 31, 2004.

[121] Months would pass before Daphne would know what had become of him. Gerard

Tuyl was arrested and taken to a German Luftwaffe prison on March 18, 1942. He had joined the Dutch underground and later was executed in a mass shooting on July 20, 1943; his body was thrown into a mass grave. The three hundred bodies were exhumed in December 1945 and given a Dutch national ceremony. Eventually, Daphne received from Holland a pathetic little snapshot of Tony, her eldest son, which Gerry had kept in his pocket in prison. On it was written a last message to his son: "Tony, love your mother. Be with her and protect her always."

[122] Daphne Joan Fry Tuyl Knox, *How Long Till Dawn* (n.p., n.d.), 3.

[123] Tuyl Knox, 3.

[124] There were many British clandestine operations in North Africa after the fall of France, and German and Italian espionage networks run by competing powers among the Nazis. Daphne never knew that Captain Galrow, the British consul general in Algiers and the first of many mentors to this startlingly beautiful blonde mother of two, was the MI6 top agent in place in Algiers. Galrow worked for Commander Wilfred "Biffy" H. Dunderdale, head of the British Secret Intelligence Service (SIS) in London. Dunderdale's mission was to spy on Vichy France, but independent of Gen. de Gaulle's Free French espionage network. The British applied the equation: divide and conquer. Another SIS section did cooperate with the Free French intelligence service in London. Dunderdale tapped a fifty-three-year-old Polish major (later general) intelligence officer named Rygor Slowikowski to form Agence Afrique. The scale of this SIS-financed network was considerable, covering all of French North Africa and including Dakar, all main ports, administrative and military centers, and airfields. The Poles had recruited eighty-nine French agents. On the eve of Torch, their networks were able to provide "intelligence of inestimable value" through two clandestine radio stations. Brooks Richards, *Secret Flotillas: Clandestine Sea Lines to France and French North Africa 1940–1944* (London: HMSO, 1996), 557; and Rygor Slowikowski, *In the Secret Service: The Lighting of the Torch* (London: The Windrush Press, 1988), 250–253.

[125] Algiers was known in French as *Alger la blanche*, because of the city's brilliant white building facades.

[126] Bernard Metz, British Consular Officer, "The North African Imbroglio," *The American Foreign Service Journal*, November 1943 (n.p.).

[127] Gosset, 1–2.

[128] Tuyl Knox, 10.

[129] Tuyl Knox, 18.

[130] Tuyl Knox, 3

[131] Colonel John Knox said, "The Polish network under Rygor's expert guidance and constant supervision was by all odds the most efficient and professional in its field, supplying the Allies with a wealth of valuable and proven material." Before the invasion, Slowikowski supplied SIS with the "main insight on military targets." Slowikowski's intelligence services in North Africa followed on his work for the Polish army and later, the Polish government in exile. He was part of the successful effort

to evacuate thousands of Polish troops from France to England. Maurice Escoute, agent 1847, introduced Daphne to Slowikowski, codename "Curley." It is characteristic of how SIS operated, for neither Daphne nor Slowikowski ever knew, until well after the Torch invasion, that they were both working for Commander Dunderdale and British SIS. Gosset, 1; Richards, 349, 452, 557; Slowikowski, xiv; and Anthony Verrier, *Assassination in Algiers: Churchill, Roosevelt, De Gaulle and the Murder of Admiral Darlan* (New York: Norton, 1990), 96–97.

[132] Tuyl Knox, 48.

[133] Tuyl Knox, 38–54; Slowikowski, 21, 91; Richards, 557; and Pendar, 121–127.

[134] The Germans eventually forced the Vichy French to have Achiary fired and confined to his home. But Daphne's and Slowikowski's network remained untouched, transmitting through their secret radios, or pouching out via the "neutral" U.S. Consulate in Algiers and Tangier. It reported military and naval intelligence and information about German agents in Casablanca, Algiers, and Tunis. Murphy had Achiary freed just before the Torch landings. Tuyl Knox, 40–56; and Knight, 88.

[135] Paraphrase from Shakespeare, *Julius Caesar*, V, iv, 1.

[136] French National Archives, Paris, 2004.

[137] Murphy, 79.

[138] Murphy, 73. Few knew in December 1940 that Adolf Hitler had already issued orders for the invasion of the Soviet Union instead of the feared cross-channel invasion of England.

[139] Murphy, 80.

[140] These misunderstandings sprung from simplistic thinking in Washington, D.C., and from ignorance about the real character and mission of Gen. Weygand. The general was absolutely loyal to Marshal Pétain. He was sent to North Africa with orders from the Marshal to "aggressively root out dissidents" in the civil and military administration, and those suspected of being disloyal to Pétain and Vichy's dedication to stay out of the war. For Weygand, the Franco-German armistice was in fact his design and "the culminating moment of his life." Philip C. F. Bankwitz, *Maxime Weygand and Civil-Military Relations in Modern France* (Cambridge, MA: Harvard University Press, 1967), 328; Hoisington, 63, 155; and Murphy, 74.

[141] Knight, 86.

[142] Ousby, 63.

[143] A month later Darlan would become Vichy foreign minister and vice president of the French Vichy Council of Ministers. It was Hitler's game. He hoped that Darlan would create stability in North Africa, and aid and prevent a Gaullist secession—an event Laval's pro-Nazism might have provoked. Melton, 102.

[144] Hoisington, 63.

[145] Weygand was never committed to anything other than Pétain's politics; of course, the "Armistice was the culminating moment in Weygand's life." Hoisington, 62.

[146] Later, Daphne would write, "I had some slight differences of opinion, of a political kind, with him, but when the almost insoluble intricacies of intrigue are considered, no one man could have done better. He strove for the greatest good for the greatest number. Pressure was brought upon him from all sides, and at the end he was held responsible for the mistakes of others." Tuyl Knox, 42.

[147] Knight, 88; André Beaufre, *La Revanche de 1945* (Paris: Plon, 1966), 68, 74, 79; and Hoisington, 155.

[148] The major historian of the period, Arthur Layton Funk, believes that the most transparent quality of Lemaigre Dubreuil was his "passionate . . . almost childlike ambition to rehabilitate France and to restore the country to a position of dignity . . . Lemaigre Dubreuil admired the non-democratic sociopolitical structure of Marshal Pétain's revolution" (Funk, *The Politics of Torch*, 13). Others saw Lemaigre Dubreuil as more of an opportunist than a patriot—though no doubt he loved France. As a militant anti-communist and anti-socialist he was ready to broker a deal following the German invasion of the Soviet Union, and assuming a German victory, between England and Germany that would restore France to a "great power status" (Hoisington, 63). Lemaigre Dubreuil "would play a very controversial part in North African politics—a friend of Laval's, he would be castigated in Gaullist propaganda as pro-Nazi . . . [as] a wealthy industrialist, he would be accused of serving only his own economic interests." As a friend of Robert Murphy's, "he would be charged with duping the American diplomat into a fascist conspiracy." Funk, *The Politics of Torch*, 13.

[149] French National Archives, Paris, June 2005: official French telephone and physical surveillance reports, 1942–1944 of Murphy, his family, and Lemaigre Dubreuil.

[150] The new White House agency, Coordinator of Information (COI), later the Office of Strategic Services (OSS), under the Joint Chiefs of Staff, was officially established by FDR on July 11, 1941.

[151] With the help of British secret services (SI) and Special Operations Executive (SOE), Donovan quickly pulled into his embryonic agency the "K" organization run by Wallace Banta Phillips, a fledgling unit operating out of U.S. naval intelligence that recruited secret agents. Donovan also arranged for British intelligence and Special Operations to cooperate with COI agents whom he would place in North Africa.

[152] Donovan's wire to Eddy, December 1942, in Cave Brown, *Wild Bill Donovan: The Last Hero*, 321.

[153] Donovan had to produce; he was locked in battle with the U.S. military intelligence establishment that sought "operational elbow room" and the power (and not the least, the millions of dollars in funding) that went with an FDR mandate to carry out secret and subversive activity. Eddy: Secret Memo to Donovan, June 9, 1942, OSS Files, RG 226, Entry 92A, Folder 25.

[154] Murphy, 83.

CHAPTER 3 ENDNOTES

[155] Francisco Franco played dumb and never answered Hitler's propositions directly. Hitler told Mussolini he would prefer to have several teeth pulled rather than undergo the pain of Franco's silence. Howe, 5.

[156] FDR and Murphy trusted Weygand out of desperation. The general was an Anglophobe, and they had earlier rejected Churchill's offer to back Weygand as the head of a dissident French North African government. Churchill had written a letter to Weygand, which Weygand then forwarded to Pétain in Vichy. (Murphy, 77, 115; and Black, 777.)

[157] "U.S. Secrets Leak to Nazis Hinted: State Department Book on 1941 Shows Germans Got Classified Information," *The New York Times*, 11 May 1959: 6.

[158] Murphy, 90–91.

[159] In *Diplomat Among Warriors*, Murphy was in error when he wrote, "they all crossed the Atlantic by ship." Eleven of the vice-consuls traveled to Lisbon, and on to Casablanca, by air. Only one sailed by ship. Murphy, 91.

[160] Pendar, 20.

[161] In 1927, King recorded his life in the French Foreign Legion in a book titled, *L.M. 8046* (the designation of his first unit, "Legion de Marche"). The book, published by Duffield and Company of New York, carried an alternate title: *Ten Thousand Shall Fall.*

[162] U.S. Foreign Service Personnel Files and Efficiency Reports: Consul General H. Earle Russell, October 10, 1941; Robert Murphy, Foreign Service Report, April 30, 1942.

[163] W. Stafford Reid's report to History Office, U.S. Department of State, May 12, 1945, 2. NARA.

[164] Knight, 35.

[165] W. Stafford Reid's report to History Office, 3.

[166] Murphy, 91.

[167] This may be the first time the U.S. Department of State allowed military officers to serve in civilian functions under diplomatic cover, albeit with "special passports," rather than with diplomatic ones. Even today, CIA officers serve in U.S. diplomatic posts abroad as Foreign Service reserve officers.

[168] Reid, 5.

[169] Reid, 5.

[170] State Department memos, April 9–17 and May 1, 1941. NARA.

[171] Knight, 32.

[172] Knight, 33.

[173] Knight, 16.

[174] Later, when stationed at Oran, Algeria, Ridgway and his fellow vice-consul, Leland Rounds, the fifty-year-old rotund veteran of World War I, continued to enjoy the good life. With Ridgway's refined palate, they always managed to have the best wines of North Africa for their table. Knight, 23.

175 The U.S. Air Force was part of the U.S. Army all throughout World War II.

176 Years later, Ridgway told the author that his "cover" story as a humdrum merchandise control officer, inspecting cargoes of tea and condensed milk, never satisfied his wife, who could not understand how the job fitted with his previously professed desire to go to war. It was hardly sufficient to justify, in her eyes, his leaving home and hearth and a very lucrative wine-import business. Ridgway claimed he scrupulously respected the orders for secrecy, despite the effect it had on his marriage. Conversation between Knight and the author, June 1999.

177 Knight, 59.

178 Even today, State Department "Post Reports," written by Foreign Service officers, often exaggerate local conditions. The reports play a role in determining what extra funds will be paid to officers and clerks as "hardship allowances."

179 Three years later, U.S. Marine Herbert Wildman would be killed in the assault on Iwo Jima.

180 Pendar, 11; and Knight, 54–57.

181 "Americans Reach Spain: Ninety-four in Madrid After a Six-Day Trip From Marseille," *The New York Times*, 11 July 1940: 5.

182 Reid, 6.

183 Reid, 6.

184 "Two U.S. Vice–Consuls Off to Morocco: Their Departure on Clipper for Lisbon Recalls Plan to Send Food to French Colonies," *The New York Times*, 1 June 1941: 7.

185 Franklin O. Canfield, *Memoirs of a Long and Eventful Life* (n.p., n.d.), 17. Portions of Canfield's unpublished memoirs were shared with the author through the courtesy of Peter M. F. Sichel, a former OSS officer and CIA station chief, and through the offices of Jacques Tétrault, a member of the firm McCarthy Tétrault, Barristers & Solicitors, Montreal, Canada.

186 Knight, 58–60.

187 Reid, 6.

188 The United States had never recognized the French Protectorate over the city of Tangier. The international city was run by a sultan, and the American representative was a minister of the legation.

189 Knight, 66.

190 Present company excluded, Knight professed contempt and ridicule for diplomats and their alleged "striped pants softness." Knight, 23.

191 Knight, 67.

192 For a description of the one-time pad cipher, see Simon Singh, *The Code Book* (London: Fourth Estate, 2000), 120–121.

193 Traveling in North Africa at the time was next to impossible. Gasoline was a luxury doled out liter by liter to priority users: hospitals, the armed forces, and senior officials. Most cars, trucks, and buses were converted to using "gazogene," a charcoal-based poor

fuel that burned in a four-to-six-foot-high cylinder added to the vehicle. The charcoal was lighted, and when combustion was reached, air was blown over the burning charcoal, resulting in a poor gas that retained explosive properties. The by-product was then piped into the motor's cylinders instead of gasoline. The result was a foul-smelling, loud "farting" vehicle that moved in lurches and never attained half of the engine's theoretical rating. Knight, 70.

[194] Knight, 70.

[195] Knight, 73.

[196] Knight, 147.

[197] David Wooster King, OSS Report, RG 226, Entry 99, Box 49, NARA.

[198] "Daniels Commends Two for Rescues: Lieut. Commander Maxwell and Lieut. Culbert Showed Heroism When Dirigible Went Down," *The New York Times*, 15 July 1918: 7.

[199] Shakespeare's *Henry V*, III, I, 32 and *The Merchant of Venice*, V, I, 85.

CHAPTER 4 ENDNOTES

[200] Pendar, 13. Vichy had already proclaimed that a German invasion (or an Allied invasion) of North Africa would be repelled by French forces using the native Arab and Berber warrior troops. It was only when Germany invaded the Soviet Union and British–de Gaulle forces took Syria that a certain hesitant calm returned to North Africa.

[201] Murphy, 91.

[202] Gestapo report passed to Murphy by a friendly French police officer in Morocco. Murphy, 91.

[203] Pendar, 22.

[204] From the files of William A. Eddy, found in NARA, RG 226, Entry 92A, Folder 25: Secret Memo to Donovan, June 9, 1942.

[205] Reid, 11.

[206] The German and Italian Armistice Commission reported any signs of French efforts to rearm, collecting every scrap of information about the Vichy bureaucracy and whatever they could learn about the work at the U.S. Consulate. They had entrée into French military installations, equipment, and personnel. Their agents—police, military, and naval officers, technicians, and businessmen—did their best to remind everyone that France was a beaten country. They had no direct power over Vichy officers in Morocco, but their recommendations were transmitted for action to Berlin and Rome and then to German and Italian agencies in Paris and in Vichy. The commission mostly ran an efficient espionage and propaganda organization targeting the French community and the Arab and Berber peoples.

[207] Reid, 13–15.

[208] Atkinson, 131.

[209] Howe, 40.

[210] Reid, 19.

[211] Reid, 22a.

[212] Reid, 13.

[213] Reid, 14.

[214] Coon, OSS files, RG 226, Entry 99, Box 43.

[215] Pendar, 63.

[216] Pendar wrote after the war that he and his colleagues felt that they had been dropped like so many "Alices" into a North African wonderland. "I wanted to do something useful for my country, for the anti-Nazi cause, and for France." Pendar, 12.

[217] Pendar, 23.

[218] *Time* Magazine, 1 September 1941: 24.

[219] Pendar, 46; Russell, U.S. FSO efficiency Report, Oct. 16, 1941; *Time* Magazine, 1 September 1941: 24; and Canfield's memoirs.

[220] Pendar, 38–45; Dept. of State memo of conversation between Kitchel and Villard, April 15, 1943; and Knight, 80.

[221] *Time* Magazine, May–June 1941.

[222] Field Marshall Alan Brooke, *War Diaries 1939–1945* (London: Weidenfeld & Nicolson, 2001), 26.

[223] In the summer of 1941, Britain's strength in Africa lay in holding East Africa and the Red Sea. As de Gaulle's Free French forces fought in Africa, British forces seized Basra, Iraq, and secured the Mosul oil fields and Turkey's back door.

[224] In fact, Franco had refused Hitler's request for passage of German troops through Spain on December 7, 1941. *Time* Magazine, 26 May 1941.

[225] French officers meant to defend against a German landing but were not ready to seize North Africa and fight on the Allied side—an attitude not necessarily understood in Washington.

[226] He was also codenamed "Mr. Mole," though his real name was "Pelabon." From the National Archives, OSS Files, RG 226, Entry 99, Box 49.

[227] OSS Files, NARA. There is no record of the nationality of Miss Ellis, but she was probably English.

[228] King, OSS Files, RG 226, Entry 99, Box 49, no page number; Reid, 63.

[229] Tangier was acquired by the British in 1662 when the "amorous comedian" Charles II married the Portuguese princess, Catherine de Braganza. The lady apparently had the city in her purse. It was later abandoned to the Moors, and, in 1905, the German Hohenzoller took the city. After the Great War, Tangier was administered by England, France, Spain, and Italy.

[230] From a photocopy of a book entitled *Wartime Spymaster*, 343.

[231] Eddy, Monogram, "Spies and Lies in Tangier," Papers of William Alfred Eddy, Box 13, Seeley G. Mudd Manuscript Library, Princeton University, Princeton, NJ.

232 Carleton S. Coon. *A North African Story: The Anthropologist as OSS Agent 1941–1943* (Ipswich, Mass., Gambit Publications, 1981), 12.

233 Randolph Mohammed Gusus.

234 O'Donnell, 34–35.

235 Coon never revealed the real names of Strings and Tassels. Later, when working with the British Army, Browne and Coon would perfect a "mule turd" explosive device shaped to look like mule droppings and loaded to destroy Axis tires.

236 Ed Cray, *General of the Army: George C. Marshall, Soldier and Statesman* (New York: W. W. Norton & Company, 1990), 197.

237 Cray, 197–198.

CHAPTER 5 ENDNOTES

238 Knight, 183–185, and as told to the author by Knight at Inxent, France, spring 1999. One wonders if the story of the German's murder might be apocryphal. The only confirmation the author can find outside of Ridgway Knight's memoirs is the reference to codename "Necktie" in OSS files, which referred to Abbé Cordier.

239 Knight, 83–87; and Rounds, OSS Files, RG 226, Entry 99, Box 49.

240 Knight 75–76; and Rounds, Foreign Service biographic and personnel records.

241 Knight, 121.

242 From a WWI pejorative word used to describe Germans: an alteration of *hinder:* the human buttocks; and Dago: an offensive term used to describe Italians.

243 Knight, 92–95.

244 Knight and Rounds found these borderline fascist sentiments typical of what European Algerians thought in 1941. The moral values proclaimed by the Marshal: Work, Family and Country ("Travail, Famille, Patrie") appealed to the essentially bourgeois mood of the people and fitted in with their resolute anti-communist attitude and fear of the Soviets. (The only group hostile to Vichy was the Jews, who were relatively more numerous in Algeria than in Metropolitan France. While only a little over 1 percent in France, Jews numbered about 10 percent of the non-Moslem population in Algeria.) The Jews were uneasy on two scores: because of the Nazi anti-Jewish so-called "Nuremberg laws," which the Vichy regime was to introduce piecemeal in France, and because in October 1870, during the Franco-Prussian war, as the Prussians were besieging Paris and France's defeat seemed probable, the government adopted the "Cremieux law." This measure automatically gave French nationality to all Algeria's native Jews. (Moslems were denied this status.) Intended to strengthen France's hand against the Moslems, who might be tempted to take advantage of her defeat and revolt, this measure was to contribute to their subsequent alienation because of its patent inequity. After the 1940 Armistice, what with the state of mind prevailing in Vichy, the Jews feared the abrogation of the "Loi Cremieux"; and Vichy repealed the law in 1942. Knight, 98, 117.

245 Knight, 197, 212.

[246] OSS Algiers Files.

[247] Knight, 129–132; and Rounds, OSS Files, RG 226, Entry 99, Box 49.

[248] Knight, 140–145.

[249] Knight, 147.

[250] Knight, 147–148.

[251] Quotation attributed to Justice Felix Frankfurter in Walter Issacson and Evan Thomas, *The Wise Men* (New York: Simon and Schuster, 1986), 456.

[252] *Time* Magazine, 1 September 1941: 24.

[253] *Time* Magazine, 8 September 1941: 1.

CHAPTER 6 ENDNOTES

[254] The tale of John Knox and Daphne Joan Fry Tuyl is a "love story" that ends well—and the subject for another book. Suffice to say that Knox was born to a wealthy "high-society" Bostonian family that traced its ancestry back to the *Mayflower*. He lost his father at age three, and was raised in wealth in the United States and Europe, attending for a time Groton, Harvard, Oriel College, Oxford, and then entering the French military academy at Saint-Cyr (the West Point of France). From there, he graduated as a second lieutenant and joined the French Foreign Legion. Knox fought in the battles of the Moroccan Riff as a Legion officer (something out of the film *Beau Geste*, starring Gary Cooper, whom Knox resembled). He was wounded twice, retiring as a captain to begin a carefree life in Paris and southern France. He was for a time one of the acquaintances of Ernest Hemingway and his "lost generation" crowd. As World War II loomed, Knox returned to the United States, was commissioned a captain in the United States Army, and was recruited as one of the original Twelve Apostles. After his adventures in North Africa, John Knox married Daphne Joan Fry Tuyl, a British spy who aided the French Resistance and the vice-consuls in their work. At their wedding, Robert Murphy gave the bride and groom away. (FSO personnel records; and from an unpublished biography by A. Derek Knox and Alexandra Curley.)

[255] A daughter, Alexandra, was born in 1944 when Daphne and John married.

[256] Tuyl Knox, 85–91.

[257] Tuyl Knox.

[258] Murphy, 79.

[259] Eddy, OSS Files, RG 226, Entry 99, Box 49; and Murphy, 101.

[260] Slowikowski, Appendix B.

[261] The term "Gestapo" is used here as an umbrella term for all the Nazi security services working in North Africa before the Allied invasion. In fact, there were at least five official German security services there, concerned with the collection of intelligence, counterintelligence, security, and radio surveillance. In addition, the Italian security services, OVRA and SIM, were involved in espionage and dirty tricks against Vichy French, Allied forces, and their agents and Americans. SS *Reichsführer* Heinrich

Himmler was chief of the principal Reich security services: the *Reichsicherheitshauptamt* under SS Chief Ernst Kaltenbrunner. Their organization was composed principally of the SD (*Sicherheitsdienst*) Inland (*Amt III* counterespionage), the Gestapo (*Amt IV*, political police), the Kripo (*Amt V*, criminal police), and the SD *Ausland* (*Amt VI*, foreign espionage services). They were a separate unit from Admiral Wilhelm Canaris's *Abwehr* foreign intelligence service until Canaris was murdered in 1944.

262 There were well over 100,000 Polish officers and servicemen stranded in France or prisoners in German camps in France after the French-German armistice. Slowikowski, 7.

263 Slowikowski, 22.

264 Knight, 99.

265 Knight, 146; and Pendar, 20.

266 Twelve men—the original Twelve Apostles—were recruited in Washington to serve under Murphy in North Africa. Over time some of them would be replaced for various reasons.

267 Italian Foreign Ministry report, 1931–1945, 57. Carmel J. Doublet, connected with the U.S. mission in Tunis, was also involved. Eddy, secret memo to Donovan in OSS files RG 226, Entry 92A, Folder 25; and King and Coon reports, Entry 99, Box 49.

268 Knight, 90.

269 Warren Tute, *The Reluctant Enemies: The Story of the Last War Between Britain and France, 1940–1942* (London: HarperCollins, 1990), 189.

270 Knight, 82; and Coon, OSS Files, RG 226, Entry 99, Box 43.

271 Pendar, 78.

272 Author's teleconference with Rosemary Murphy, New York, October 5, 2004.

273 Correspondence, Department of State personnel files, HI 296-300, April–May 1941.

274 Correspondence, Department of State personnel files, HI 295, August 1941.

275 Pendar, 19.

276 Ridgway Knight's words were a cutting observation made by an astute and successful diplomat almost fifty years after the cloak-and-dagger events and dangers he shared with his boss, Robert Murphy. Knight served as U.S. ambassador to Syria, Belgium, and Portugal after being deputy chief of mission in Karachi. Knight, 85.

277 FSO Efficiency Reports: Russell, 1941 and Murphy, 1942. From a memo dated August 25, 1945, from a State Department Officer whose initials were penciled in as "MVD."

278 Paxton, *Vichy France: Old Guard and New Order 1940–1944*, 93.

279 Pendar, 78–79.

280 On pages 576–577 of his book, *Wild Bill Donovan: The Last Hero*, author Anthony Cave Brown claims that Murphy's life "had been blotched by tragedy because Murphy's wife was an incurable manic-depressive." Cave Brown goes on to say: "A lonely man, he

had early in his work encountered the Princess de Ligne, the representative in North Africa of the Comte de Paris . . . Their relation had deepened from one of politics to a matter of the heart." La Princess Marie de Ligne, wife of Prince Alexandre de Turin et Taxis and the mother of two sons, moved to Algiers before the occupation and was there during Murphy's stay. To the contrary, Donovan (or Cave Brown) may have been deceived by disinformation aimed against Murphy. In *The Unseen War in Europe*, author John H. Waller writes: "In the subterranean war of French North African politics, people opposing Murphy spread salacious gossip linking him romantically with the Princess de Ligne, an agent of the Comte de Paris" (Waller, 254). The author can find no evidence that Murphy had love affairs in Algiers with anyone, including the Princess as cited in Cave Brown. Boule Rodier married Comte de Breteuil and lived at Villa Taylor, Marrakech. (Conversations with Christine Guerlain, Paris, 2004.)

[281] Tute, 227.

[282] One of the partisans to insurrection known to Murphy and his vice-consuls included the fascist Jean Rigault, whom Dave King in Casablanca spotted as an "authoritarian, high handed" blowhard. He was Lemaigre Dubreuil's "man Friday" and editor of the newspaper *Le Jour-Echo de Paris,* which Lemaigre Dubreuil owned. Another major insurrectionist was Colonel A. S. Van Hecke, who became close to vice-consul John Knox. A former French legionnaire, Van Hecke was the North African commissioner of the unarmed *Chantiers de la Jeunesse* (Youth Workshops), a group not unlike the American Civilian Conservation Corps. The group wore a distinctive and dramatic uniform: short jackets, baggy trousers, and blue-green berets. They were not unlike a grown-up version of the Boy Scouts. Van Hecke touted them as potential shock troops to augment the regular army; but the leadership was mediocre and their military training spotty. Van Hecke, however, "possessed ideal qualifications for organizing a clandestine movement: he controlled transport and gasoline, had authorization to travel, and developed contacts with the military and civilian leadership. This enthusiasm was not counterweighed with that circumspection necessary for underground conspiracy, and he had several close calls with security officers." Funk, *The Politics of Torch*, 20. Other major players in the insurrection plan included army major Germain Jousse along with the diplomat Jacques Tarbé de Saint-Hardouin; the Catholic priests, Fathers Théry and Abbé Cordier; Lt. Bernard Karsenty; Colonel Tostain (who later turned out to be a traitor); plus some young Jews such as Roger and Pierre Carcassonne, who were militantly opposed to Vichy anti-Semitism.

[283] Murphy would become a lifelong friend of the Lemaigre Dubreuil family. His postwar written testimony to a Paris court on behalf of Lemaigre Dubreuil probably saved the man from prison as an anti–de Gaulle collaborator. Hoisington, 65; note dated March 26, 2005, from Mme. Christiane Guerlain (family Lesieur), who lived with her sister, the wife of Jacques Lemaigre Dubreuil in Algiers, where she worked with the French Red Cross from 1941–1942; and Foreign Relations of the United States (FRUS) 1942, 2:232–233 found in Hoisington, 155.

[284] Funk, *The Politics of Torch*, 20–21; and Knight, 12.

[285] King's Report, July 19, 1944, OSS Files, RG 226, Entry 99, Box 49, unnumbered.

286 Wilkes had powerful friends in the nation's capital, and once there, he was hired by COI (OSS) to be the assistant to Wallace Phillips, chief of K section of COI Secret Intelligence. FS Efficiency Report, Consul General H. Earl Russell, October 16, 1941; and King's Report, July 19, 1944, OSS Files, RG 226, Entry 99, Box 49, unnumbered.

287 Murphy would assign Canfield to Dakar, West Africa, but he refused to go and returned home. Like Wilkes, he had nothing to fear for his future. He was a close friend of John Foster Dulles, the future U.S. secretary of state and the brother of Allen Dulles, who was just then trying to enter Switzerland to take up the prime Europe listening post for the OSS. In Washington, Canfield, too, was immediately hired by OSS. In 1945, "Colonel Canfield" was assigned by Donovan to be the OSS representative at Supreme Headquarters in Europe at Berlin, where he served with Murphy. His job was to push an aggressive American secret intelligence policy: the penetration of Russian and British sectors. Such are the vagaries of the Foreign Service and spying. "Torch History," edited by Carleton Stevens Coon for General William Donovan's eyes, Washington, D.C., September 6, 1944. NARA, Record Group 226, Entry 99, Box 49, OSS files; and Cave Brown, *Wild Bill Donovan: The Last Hero,* 635.

288 A year later, Bartlett was back in North Africa as a U.S. Air Corps Major. FS Efficiency Reports, Consul General H. Earle Russell, July 8, 1942. Transcript of telephone message from Arnold to Shapiro, signed M. Schumann, March 13, 1943, State Department Personnel Files.

289 Coster was highly decorated for his service in WWII. King, OSS Files; and "Donald Q. Coster, 76, Former A.I.D. Official," *The New York Times,* 8 June 1984: 19.

290 Whirlwind's function was to monitor and decipher radio traffic. The center managed to exist in Algiers and unoccupied France due to the efforts of French Colonel Rivet, the head of the Vichy Intelligence Services, who was anti-Nazi and pro-Allies. The network's existence was known to only a handful of persons selected by MI6 officers in London. Officers reading Slowikowski's reports never knew how they were transmitted. Slowikowski, 60–61.

291 Slowikowski, 43.

292 Single-source intelligence and its collection, analysis, and dissemination had its hazards. One constantly had to keep in mind that though the information originated from Slowikowski's network, it reached Washington and London by two different routes: to the vice-consuls in Algiers and then onto Washington via Tangier for analysis and dissemination there; and to London, where it may have been digested and then re-fed to Washington. This led to the belief that the information came from different sources. The CIA today demands that their agents produce documents copied from original papers directly from a source's safekeeping. Author's experience.

293 Melton, 48.

294 FRUS (1941) 2:185 in Melton, 129.

295 Weygand told Murphy that the U.S. would have to provide modern arms to equip the eight French army divisions he commanded in Algeria, Morocco, and Tunisia.

Maxime Weygand, *Rappele au Service* (Paris: Flammarion, 1950), 492.

[296] Weygand's dismissal was part of a settlement that Darlan negotiated with the Germans. Melton, 133. Under the Murphy-Weygand aid agreement, North Africa received: 12,000 tons of diesel fuel; 10,000 tons of gasoline; 6,000 tons of other petroleum products; 4,000 tons of coal; 900 tones of cotton products; 300 tons of canned milk; and 1,250 tons of yarn. Another 60,000 tons of petroleum products were on the high seas by the time Weygand was recalled to Vichy. Weygand, 488.

[297] Murphy, 94–95.

[298] Murphy, 94–95.

[299] Murphy, 94–95.

[300] Darlan retained his authority as commander in chief of all French forces—navy, army, and air—when Laval replaced him in April 1942 at the Germans' insistence. Murphy, 62, 111; and Ousby, *Occupation* 76–77.

[301] William L. Langer, *Our Vichy Gamble* (New York: Knopf, 1947), 123 and footnotes 10–11; captured German documents: report of the meeting of Hitler with Darlan, December 24, 1940; State Department and War Department interrogations of Dr. Paul Schmidt and the manuscript study of German foreign policy by Erich Kordt from Leahy File, 7, supplemented by tel. (January 21, 1941) from Leahy.

[302] Melton, 159–161.

PART TWO

[303] *Bartlett's Familiar Quotations*, 432.

CHAPTER 7 ENDNOTES

[304] For Dave King and many OSS officers, the U.S. State Department and its overseas components were a "snake pit" (OSS Files, RG 226).

[305] *Wartime Spymaster*, 342.

[306] When it came to French territory de Gaulle would not give an inch. Thus, after receiving a call for help from the residents of the Vichy-French–controlled islands of Saint-Pierre-et-Miquelon, north of the Grand Banks and west of St. Johns Newfoundland in the Atlantic, he decided to bring the islands under the Free French banner. De Gaulle initially obtained approval from Churchill and the British Foreign Office, but at the last moment on December 15 Churchill asked de Gaulle to wait thirty-six hours while the Foreign Office checked with the U.S. State Department. As strange as it may seem, although the U.S. was now at war with Germany and Japan, Roosevelt wanted to personally assure Marshal Pétain that the United States would respect the integrity of French possessions. He asked Canada to send monitors to the island to screen broadcasting from there. De Gaulle would not stomach the presence of Canadians (a foreign power) on the island. He ordered the island seized by Free French marines on Christmas Eve. In acting against Roosevelt's wishes, de Gaulle earned the eternal antagonism of FDR; and his secretary of state, Cordell Hull, was

furious and insisted that he would not tolerate any action that would compromise U.S. relations with Marshal Pétain. This storm in a teacup would have enormous future costs for U.S. relations with Gen. de Gaulle. Kersaudy, 174.

With America in the war De Gaulle instinctively knew that from December 7 onward Churchill would never act without Roosevelt's approval. He also knew he would be excluded from the intimate circle of the two Princes—and from the political decisions of the Anglo-American-Soviet superpowers. De Gaulle knew how hard it was to recruit French officers to his Free French movement—for that meant choosing between "legality and honor": whether to follow de Gaulle's Free French in London and go on fighting the Germans or obeying their legal oaths to Marshal Pétain—which meant collaboration with the occupier. The choice may seem clear (to join de Gaulle) sixty years later; but in 1940 it often came down to how a man would deal with the loss of family, friends, and career. Fleeing to England or some other Free French base meant leaving wife, children, and family in occupied France and being labeled a traitor by fellow officers and prosecuted as one by the state. Paxton, *L'Armee de Vichy*, 154; and Jean-Louis Crémieux-Brilhac, 368–375. De Gaulle and his Free French movement, though backed by Churchill, would eventually be accepted but would never be popular in the White House. Murphy and his vice-consuls misestimated the de Gaulle phenomena in North Africa until 1943. Still, Gen. de Gaulle was regarded as untrustworthy and likely to impose a Gaullist regime on the French people after the war. Kersaudy, 174.

[307] Jenkins, 647.

[308] Deleted from Churchill's quotation: ". . . except for the changes in Syria and certain adjustments which may be necessary on the frontier of Spanish Morocco." Verrier, 70–71. "Enigma" was a secret British code-breaking operation that permitted the Allies to read German signals. Churchill knew from Enigma that a German occupation of Vichy France in the event of an Anglo-American force descending on North Africa was more likely than not.

[309] Atkinson, 16. Churchill suffered a heart attack on December 26 after successfully addressing both houses of Congress.

[310] Dakar's strategic port guarded the Atlantic routes used by U.S. convoys carrying tanks, arms, and foodstuffs through the southern routes, via South Africa, to British armies in Egypt. If American ships had been attacked by German warships operating from Dakar and Casablanca, the American freighters would have been cut to ribbons and the 8th Army would probably have continued to retreat through Egypt.

[311] Bulletin n.12–14: French Overseas Territories Under Italian Control 1941. Original source: *Notiziario n. 12 relativo ai territori francesi oltremare sotto controllo italiano dal 1941. Notiziario n. 14 relativo ai territori francesi oltremare sotto controllo italiano dal 1 al 15 giugno 1941.* Author's translation.

[312] Paxton, *Vichy France*, 44.

[313] King, OSS files, RG 226, Entry 99, Box 49, 5.

[314] FSO Efficiency Reports 1941-1942; King OSS Files, RG 226.

[315] Pendar, 20–21.

[316] The author has only briefly mentioned Robert Solborg, a U.S. military intelligence and OSS agent involved in agent recruitment and espionage in Algeria, Morocco, and Tunisia. In 1942 his unsanctioned activities would cause his recall to Washington and separation from OSS. Solborg then returned to Spain to work for U.S. military intelligence. Cave Brown, *Wild Bill Donovan: The Last Hero,* 225–226.

[317] Today, the American Legation building in Tangier is a museum and research center.

[318] Cave Brown, *Wild Bill Donovan: The Last Hero,* 321–322.

[319] To this day, the British claim they tried to land ten tons of arms and explosives at various locations in Algeria (Brandon mission) but that their boats failed to make contact with shore parties. Richards, 582–583.

[320] Murphy, 92.

[321] Murphy, 92.

[322] As late as 1944, Reid would not reveal the real name of his French wireless operator.

[323] After being transferred to Tangier, Coster returned home when he failed to satisfy Eddy and Murphy. COI cable: Raichle to Donovan S.I., May 4, 1942; and COI letter, David Williamson to W. E. DeCourcy, June 24, 1942.

[324] Reid, author-edited, 58–69.

[325] Funk, *The Politics of Torch,* 27, 35.

[326] Knight, 197.

[327] Many years after the war, one of Knight's colleagues who had been stationed in Tangier at the time told Ridgway that the British service, MI6, which was supposed to make arms deliveries, had sabotaged the efforts out of distrust of the French. Ridgway Knight held that the British were always lukewarm toward the entire Murphy mission. At a meeting in Paris in 1999, he told this author that Robert Murphy always believed that the British had intentionally bungled the arms deliveries because of their dislike for the French groups with whom the Americans were working. See also Richards, 568.

[328] Murphy, 117. (written some twenty years after the events). After Pearl Harbor, FDR would send Douglas MacArthur II to propose that Weygand head a separatist movement in North Africa. The general refused, and later, was imprisoned by the Nazis.

[329] The holdup was due to British Board of Trade objections. The British did not trust Murphy; they thought him both "Anglophobe and Vichyphil." Verrier, 66.

[330] Through Knox, Boyd, and Daphne Joan Fry Tuyl.

[331] Slowikowski, 117, 152.

[332] *The New York Times,* 22 June 1942: 1.

[333] *The New York Times,* 22 June 1942: 1.

[334] James B. Reston, "News Puts Damper on Churchill Visit: But Washington Sees Mid-East Crisis as Incidental in His Planning With Roosevelt," *The New York Times,* 22 June 1942: 1.

335 Prior to Torch, Murphy and the vice-consuls dealt with many potential insurgency groups in North Africa, though the principal leaders remained Jacques Lemaigre Dubreuil, Henri d'Astier de la Vigerie, Jean Rigault (Lemaigre Dubreuil's associate, whom Dave King distrusted), Colonel Germain Jousse (whose plan was rejected by Eisenhower in London), and Colonel Van Hecke, leader of the *Jeunesse*. Murphy and the vice-consuls believed that the Gaullist Free French movement was not acceptable to the North African officer corps, and had a weak civilian following in North Africa. It is true that with the anti–de Gaulle sentiment in Washington, they had little incentive to seek out or include Free French resistance units into their planning. But Murphy could be faulted for not making a greater effort to bring French generals Juin and Nogues to the American side. Likewise, Murphy never received a response from his report to Washington about his contacts with Adm. Darlan's representatives in Algiers. FRUS (1942) 2:331–334; Funk, *The Politics of Torch*, 34, 37–39; and Murphy, 111–112, 115.

336 Murphy had met Giraud in Paris.

337 Mark W. Clark, *Calculated Risk* (New York: Harper and Brothers, 1950) 70–71. In October, Murphy told Clark in London that "Darlan was expected to arrive in Algiers in the following week." Darlan did indeed visit North Africa in October for an inspection trip.

338 Funk, *The Politics of Torch*, 43.

339 Murphy, 117–118. Darlan was later declared an anti-Semite fascist. He was no more an anti-Semite—a congenital disease in France at the time (and still today)—than other French officers Murphy dealt with in North Africa, including Weygand. And he was neither fascist nor pro-German. Darlan was an opportunist patriot attuned to changing political climate in Europe after Germany attacked the Soviet Union and after Pearl Harbor. See Funk, *The Politics of Torch*, 23–24, 35; and Melton, 74, 77.

CHAPTER 8 ENDNOTES

340 FRUS (1942) 2:343, 345; and Murphy's cables to Washington, August 9 and 14, 1942, HI 293 and 295.

341 The Torch decision was debated for months in Washington and London. The military was opposed, preferring to wait and invade Europe cross-channel. They were overruled by Roosevelt and Churchill, who feared the collapse of Russia, hard pressed by the Germans on the Soviet front, and because Torch had become Roosevelt's baby (as FDR wanted action in a congressional election year). Funk, *The Politics of Torch*, 91; and Murphy, 103.

342 Donovan's work was now complicated by the fact that his embryonic organization had been removed from the White House and placed under the Joint Chiefs of Staff. The COI became the OSS. But there is some evidence that Gen. Donovan's agents came to the same conclusion about Giraud, who had escaped from a German prison camp and who was on record as being anti-Nazi and seeking to kick the Germans out of France. Cave Brown, *Wild Bill Donovan: The Last Hero*, 234–235. At the same

time, Donovan began looking into Jacques Lemaigre Dubreuil's past history. What he found was hair-raising (see Appendix). Still, Murphy insisted that his friend was pro-American and anti-Nazi and was working in the best interest of the United States.

343 Murphy, 103.

344 The result of Solborg's (unauthorized) talks resulted in a detailed three-part agreement that Murphy and Solborg negotiated with the Group of Five and Mast. A memorandum was prepared (*proces-verbal*) specifying Gen. Giraud's role in a North African putsch, and protocols that would govern the military, political, and economic future of a liberated North Africa. These were taken by Solborg by hand to Washington. For an elaboration of these complicated negotiations, deceptions, and the "explosive implications" of the protocols, see Funk, *The Politics of Torch*, 53–55.

345 Funk, *The Politics of Torch*, 42; and FRUS (1942) 2:331–343.

346 Murphy, 101.

347 There is an amusing entry in FDR's secretary William D. "Bill" Hassett's diary for September 8, 1942: "Major Frank McCarthy flew up with two off-the-record bigwigs, who conferred with the President." Could "Major Frank McCarthy" be an earlier alias of Murphy's—perhaps an alternative to "Lt. Colonel MacGowan"? Murphy apparently flew from Washington, D.C., into the airfield at New Hackensack, New York (today's Duchess County Airport), thirteen miles from Roosevelt's home at Hyde Park. If this entry truly refers to Murphy's visit, then in his book *Diplomat Among Warriors*, Murphy erred in the date he met with the president. Moreover, if Hassett is accurate about Murphy's meeting with FDR and Harry Hopkins, then who were the two "off-the-record bigwigs"? We may never know. FDR kept no notes, transcripts, or memoranda of his conversation with visitors. Information thanks to Robert H. Parks, Franklin D. Roosevelt Presidential Library and Museum, March 9, 2006.

348 Joseph Persico, *Roosevelt's Secret War* (New York: Random House, 2001), 208.

349 Murphy, 102, 108.

350 Leahy, 114–116.

351 Professor Arthur Layton Funk says that after leaving Casablanca, "Coster was being transferred to the Air Force and thereafter helped plan Torch" in London. We do know that Coster was a problem to Eddy and "somewhat disgruntled" in Casablanca. He refused to stay in Casa and "went up to Algiers, saw Murphy before his departure for Washington, then returned to America." Murphy had now lost four of the original group of FDR's Twelve Apostles. It is possible the Coster switched from a State Department role in January 1942 to a job with the OSS under Eddy. Murphy, 103; Funk, *The Politics of Torch*, 288, fn 36; OSS files, RG 226, Entry 99; and Coster's Foreign Service and OSS personnel file.

352 Murphy did not know, or would not say, that Giraud had Pétainist sympathies, had no place in the hierarchy of the French army, no popular following, no organization, no social imagination, no interest in politics, no program, and no administrative abilities. All of this would only be known to Eisenhower later. Eisenhower apparently did not have at hand an analysis of the political and military intelligence reports that the

U.S. vice-consuls and Rygor Slowikowski had forwarded to Washington and London in the past year. He relied on briefings from Eddy and Murphy. Later, Ike would have the benefit of both sophisticated American and British intelligence and civil affairs advisers W. H. B. Mack for the British and Murphy as his chief.

353 This crucial assurance is fudged in Murphy's book, *Diplomat Among Warriors*. But Eisenhower was forewarned by William Eddy in their London meeting, when Patton had remarked of Eddy, "the son-of-a-bitch has really been shot at, hasn't he"—that American forces could expect considerable resistance from specific French units. Eddy had been very clear: "We believe the area in which the French will be most favorable to us is around Algiers, with the areas in which we will probably encounter resistance, those between Oran and Casablanca and in Tunis . . . the chances of effecting initial landings is better than even but that the chances for overall success of operation, including capture of Tunis before it can be forced by the Axis, are considerably less than 50 percent." Funk, *The Politics of Torch*, 94.

354 Darlan was opposed to any relations with or the involvement of Great Britain in North Africa.

355 One must wonder if anyone in that smoke-filled cottage, with wine corks popping, brought up that the United States would soon launch an invasion on the territory of a neutral nation without a declaration of war; that Roosevelt did not want to make war against the fascist-oriented Vichy, preferring an alliance with Pétain's Vichy government; that most of France's colonial administrators and soldiers remained loyal to Pétain; and that there was slim hope of getting Pétain's secret support for an American invasion. Nor did the group at Telegraph Cottage discuss the consequences of an invasion; the total Nazi occupation of all France; and the possible seizure of the French fleet lying at Toulon.

356 Ike knew that Murphy was a conservative Catholic—basically, like Roosevelt, not unpleased with the Vichy government's domestic policies, condemning collaboration with the Nazis but accepting Pétain's slogans about work, family, and country. Murphy, like his masters, blamed France's troubles on earlier Popular Front liberalism and left-oriented politics. But Eisenhower may not have realized, as Churchill and Charles de Gaulle did, that his new political counselor had passed much of his working life in prewar Paris among aristocrats, Roman Catholic monarchists, and political hard-line "rightists" if not fascists. These included the likes of Jacques Lemaigre Dubreuil, d'Astier de la Vigerie, and the men who made up the Group of Five and their fringe organizations.

357 Steven E. Ambrose, *Ike's Spies* (Jackson, MS: University of Mississippi, 1981), 17fn.

358 As a result the U.S. Department of State would be deprived of seeing important communications for several months in 1942 and 1943. Ambrose, *Ike's Spies*, 27.

359 Letter to "Katinka" dated Algiers, October 16, 1942.

360 Ambrose observes in *The Supreme Commander* that "even though Murphy made promises he could not keep and predictions that were hopelessly mistaken, even

though he got the United States to back the wrong forces in North Africa, Murphy always bounced back and ended up on top." Ambrose, 100–101.

361 Funk, *The Politics of Torch*, 109.

362 OSS Files, RG 226, Entry 99, Box 49.

363 King, OSS Files, RG 226, Entry 99, Box 49. Malevergne may have escaped with a partner, another French marine pilot named Carl Victor Klopper.

364 At a time when the Germans were murdering innocent civilians in Europe, the American military, to its credit, was observing the rules of conventional warfare.

365 It was at this time that Winston Churchill swore Eisenhower to secrecy, dramatically extracting a promise that the Torch commander would never go into a war zone or fly over one (a promise Eisenhower made but never kept), and never expose himself to capture (the enemy had ways to make captured men talk).

366 Murphy, 109.

367 Murphy, 99.

368 Murphy, 112.

369 Tuyl Knox, 100–101.

370 Harry Woodruff letter dated Algiers, November 2, 1942, and supplied by his daughter, Mrs. Edith Kunhardt.

371 Knight, 186.

372 Knight, 228.

373 Murphy makes no mention of the Chrétien meeting in his memoirs.

374 Murphy, 118.

375 OSS Files, RG 226, Entry 99, Box 49.

376 From an anonymous, photocopied document titled, "Sub Rosa," 89–90, n.d.

377 OSS Files.

378 See Richards, 567–568 and "Brandon" operations.

379 The agreements of October 15, 18, 19, and a final version dated November 2 were never satisfactory to either Murphy or the Group of Five, mainly because the issue of who would command the invasion was never settled.

380 Murphy, 119. A final version of the agreement assured Gen. Giraud (in absentia) that "the restoration of France to full independence, in all the greatness and vastness which it possessed before the war in Europe as well as overseas, is one of the war aims of the United Nations." And that "French sovereignty will be established as soon as possible throughout all the territory, metropolitan and colonial, over which flew the French flag in 1939. . . . The Government of the United States considers the French nation as an ally and will treat it as such." (This was clearly an inconsistency, as the French nation was represented in Marshal Pétain and Vichy France. And the United States was about to invade French territory.) FRUS (1942) 2:397.

CHAPTER 9 ENDNOTES

381 The material in this chapter is essentially drawn from Clark, 79–88; Knight 246–252; Richards, 562–66; and from notes taken at meetings with Knight and the author at Inxent and Paris, June 1998.

382 Clark, 67.

383 Knight, 231.

384 The party also included a Mr. Queyrat, a Cherchel lawyer and friend of Jacques Teissier's, and members of d'Astier's group; a Mr. Watson; José Aboulker; and Lieutenants Le Hen and Michel, serving with the *Douairs*, an auxiliary native Algerian military force—the strong-arm men.

385 Knight, 237.

386 It would be interesting to know what the usually anti-Semitic French reaction to Clark would have been had they known at Cherchel, and later, that the "American Eagle" was half Jewish by his mother, Becky Ezekiel. Black, 779.

387 SBS Crew: Captain G. B. Courtney, Captain R. P. Livingston, Lt. J. P. Foot.

388 Lemnitzer finished his career as Supreme Allied Commander of NATO; and Wright, a high-ranking U.S. Navy admiral.

389 Funk, *The Politics of Torch*, 134.

390 Ibid.

391 Alan Brooke, 362.

392 Funk, *The Politics of Torch*, 158; and Clark, 80.

393 Knight, 246.

394 Clark, 83.

395 Clark, 84.

396 Clark, 84.

397 Much later, Knight and Murphy learned that the police commissioner did return that next morning. He carefully searched the villa and grounds—but only Teissier was present, quietly at home.

398 Knight, 252.

399 Funk, *The Politics of Torch*, 164.

400 Funk, *The Politics of Torch*, 164.

401 Lemaigre Dubreuil would make three round trips to France as Murphy's emissary between October 23 and November 7. He was able to do so because he held special German and Vichy travel documents. See Appendix.

402 Funk, *The Politics of Torch*, 167.

403 If Giraud had known the facts, undoubtedly he would have refused to associate himself with the Allied venture. Even if Giraud had dropped out, Rigault and Lemaigre Dubreuil had foreseen that the Allies would land anyway. "Thus the Americans must

be persuaded that Giraud was Iman [sic], and Giraud must be persuaded that the Allied venture could not be ignored—it was the last chance for France to redeem its honor." Funk, *The Politics of Torch*, 167; and Cave Brown, 241.

[404] President Roosevelt would state after the Torch invasion that Murphy had exceeded his authority in the agreement. But though Murphy may have exaggerated American promises, he was following what he believed to be his latest instructions and what he thought to be Roosevelt's policy. Hoisington, 73; Funk, *The Politics of Torch*, 114–115, 177–178; and Murphy, 118.

[405] Murphy then went on, "A few days after the invasion, Clark gave a picturesque account of the Cherchell [sic] meeting to war correspondents attached to Eisenhower's temporary headquarters in Gibraltar. Since wartime security made it advisable to conceal the serious complications which had arisen at Cherchell, Clark diverted attention from the political aspects by describing some comical aspects of the venture . . . [stressing] the American visitors [had to] to hide in a wine cellar . . . This incident made lively newspaper copy, a welcome diversion from the war's somber happenings, and Clark further embellished his tale by relating how he lost his pants while getting back into the submarine." Murphy, 119.

[406] The U.S. Navy agreed that Torch "was blessed by an almost providential good fortune . . . beyond all justifiable hope." Norman Gelb, *Desperate Venture: The Story of Operation Torch, the Allied Invasion of North Africa* (New York: William Morrow & Co, 1992), 250–251.

[407] Churchill told Ike about ULTRA and how the British were reading and decoding secret German military and diplomatic radio transmissions; and about the German Enigma code machine brought to Britain by Polish and French scientists. Churchill announced that Eisenhower would now have access to the most treasured secret of the war; and that the ULTRA radio intercepts were far better than relying solely on human intelligence.

[408] Arab conspirators for their independence played the spy game, too. In Rome, Colonel Franz Seubert of the German Abwehr met with the pro-German Muslim leader Haji Amin al-Husseini—the Grand Mufti of Jerusalem. Amin gave Seubert, for the Nazi Admiral "Wilhelm Canaris's eyes only," an amazingly detailed report on the imminent Allied invasion of North Africa. The Japanese ambassador in Rome reported to Tokyo that the Grand Mufti and other Arab leaders had asked for German and Italian assurances that if the Axis won the war, Arabs would be rewarded with independence.

CHAPTER 10 ENDNOTES

[409] Atkinson, 3.

[410] Three days later on Sunday, November 1, as *Seraph* prepared to pick up Giraud, a secret courier arrived from France with an "alarming" written protest from Giraud.

[411] Murphy, 121.

412 Murphy, 121.

413 Dependents of French officials were just then evacuating the city. A month before the U.S. chargé d'affaires in Vichy had cabled Washington to advise that "the French Army Staff were preparing plans for possible operations on the continent in cooperation with Anglo-American forces," Darlan's wish to cooperate with the U.S. was by now clear to Washington and London. This was despite his caution against premature or weak U.S. operations that could have disastrous results on the continent. Funk, *The Politics of Torch*, 179; and Melton, 163.

414 Funk, *The Politics of Torch*, 184.

415 Lemaigre Dubreuil in Professor Funk's words thought that after the invasion, "cut off from Vichy, North Africa would become a headless creature requiring a strong political leash." Lemaigre Dubreuil could not permit Vichy officials, Juin, Nogues, and company to establish themselves as "viceroys." Professor Funk even postulates that Lemaigre Dubreuil saw the possibility of bringing Pierre Laval (his friend and sponsor) to North Africa to head "a civil government in a truncated colony." Thus Adm. Darlan and Gen. de Gaulle were poison to Lemaigre Dubreuil and his clique. Funk, *The Politics of Torch*, 184–185.

416 Ibid.

417 Renée Gosset in *Conspiracy in Algiers* states that Murphy saw Darlan on October 30, implying that Darlan knew an invasion of North Africa was imminent and failed to warn Vichy. She concludes that Darlan was already prepared to cooperate with Murphy. Gosset, 208.

418 Slowikowski, 121.

419 Slowikowski, 212–214; and Funk's personal notes, October 1942.

420 Pendar, 97.

421 Rigault actually called Murphy a *chameau*, literally a "camel driver." Pendar, 97.

422 Reid, Coon, OSS Files, RG 226, Entry 99, Box 43.

423 Pendar, 97–100.

424 Knight, 300.

425 Browne and Coon's main work in Morocco was to lay the groundwork for an Arab and Berber insurrection against the Spaniards in the Riff. Knight, 310.

426 Knight, 270.

427 Ibid.

428 Later Roger Carcassonne, "the Duke," and d'Astier's choice for a leader, confirmed this.

429 Knight, 283.

430 Knight, 300–320. Author's note: In order to maintain continuity, the time frame related here has been compressed to include only the high points of Knight's narrative of the events of the last seventy-two hours before the Torch landings. No facts have been altered in any way.

[431] Ducrot conducted himself with such bravery in the two ensuing days that Gordon was ecstatic in his praise. Ducrot was decorated with the U.S. Silver Star for his work.

[432] Atkinson's, "In Barbary," 78.

[433] Howe, 70; Atkinson, 132-133.

[434] Ambrose, *The Supreme Commander*, 179.

[435] Rounds's personnel documents, courtesy of the Hoover Institution, Stanford, Calif.

[436] Rounds's personnel documents, courtesy of the Hoover Institution, Stanford, Calif.

[437] Atkinson, 52.

[438] John Crawford Knox's memoirs: *The First 36 Hours* (n.p., n.d.); and Daphne Joan Fry Tuyl's (JFT) memoirs, approximately p. 69. (Some of Mrs. Knox's manuscript pages in the author's possession are unnumbered.)

[439] No one has come up with an exact count of the number of partisans that participated in the insurrection. Some reports state that only 200 showed on the night of November 7–8, ready to fight. Others maintain a maximum of 500 young men were present for duty. Funk, *The Politics of Torch*, 174–175.

[440] The material for this section is extracted from Reid's and King's narrations of events found in OSS Files, RG 226, Entry 99, Box 43, and Reid's Summary files.

[441] Reid's Summary, OSS Files, Entry 99, Box 49. Reid never identifies French partisan Captain X.

[442] King, OSS Files.

[443] Reid's Summary.

[444] Very much as marine security guards do today at U.S. embassies and consulates.

[445] Reid Summary.

[446] Reid Summary.

[447] Howe, 125. For a brief and fine description of the Fedhala action, see Atkinson, 109–111.

[448] Clark, 96.

[449] Murphy, 122.

[450] Hoisington, 55.

[451] Ambrose, *The Supreme Commander*, 119.

[452] Ambrose, *The Supreme Commander*, 119; and Atkinson, 61.

CHAPTER 11 ENDNOTES

[453] Funk, 205; and Pendar, 102–103.

[454] For a description of U.S. and British convoys and assault forces, see Samuel Eliot Morison, *Operations in North African Waters: October 1942–June 1943* (Edison, NJ: Castle Books, 1947). Patton's western assault forces (some 33,000 men) would attack

Casablanca-Fedala, Safi, and Port Lyautey. The U.S.-British force under Generals Ryder and Fredendall (some 72,000 men) aimed for Algiers and Oran. The western assault convoys comprised some 30 ships laden with 33,843 mostly green National Guard troopers, 3,000 vehicles, and 46,000 tons of supplies. Eastern assault forces comprised some 73 ships laden with 72,000 American and British troops and carrying 7,000 vehicles and 54,000 tons of supplies.

[455] Murphy, 128.

[456] Eisenhower had all along wanted Darlan (as Churchill did); Ike wanted the admiral who controlled the French fleet on the U.S. side, and he wanted Giraud to work with Darlan to promote the Allied cause. Funk, 257. Churchill later called Darlan's arrival in Algiers, "a strange and formidable coincidence." Verrier, 118. Roosevelt had cabled Murphy on October 17, 1942, via Leahy, authorizing Murphy "to initiate any arrangement with Darlan which in my judgment might assist the military operations." Murphy, 129.

[457] Atkinson, 95.

[458] Melton, 172.

[459] Murphy, 129–130.

[460] Atkinson, 136.

[461] Murphy, 131.

[462] Murphy, 131.

[463] Funk, 219.

[464] Knox, *The First 36 Hours of November 8, 1942*, 14.

[465] Knox, *The First 36 Hours of November 8, 1942*, 13.

[466] Atkinson, 164.

[467] Murphy, 133.

[468] Knox, *The First 36 Hours of November 8, 1942*, 14.

[469] Historians have noted that Ken Pendar's description of the meeting with Gen. Ryder at Beach Beer White and the French ceasefire ceremony differs dramatically from Murphy's narrative. In Pendar's version, which neither Professor Arthur Layton Funk nor Rick Atkinson treated in their books, Pendar wears the laurels of the peacemaker and adventurous vice-consul. (Pendar's book, *Adventure in Diplomacy*, was first published in 1945 but was reissued with "new material" in 1966. Murphy's autobiography and account of the events, *Diplomat Among Warriors*, was brought out in 1964.)
  The Pendar version is worth reading for color:
  ". . . I decided to try to locate the American commanding general for d'Orange and Juin. This time, I tried the Villa Sinetti where our secret radio station was hidden. Cole and Boyd were there, and told me the Allies were at Sidi Ferruch [Algeria]. We got into our cars, and they guided me until I was safely on the back road to our beaches. It was a big moment to see the little harbor off Cheragas filled with what seemed to be hundreds of grey ships, the roads

filled with companies of Americans marching to Algiers. (Paradoxically the Allies were landing in almost the same spot where a hundred years before the French had landed.) In every little crossroad town, Arabs and French had lined the roadside to watch them. The Arabs were particularly fascinated by the commandos with their black faces: they thought they were a new, and interesting, type of native.

"At his temporary headquarters, behind a roadside hedge under a tree, I found our commanding Gen. Ryder, a very tall, thin, stooped and handsome man, with great personal charm. Gen. Mast and, surprisingly, Captain Randolph Churchill, son of the prime minister, were with him. He gave me his terms: easy ones if the French surrendered at once, tough if they didn't, and a postscript that Murphy must be present at all negotiations. I started back to Algiers. Near Juin's villa, I met Murphy on his way to find Ryder, too. We turned back together, got Ryder, turned again, and met d'Orange just leaving El Biar to surrender Fort Lempereur to us on behalf of the French.

"The surrender was wonderfully French, like a historical painting in some European museum. D'Orange stood before six French soldiers, lined up in arrow shape, and handed the sword of surrender by the blade, hilt extended, to Gen. Ryder, announcing that, with this sword he surrendered Fort Lempereur, and the city of Algiers, to the American general." Pendar, 113–114.

[470] Murphy, 133.

[471] Melton, 175. For an insight into of Darlan's outlook and his deference to Marshal Pétain at this time, see Melton, chapter 19.

[472] Melton, 177.

[473] The French delegation besides Adm. Darlan and Gen. Juin included Navy: Vice Admiral d'Escadre Moreau, maritime commander of the Fourth Region; Vice Adm. Fenard, Secretary-General of the North African government; Rear Admiral Battet, Chief of Cabinet to Darlan; and Rear Admiral Reboul Hector Berlioz, Chief of Staff of the Fourth Region; Army: General Koeltz, commander of the 19th Military Region, and General de Brigade Sevez, Chief of Staff to Juin; Air: General Mendigal, Superior Commandant of Air in North Africa. The Americans present were Murphy, who acted as interpreter, Colonel Holmes, Captain Wright, Commodore Dick, and Lieutenant Jack Beardwood, Clark's aide. Clark, 106.

[474] Funk, 238.

[475] Melton, 177–178; Murphy, 138.

[476] Clark, 106.

[477] Morison, 129.

[478] Morison, 130–131.

[479] Morison, 131.

[480] War Cabinet Minutes, 3–21 December: W.M. (42): 164th/165th/171st meeting.

[481] War Cabinet Minutes, 3–21 December: W.M. (42): 164th/165th/171st meeting.

482 War Cabinet Minutes, 3–21 December: W.M. (42): 164th/165th/171st meeting.

483 Atkinson, 90–91.

484 Reid, 106.

485 Morison, 164.

486 Morison, 164.

487 Landing Ship Tank, Landing Craft Tank, and Landing Craft Infantry.

488 Morison, 164–165, 258, 273.

CHAPTER 12 ENDNOTES

489 Ridgway reveals in his memoirs that Murphy had told Eisenhower about this strange business—the new d'Astier plot—and that Ike had given a firm "no" to the affair.

490 Pendar, 123.

491 General Nogues and Yves Chatel would continue as governors of Morocco and Algeria, respectively. General Giraud would head the reorganized French armed forces, recruiting the regular French army and navy to fight alongside Allied forces in the Tunisian campaign.

492 Funk, 239.

493 For the ten months from the time of his "invention" of Giraud in May 1942, until his resignation from Giraud's staff in March 1943, Lemaigre Dubreuil remained steadfast in his commitment to Giraud. In part, he valued the Murphy-Giraud Agreement as the surest instrument for France's reemergence as an independent and sovereign state on the Allied side. And after two years of relentless work for the liberation of French Africa, Lemaigre Dubreuil still clung to the ambition that he was destined to play an important political role, perhaps as Giraud's civilian chief of staff or even as "prime minister" in a future Giraud government. Lemaigre Dubreuil had always opposed Darlan and favored Laval as the Vichy politician best able to manipulate Pétain and the Nazis for the good of France.

494 Hoisington, 82.

495 Hoisington, 82.

496 Hoisington, 82.

497 With Giraud's approval, Lemaigre Dubreuil prepared a plan to create a French Imperial Federation of all French territories. Darlan took it up.

498 The addresses are not clear. In *Wild Bill Donovan: The Last Hero*, author Anthony Cave Brown suggests that the memo was destined for FDR, Secretary of State Cordell Hull, and the joint chiefs—Donovan's usual "customers."

499 Cave Brown also states in his book, *Wild Bill Donovan: The Last Hero*: "The extent to which this document played a part in the assassination of Darlan, which soon followed, is impossible to estimate with confidence, if indeed it played any part. In the

first place, there is no indication to whom the memo went, if it went to anybody, nor is there any evidence of reply or discussion with WJD's [Donovan's] "customers." In the second place, while WJD would not have stopped at assassination in wartime if the situation had warranted such an action, there is no evidence in the Donovan papers, which included his cable files, that he contemplated or recommended such action. Certainly there is none that he authorized such a measure.

500 Cave Brown, *Wild Bill Donovan: The Last Hero*, 261; Gelb, 279.

501 Anthony Eden, *The Memoirs of Anthony Eden: Earl of Avon: The Reckoning* (Boston Houghton Mifflin Company, 1965).

502 Coon, *A North African Story: The Anthropologist as OSS Agent 1941–1943*, (Ipswich, Mass., Gambit Publications, 1981), 61.

503 Richards, 582-583, 610–611.

504 Richards, 582-583, 610–611.

505 Richards, 582.

506 They included Alfred Pose, Jean Van Hecke, Marc Jaquet, and Pierre Alexandre (representing the Jewish community of Metropolitan France).

507 Pendar, 46, 126.

508 The following is taken from Renée Gosset, *Conspiracy in Algiers* (New York: The Nation, 1945), and from Mario Faivre (one of d'Astier's partisans), *We Killed Darlan: A Personal Account of the French Resistance in North Africa, 1940–1942*, translated by Douglas W. Alden (Manhattan, Kansas: Sunflower University Press, 1999), 122–126. While Faivre is not always reliable about political matters, his description given here concords with fact as reported in a number of histories and in the press.

509 Faivre, 116–132.

510 Carleton Coon tells us that around noon on Christmas Eve day, Coon drove his Studebaker from Algiers to Ain Taiya. He was held up in midtown traffic; and he impatiently, "skirted the jam" in the diplomatic Studebaker, "only dimly aware he was circumnavigating Darlan's assassination." When he arrived at Ain Taiya (a half-hour to an hour's drive), "a French officer hurried in and announced that Darlan had been killed. He added that the killer was Fernand Bonnier de la Chapelle, a twenty-year-old student of Coon's.

Coon's relating this is very odd. The Algiers press on December 25 attributed the assassination of Darlan to an Axis fanatic; not a word was written or said about Bonnier. Author's note: News must have traveled fast to the camp at Ain Taiya. It is a wonder that in an hour's time, "a French officer" knew that it was Bonnier de la Chapelle [correct] who had killed Darlan—for Darlan lay in an Algiers hospital just then, dying. Mark Saxton in chapter 3, preface to Coon's *A North African Story*, 47–48 and Coon himself, 60–61.

511 Tute, 308.

EPILOGUE ENDNOTES

512 Italics original. Walter Lippmann, *Toward Tomorrow*, syndicated feature, January 19, 1943; Funk, *The Politics of Torch*, 256.

513 Edgar Ansel Mowrer, "More on Mr. Murphy," Editorial, *The Washington Post*, 12 September 1944: 6.

514 "Team Play," Editorial, *The Washington Post*, 5 Sept. 1944: 8; "Mr. Hull's Defense," Editorial, *The Washington Post*, 7 Sept. 1944:8.

515 Funk, *The Politics of Torch*, 256.

516 Funk, *The Politics of Torch*, 256.

517 Yves Maxime Danan, *La vie politique à Alger, de 1940 à 1944* (Paris: L.G.D.J., 1963), 130.

518 *The New York Times*, 10 January 1978:10.

APPENDIX ENDNOTES

519 Cave Brown, *Wild Bill Donovan: The Last Hero*, 243.

520 Cave Brown, 243.

521 Donovan interrogated him at the St. Regis Hotel in New York. Cave Brown, 243-248.

522 Cave Brown, 776-778.

523 Conrad Black, *Franklin Delano Roosevelt: Champion of Freedom* (New York: PublicAffairs, 2003), 795.

524 From material collected at the French National Archives and evaluated by Professor Charles Robertson, November 2005.

525 Cave Brown, 243-248; Hoisington, 86-100.

INDEX

Lemaigre Dubreuil, Simone Lesieur, 41, 248
Lemnitzer, Lyman, 165
Lescroux, General, 198, 200
Lesieur Guerlain, Christiane, 41, 110, 281n
Lesieur, Georges, 248
Libyan Desert, 69, 182, 221, 266n
liquor, 92–93
Lubienski, Henry (Banuls), 101–2
Ludendorff, Erich, 16
Lutzina, 106, 162

M
MacArthur, Douglas II, 285n
MacArthur, Douglas, 83
"MacGowan," 143–44, 287n
Mack, W. H. B., 288n
Madame "S," 87
Malcolm, 211
Malevergne, René, 148–49, 217, 289n
Mandel, Georges, 263n
manic depression, 262n
Marianna, 106
Marshall, George C., 123, 136, 142–43, 146, 149–50, 161, 180, 202, 224
Martin, General, 184
Mast, Charles Emmanuel
  Cherchel, 137, 161–62, 166–68, 172
  Darlan and, 175
  Giraud and, 136, 142, 144, 151
  Juin and, 181
  Murphy and, 140, 158–59
  on D-Day, 203, 209–10
  Torch, 174, 179, 185, 189
  Tostain and, 186, 189
Matthews, Freeman, 145
Maugham, William Somerset, 13
McCarthy, Frank, 287n
Méchéria, 90
Medals of Merit, 240–44
Mein Kampf (Hitler), 16
Mers-el-Kebir, 30, 35, 71, 82, 266n
MI6, 113–14, 285n

Michelier, François, 142, 200, 211, 220
Midway station, 104
Military Intelligence Services (MIS), 47
milk, 99–100
minerals, 65–66, 270n
Mockler-Ferryman, Edward, 145
Morocco, 93–94, 123–24
Moslems, 278n
murder, 81, 97–98, 278n. *See also* assassination.
Murphy, Catherine, 20, 33, 107, 126, 146, 270n
Murphy, Mildred (daughter), 126
Murphy, Mildred Taylor, 5, 9, 15–18, 20–21, 33, 48, 262n, 264–65n
Murphy, Robert Daniel, ix, xiii
  after Pearl Harbor, 124
  after Torch, 225–26
  agreement with Giraud, 291n
  and insurgent groups, 286n
  and the coup d'état, 234–35, 296n
  and the dairy cow, 100
  and the Group of Five, 133–34
  and the resistance, 196
  armistice conference, 215–17
  as Lt. Col. MacGowan, 143–47, 287n
  before Torch, 139–42, 149–51, 154–55, 174, 179–80, 183
  Canfield and, 124–25
  Catholicism, 32, 108, 288n
  ceasefire, 212–13
  Cherchel, 161–73
  Darlan and, 221
  Distinguished Service Medal, 240
  during the occupation of Paris, 4–11, 261–62n
  Eddy and, 129
  Eisenhower and, 144–47, 223
  family, 126, 142, 264–65n, 280–81n
  formation of the Twelve Apostles, 45–47, 57
  Giraud and, 202
  in Algiers, 31–33, 36–43, 106–8
  in Bern, Switzerland, 13–15